FEDERAL LAW AND SOUTHERN ORDER

STUDIES IN THE
LEGAL HISTORY OF THE SOUTH
Edited by Paul Finkelman and Kermit L. Hall

This series explores the ways in which law has affected the development of the southern United States and in turn the ways the history of the South has affected the development of American law. Volumes in the series focus on a specific aspect of the law, such as slave law or civil-rights legislation, or on a broader topic of historical significance to the development of the legal system in the region, such as issues of constitutional history and of law and society, comparative analyses with other legal systems, and biographical studies of influential southern jurists and lawyers.

Federal Law and Southern Order

RACIAL VIOLENCE AND CONSTITUTIONAL

CONFLICT IN THE POST-*Brown* SOUTH

Michal R. Belknap

THE UNIVERSITY OF GEORGIA PRESS

ATHENS AND LONDON

© 1987 by the University of Georgia Press
Athens, Georgia 30602
Preface to the New Edition
© 1995 by the University of Georgia Press
All rights reserved
Set in Linotron Garamond No. 3
The paper in this book meets the guidelines for permanence and durability
of the Committee on Production Guidelines for Book Longevity of the
Council on Library Resources.

Printed in the United States of America
91 90 89 88 87   C   5 4 3 2 1
99 98 97 96 95   P   5 4 3 2 1

Library of Congress Cataloging in Publication Data

The Library of Congress has cataloged the
cloth edition as follows:
Belknap, Michal R.
   Federal law and Southern order.
   Bibliography: p.
   Includes index.
   1. Afro-Americans—Civil rights—Southern States—
History. 2. Intervention (Federal government)—
United States—History. 3. Racism—Southern States—
History. 4. Southern States—Race relations—History.
5. Violence—Southern States—History. I. Title.
KF4757.B346 1987   342.75'0873   86-19237
ISBN 0-8203-0925-7 (alk. paper) 347.502873
ISBN 0-8203-1735-7 (pbk.: alk. paper)

British Library Cataloging in Publication Data available.

For my cousin Robert Stuart Belknap,
who, like the martyrs of the civil rights movement,
died much too young

CONTENTS

PREFACE
TO THE NEW EDITION

On February 5, 1994, a predominantly black state jury in Jackson, Mississippi, convicted a white racist, Byron De La Beckwith, of murder in the 1963 slaying of an African-American civil rights leader, Medgar Evers.[1] This was not the first time De La Beckwith had stood trial for that crime. As the original edition of *Federal Law and Southern Order* reported, he was tried twice for the murder in 1964. Both times, although prosecutors presented them with more than ample evidence to justify a conviction, all-white juries could not agree on a verdict. Indeed, in one of these trials, and perhaps in both, when the jury hung and the judge declared a mistrial, a majority of the jurors were holding firm for outright acquittal.[2]

The 1994 conviction of De La Beckwith for an act of racial violence committed more than three decades earlier—at the height of the turmoil unleashed by the Supreme Court's historic ruling in *Brown v. Board of Education* (1954)—provided dramatic proof of how much things have changed in the South since the era discussed in *Federal Law and Southern Order*. Whites are no longer free, as they were in 1963, to employ assault and even murder to enforce the subordination of African Americans. The southern legal system, no longer operated exclusively by whites, now punishes crimes of a type that three decades ago it tolerated and even encouraged. Federal intervention in the South no longer seems essential, as it did then, to enable African Americans and defenders of their rights to enjoy simple physical safety. Nor is uncontrolled racial violence any longer calling into question the efficacy of the American federal system. Yet, the legal and political battles of the 1950s and 1960s over whether Washington should move against the rampant racist terrorism that threatened the civil rights movement, or whether the Constitution precluded the national government from acting and required that the targets of this terrorism be left to seek protection from the hostile law enforcement agencies and judicial institutions of the southern states, remain significant. Although products of a now by-gone era, the events chronicled in this book continue to demand attention because they affected decisively the evolution of both American federalism and the American South. Recognizing their continuing significance, the University of Georgia Press has chosen to publish this paperback edition of *Federal Law and Southern Order* as part of its series on southern legal history.

No exploration of the legal history of the South can ignore the issue of violence—nor can any student of southern race relations. Indeed, even today, when, as Julius Chambers points out, "Most Americans no longer countenance flagrant racial violence," it still occurs.[3] Such events as the 1982 killing of a Chinese American by Michigan auto workers who mistakenly believed him to be Japanese, the 1986 baseball bat attack on four black men by members of a white gang in the Howard Beach section of Queens, New York, that resulted in the death of one of the victims, and the 1992 beating of African-American motorist Rodney King by white police officers in the Los Angeles show that this phenomenon is not confined to the former Confederate states.[4] While southern whites are not the only perpetrators of racially motivated violence, it is undeniable that they have not abandoned entirely the type of behavior that triggered widespread demands during the 1960s for federal intervention in the South.

To be sure, lynchings of the type that once left scores of black bodies hanging from southern trees no longer occur; they were already a thing of the past by the time of the *Brown* decision in 1954. The classic lynching was a community ritual in which the white community as a whole assembled as a mass mob to participate in the apprehension, execution, and torture of the black victim. In the 1950s whites still beat and killed African Americans in order to avenge private grievances and enforce white supremacy. But while tolerating these acts of racist violence and refusing to punish the perpetrators, the vast majority of southern whites abstained from personal participation in such brutality.[5] "There is an important difference," asserts W. Fitzhugh Brundage, "between community approval for lynching in the form of open community participation and community acquiescence in the form of refusal to investigate or prosecute lynchers."[6] While community participation was a thing of the past by the 1960s, community acquiescence persisted through much of that troubled decade.

Fear of a breakdown of law and order eventually destroyed this toleration of racist violence, inspiring other white southerners to crack down on Ku Klux Klan terrorists, even though they shared the Klansmens' determination to preserve segregation. Killings and beatings inspired by a desire to preserve the South's traditional racial caste system declined in the late 1960s, but they did not entirely disappear. In 1981 Klansmen randomly abducted a nineteen-year-old black man, Michael Donald, in Mobile, Alabama, beat him to death, and then strung his body up in a camphor tree. This crime and others that occurred at about the same time inspired Ronald Reagan, hardly noted for his vigorous support of civil rights, to express concern about "a disturbing reoccurrence of bigotry and violence."[7] Seven years later, the white police chief of tiny Hemphill, Texas, Thomas Ladner, beat to death in the Sabine County jail an African-American motorist, Loyal Garner, whom he and a deputy sheriff had arrested for drunken driving.[8]

Although even today white bigots occasionally resort to violence in a futile attempt to perpetuate by force the subordination of the black race outlawed by the court decisions and federal legislation of the 1950s and 1960s, the South is now far less tolerant of such conduct than it once was. On June 21, 1989, twenty-five years to the day after the murders of civil rights workers Michael Schwerner, James, Chaney, and Andrew Goodman near the Neshoba County, Mississippi, town of Philadelphia (an event that sparked outrage across America and generated irresistible political pressure for federal intervention to combat racist violence in the South), Mississippi Secretary of State Dick Molpus addressed a memorial service for the three murdered men in the community where they had died. "We deeply regret what happened here twenty-five years ago," declared Molpus, who had grown up in Philadelphia. "We wish we could undo it. . . . Every decent person in Philadelphia and Neshoba County and Mississippi feels that way." Molpus had done what it was once assumed no "elected official in Mississippi would ever do: he had apologized for the racial violence that his state once condoned." Yet Gov. Ray Mabus Jr., who also addressed the memorial service, echoed his sentiments.[9]

They spoke as the elected leaders of a state that in the 1960s had not even tried the killers of Schwerner, Chaney, and Goodman. Then racist murderers had to be brought to justice by federal prosecutors. Today the criminal justice systems of the southern states reflect the alteration in southern attitudes that Molpus's speech exemplifies. Verdicts in state

courts offer evidence that indeed the times have changed. To be sure, after
a trial before a biased judge, a Hemphill, Texas, jury, which included
several individuals who should never have been permitted to serve, did
acquit on state civil rights charges both Chief Ladner and the deputy who
had assisted him in beating Garner. The two men were subsequently tried
for murder in an adjacent county where the victim had died, however.
That trial ended with convictions. Ladner received a twenty-eight-year
prison sentence, and the deputy got ten years. After the Texas Court of
Criminal Appeals rejected their claim that they been subjected to double
jeopardy, a state appellate court affirmed the convictions. One of the
Klansmen responsible for the killing of Michael Donald pleaded guilty to
federal civil rights charges and accepted life in prison in order to avoid
being tried by the State of Alabama, because he feared the "state would
electrocute him." His fears were justified. Another of Donald's killers,
who stood trial in an Alabama court, was convicted of capital murder and
sentenced to death.[10]

In addition, Donald's mother won a $7 million judgment against the
United Klans of America in a civil suit filed by Morris Dees's Southern
Poverty Law Center. Although Dees won that victory in federal court, the
quality of federal justice in the South is no longer notably superior to that
available in state courts. Probably the most controversial cases involving a
crime of racist violence tried during the 1980s arose out of a November
1979 clash that pitted a group of Ku Klux Klansmen and Nazis against
participants in a "Death to the Klan" march through black neighborhoods
in Greensboro, North Carolina. That procession, organized by a Communist group called the Workers Viewpoint Organization, ended in a gun
battle that claimed the lives of five radicals. Pres. Jimmy Carter dispatched a team of twenty FBI agents to investigate, and the Guilford
County District Attorney assigned his two most experienced homicide
prosecutors to the case. Seeking first degree murder convictions and the
death penalty, they eventually tried fourteen white racists on murder and
felony riot charges. After initially voting 7-5 to convict, however, a state
jury acquitted all the defendants.[11]

These acquittals spawned public outrage and triggered demands for
federal intervention. The Department of Justice sent Michael Johnson,
the most experienced attorney in the Criminal Section of its Civil Rights
Division, to North Carolina to prosecute the Klansmen and Nazis. He
secured indictments charging nine of them with violating the general

federal conspiracy statute and with conspiring to violate civil rights of persons because of their race or religion and because the victims had been participating in an integrated activity. The latter kind of conspiracy constituted a violation of 18 U.S.C., section 245, a statute that had been enacted in 1968 after a long campaign to give the federal government a weapon with which to combat the sort of racially motivated violence that had tormented the South during the 1950s and 1960s. But that weapon misfired in Greensboro; after three days of deliberations, an all-white jury acquitted all defendants on all charges. Although the radical victims had cooperated with federal prosecutors, as they had not with lawyers for the state, the government apparently was unable to persuade jurors that the Klansmen and Nazis had not acted in self-defense or that they had possessed the racial motivation required by section 245. Both trials aroused suspicions about the persistence of racist justice in the South, but probably both ended in acquittal because the cases presented to the juries simply were not strong enough to establish guilt beyond a reasonable doubt. Certainly, the Greensboro trials failed to prove that in the modern South federal law and the federal judicial system are any more effective than state law and state legal institutions in punishing racist violence.[12]

Ironically, section 245 and its companion statutes seem to have become at least as important for redressing failures of local institutions to deliver justice in the North and West as in the South. In 1986, for example, the Chinese-American community reacted angrily when a white man in Michigan, who had killed a Chinese for racial reasons, was allowed to plead guilty to manslaughter and sentenced by the Wayne County Circuit Court only to probation and a $3,720 fine. Responding to its outrage, the Department of Justice overruled the decision of the local United States Attorney not to prosecute and instituted proceedings against the killer, Ronald Ebens, under section 245. A jury convicted Ebens, and he was sentenced to twenty-five years in prison. The United States Court of Appeals for the Sixth Circuit subsequently reversed the conviction, because it felt the trial judge had erred in permitting certain testimony and in refusing to admit into evidence tapes of interviews with three government witnesses. While doing so, however, it rejected the contention that "in enacting section 245, Congress . . . intended to limit its application exclusively to vindicate the rights of blacks and of white civil rights workers who aid blacks. . . ."[13]

Unlike the Ebens case, the Rodney King affair involved an African-

American victim, but it too arose out of a context very different from that which concerned those who had campaigned during the 1960s for the enactment of federal legislation to combat racist violence. King, a black motorist being arrested on a traffic charge, was savagely beaten by white Los Angeles police officers in an incident that received widespread publicity because a bystander recorded it with a home video camera. Although the videotape seemed to most of the millions who saw it on television to be conclusive proof that the policemen were guilty, an all-white state jury in the suburban California community of Simi Valley acquitted them. Its verdict sparked rioting in Los Angeles, and the Department of Justice entered the case, prosecuting the officers under 18 U.S.C., section 242 for violating King's civil rights. In April 1993 a federal court jury convicted two of the four indicted officers on that charge. This was not the sort of case that had concerned the activists of the 1960s who demanded increased federal intervention in local law enforcement to protect the victims of racist violence, but by the 1990s it was the kind that most demanded the attention of federal prosecutors.[14]

Although the relationship between racial violence, state criminal justice, and the enforcement of federal civil rights laws has changed significantly since the era depicted in *Federal Law and Southern Order*, the problems that this book addresses continue to excite scholarly interest. Since this book appeared in 1987, the literature on subjects treated in these pages has expanded significantly. For example, there are numerous new books and articles on lynching. That subject remains fascinating to sociologists, who continue to write extensively about it.[15]

Since 1987, however, historians have also made an impressive number of contributions to the literature on lynching. A number of these books and articles, like most of those that had appeared prior to the publication of *Federal Law and Southern Order*, deal with the era prior to World War II, and particularly with the decades around 1900 when the extralegal execution of African Americans was at its zenith. Brundage's study of Georgia and Virginia between 1880 and 1930, which carefully distinguishes among various types of lynchings and shows that these died out at different rates, is somewhat disjointed and uneven, but extremely insightful.[16] Also excellent is George C. Wright's study of Kentucky between 1865 and 1940, which revises earlier notions about the frequency of lynchings before 1880 and makes it clear that, at least in the state its author studied,

". . . the entire legal system upheld white violence by refusing to apprehend, charge, and convict white offenders of blacks, thus ensuring that
all Afro-Americans were at the mercy of whites."[17] Ann Field Faulkner has
written an impressive article on the 1893 lynching of Thomas Smith in
Roanoke, Virginia, and the deadly rioting that accompanied it, in which
she argues that this incident provoked a reaction that was partially responsible for a rapid decline in the frequency of extralegal executions in the
Old Dominion. Also worth noting are Michael J. Pfeifer's brief study of
developments in Missouri between 1890 and 1942 and Walter T. Howard's detailed account of a double lynching in Tallahassee, Florida, in
1937. Although focusing on other matters, Nancy Maclean's book on the
second Ku Klux Klan provides dramatic accounts of lynchings in the
Athens, Georgia, and Aiken, South Carolina, areas, along with valuable
insights into the extent of community support for such crimes and the
reasons why those who perpetrated them were so seldom punished.
William L. Ziglar has assessed Theodore Roosevelt's contributions to the
decline of lynching, and Mark Ellis has investigated the efforts of the
NAACP's Joel Spingarn to persuade the federal government to take action
against it during World War I.[18]

While continuing to study the era when lynching was most common,
since 1987 historians have given increasing attention to post-1940 manifestations of that phenomenon. Although beginning his massive study,
White Violence and Black Response, with Reconstruction, Herbert Shapiro
carries it all the way to 1957. Much more narrowly focused is Jack E.
Davis's article on the October 1945 slaying of a black tenant farmer, Jesse
James Payne, by his landlord and the resulting libel suit filed by Florida's
Gov. Millard F. Caldwell against *Collier's* magazine for accusing him of
advocating lynch law. The best recent work on a case from the World War
II era is Dominic J. Capeci Jr.'s in-depth analysis of the Cleo Wright
lynching. That brutal slaying of an African-American man accused of
trying to rape a white woman in Sikeston, Missouri, in 1942 "drew the
United States Department of Justice directly into the area of civil rights
for the first time."[19]

Two lynchings during the 1950s also generated powerful pressures for
Washington to take action against racist violence, as *Federal Law and
Southern Order* reports.[20] Now there are excellent monographs on both of
those post-*Brown* cases. In *A Death in the Delta: The Story of Emmett Till*,
Stephen J. Whitfield recounts the saga of a black teenager from Chicago,

who was shot and dumped into the Tallahatchie River in 1955 for making what her husband and his half-brother regarded as improper advances toward a Mississippi white woman. Whitfield provides readers with a brilliant analysis of the significance of the Till case and an insightful discussion of the demise of lynching. Howard Smead's *Blood Justice: The Lynching of Mack Charles Parker* recounts the abduction from the Poplarville, Mississippi, jail of an African-American man accused of raping a white mother in front of her child, and discusses both the summary execution of Parker and the legal proceedings that followed it.[21]

Like the Till and Parker lynchings, other acts of racially motivated violence committed during the period between 1954 and the early 1970s have received increasing scholarly attention in recent years. To be sure, not all those writing on the civil rights movement have exhibited an awareness of the importance of this issue. Two general studies by Hugh Davis Graham rather largely ignore it, and David R. Goldfield devotes only minimal attention to the subject in his study of race relations and southern culture since 1940. Robert Weisbrot's history of the civil rights movement, however, deals extensively with the violent resistance the movement encountered and the legal system's response to it, as do John Dittmer's study of civil rights struggles in Mississippi and Donald Nieman's brief constitutional history of African Americans.[22]

Perhaps not surprisingly, among works that have appeared since 1987, it is the numerous books on the Mississippi Freedom Summer that deal most extensively with the topic of anti–civil rights violence. As Weisbrot observes in his discussion of that tragedy-plagued campaign to register African Americans to vote and to educate them about their rights, "The South's most conservative state also proved to be its most violent."[23] The Freedom Summer accelerated a trend that had begun soon after *Brown*, revealing once again that, "For black Mississippians who sought to exercise their political rights, the peril from white violence increased many fold."[24] Mississippi was a dangerous place for white civil rights workers as well as for the African Americans they tried to help. Doug McAdam makes this clear in his chronicle of the Freedom Summer, which contains accounts by a number of participants of the violence they encountered. His *Freedom Summer* and Nicholas Mills's *Like a Holy Crusade* both highlight the terrifying focal point of the civil rights campaign in Mississippi: the disappearance of CORE volunteers Schwerner, Chaney, and Goodman and the eventual discovery of their bodies buried under an earthen dam in Neshoba County. That tragic turning point in the long saga of racial

violence in the South also receives substantial attention in the autobio-
graphical *Freedom Song*, a book whose author, Mary King, manned a
WATS line at the headquarters of SNCC in Atlanta during the tense hours
after the three young men vanished following their release from jail in
Philadelphia. King also handled much of the communication between the
civil rights movement and the federal government concerning the incident.[25]

By far the most detailed account of the Neshoba County murders is
Seth Cagin and Philip Dray's *We Are Not Afraid*. Although subtitled *The
Story of Goodman, Schwerner and Chaney and the Civil Rights Campaign in
Mississippi*, their book is much more than that. In sketching the background and context of the Philadelphia murders, Cagin and Dray recount
a whole series of beatings and killings in Mississippi, reaching back to the
Till and Parker lynchings of the 1950s.[26] Furthermore, they make it clear
that beatings of civil rights workers were "a powerful discouragement to
local blacks who might have considered attending voter registration
classes."[27] While *We Are Not Afraid* paints the most graphic and gripping
picture of the violence that beset the civil rights movement, it is only one
of a growing number of books and articles that highlight the problem.

Cagin and Dray also join other writers in calling attention to the failure
of state and local authorities in the South to prevent or punish the crimes
they describe. *We Are Not Afraid* points out that Mississippi could not
possibly have prosecuted the killers of Schwerner, Chaney, and Goodman
because neither county nor state authorities ever conducted a serious investigation of the crime.[28] Writing about one racially motivated murder,
Cagin and Dray declare that "a stone wall of local white complicity prevented any charges from being brought. . . ."[29] These authors are particularly effective in capturing the frustration felt by civil rights activists,
such as Bob Moses of SNCC, as it became increasingly obvious to them
that Mississippi would never bring perpetrators of racist violence to justice. Moses became the first African American ever to press criminal
charges against a white man in Amite County for beating him, but predictably, his assailant, a cousin of the sheriff, was acquitted. Furthermore,
Moses's "willingness to challenge white violence in court was not enough
to prevent its recurrence"; a few days later in his presence a SNCC field
secretary was beaten on the courthouse lawn. The utter futility of his
efforts and the blatant complicity of local officials in racially motivated
assaults and murders filled Moses with a sense of impotence.[30]

While Cagin and Dray's description of Moses's encounters with Mississippi's criminal justice system is particularly effective in highlighting the futility of reliance on local authorities in the South to control racially motivated violence, it is Mills who summarizes the problem most bluntly and concisely: "The threat of violence, coupled with the fact that Mississippi juries . . . would not convict a white man accused of racial murder was the most chilling obstacle SNCC faced in trying to build a political movement in Mississippi."[31] Whitfield's account of the Emmett Till case conveys a similar picture of "justice" in the Magnolia state. Seeking to explain how a jury could find not guilty two defendants who later admitted to a magazine writer that they had killed Till, he theorizes "that the jurors deemed the probable motives for such a homicide justifiable."[32] Their verdict, Whitfield notes rather cynically, "match[ed] the pattern of crimes of violence in the South, which was scaled according to caste . . . and . . . held the violence of whites against blacks usually justified. . . ."[33] Weisbrot is less universal in his condemnation of the white-controlled criminal justice systems of the southern states. But while commending the efforts of Alabama highway patrolman Eli Cowling to protect the Freedom Riders, he sharply criticizes the likes of Dallas County, Alabama's, Sheriff Jim Clark, whom he sees as fitting "a common mold of Southern lawmen, given to proud self-assertion and raised to equate the public welfare with the maintenance of a caste tradition."[34] In an article on the Dallas County community of Selma, J. Mills Thornton points out that police officers there actively participated in an effort to intimidate a black businessman that included shooting, kidnapping, and arson, and that the grand jury refused to indict anyone for the crimes in which these law enforcement officers participated.[35]

It is little wonder, then, that participants in the civil rights movement sought protection from the federal government. They seldom got what they asked for. Recent writing on the movement reenforces one of the central themes of *Federal Law and Southern Order*: the extreme reluctance of the national government to involve itself in the suppression of anti−civil rights violence. Throughout his book, Weisbrot describes situations in which Washington responded to attacks on civil rights activists either by doing nothing at all or by acting only belatedly. In his biography of Alabama's noted federal district judge, Frank M. Johnson Jr., Jack Bass reports that Johnson felt compelled, before issuing a sweeping injunction protecting Dr. Martin Luther King Jr.'s Selma-to-Montgomery voting rights march, to wring from Atty. Gen. Nicholas Katzenbach and Pres.

Lyndon Johnson a commitment that, if he issued such an order, they would actually enforce it. David Garrow's biography of King, while devoting more attention to the civil rights leader's efforts to force the national government to intervene in the South and noting several instances in which federal officials acted to thwart attempts on his life, also highlights the reluctance of the FBI and both the Eisenhower and Kennedy administrations to respond to the movement's calls for protection from physical violence.[36]

Perhaps because he deals almost entirely with the 1950s, rather than with the following decade, during which Washington finally acceded reluctantly to demands that it take action against racist murders and assaults, Whitfield is even more critical of federal inaction than are such writers as Garrow and Weisbrot. He faults the national government for being "quite indifferent to the 'jungle fury' that the NAACP charged was prevailing in the state of Mississippi," and excoriates what he characterizes as "the callousness of the Eisenhower administration to the plight of black victims of racist brutality. . . ."[37] Smead echoes Whitfield's sentiments. In criticizing the initial decision of the Justice Department not to prosecute anyone for the Mack Charles Parker lynching, he castigates "the conservative and somewhat timid" officials who made that decision and also faults the FBI for equivocating concerning the quality of the evidence it has unearthed.[38]

Those writing about the Mississippi Freedom Summer have been even more critical of the federal government's reluctance to do anything about racist violence than have students of the two most notorious lynchings of the 1950s. Participant Mary King and scholars Mills, McAdam, and Cagin and Dray all echo the complaints of civil rights activists and their supporters in 1964 that Washington was shirking its responsibilities. "The fundamental goal of the project," as McAdam points out, "was to focus national attention on Mississippi as a means of forcing federal intervention."[39] Yet, not until Schwerner, Chaney, and Goodman disappeared did the national government do anything about the rampant terrorism threatening participants in the Freedom Summer. While commending the steps it took following their disappearance, he and other recent writers agree that Washington should have acted much sooner than it did.[40]

A particular target of their criticism is the Federal Bureau of Investigation. "Practically everyone working in the civil rights movement knew from firsthand experience of the duplicity of the FBI," Mary King writes.[41] The cynicism of civil rights activists about the Bureau was thoroughly justified, as Kenneth O'Reilly has demonstrated in an article and in his slashing monograph, *"Racial Matters."* According to O'Reilly, the Bureau's longtime director, J. Edgar Hoover, was a racist, who shared the views of die-hard southern segregationists. Hoover considered the civil rights movement subversive, and after Martin Luther King Jr.'s 1963 March on Washington, he determined to destroy it. Even during the Eisenhower administration, however, the director had sought to reduce his agency's civil rights caseload. While John Kennedy was in the White House and his brother ran the Justice Department, the Bureau investigated fairly vigorously some prominent acts of anti-civil rights violence, such as the attacks on Freedom Rider buses in Alabama, the bombing of Birmingham's black Sixteenth Street Baptist Church, and the murder of Medgar Evers. But even when the FBI had advance knowledge of planned onslaughts against civil rights activists, it did nothing to prevent these. Indeed, by sharing information with local police departments that had been infiltrated by the Klan, the Bureau frequently facilitated acts of racist terrorism.[42] Even when voter registration workers were beaten in their presence, Hoover's agents would not arrest the Klansmen and southern sheriffs responsible for these crimes.[43] The Director did not condone such violence, but he did argue "that the FBI had no constitutional right to usurp the responsibilities of state and local police to maintain law and order."[44]

Although unwilling to protect the civil rights movement, Hoover was anxious to gather intelligence concerning its activities. He met with little resistance from the Kennedys, who "sanctioned FBI notions about the proper role of the federal government—the idea that the government had de facto authority to spy on civil rights activists but had little authority to protect them from segregationist terrorists. . . ."[45] According to O'Reilly, "Neither Robert Kennedy nor the attorneys in the Civil Rights Division were struck by the contradiction between the FBI's strict-constructionist posture on civil rights enforcement and its anything-goes activities in surveillance."[46]

O'Reilly does concede that the FBI grew somewhat more vigorous after the disappearance of Schwerner, Chaney, and Goodman. However, he attributes Hoover's sudden interest in the situation in Mississippi, as I did in the original edition of this book, to political pressure applied by President Johnson.[47] In O'Reilly's opinion the horrors of the Freedom Summer did not change FBI priorities. While discussing in considerable detail the attack on the Ku Klux Klan that the Bureau launched in 1964, he contends, "From the beginning to the end, the Klan wars remained a sideshow to the real war against the black struggle for racial justice."[48] "The movement sought the relief of law," O'Reilly observes, "and received a lawless counterintelligence program."[49]

Although less savage than his condemnation of the FBI, Nieman's discussion of the federal failure to protect the targets of anti–civil rights violence is critical too. Nieman views the inaction of the national government, at least during the Kennedy administration, as politically motivated. He concedes that Washington lacked sufficient law enforcement personnel to police the entire South and acknowledges that, because of some old Supreme Court decisions, prosecution would have been problematic. Nevertheless, explicitly endorsing the analysis of *Federal Law and Southern Order*, Nieman concludes, "Federal intervention was neither impossible nor a potential threat to liberty."[50]

Nieman's *Promises to Keep* is one of the few recent works that, like the first edition of this book, views the violence that convulsed the South during the post-*Brown* era from a constitutional perspective. Other scholars have added to our knowledge of what the national government actually did in response to various violent incidents discussed in *Federal Law and Southern Order*. For example, Cagin and Dray supply substantially more detail concerning the FBI's investigation of the kidnapping and murder of Schwerner, Chaney, and Goodman than I did, and O'Reilly adds to my account the extremely important information that the Bureau broke the case by paying an informant $30,000. Recent accounts also enrich our understanding of how really rampant racist violence was during the decade after *Brown*. *We Are Not Afraid* is particularly effective in this regard. For example, Cagin and Dray reveal that while looking for Schwerner, Chaney, and Goodman, searchers found several black corpses that proved to be victims of previously unknown killings perpetrated by the Klan and Mississippi lawmen.[51]

Although adding significantly to our knowledge of the anti–civil rights violence that generated the crisis in federalism with which *Federal Law and Southern Order* deals, however, recent scholarship has slighted the judicial proceedings to which that crisis gave rise. It has also ignored the constitutional significance of those cases. Cagin and Dray devote only 12 pages of a 457 page book to the federal prosecution of the perpetrators

of the Neshoba County killings and just one paragraph to the important
Supreme Court decision that made it possible for the prosecution of that
case to proceed after a federal district judge dismissed most of the charges
against the defendants. Although Judge Frank Johnson presided over the
federal trial of the Klansmen who killed Viola Liuzzo, Bass devotes less
than three pages of his biography to that proceeding, neglecting to mention Johnson's daring refusal to dismiss the indictments, which required
him to ignore precedent and anticipate a future change in direction by the
Supreme Court. My own 1984 article in the *Howard Law Journal* remains
the most complete discussion of the Lemuel Penn case, *United States v.
Guest*, outside the pages of *Federal Law and Southern Order*.[52]

Indeed, except for Nieman, recent writers have overlooked *Guest* entirely. Nieman is also the only scholar to publish since 1987 who has
addressed the significance of the other case that the Supreme Court decided the same day, *United States v. Price*, although that ruling not only
reinstated the indictments in the Neshoba County prosecution but also
significantly broadened the coverage of the criminal civil rights laws then
on the books. *Promises to Keep* is unique in devoting significant attention to
the enactment of those parts of the Civil Rights Act of 1968 designed to
expand the capacity of the federal government to combat anti–civil rights
violence.[53]

Nieman bases his discussions of all these matters on *Federal Law and
Southern Order* because, unlike other works, it focuses on the constitutional
dimensions of the crisis over anti–civil rights violence. Since 1987, Cagin
and Dray, Weisbrot, and Garrow, joined by other scholars, such as Adam
Fairclaugh and James H. Laue, have called attention to the determination
of civil rights activists to provoke federal intervention in the South. Many
of these writers have stressed the movement's deliberate exploitation of
white violence to advance that objective.[54] While demonstrating an awareness that there was a relationship between violent resistance to civil rights
and the division of responsibility between the states and the national government, however, they have not focused on federalism, but instead have
treated it as a somewhat peripheral issue. The only recent writer, with the
partial exception of Nieman, to give federalism a central place in his
analysis is Julius Chambers, and he does so in a review of *Federal Law and
Southern Order*. Although critical of the book, Chambers at least recognizes
the essence of the problem with which it deals: whether "the national
government was [or was] not powerless to prevent the pervasive racial
violence and discrimination suffered during the 1960s."[55]

Contrary to what Chambers contends, *Federal Law and Southern Order* does not endorse nonintervention as a constitutional principle. This book does conclude, however, that by the time the Supreme Court and Congress got around to equipping the Justice Department with an appropriate legal weapon for combatting racist violence in the South, white southerners were already cracking down on such violence themselves.[56] The problem of uncontrolled white terrorism was once very real and very serious, and it demanded the attention of the national government. But federal intervention in southern law enforcement, while constitutionally admissible, has not been necessary for nearly a quarter of a century.

That does not mean we can ignore today the voices of those who demanded it in the 1950s and 1960s. As Chambers points out, federalism can easily become a "pretext for quiescence."[57] The Eisenhower and Kennedy administrations, and for a time the administration of Lyndon Johnson as well, used federalism for that purpose. In the 1950s and 1960s federalism provided government leaders with a constitutional justification for politically convenient inaction. The temptation to exploit it for that purpose remains. The danger that federalism will be used as an excuse for declining to deal with difficult social problems is as real today as it was a quarter of a century ago. The specific dilemma with which *Federal Law and Southern Order* deals is no longer with us, but the broader issues that this book raises remain very much alive.

Notes

1   *Los Angeles Times*, February 6, 1994.

2   Michal R. Belknap, *Federal Law and Southern Order: Racial Violence and Constitutional Conflict in the Post-"Brown" South* (Athens, Ga.: University of Georgia Press, 1987), pp. 123–24.

3   "Protection of Civil Rights: A Mandate for the Federal Government," *Michigan Law Review* 87 (May 1989): 1613.

4   "Combating Racial Violence: A Legislative Proposal," *Harvard Law Review* 101 (April 1988): 1270; United States v. Ebens, 800 F.2d 1422, 1425 (6th Cir. 1986).

5   Stephen J. Whitfield, *A Death in the Delta: The Story of Emmett Till* (Baltimore: Johns Hopkins University Press, 1988), pp. 131–33, 144; W. Fitzhugh Brundage, *Lynching in the New South: Georgia and Virginia, 1880–1930* (Urbana: University of Illinois Press, 1993), p. 48.

6   Brundage, *Lynching in the New South*, p. 48.

7   James Mann, "Tremors of Bigotry that Worry America," *U.S. News & World Report*, July 13, 1981, p. 48.

8   Miriam Rozen, "Town on Trial," *American Lawyer*, June 1989, p. 80.

9   Nicholas Mills, *Like a Holy Crusade: Mississippi 1964—The Turning of the Civil Rights Movement in America* (Chicago: Ivan R. Dee, 1992), pp. 185–86 (Milpas is quoted at 186).

10   Rozen, "Town on Trial," p. 80; Howard Swindle, *Deliberate Indifference: A Story of Murder and Racial Injustice* (New York: Viking, 1993); Ladner v. State, 780 S.W.2d 247 (Tex. Crim App. 1989); Ladner v. State, 868 S.W.2d 417 (Tex. App. 1993); Frank Judge, "Slaying the Dragon," *American Lawyer*, September 1987, p. 83.

11   Judge, "Slaying the Dragon," p. 83; Elizabeth Wheaton, *Codename GREENKILL: The 1979 Greensboro Killings* (Athens: University of Georgia Press, 1987), pp. 10, 101–4, 108, 136–48, 153, 170, 175, 180–82, 202–3, 225–28.

12   Wheaton, *Codename GREENKILL*, pp. 212–13, 227–28, 231, 233–34, 253–54, 256–80.

13   United States v. Ebens, 800 F.2d at 1425, 1429, 1430–37 (quote at 1429).

14   United States v. Koon, 34 F.3d 1416 (9th Cir. 1994).

15   See for example, E. M. Beck and Stewart E. Tolnay, "The Killing Fields of the Deep South: The Market for Cotton and the Lynching of Blacks, 1882–1930," *American Sociological Review* 55 (August 1990): 526–39; Jay Corzine, Lin Huff-Corzine, and James C. Creech, "The Tenant Labor Market and Lynching in the South: A Test of Split Labor Market Theory," *Sociological Inquiry* 58 (Summer 1988): 261–78; Susan Olzak, "The Political Context of Competition: Lynching and Urban Racial Violence, 1882–1914," *Social Forces* 69 (December 1990): 395–421; Stewart E. Tolnay and E. M. Beck, "Racial Violence and Black Migration in the American South 1910 to 1930," *American Sociological Review* 57 (February 1992): 103–16; Charlotte Wolf, "Constructions of a Lynching," *Sociological Inquiry* 62 (Winter 1992): 83–97.

16   Brundage, *Lynching in the New South*. See also "To Howl Loudly: John Mitchell Jr. and his Campaign Against Lynching in Virginia," *Canadian Review of American Studies* 22 (Winter 1991): 325–41.

17   George C. Wright, *Racial Violence in Kentucky, 1865–1940: Lynchings, Mob Rule and "Legal Lynchings"* (Baton Rouge: Louisiana State University Press, 1990), pp. 1, 13 (quote at 1).

18   Ann Field Faulkner, "'Like an Evil Wind': The Roanoke Riot of 1893 and the Lynching of Thomas Smith," *Virginia Magazine of History and Biography* 100 (April 1992): 173–206; Michael J. Pfeifer, "The Ritual of Lynching: Extralegal Justice in Missouri, 1890–1942," *Gateway Heritage* 13 (Winter 1993):

22–33; Walter T. Howard, "Vigilante Justice and National Reaction: The 1937 Tallahassee Double Lynching," *Florida Historical Quarterly* 67 (July 1988): 32–51; Nancy Maclean, *Behind the Mask of Chivalry: The Making of the Second Ku Klux Klan* (New York: Oxford University Press, 1994), pp. 34, 149–52, 171–73; William L. Ziglar, "The Decline of Lynching in America," *International Social Science Review* 63 (Winter 1988): 14–25; Mark Ellis, "Joel Spingarn's 'Constructive Programme' and the Wartime Antilynching Bill of 1918," *Journal of Policy History* 4 (1992): 134–61.

19   Herbert Shapiro, *White Violence and Black Response: From Reconstruction to Montgomery* (Amherst: University of Massachusetts Press, 1988); Jack E. Davis, "'Whitewash' in Florida: The Lynching of Jesse James Payne and Its Aftermath," *Florida Historical Quarterly* 68 (January 1990): 277–98; Dominic J. Capici Jr., "The Lynching of Cleo Wright: Federal Protection of Constitutional Rights during World War II," *Journal of American History* 72 (March 1986): 859–87 (quote at 859).

20   Belknap, *Federal Law and Southern Order*, pp. 31–32, 36–37, 61–62.

21   Whitfield, *A Death in the Delta*; Howard Smead, *Blood Justice: The Lynching of Mack Charles Parker* (New York: Oxford University Press, 1986).

22   Hugh David Graham, *The Civil Rights Era: Origins and Development of National Policy, 1960–1972* (New York: Oxford University Press, 1990); ibid., *Civil Rights and the Presidency: Race and Gender in American Politics 1960–1972* (New York: Oxford University Press, 1992); David R. Goldfield, *Black, White, and Southern: Race Relations and Southern Culture 1940 to the Present* (Baton Rouge: Louisiana State University Press, 1990), pp. 88–89, 128–29; Robert Weisbrot, *Freedom Bound: A History of America's Civil Rights Movement* (New York: W. W. Norton, 1990), pp. 57–60, 67–68, 93–99, 113, 196–203; John Dittmer, *Local People: The Struggle for Civil Rights in Mississippi* (Urbana and Chicago: University of Illinois Press, 1994), *passim*; Donald G. Nieman, *Promises to Keep: African-Americans and the Constitutional Order 1776 to the Present* (New York: Oxford University Press, 1991), pp. 155–72.

23   Weisbrot, *Freedom Bound*, p. 93.

24   Ibid.

25   Doug McAdam, *Freedom Summer* (New York: Oxford University Press, 1988), pp. 4, 26–27, 96–101; Nicholas Mills, *Like a Holy Crusade: Mississippi 1964—The Turning of the Civil Rights Movement in America* (Chicago: Ivan R. Dee, 1992), pp. 133–34, 141–44; Mary King, *Freedom Song: A Personal Story of the 1960s Civil Rights Movement* (New York: William Morrow, 1987), pp. 367–98.

26   Seth Cagin and Philip Dray, *We Are Not Afraid: The Story of Goodman, Schwerner and Chaney and the Civil Rights Campaign in Mississippi* (New York: Macmillan, 1988). For Cagin and Dray's discussion of other violent incidents in Mississippi and elsewhere in the South in addition to the anti–civil rights murders

that are the focus of the book, see particularly pp. 23–25, 31, 49, 54, 70–74, 108–11, 116–19, 150, 157, 191–92, 205, 207–8, 215–16, 220, 223, 227–28.

27 Ibid., p. 151.
28 Ibid., p. 435.
29 Ibid., p. 228.
30 Ibid., pp. 150–54, 192–93 (quote at 150).
31 Mills, *Like a Holy Crusade*, p. 46.
32 Whitfield, *A Death in the Delta*, p. 43.
33 Ibid., p. 44.
34 *Freedom Bound*, pp. 57, 139 (quote at 139).
35 "Selma's Smitherman Affair," *Alabama Review* (April 1991): 122–23.
36 Weisbrot, *Freedom Bound*, pp. 58, 60, 67, 129–30, 202; Jack Bass, *Taming the Storm: The Life and Times of Judge Frank M. Johnson, Jr. and the South's Fight Over Civil Rights* (New York: Doubleday, 1993), p. 251; David J. Garrow, *Bearing the Cross: Martin Luther King, Jr., and the Southern Christian Leadership Conference* (New York: William Morrow, 1986), pp. 86–87, 157, 187–88, 341, 361, 392. Garrow does point out, however, that King was so impressed with how quickly the FBI arrested the killers of Viola Luizzo that he sent J. Edgar Hoover a congratulatory telegram. (Ibid., p. 413). In his biography of King, which ends in 1963, Taylor Branch pictures the FBI and the national government in general as somewhat more sympathetic and responsive than does Garrow. See *Parting the Waters: America in the King Years, 1954–1963* (New York: Simon & Schuster, 1988), pp. 64, 257–58, 521, 638–39, 718, 891–92.
37 Whitfield, *A Death in the Delta*, pp. 71, 75. For further critical discussion of the Eisenhower administration's failure to do anything about the Emmett Till lynching, see ibid., pp. 71–75.
38 Smead, *Blood Justice*, p. 160. Smead, however, does go on to point out that the federal government did reenter the case after Mississippi failed to indict anyone in it. Rulings by Judge Sidney Mize crippled its case, and a federal grand jury, sitting in Biloxi, also failed to indict anyone. (Ibid., pp. 177, 194–95).
39 McAdam, *Freedom Summer*, p. 39.
40 Ibid., p. 103; King, *Freedom Song*, pp. 384, 388–89, 393–94; Mills, *Like a Holy Crusade*, pp. 16, 97–102, 111–12; Cagin and Dray, *We Are Not Afraid*, pp. 42, 154, 304–6, 308–9, 331–33, 339, 354–55, 369–70.
41 King, *Freedom Song*, p. 384.
42 Kenneth O'Reilly, "The FBI and the Civil Rights Movement During the Kennedy Years—From the Freedom Rides to Albany," *Journal of Southern History* 54 (May 1988): 208–14, 220–25; Kenneth O'Reilly, *"Racial Matters": The FBI's Secret File on Black America, 1960–1972* (New York: Free Press, 1989), pp. 37, 39–40, 80, 87–90, 110–11, 355.

43 O'Reilly, *"Racial Matters,"* p. 61.

44 Ibid., p. 5.

45 O'Reilly, "FBI and the Civil Rights Movement," p. 203.

46 O'Reilly, *"Racial Matters,"* p. 103.

47 Ibid., pp. 163, 167–68. Compare Belknap, *Federal Law and Southern Order*, pp. 153–55.

48 Ibid., pp. 177–78, 195–227 (quote at 200).

49 Ibid., p. 201.

50 Nieman, *Promises to Keep*, p. 165.

51 Cagin and Dray, *We Are Not Afraid*, pp. 339–72; O'Reilly, *"Racial Matters,"* p. 175.

52 Bass, *Taming the Storm*, pp. 256–58; Michal R. Belknap, "The Legal Legacy of Lemuel Penn," *Howard Law Journal* 25 (1982): 457–524; United States v. Guest, 383 U.S. 745 (1966).

53 Nieman, *Promises to Keep*, pp. 174–76; United States v. Price, 383 U.S. 787 (1966). Whitfield comments briefly on the enactment of the antiviolence provisions of the Civil Rights Act of 1968, but is confused concerning their contents. (*A Death in the Delta*, pp. 106–7). Weisbrot discusses enactment of the statute but deals only with its open housing and antiriot provisions, ignoring those directed at the sort of violence and intimidation to which the civil rights movement had been subjected in the South (*Freedom Bound*, pp. 271–72).

54 Cagin and Dray, *We Are Not Afraid*, p. 318; Weisbrot, *Freedom Bound*, p. 96; Garrow, *Bearing the Cross*, pp. 156–57, 228–29; Adam Fairclough, *To Redeem the Soul of America: The Southern Christian Leadership Conference and Martin Luther King, Jr.* (Athens: University of Georgia Press, 1987), pp. 7–8; James H. Laue, *Direct Action and Desegregation, 1960–1962: Toward a Theory of the Rationalization of Protest* (Brooklyn, N.Y.: Carlson Publishing, 1989), p. 110.

55 Chambers, "Protection of Civil Rights," p. 1603.

56 Ibid., p. 1603 n. 19; Belknap, *Federal Law and Southern Order*, pp. 229, 233–51. Chambers is simply wrong when he states: "Belknap maintains throughout the book that responsibility for the protection of civil rights rests with state and local authorities." (Chambers, "Protection of Civil Rights," p. 1603). I characterize that as the traditional American position, but I certainly do not endorse it.

57 Chambers, "Protection of Civil Rights," p. 1614.

"The federal government must protect its citizens," James Farmer of the Congress of Racial Equality (CORE) declared in a 1963 telegram to Attorney General Robert F. Kennedy.[1] That same year Assistant Attorney General Burke Marshall, who headed the Civil Rights Division of the United States Department of Justice, argued with equal fervor, "There is no substitute under the federal system for the failure of local law enforcement responsibility."[2] Farmer and Marshall spoke for the opposing sides in a vigorous and often emotional political and constitutional debate that raged for nearly a decade and a half during the 1950s and 1960s.[3] The issue that divided them was what the national government could and should do about racial violence in the South. The drive to expand black civil rights, which accelerated so dramatically in the years following the Supreme Court's 1954 decision in *Brown v. Board of Education*, met violent resistance from a militant minority of southern whites. Although those who committed this anti–civil rights violence were guilty of murder, assault, arson, and numerous other crimes proscribed by state law, their offenses generally went unpunished. With disturbing regularity, persons responsible for enforcing the law in the South acquiesced in such crimes, and sometimes they even joined in attacking assertive blacks and white civil rights activists from the North. Farmer's was only one of hundreds of voices demanding that the national government do what southern policemen, prosecutors, judges, juries, and public officials would not: protect participants in the struggle for racial justice from physical violence. Marshall and other federal officials responded to these demands with warnings that if Washington filled the vacuum created by this abdication of responsibility by state and local authorities it would destroy American federalism. Numerous government leaders, both Democratic and Republican, resisted any substantial expansion of the federal role in southern law enforcement.

The controversy bubbled through the presidencies of Dwight D.

Eisenhower, John F. Kennedy, and Lyndon B. Johnson. Civil rights activists and Justice Department lawyers were not the only participants. The
White House, Congress, and a substantial segment of the American public became embroiled in the dispute, and even the Supreme Court addressed the issue.

The problem that concerned them all was not unique to the years after
1954. The South had always been a violent region where force and threats
of force helped whites maintain supremacy over blacks. During the days of
slavery such racially motivated violence enjoyed formal legal sanction.
After the Civil War, it became nominally unlawful, but the lynchings
which grew increasingly common as the nineteenth century neared its end
generally went unpunished anyhow. The reason was that whites controlled
the legal system, and most of them continued to view a certain amount of
force as necessary to keep blacks in "their place." Although the federal
government intervened briefly but effectively in southern law enforcement
during Reconstruction, using troops and criminal prosecutions to stamp
out white terrorism, it soon withdrew from the field. Thereafter, blacks
threatened by racist violence could seek protection only from unsym-
pathetic state authorities. By the middle of the twentieth century federal
nonintervention had become, with considerable assistance from the Supreme Court, not merely government policy but constitutional dogma.

It was a gospel the Eisenhower administration did not challenge. Although southern racial violence escalated dramatically after the *Brown* decision, the president and the Justice Department insisted that controlling
it was a state and local responsibility. The administration took this position even with respect to riotous resistance to school desegregation ordered by the federal courts. Only when this policy and the efforts of
Arkansas Governor Orval Faubus to exploit it for the purpose of preventing the integration of Little Rock's Central High School produced a major
constitutional crisis did the federal government act. By then Eisenhower's
only option was to use the army. While he was president, Congress did
enact some legislation that enabled the FBI to assist in combating the
racist bombings that were plaguing the South, but Eisenhower provided
the legislative branch with little leadership.

His successor, John F. Kennedy, was also reluctant to depart from the
established custom of federal nonintervention in southern law enforcement, for this tradition served the political needs of a Democratic president anxious to avoid alienating the usually Democratic white South. Un-

der Kennedy the Justice Department, headed by his brother Robert, sought to implement the views of Burke Marshall. During several riotous crises ignited by events such as the Freedom Rides and the court-ordered integration of the University of Mississippi, blatant abdication of responsibility by southern officials forced the Kennedy administration to take dramatic and forceful action to keep racist violence from thwarting the exercise of constitutional rights by blacks and their supporters. The White House and Justice Department leaders regarded these gestures as isolated and temporary departures from a general policy of leaving the problem of racist terrorism to the states. When civil rights workers, subjected to violence and intimidation because of their efforts to register black voters in the South, begged the national government for help, the Justice Department proved unresponsive. Federal officials advised activists to seek protection from state and local authorities, some of whom were participating in the attacks upon them.

The national government's policy of refusing to assume responsibility for controlling anti–civil rights violence was a casualty of the bloody Freedom Summer of 1964. Murders of blacks and civil rights workers in Mississippi and Georgia generated irresistible political pressures which forced Washington to reassess its approach to the problem. The FBI launched an attack on the Ku Klux Klan, and the Justice Department initiated federal prosecutions against klansmen responsible for anti–civil rights killings. The Supreme Court supported these efforts by reinterpreting old statutes and the Constitution so that the cases could go forward. Federal prosecutions resulted in convictions of some of those implicated in the Georgia and Mississippi killings. In addition, a federal jury in Alabama returned guilty verdicts against klansmen who had committed a 1965 murder there. Assured by the Supreme Court that it was willing to uphold any new legislation that might be enacted to deal with the problem, Congress in 1968 passed a sweeping statute which made virtually all conceivable forms of racially motivated violence and intimidation federal crimes.

Although dramatic, this change in federal policy has been largely ignored by scholars. So has the way the South itself, and the criminal justice systems of the southern states, reacted to the epidemic of racist violence that the region experienced during the late 1950s and early 1960s. Historians and popular writers alike have dealt with the violent incidents of those years as isolated episodes. This book examines them collectively, treating the failure of state and local authorities in the South to control and punish a variety of violent acts against the civil rights movement as what contemporaries considered it: a challenge to American federalism. The pages that follow also explore the changes in the attitudes of southern whites produced by what many of them came to view as the threatened collapse of law and order in their communities and the effects of those changes on law enforcement and the performance of judicial institutions.

In examining these matters, this book focuses on the eleven states that once comprised the Confederate States of America. There was, of course, some anti–civil rights violence elsewhere (in Maryland and Kentucky, for example), but it was in the region stretching from Virginia south and west to Texas that the problem was most serious. More important, it was in that area that the failure of state criminal justice systems to control anti–civil rights violence provoked a constitutional crisis and undermined law and order.

One person deserves most of the credit for the fact that this facet of the history of the post-*Brown* South is now being laid out in a full-length monograph. After reading the manuscript of an article I had written on one of the most legally significant racial murders of the 1960s (the slaying of Lemuel Penn near Athens, Georgia) my University of Georgia colleague Numan V. Bartley expressed the opinion that there was a need for a book on the violence against the civil rights movement and the political and constitutional controversies it ignited. Although I was already well into a totally unrelated project, his suggestion intrigued me. A little secondary reading established that, as always where the post–World War II South is concerned, Bud Bartley was right on the mark. Persuaded by him that I could do the book he had in mind, I commenced the research that has finally yielded *Federal Law and Southern Order*. Graciously accepting paternal responsibility for the project, Bud read and made invaluable comments on the manuscript. Indeed, several chapters have benefited from more than one of his critiques. For whatever merits this book may have, much of the credit belongs to him.

I also owe debts of gratitude to several other members of the history department at the University of Georgia. Peter C. Hoffer, William M. Leary, Jr., and William Whitney Stueck, Jr., all read and commented on the manuscript. So did Steven F. Lawson of the University of South Florida, who provided a superb substantive critique, and my father, Robert

Harlan Belknap, who did a great deal to improve the readability of the manuscript. I also wish to thank Professor Eugene Watts of Ohio State University and Dorothy Landsberg of the Washington, D.C., law firm of Shea & Gardner, who commented helpfully on a paper that became chapter 10, and Professor Paul Kurtz of the University of Georgia School of Law, whose critique greatly improved chapters 1 and 7.

I also owe special debts of gratitude to two other law professors, David B. Filvaroff of the University of Texas and Milner Ball of the University of Georgia. Professor Ball, one of the few legal scholars with the breadth of vision to see that lynching might have something to do with jurisprudence, helped me develop the core of chapter 1 as a paper for his course on that subject. Professor Filvaroff also indulged research interests that were much more historical than those of most law students, allowing me to work on the twenty-five-year-old Lemuel Penn case in his civil rights seminar. The paper I did for him was later published by the *Howard Law Journal*. I would like to thank its editors for allowing me to include at various places in this book material drawn from "The Legal Legacy of Lemuel Penn." I am also grateful to the editors of the *Emory Law Journal* for giving me permission to publish in chapter 10 much of my article "The Vindication of Burke Marshall: The Southern Legal System and the Anti–Civil Rights Violence of the 1960s."

I wish to express my gratitude to the many people who assisted me in my research for this book. My student research assistants, Sidney Smith III and Melissa Tufts, spent long hours culling items on racial violence from microfilmed newspaper clipping files. Particularly helpful were the members of the staff of the Lyndon B. Johnson Presidential Library, especially Nancy Smith, David Humphry, and Michael Gillette. I also wish to thank David Haight and his associates at the Dwight D. Eisenhower Presidential Library and Henry J. Gwezda and the rest of the staff at the John F. Kennedy Presidential Library. David Wigdor of the Library of Congress, Philip Shipman of the Senate Judiciary Committee staff, and Helen Near of the Federal Bureau of Investigation all helped me gain access to valuable documents in Washington, D.C. I also want to thank Mary Ceville of the reference department at the *Atlanta Journal and Constitution* for her valuable assistance in locating relevant photographs. I am especially grateful to Minnie Clayton of Atlanta University and to Louise Cook of the Martin Luther King, Jr., Center for Nonviolent Social Change, who, despite inadequate staff and funding, do a fantastic job of making available to researchers the records of some of the South's most important civil rights organizations.

The Georgia history department financed part of my research with a summer grant, for which I am grateful. I would also like to thank the Office of the Vice-President for Research at the University of Georgia, which provided me with funding for computer work, and Henry and Jane Halko, whose kindness in lending me their lovely Chesnut Hill home made my research at the Kennedy Library possible.

I also wish to offer a word of appreciation to David Moritz, longtime aide to Congressman Doug Barnard (D-Ga.) for his persistence in seeking to get me access to case files of the Justice Department's Civil Rights Division, as well as to microfilm records of that agency housed in the Kennedy Library. Unfortunately, his extensive efforts on my behalf proved unavailing. It is ironic that while the Civil Rights Division was being persistently unhelpful, the much-maligned FBI was making available to me files on three politically charged cases and a COINTELPRO operation.[4] Indeed, much of my information about what Civil Rights Division lawyers were doing comes from reports about their activities written by FBI personnel. Also extremely helpful was a Bureau report on the situation in Little Rock, Arkansas, in 1957, which Professor Tony Freyer of the University of Alabama obtained and was kind enough to share with me.

If Numan Bartley is the father of *Federal Law and Southern Order,* then Charles East is at least its godfather. During his tenure as editor of the University of Georgia Press he repeatedly encouraged me to write this book. Sometimes Charles seemed to have more faith in the project than I did. Upon his retirement from the press, he paid me the supreme compliment of asking to copyedit my manuscript on a free-lance basis. He is also responsible for the fact that the book reached completion as quickly as it did. When Charles left Georgia, he left the job of prodding me along in the capable hands of Malcolm Call, to whom I am also grateful.

I would also like to express my appreciation to Kathy Coley and Donna Marshall, who worked harder on this book than anyone else but me. The good humor with which they word-processed draft after draft for an author who never seemed to stop revising deserves all the praise I can offer. I suspect the thing they will appreciate more, however, is never having to see the manuscript again.

My wife is no doubt also glad the book is finished. Some aspects of this project, such as a wonderful summer research trip to Boston, were fun for her too. Mostly, though, what *Federal Law and Southern Order* has meant to Tricia is long hours without a husband, who seemed to have more time for the participants in the civil rights conflicts of the 1950s and 1960s than for her. I may have written this book, but Tricia's love and understanding made it possible.

ONE

Law and Violence in the Lynching Era

In May 1916 a mob dragged Jesse Washington, a black man just convicted of sexually assaulting and murdering a white woman, from a Waco, Texas, courtroom. While 10,000 persons watched and cheered, the lynchers cut off his fingers, ears, and genitals. Using a chain, they hoisted their dying victim into a tree, then lowered him several times into a raging fire. Having completed this brutal execution, they tied Washington's charred remains to a horse and dragged them through the streets of the town. Both the mayor and the police chief watched the black man die, but local authorities made no move to prosecute the killers. Nor did the federal government take any action against them.[1] The "Waco Horror" exemplified a southern problem that had originated long before 1916. It was one which would persist for more than half a century after the Waco lynching and which, during the decade and a half of rapid expansion in the civil rights of blacks that began in 1954, would severely strain the fiber of American federalism.

The essence of the problem was that in the South whites could maim and kill deviant or assertive blacks with impunity because their race controlled the criminal justice system. Extralegal violence against blacks was a bulwark of the southern system of white supremacy, and even those white southerners who refrained from such conduct themselves were disinclined to punish those who did engage in it. Although lynching became less common in the decades which followed 1916, the attitudes that had produced the Waco Horror survived into the 1950s. So did a notable reluctance on the part of the national government to interfere with the vigilante methods of racial control practiced in the southern states. Although the Fourteenth Amendment appeared to provide a constitutional basis for action by the national government against the racist violence which authorities in the South refused either to prevent or punish, the federal role in combating interracial terrorism remained extremely limited.

Extralegal executions did not become a prominent feature of black-white relations in the South until after the Civil War. In the days of slavery the positive law of the southern states sanctioned—indeed required—the use of force by private individuals to enforce the subordination of the Negro race. Whites, who totally controlled the antebellum legal system, believed self-preservation justified all measures necessary to prevent servile insurrection. Consequently, southern colonies, and later southern states, adopted slave codes which required masters to maintain discipline among their Negro chattels and authorized them to use corporal punishment to do so. The whip became a symbol of the planter's authority. The principal limitation upon its use was the master's own discretion, for in many places the law was more concerned with prodding permissive owners toward firmness than with restraining those who might carry discipline too far.[2] As North Carolina Chief Justice Thomas Ruffin acknowledged in 1829: "We cannot allow the right of the master to be brought into discussion in the courts of justice. The slave, to remain a slave, must be sensible that there is no appeal from his master."[3]

Southern law placed blacks at the mercy not only of their owners but of an entire race. Every white was authorized to apprehend any Negro unable to give a satisfactory account of himself. In South Carolina, if a slave found off the plantation refused to submit to interrogation, his white questioner could summarily execute him. Even for mere insolence, a member of the master race had the right to beat either a slave or a free Negro.[4]

While antebellum southern law legitimated and incorporated into the legal system a vast range of violent acts by white private citizens, it did impose some restraints on the use of force against blacks. Early colonial slave codes either failed to punish the killing of a bondsman or imposed only very modest penalties for that offense, but a dramatic policy change occurred following the Revolution. One state after another declared, in either its statutes or its constitution, that the malicious killing of a slave was murder. By 1821 every slave state had taken this step.[5] While still a republic, Texas adopted a statute making the killing of a slave murder, and in 1845 it provided in its first state constitution that any person maliciously dismembering or taking the life of a bondsman should "suffer such punishment as would be inflicted, in case the like offense had been committed upon a free white person."[6] The Texas Supreme Court found in these measures an "intention of our legislation . . . to throw around the *life* of a slave the same protection which is guaranteed to a freeman."[7]

On the basis of similar reasoning, judges in several other states held that slave killers could be indicted for common-law murder.[8] In one such case, Justice J. G. Clark of the Mississippi Supreme Court expressed the view that "it would be a stigma upon the character of the state, and a reproach to the administration of justice, if the life of a slave [could] be taken with impunity."[9] In 1853 the Texas Supreme Court announced: "Slaves are persons within the meaning of the statutes concerning crimes; and . . . where not otherwise provided . . . the statutes enacted for the punishment of . . . crimes committed by violence to the person, apply equally to . . . a slave."[10] In addition, by the 1850s most slave codes had made cruelty a criminal offense.[11]

Not many whites actually suffered punishment for abusing or killing blacks. The statutes which supposedly protected slaves contained large loopholes. For example, the accidental killing of a slave while he was receiving "moderate correction" was not a homicide. Nor was it an offense to kill a slave who was resisting arrest or rebelling. Courts often took the position that the line between permissible correction and cruelty was impossible to draw. Further reducing the possibility of conviction was the prohibition against slaves giving testimony, which was common to the law of all southern states. A detailed study of eighteen judicial districts in South Carolina reveals that few whites were prosecuted for murdering slaves, and of those who were, only 22.5 percent were convicted.[12] One jury foreman forthrightly admitted he "would not convict the defendant or any other white person for murdering a slave."[13] Nevertheless, fifty-five convictions for killing or abusing blacks were appealed to the supreme courts of the southern states during the period 1830–1860. Most were affirmed, even when tenable grounds existed for granting the white defendant a new trial.[14] In announcing one of these decisions, Justice Wheeler of the Texas Supreme Court expressed what seems to have been the fundamental assumption of the antebellum legal system concerning interracial violence: "The interest of the master, as well as the dictates of humanity, require that [slaves] should be within the protection of the law."[15]

Although blacks enjoyed only limited legal protection from white attack during the antebellum period, they seldom experienced extralegal violence. Lynching was common, but the victims were much more often white than Negro. White abolitionists, viewed as threats to the economic and social structure of the region, were frequent targets of mobs and vigilance committees, egged on by the southern press. Neighbors of a man believed to have incited a slave to insubordination might well hang him from the nearest tree. Such summary executions often accompanied the insurrection scares which periodically sent a shiver of terror through the antebellum South. These episodes also produced most of the relatively small number of black lynchings that occurred. Generally, bondsmen and women were safe from summary execution, in part because of planter paternalism, but even more because of their value as property. Slaying a slave might well subject the killer to a suit for damages by the victim's owner. The economic self-interest of whites protected blacks from lynchings.[16]

By eliminating slavery the Civil War removed this effective restraint on interracial killing. It also resulted in a substantial reduction in the legal autonomy of the states, making it impossible for the South any longer formally and openly to incorporate white violence against blacks into its positive law. The Civil Rights Act of 1866, and particularly the Equal Protection Clause of the Fourteenth Amendment (added to the Constitution in 1868), made it unlawful for a state to designate all members of one race as its agents for the control of the other race and to authorize them to mete out summary punishment at their own discretion.[17] If southerners were to use private force to maintain white supremacy, they would have to go outside the law to do it. Unconcerned with the legality of actions they regarded as essential for their safety, the preservation of their social structure, and the control of their black work force, whites responded violently to the assertiveness of freedmen. Their aggressions ranged from individual assaults through pitched battles to massive rioting in New Orleans and Memphis.[18]

This escalating violence quickly became organized, as secret terroristic societies sprang up throughout the South. White night riders, increasingly identified with the Ku Klux Klan, reduced many areas to virtual anarchy. Seldom did local authorities make any effort to control them. An exasperated federal army officer reported from Jefferson, Texas, that "the civil officers *cannot* and *will not* punish these outrages."[19] Nor would southern juries. One judge observed in 1868 that it was "almost an impossibility . . . to convict a white man of any crime . . . where the violence has been against a black man."[20]

Ku Kluxers enjoyed immunity from punishment because they kept the black population docile. Although lacking the legal sanction enjoyed by the slave patrols that had kept slaves from running away or rebelling before the Civil War, klansmen performed a similar function. They insisted that their terroristic methods, used for purposes ranging from discouraging Afro-American political participation to driving blacks off land that whites wanted, were necessary to preserve law and order. Actually, as Allen Trelease observes, "The overriding purpose of the Ku Klux movement . . . was the maintenance or restoration of white supremacy in every walk of life."[21]

One of the movement's principal instruments was lynching. Whites whipped and even killed blacks for often trivial reasons. A "nigger hunt" in Louisiana's Bossier Parish that took 120 lives in 1868 was only the most extreme example of a phenomenon which became widespread during Reconstruction. No longer valuable property, blacks ceased to be a minority among the victims of lynching. The epidemic of extralegal executions which began during Reconstruction grew worse in the 1880s. Lynching reached a peak in the 1890s and remained at a relatively high level through the first two decades of the twentieth century.[22]

Although at one time common in frontier areas on both sides of the Mason-Dixon line and used against members of all races, lynching became increasingly a southern phenomenon and a black problem. During the thirty-year period from 1889 to 1918 the South (including Missouri and Oklahoma) accounted for 85 percent of the lynchings in the entire country, and by the end of this period it was responsible for over 97 percent. Elsewhere, less than one-third of the persons lynched between 1888 and 1929 were Afro-Americans. In the South 85 percent were. Even in Texas, with a large Mexican-American minority that was frequently the target of white violence, all but 72 of the 355 persons lynched between 1889 and 1918 were black.[23]

Southerners often attributed the frequency with which they lynched Negroes to the inefficiency of their legal systems. They complained that law enforcement was inadequate in sparsely settled areas, that their judicial systems were slow and uncertain, and that appellate court rulings based on legal technicalities often rescued the guilty from punishment. "If criminals were promptly tried and punished for their offenses with a satisfactory degree of fairness and certainty," the *Dallas Morning News* editorialized in 1897, "the lyncher would soon find himself without a job and without encouragement." The chief justice of North Carolina and the Georgia Bar Association expressed nearly identical views. Lynching was, Mobile, Alabama, attorney Hannis Taylor insisted, "the outcry of a conservative and lawloving people against the abuses of a system of criminal procedure which has become intolerably inefficient."[24]

The frequency with which this thesis was articulated, as well as the endorsement it received in 1905 from a prominent northern lawyer, future president and chief justice William Howard Taft, suggests it may have had some factual foundation. Lynchings did tend to be more common where murders had been frequent but murderers rarely had been punished. The alleged inefficiency of the legal system, however, provides no explanation for actions such as the Waco execution of Jesse Washington, who already had been convicted and would have been put to death legally the following morning. Also undercutting this justification for summary punishment are some comparative figures from South Carolina and Rhode Island. During the period 1920–1926, South Carolina punished six persons for every ten homicides committed, while Rhode Island punished only four. Yet South Carolinians lynched four persons suspected of murder or attempted murder, while Rhode Islanders lynched none. The evidence simply does not support the contention that a weak and inefficient legal system compelled southerners to resort to summary punishment.[25]

Nor does it sustain the claim that lynching was necessary to protect white women from Negro rapists. White southerners had always exhibited a sort of paranoia about black sexual aggression and had long punished it savagely. In 1806 Georgia made death the penalty for even the attempted rape of a white woman by a Negro man, and at one time both that state and Virginia punished this offense with castration.[26] Probably, as Walter White of the National Association for the Advancement of Colored People (NAACP) observed in 1929, "The vast majority of whites in the states where lynchings are most frequently staged really believe that most mob murders are the results of sex crimes."[27] But they were not. Studies of various periods between 1889 and 1944 establish that never were more than 34 percent of lynching victims even accused of sexually assaulting a white woman; generally, the figure was below 30 percent.[28]

The real explanation for the high level of lynching characteristic of the post-Reconstruction South was the determination of whites to maintain their traditional dominance over blacks. In 1907 Mississippi's Senator James K. Vardaman declared that every Negro in the state would be lynched if such a slaughter were necessary to maintain white supremacy. Whites gradually devised institutional arrangements, such as disfranchisement and *de jure* segregation, to protect their position, but lynching served constantly to remind blacks of the raw physical power on which white supremacy ultimately rested. It was a way of terrorizing the "uppity nigger" back into his "proper place." Recognizing this, the Tuskegee Institute, which kept the best records on the subject, defined a lynching as a killing "at the hands of a group acting under the pretext of service," not only to "justice" but also to "race, or tradition." While many members of lynch mobs came from the poorer and less educated segments of the white population, whose positions were most directly threatened by black advances, members of local elites often provided both leadership and numbers. Lynching drew its repressive power from the extraordinary caste solidarity which supported it.[29]

The brutality often associated with this form of murder was a consequence of its purpose. The objective was not simply to kill a Negro but to make an example of him. After a black murder suspect was shot while allegedly resisting arrest at Honey Grove, Texas, in 1930, a mob seized his corpse and dragged it several miles in order to burn it in front of a Negro church. In Morehouse Parish, Louisiana, in 1881, whites drove home the message that their property rights must be respected by trussing up a black cattle thief inside a cow with only his head protruding, so that buzzards and crows could pick his eyes out. From the 1880s on, such relatively humane methods of execution as hanging and shooting increasingly yielded to mutilation and torture, followed by roasting over a slow fire. At Paris, Texas, in 1893, the father of the girl Henry Smith was accused of raping and murdering seared off his flesh with a hot tinner's iron, cut out his tongue, and blinded him, after which the mob set Smith ablaze.[30]

Because lynching was basically an instrument of racial control, it tended to intensify whenever something disrupted the "accommodative structure" of race relations. In the 1890s, when white Populists sought black votes in an effort to wrest political control of the South from conservative Bourbons, their opponents responded with violence and intimidation. The year 1892 witnessed 161 lynchings of blacks, the most ever. Some of these killings involved direct political repression. The others, although ostensibly punishment for crimes, were part of a generalized reassertion of white supremacy that also produced major race riots in Wilmington, North Carolina (1898), Lake City, South Carolina (1898), New Orleans, Louisiana (1900), and Atlanta, Georgia (1906). Like disfranchisement and segregation, lynching became a means of reuniting whites across class lines.[31]

By the turn of the century, whites had legislated blacks into second-class citizenship and intimidated them into quiescence. With the new caste system firmly in place, the number of lynchings recorded each year dropped steadily, falling 66 percent between 1900 and 1917. Then World War I disrupted the status quo. Black men returned from military service far less willing than they had once been to accept quietly the indignities of Jim Crow. Whites met their new assertiveness with increased violence. The number of black lynchings, down to only 36 in 1917, leaped to 76 in 1919.[32]

By 1922, however, lynching was on the decline again, the annual total falling to seven in 1929. What seemed to be a dying phenomenon revived in 1930, probably resuscitated by economic competition between the races, made bitter by the Great Depression. Lynchings became briefly more common and more brutal. But after 1935 the number of blacks summarily executed each year dropped below ten and stayed there. A race firmly locked into a subordinate caste position did not need frequent violent reminders that its place was at the bottom of the southern social hierarchy.[33]

During the period when lynching was necessary, those who engaged in it could count on the support of a majority of their fellow whites and the acquiescence of almost all the rest. For this reason, despite breaking what was nominally the law, they had little to fear from those who administered the southern legal system. Typical was the attitude of the Columbus, Texas, prosecutor who in 1935 dismissed a lynching as "an expression of the will of the people." South Carolina Governor Cole Blease, that state's chief executive from 1911 to 1915, was even more tolerant of mob violence, proclaiming himself willing to participate personally in the lynching of any black man who attacked a white woman. Like Blease, local sheriffs generally shared the attitudes of their constituents. In any event, they needed the votes of mob members and their friends to stay in office. Some southern peace officers courageously defended black prisoners from would-be lynchers, but far more typical was the one who asked rhetorically, "Do you think I am going to risk my life protecting a 'nigger'?"

Indeed, according to Arthur F. Raper, during the period 1930–1933 sheriffs or their deputies planned or participated in nearly half of all lynchings.[34]

Because lynchers often acted with the assistance of law enforcement personnel and almost always enjoyed at least the silent support of their communities, it is hardly surprising that very few of them received any punishment for their conduct. The legal system served mainly as a shield for the guilty. Although the identities of lynchers were generally a matter of common knowledge, coroners routinely reported that the victims had died at the hands of "persons unknown." Neither prosecutors nor grand juries exhibited much interest in investigating crimes of violence against blacks, and only rarely was a white indicted for such an offense. When lynchers were hailed into court, eyewitnesses often refused to testify. The judge would assist the defendants with rulings adverse to the prosecution, and the jury would nullify the law by ignoring any evidence of guilt and voting for acquittal.[35]

The failure of the southern criminal justice system to punish lynching was nearly total. As of 1933, less than 1 percent of the country's lynchings had been followed by successful prosecution of those responsible. Seven years later Mark Ethridge of the *Louisville Courier-Journal* informed Congress that since record keeping began in 1882 there had been legal action against those responsible for only 40 of the approximately 5,150 lynchings in the United States. As late as 1933, only four southern states had recorded any convictions, and most of those were accounted for by Alabama, where half of all the persons in the entire country punished for lynching in the first three decades of the twentieth century were prosecuted during Thomas Kilby's 1919–1920 gubernatorial term.[36] For years the southern criminal justice system regularly collaborated with lynching.

That system was, of course, not totally independent. The southern states were part of a larger legal order which, at least after the adoption of the Fourteenth Amendment in 1868, seemed to possess the power to ensure the security of the nation's black citizens. Traditional concepts of federalism prevented the national government from suppressing lynching.

Federal authorities did move against racial violence during Reconstruction. General Ulysses S. Grant ordered military commanders in the occupied South to arrest and try persons committing crimes against blacks if local officials failed to prosecute them. The Civil Rights Act of 1866,

which guaranteed citizens of all races the equal benefit of "laws and proceedings for the security of person" and authorized punishment of anyone
acting "under color" of law or custom who deprived someone of that
right, also seemed to provide for federal trial of crimes against blacks that
state courts would not punish. That statute was used against perpetrators
of interracial murders until the Supreme Court decided an 1871 case in
which two Kentucky white men had axed to death several members of a
black family and then mutilated the bodies. Contrary to appearances, the
court said, the statute did not give the national government jurisdiction
to try such offenses. Many members of the Republican party, which then
controlled Congress, were themselves uneasy about the sort of extension of
federal authority that the Court had refused to sanction. Most ordinary
crimes, including murder and assault, had always been outside the jurisdiction of the central government. These were offenses against state and
local law, and most Republicans would have preferred leaving punishment
of them to state and local governments. They had no desire to extend
federal authority any further than was necessary to ensure that state law
and its enforcement met certain minimum standards. On the other hand,
the Republicans were committed to guaranteeing certain civil rights to all
citizens. That required reducing somewhat the options open to states in
dealing with their own residents.[37]

It was only with great reluctance that the Republican majority in Congress moved beyond the sort of negative intervention represented by statutory and constitutional prohibitions limiting what states could do to the
enactment of legislation authorizing the federal government itself to prosecute wrongdoers who otherwise would have evaded punishment. Ani-
mated by the Ku Klux Klan's unchecked reign of terror, Congress on May
31, 1870, passed an enforcement act, intended to implement the new
Fifteenth Amendment. This statute spoke first to state election officials,
promising to inflict penalties on them if they attempted to keep blacks
from exercising the franchise. But it also provided for punishment of private citizens who committed certain kinds of election offenses, including
the use of force or intimidation to keep persons whose right to vote was
protected by the Fifteenth Amendment from exercising this right. In addition, the law's section 6, obviously inspired by the Klan's recent depre-
dations, made it a felony for two or more persons to conspire or go in
disguise with the intent to deprive a citizen of the exercise of "any right or
privilege granted or secured to him by the Constitution or laws of the

United States," or to punish him for having exercised one of these rights or privileges.[38]

A year later, still disturbed by Klan violence and determined to protect the freedmen if the southern states could not or would not do so, Congress adopted the so-called Ku Klux Act. Relying this time primarily on the Fourteenth Amendment, the House and Senate authorized the president, when an unlawful combination or domestic violence obstructed the execution of state or federal law, to utilize the militia or armed forces of the United States to meet the crisis. In addition, the Ku Klux Act subjected to fine and/or imprisonment persons who went about in disguise or entered into conspiracies with the objective of depriving others of the equal protection of the laws or of equal privileges and immunities under the law, or who conspired to employ force or intimidation to keep those entitled to vote from doing so. This 1871 law also made it an offense to conspire to deprive someone of his or her equal protection rights by hindering state efforts to secure those rights or by interfering with the due course of state justice. Congress endeavored to avoid supplanting local jurisdiction over ordinary crimes by defining as federal offenses only conduct peculiar to the Klan and similar organizations, but it did impose federal criminal sanctions on a good deal of private conduct.[39]

Although the Ku Klux Act punished private behavior, its constitutional basis was the Fourteenth Amendment, which forbade only states, not individuals, to deny privileges and immunities, due process, and the equal protection of the laws. The author of this legislation, Representative Samuel Shellabarger (R-Ohio), and several other Republican members of Congress explained their reliance on the Fourteenth Amendment by characterizing a state's failure to punish private persons who had deprived others of these constitutional rights as state action. It should be noted that Congress had written the Fourteenth Amendment following hearings at which its Joint Committee on Reconstruction took extensive testimony about the refusal of southern states to punish private wrongs against blacks, carpetbaggers, and unionists. By adopting the amendment in 1866, senators and representatives (many of whom were still serving in 1871) apparently sought to provide a constitutional basis for federal action in cases where states defaulted on their responsibility to protect all classes of citizens. Certainly, Shellabarger assumed that is what they had done. Unfortunately, when moderate and conservative Republicans objected to what they regarded as an improper attempt to extend the original jurisdiction of the federal government over the private rights of individuals, he modified his bill.[40]

The result was ambiguity. Although one authority insists that in its final form the Ku Klux Act was intended to authorize the federal government to act directly against individuals only when they sought to prevent a public official from affording equal protection, he concedes that the statutory language did not make this clear.[41] Indeed, the words of the new law seemed to authorize the central government to punish those who conspired to commit such offenses as murder and assault—normally crimes dealt with by the states—provided only that their objective had been to deprive someone of his or her federal rights. This is probably what Congress intended to do, but only with respect to situations in which a state had defaulted on its responsibility to protect the victims of such crimes. Failure to make it clear that state inaction was the constitutional basis on which the Ku Klux Act rested made it vulnerable to later attack, and by the mid-1880s had very nearly destroyed its utility.[42]

In the short run, however, the anti-Klan legislation of 1870–1871 proved extremely effective. In most areas federal prosecutors and grand juries moved with vigor against Ku Kluxers. The results were hundreds of indictments. Scores of terrorists pleaded guilty, producing conviction rates of 74 percent in 1870, 41 percent in 1872, and 36 percent in 1873. Only a fraction of those arrested were ever tried, and many convicted klansmen received suspended sentences. Nevertheless, the obvious determination of the national government struck terror into the hearts of klansmen. The federal crackdown, which lasted a mere four years, broke the back of the Ku Klux movement.[43]

Even as this campaign to control white terrorism approached a successful conclusion, its legal basis began to erode. When all federal laws were recodified and published as the *Revised Statutes* in 1873, the 1870 Enforcement Act, a related measure enacted in 1871, and the Ku Klux Act were broken up and their provisions scattered. In 1894 Congress, now controlled by the southern-based Democratic party, repealed a number of those that protected suffrage. Other provisions of the 1870–1871 legislation dropped out of the statute books when the federal criminal laws were recodified in 1909.[44]

The penal code still contained two provisions with the potential to protect blacks from violence and intimidation. Section 19 made it a crime for two or more persons to "conspire to injure, oppress, threaten, or intimidate any citizen" for the purpose of keeping him from exercising or enjoying "any right or privilege secured to him by the Constitution or laws of the United States," or to abuse him for having done so. This provision also forbade going in disguise on the highway or onto the premises of another with the intent to prevent or hinder the free exercise of any right or privilege secured by the Constitution or by federal law. Section 20 made it a crime for a *single individual* to deprive another person of some of these same rights or privileges, provided he acted willfully and "under color of any law, statute, ordinance, regulation, or custom."[45]

Although legislative action had removed some behavior outlawed in 1870–1871 from the law's explicit proscription, Congress did far less to undermine the federal government's capacity to combat southern racial violence than did the Supreme Court. Emphasizing the apparent discrepancy between laws punishing private conduct and constitutional amendments addressed only to state action, the Court began in the mid-1870s to eviscerate the anti-Klan legislation. This process commenced with *United States v. Cruikshank* (1876), a case arising out of a prosecution under the 1870 Enforcement Act for an 1873 racial massacre at Colfax, Louisiana, in which at least sixty blacks had been killed and their bodies left to rot in the parching sun.[46] Attempting to justify section 6, Joseph Bradley, a Supreme Court justice sitting as a circuit judge, expressed the opinion that "the war of race, whether it assumes the dimensions of civil strife or domestic violence, whether carried on in a guerrilla or predatory form, or by private combinations, or even by private outrage or intimidation, is subject to the jurisdiction of the government of the United States." Congress could reach such violence under the Fifteenth Amendment, he believed, provided what it targeted were attempts to keep blacks from voting because of their color which the states had failed to prosecute.[47] The Supreme Court, however, took a more restrictive view of congressional power under the Reconstruction amendments. Speaking for the Court, Chief Justice Morrison R. Waite announced that the Fourteenth Amendment added nothing to the rights of one person against another. Consequently, it could not support legislation against conspiracies to commit what were really state crimes, such as murder and false imprisonment. According to Waite, the Due Process and Equal Protection clauses authorized Congress only to forbid states to take affirmative action denying or encroaching upon individual rights.

Cruikshank boded ill for the future of the anti-Klan legislation. Its potential for destroying the capacity of the federal government to combat lynching was partially fulfilled seven years later when the Court in *United States v. Harris* invalidated section 5519 of the *Revised Statutes,* embodying that part of section 2 of the Ku Klux Act which punished conspiracies to deprive an individual or class of persons of the equal protection of the laws or to hinder state authorities in giving or securing equal protection.[48] The twenty defendants in the case had taken four prisoners from the custody of a Tennessee deputy sheriff, beaten three severely, and killed the fourth. Here was a lynching apparently attributable to just the sort of state inaction which had concerned Congress. Yet, according to Justice William Woods, because section 5519 was "directed exclusively against the actions of private persons, without reference to the laws of the state or their administration by her officers," it was "not warranted by any clause in the Fourteenth Amendment."[49]

Unlike the senators and representatives who had enacted the anti-Klan statutes, the Court could not accept the idea that merely by standing idle while a white mob deprived some black person of his or her Fourteenth Amendment rights a state could violate that amendment. The justices did not believe state inaction could make federal intervention constitutional. They seemed unable to see what was perfectly obvious to Thomas Goode Jones, a federal district judge in Alabama. While conceding in two 1909 opinions that one private individual might not be able to deprive another of the equal protection of the laws, Jones argued that he could, by taking that person out of state custody and killing him, take away his rights under the Fourteenth Amendment's Due Process Clause. That provision, Jones reasoned, imposed upon the states an affirmative duty to afford their citizens due process of law, and under its authority Congress could punish violence by private individuals which was intended to prevent a state from meeting that obligation.[50] Jones reluctantly concluded that a Supreme Court decision (which he was legally bound to follow) required rejection of his theory.[51] The Court agreed with him that it did.[52]

The justices would permit federal punishment of a lynching only when the victim was in federal custody, and the killing, consequently, interfered with the operations of the national government. Thus, in 1909 the Supreme Court cited for contempt a Tennessee sheriff, his deputies, and other members of a mob which had killed a convicted black rapist while the Court had his case under review.[53] Even more revealing was *Logan v. United States* (1882), in which a rather technical federal involvement pro-

duced a result strikingly different from that in *Harris*. Lynchers had killed
two prisoners of a Texas deputy sheriff and wounded two more, apparently
with the complicity of the men guarding them. Although the victims
were being held in connection with a murder, they had been freed on bail
earlier on a federal charge of larceny in the Indian Territory and at the time
of the attack were being transported to a safer jail on orders of a United
States marshal. That, according to the Court, made a prosecution by the
national government permissible.[54]

Unlike the prisoners in *Logan,* most potential lynching victims were
not in any sense federal prisoners. Thus, the Court's interpretation of the
anti-Klan criminal statutes left them defenseless. As a result of these rulings, laws enacted to control racist violence became almost useless for that
purpose. Well before 1900 the Supreme Court had so constricted the statute which became section 19 of the Criminal Code that the only significant conspiracies to intimidate blacks it could reach were ones to keep
them from voting in federal elections.[55]

Section 19's under-color-of-law companion, section 20, remained until
1945 at least potentially effective as a check on police brutality against
Afro-Americans. Then the Supreme Court emasculated it in *Screws v.
United States*.[56] The *Screws* defendants (a policeman, a special deputy, and
the sheriff of Baker County, Georgia) had beaten to death a black prisoner
arrested for stealing a tire. A federal prosecutor charged them with violating section 20 by willfully depriving their victim of his due process right
not to be deprived of life without a trial. The government obtained convictions, but the Supreme Court overturned them, saying the jury had
received inadequate instructions. The trial judge had erred in failing to
charge its members that, because the word "willfully" appeared in the
statute, they must find the defendants had acted with the specific intent to
deprive their victim of a particular constitutional right.

Reading a specific intent requirement into the statute considerably reduced its effectiveness, for it now became necessary to prove not only that
officers had abused a black prisoner but that they had done so for the
explicit purpose of denying him the benefit of some constitutional guarantee, rather than out of racial bigotry, personal animosity, or sheer vicious-
ness. The *Screws* retrial resulted in an acquittal. The United States Court
of Appeals for the Fifth Circuit subsequently managed to finesse the Supreme Court's ruling to a certain extent by coupling the hornbook legal
maxim that one is generally presumed to have intended the normal and

reasonable consequences of one's actions with an assertion that deprivation of the right to life is an inexorable consequence of a willful homicide. This, and deference to a jury finding on the question of intent, enabled it in 1949 to uphold the conviction (under section 20's successor statute, 18 U.S.C. section 242) of a Bradford, Florida, town marshal who had forced a black prisoner to jump to his death from a bridge. Although that decision held out some hope for the future of section 242, the Supreme Court, which had the final word on the statute's meaning, never endorsed it, and federal trials of southern law enforcement officers for brutality against Negroes generally ended in acquittal.[57]

Given the nature of the jury instructions required by *Screws,* such verdicts were hardly surprising. The Supreme Court had not dealt black victims of white violence as hard a blow in that case as it might have, though. Justices Owen Roberts, Felix Frankfurter, and Robert Jackson had wanted to hold section 20 unconstitutional (regarding it as too indefinite in identifying the conduct proscribed to satisfy the demands of due process) and thus leave the prosecution of such crimes entirely to the states. Their dissenting opinion indicated that the majority also entertained doubts about the statute's constitutionality and that it had injected the specific intent requirement as a means of saving section 20 from invalidation.[58]

Justice Wiley Rutledge, who cast the deciding vote in a 4–3 case, rejected the reasoning of both sides, arguing that the challenged statute was constitutional as it stood. He also took the position that sections 19 and 20 protected the same rights. Thus, "If one falls for vagueness in pointing to these, the other also must fall for the same reason." Conversely, "If one stands, so must both."[59]

In *United States v. Williams* (1951), a nonracial case involving the beating of theft suspects by private detectives and a Miami police officer, four justices, speaking through William O. Douglas, accepted Rutledge's contention and voted to affirm the conviction while endorsing the second of his two alternatives.[60] Four other members of the Court took the opposite position. Their spokesman, Justice Frankfurter, was determined to keep the federal government from taking over law enforcement responsibilities which he believed properly belonged to the states. Although having to admit that his position was not entirely consistent with some early case law, he insisted that section 19 did not protect Fourteenth Amendment rights. According to Frankfurter, it covered only conduct which interfered with rights that arose "from the relationship between the individual and the Federal Government," or, in other words, those derived from substantive national powers (the example he gave was the right to vote in a federal election).[61] Hugo Black joined Frankfurter in voting to reverse the convictions, but for entirely different reasons.[62] On the crucial issue of what rights section 19 protected, the Court split 4 to 4, with Black expressing no opinion.

Williams made it at best highly doubtful whether the national government could constitutionally prosecute under section 19's successor statute, 18 U.S.C. section 241, persons who conspired to deprive others of their rights to due process and equal protection of the laws. The Court had left the Justice Department's authority "meager and hedged with technicalities." In the opinion of A. B. Caldwell, who supervised the department's civil rights enforcement efforts in the early 1950s, the effect of *Williams* was to make section 241, except in most unusual circumstances, "a useless weapon in lynching or other mob violence cases."[63]

The Supreme Court was not alone in refusing to sanction a national attack on lynching. For decades Congress spurned pleas from the NAACP for enactment of a law making it a federal crime. The NAACP's campaign to win passage of such legislation began in 1918 when Representative Leonidas Dyer (R-Mo.) introduced a bill which proposed to protect citizens against denial of their Fourteenth Amendment right to equal protection of the laws by subjecting mob members to federal penalties when a state defaulted on its responsibility to punish them. His measure also would have imposed criminal sanctions on officials who permitted a lynching to take place, and would have allowed the victim's heirs to recover damages from the county where the crime occurred. The Dyer bill encountered stiff opposition from southerners. Led by five members of the House Judiciary Committee, including its chairman, Hatton Sumners of Texas, they argued that such a statute would destroy local responsibility for law enforcement and the traditional balance between state and federal jurisdiction. Despite their efforts the bill passed the House in 1922 by a vote of 231–119, only to die in the Senate. The Republican leadership there, more concerned about the fate of other legislation, abandoned the antilynching proposal when Alabama's Oscar Underwood threatened a filibuster.[64]

In 1934 the NAACP tried again. Senators Robert Wagner (D-N.Y.) and Edward Costigan (D-Colo.) introduced legislation to punish officials who permitted lynchings to take place and to impose civil liability on the counties where they happened. Three years later, now sponsored by Representative Joseph Gavagan of New York, their proposal passed the House 277–120. Again, its Senate opponents (mostly southerners) killed it, their filibuster forcing the Democratic leadership to abandon the bill in order to pass an important administration relief measure. Antilynching legislation passed the House once more in 1940, but for a third time the Senate failed to act.[65]

After an upsurge of racial violence at the end of World War II, Harry Truman, prodded by the NAACP's Walter White, created the President's Committee on Civil Rights. It recommended enactment of legislation to strengthen the laws that would soon be known as sections 241 and 242, and in 1948 Truman sent these proposals to Capitol Hill. A Gallup poll the previous year had disclosed that 56 percent of southerners believed the national government should have the right to step in and deal with lynching if the states did not do so.[66] Although a Texan, Truman's attorney general, Tom Clark, vigorously supported the president's proposals, arguing that the federal government had an "obligation to protect its citizens . . . from forcible deprivation by mob action of the right to a fair trial" and from "mob action directed against individuals by reason of their race."[67] Nevertheless, Congress continued to do nothing. Between 1882 and 1951 opponents of lynching introduced 248 bills on the subject. Not one passed.[68]

Even had Congress and the Supreme Court not combined to deprive the national government of any effective legal weapon against lynching, it probably would not have done much about the problem until after World War II, for the executive branch long shared the aversion of the legislative and judicial branches to federal intervention in southern affairs. When confronted with extralegal violence against blacks, late-nineteenth-century presidents generally did nothing about it. Benjamin Harrison justified inaction by emphasizing the limitations on federal power and the need for sectional harmony. After Congress received numerous petitions during the 1890s calling for action against southern mob violence, William McKinley did declare in his inaugural address that lynching could not be tolerated in a civilized country. The McKinley administration, however, did nothing to protect a black postmaster in Lake County, South Carolina, when he was threatened by hostile whites who eventually set fire to his house, burning him to death. Inaction also characterized the early-twentieth-century administrations of Theodore Roosevelt and William Howard Taft. When approximately twenty black plantation workers were murdered in Palestine, Texas, in 1910, a federal investigation was requested, but the Justice Department insisted it was powerless to act because no federal law had been violated.[69]

The deference to southern states which had developed in the decades after Reconstruction survived even the vast increases in the powers and activity of the national government brought about by the Progressive reform movement, the World War I mobilization effort, and Franklin D. Roosevelt's New Deal. The Justice Department remained extremely reluctant to move against racial violence in the South. In 1934 and 1935 Florida and Mississippi lynchers violated the letter of the Lindbergh Kidnapping Act by transporting their victims across state lines before killing them. Although there was a statutory basis for federal intervention in these cases, Attorney General Homer Cummings refused to prosecute or even investigate southern lynchings unless Congress gave the Justice Department more authority.[70]

Only during World War II did the attitude of the executive branch begin to change. In July 1942, bothered by the use enemy propagandists were making of the mob murder of a black prisoner in Sikeston, Missouri, as well as by the growing militance of American blacks, and prompted by a recent lynching in Texarkana, President Roosevelt instructed the Justice Department to investigate all such killings of Negroes automatically to determine whether there was any basis for asserting federal jurisdiction. The department attempted to prosecute the Sikeston case but failed to persuade a grand jury to return indictments. It did manage to bring to trial a jailer and four mob members implicated in a Mississippi lynching, but local politicians denounced that prosecution as an invasion of states' rights, and a trial jury acquitted the defendants. The government obtained convictions in the first *Screws* trial, but not in the one which followed the reversal by the Supreme Court.[71] Perhaps because success seemed so unlikely in such cases, Justice continued to deal with most civil rights violations by urging state officials "to take appropriate action under state law." As late as 1945, it characterized its own policy as one of "strict self-limitation."[72]

That policy changed somewhat under the Truman administration, which was disturbed by an outbreak of racial violence that followed the war. Although the Justice Department still considered itself handicapped by inadequate laws, Attorney General Clark, under pressure from the public and from black Congressman Adam Clayton Powell, did insist that all lynchings be investigated by the FBI, even if there was no possibility of federal jurisdiction. Clark hoped in this way to prod state and local authorities into vigorous prosecutions of their own.[73] FBI Director J. Edgar Hoover did not like the attorney general's policy, complaining bitterly about having to expend "a considerable amount of manpower investigating murders, lynchings and assaults, particularly in the Southern states, in which there cannot conceivably be any violation of a federal statute."[74] The Bureau's investigative work proved more productive than Hoover expected, making possible successful prosecutions of a number of klansmen under the Lindbergh Act and on charges of perjury and giving false statements.

Those who headed the Justice Department during the Truman administration were more willing than Homer Cummings had been to use available federal laws to combat mob violence and terrorism. They achieved most of their successes, however, in cases involving white victims who had aroused the ire of the Klan for moral and religious reasons.[75] The 1946 prosecution of six whites who had taken two blacks out of a Minden, Louisiana, jail and beaten them severely, leaving one dead and the other unconscious, ended with the acquittal of all defendants. Despite a thorough investigation by the FBI and the enthusiastic support of Governor Ellis Arnall, the federal government could not even obtain indictments against the whites responsible for four lynchings in Monroe, Georgia. The same thing happened when it tried to prosecute those who attacked blacks during a 1945 race riot in Columbia, Tennessee. Perhaps cowed by such failures, when confronted in 1947 with a lynching in South Carolina, the Justice Department deferred to state prosecutors. Even after a state jury returned what Clark regarded as outrageous not guilty verdicts in that case, Justice chose not to seek federal indictments. The government did manage to achieve some success in using section 242 against law enforcement officers who participated in an attack on black youths in Hooker, Georgia, but it could not obtain the conviction of their private-citizen accomplices.[76] As Hoover acknowledged in 1953, "Despite . . . efforts made, justice does not always triumph in civil rights cases."[77]

The prejudices of southern jurors were not the only reason. Equally important was the persistent reluctance of federal judges, legislators, and bureaucrats to dispute the legal autonomy of the southern states by using the power which the Fourteenth Amendment gave the national government to combat racist violence. When lynching eventually died out in the South, both the FBI and the Justice Department's Civil Rights Section claimed the credit.[78] In fact, white southerners were primarily responsible.

By as early as 1929 a steady downward trend in the number of lynchings was evident. That year Walter White of the NAACP reported a decline in the annual average from 166.5 in the 1890s to 92.1 in the early 1900s, 84.0 in the period 1910–1919, and 38.0 for the period 1920–1927. His figures included the minority of lynchings whose victims were white, and also the small number occurring outside the South, but obviously the principal beneficiaries of this trend were southern blacks. A brief acceleration at the beginning of the Great Depression temporarily interrupted the decline. Then a steady downward trend began in 1936, broken only briefly by a leap from one lynching in 1945 to six in 1946. The number dropped to nine for the entire period 1947–1951, including two with nonblack victims. In December 1952 the Tuskeegee Institute reported that for the first time since it had begun keeping records in 1882 the country had managed to get through an entire year without a single lynching. There were none in 1953 or in 1954.[79]

The virtual disappearance of lynching was due in part to the agitation for enactment of a federal law against it. Congressional debate on the Dyer and Costigan-Wagner bills revealed to southerners that if they did not do something about the problem Washington might.[80] Arguing against federal antilynching legislation, the *Memphis Commercial Appeal* insisted, "The states can do this job themselves." Furthermore, "It is their duty to do it."[81]

That had not always been the southern attitude. Although the statute books of the region contained numerous laws supposedly enacted to prevent lynching, these long lay moribund. By 1933 lynching was a distinct statutory offense in Alabama, Virginia, and North Carolina. Alabama, as well as Tennessee and South Carolina, provided for the removal from office of lawmen who failed to prevent lynchings. Both North Carolina and South Carolina authorized personal representatives of victims to recover damages from the counties responsible for their deaths. Georgia allowed a change of venue in any case which threatened to provoke a lynching, and

Arkansas made provision for calling a special term of court to try inflammatory offenses. The most notable thing about almost all of these laws was how rarely they were used, especially in cases involving blacks.[82]

By the late 1930s the attitudes which had rendered these statutes moribund were changing. A growing number of southerners shared the *Commercial Appeal*'s conviction that the lynching of blacks had to be halted. Led by Julian Harris's *Columbus* (Ga.) *Inquirer-Sun,* much of the region's press campaigned relentlessly against the practice. By 1929 "hardly a paper of the South, save in the most benighted rural section [would] openly defend lynching."[83]

Nor would most responsible southerners. This was largely due to the efforts of two spin-offs from the Atlanta-based Commission on Interracial Cooperation. The Southern Commission for the Study of Lynching was a fact-finding organization which collected data and published books and pamphlets. While the commission did research, the Association of Southern Women for the Prevention of Lynching "spread the word." Organized by Georgetown, Texas, native Jessie Daniel Ames in the early 1930s, the ASWPL sought to create a new climate of opinion by challenging the long-standing association between summary punishment and sexual attitudes. As a result of the stand taken by Ames and her associates, "it simply wasn't respectable to use protection of Southern women as a defense for lynching any longer." By the early 1940s the ASWPL had enlisted 43,000 women and 109 organizations in its crusade.[84]

The pressure which that organization brought to bear on southern lawmen to protect their prisoners produced results. By presenting sheriffs with petitions from local citizens, to prove how much support they would have if they upheld the law and how much opposition they would face if they did not, the ASWPL managed by 1941 to get 1,355 peace officers to sign statements declaring lynching was never justified. By then, Ames and her associates were able to point to a number of specific instances in which sheriffs had protected their prisoners from threatening mobs.[85] In 1952 the Social Service Commission of the Southern Baptist Convention reported that law enforcement personnel in the South were beginning to win "merited acclaim for averting mob violence, safeguarding unpopular prisoners, [and] protecting the innocent."[86]

Their improved performance probably pleased most southerners. As Arthur Raper observed, "The Lynching Commission and the Southern

Women's Association for the Prevention of Lynching simply made lynching no longer respectable in the South."[87] By the early 1940s "no white man with any self-respect" would engage in such activity. Writing then, Ames noted that hostility towards the lynching of blacks had become so widespread that even in rural areas, where people had once boasted of extralegal executions, these were now considered a source of shame. Although the South experienced a brief revival of Ku Klux Klan activity just after World War II, those involved enjoyed little prestige, and in many communities they met with open resistance. Between 1949 and 1951 Alabama, Florida, Georgia, and South Carolina all enacted antimask laws designed to suppress the Klan, and fifty-two cities adopted ordinances of a similar nature.[88]

Several factors accounted for this change in southern attitudes. For one thing, southerners eventually discovered that as a technique for controlling black labor, lynching was counterproductive. While it cowed some Negroes into working quietly for whites, others reacted to mob violence by packing up and moving North. Thus, as Walter White observed, "Enlightened selfishness led the South to renewed efforts to put down lynching and ensure a larger measure of immunity from attack to Negroes."[89]

Hangings and burnings of blacks also damaged the regional image. Liberals expressed concern about their effect on the honor of the South, while advocates of industrialism worried about how the world's reaction would affect prospects for economic growth. Both shared a conviction that lynching must end if the region were ever to shake off its reputation for backward-looking barbarism.[90]

Even more important than concern for the regional image was a growing conviction that lynching was subversive of public order and of the rule of law. As early as 1897 the *Dallas Morning News* worried that mob violence was exposing "the state and law . . . as barren abstractions" and causing a "gradual dissolution into anarchy." Nearly four decades later Raper echoed its concern, insisting that until lynching (which he considered a relapse to the law of the jungle) was eliminated, "we have no assurance that ordered society will not at any moment be overthrown by the blind passion of a potentially ever-present mob." Summary punishment could no longer be tolerated, the *Cordele* (Ga.) *Dispatch* argued, because it tended to tear down laws, and "without upholding laws there can be no worthwhile government. A respect for law and order is absolutely essen-

tial for any safe and sensible government."[91] By 1947 even such an outspoken champion of white supremacy as South Carolina's Governor J.
Strom Thurmond was condemning lynchings as "flagrant violations of
every concept of law and order."[92]

By 1947, of course, lynchings were no longer needed to keep blacks
down. But should Negroes ever attempt to challenge the racial status quo,
renewed violence was likely, for white southerners retained the values and
attitudes that had given rise to lynching. One of these was a preference for
personal violence over law as a method of resolving disputes. To a certain
extent this predilection was an outgrowth of attitudes long common to
Americans generally. In Europe, where laws had evolved out of tradition
and ancient custom, they tended to be revered. Americans' attitudes were
more utilitarian. They considered laws useful instruments for regulating
human conduct in a manner calculated to secure the greatest good for the
greatest number, but did not look upon them with any sense of awe.
Americans picked and chose among their laws, obeying those they liked
and ignoring the ones of which they disapproved.[93]

Conditions in the antebellum South had served to magnify this general
American tendency toward lawlessness. Because of the plantation system,
frontier conditions persisted there long after they had disappeared in the
free states. This, along with a cultural emphasis on the importance of
defending one's honor, inhibited the growth of governmental institutions
and law enforcement agencies. Consequently, southerners developed the
habit of settling disputes with fists, knives, and dueling pistols, rather
than asking the law to do it for them. Slavery reinforced their tendency to
minimize the role of the legal system. Charles Sydnor errs in asserting that
slavery placed the planter above the law; actually it made him an agent of
the legal order. The range of discretion which he enjoyed in dealing with
his chattels was so great, however, that he could make most decisions
about how to treat them without any real reference to positive law. Plan-
ters tended to view themselves as freed from the constraints that the legal
order imposed on others and as operating in what amounted to a state of
nature. To prevent impingement on their autonomy, South Carolina's
planter-controlled government deliberately kept the state's formal legal
system weak. In northern states, such as Massachusetts, the tendency was
to discourage development of other centers of authority which might com-
pete with the government. South Carolina not only tolerated but encouraged the exercise of informal authority that was tenuously tied to and

legitimated by the legal order. Southerners respected the law, but they came to view it as controlling a rather small portion of their lives.[94]

Consequently, when disagreements between them arose, they were likely to settle these personally, often by fighting it out. By 1878 the South had firmly established itself as the most murderous part of the United States. It retained this dubious honor during the period 1920–1924, with a homicide rate two and one-half times greater than that for the rest of the country. Southerners continued killing each other far more often than other Americans in the 1930s and during the period 1946–1952.[95]

The reason appears to be that personal violence in general, and homicide in particular, continued to enjoy a cultural sanction in the South which they had lost in other areas with the passing of the frontier. The methodology of some scholars who have attributed the region's phenomenal murder rate to its cultural peculiarities has been questioned, and, of course, most southerners were seldom violent and never killed anyone. The fact remains, however, that over a long period of time the South produced far more killings per capita than the rest of the country, and it also demonstrated a far greater willingness to excuse those who took the lives of their fellow men. Time and again, southern juries returned verdicts of justifiable homicide on the basis of evidence which in the North would in all likelihood have produced murder convictions.[96]

Inclined toward resort to force, rather than law, and tolerant of all killing, southerners found it particularly easy to excuse slayings which seemed to contribute to the maintenance of white supremacy. That is why, even as opposition to lynching mounted, most of those who resorted to it continued to avoid punishment. As late as 1947 the President's Committee on Civil Rights found it "still possible for a mob to abduct and murder a person in some sections of the country with almost certain assurance of escaping punishment for the crime."[97] In May of that year a Greenville, South Carolina, jury dramatically illustrated the committee's point by acquitting the thirty-one men accused of lynching black murder suspect Willie Earle, despite the fact that the FBI had obtained confessions from twenty-six of the defendants.[98]

During the years after 1920 southerners abandoned the use of rope and faggot for pragmatic reasons, but they continued to support the objective for which lynching traditionally had been employed: the maintenance of white supremacy. Other methods of racial control, less subversive of law and order generally, came to be regarded as preferable. Because lynching advanced the strategic interests of the white community, however, when and where it was actually employed, it continued to be "regarded as an expression of popular justice."[99]

Those who engaged in a generally discredited practice escaped conviction, or received only light sentences, because most southerners remained, even in the middle of the twentieth century, extremely reluctant to punish a white person for killing a black one. As an observer noted in 1930, white opinion was frequently in sympathy "privately with murder when this has as its object the suppression of 'sassy niggers.' "[100] As late as 1959, veteran reporter Bicknell Eubanks of the *Christian Science Monitor* could not remember, in twenty-five years of covering his native South, ever having seen a Caucasian convicted of a major crime against a Negro.[101] So long as the caste solidarity which shielded those whites who committed acts of violence against members of the other race persisted, the southern legal system could afford blacks no real protection. The demise of lynching meant a decline in the immediate danger they confronted, but it left their physical safety dependent on nothing more reliable than white whim.

When a vigorous civil rights movement arose to challenge the existing pattern of race relations during the 1950s and 1960s, the result was an orgy of violence. Following well-established tradition, some southerners resorted to force to preserve white supremacy. A regional legal order which had once sanctioned, and never punished, private violence employed for purposes of racial control acquiesced in, and sometimes even aided and abetted, the actions of these vigilantes. Its inaction inspired renewed calls for federal intervention, but, like the South, the national government clung to the traditions of the past. Eventually, Washington took vigorous action against racist violence, as did the South itself. Neither moved quickly, for the habits of the lynching era proved hard to break.

The Violent Aftermath of the *Brown* Decision

"Racial tension," FBI Director J. Edgar Hoover informed President Dwight Eisenhower and the members of his cabinet in March 1956, "has been mounting almost daily since the Supreme Court banned segregation in public schools on May 17, 1954, and later, on May 31, 1955, required that integration be established at the earliest practicable date."[1] Like earlier challenges to white supremacy that had disrupted established patterns of race relations in the South, the Court's landmark ruling in *Brown v. Board of Education* produced a violent reaction. Although many white southerners expressed opposition to the violence, criminal justice systems in the region often failed to punish those who committed it, and some public officials even used the turmoil caused by racist hoodlums to justify denying blacks their constitutional rights. Following the example of its predecessors in the late nineteenth and early twentieth centuries, the Eisenhower administration showed little inclination to protect Afro-Americans. Nor would it accept responsibility for preserving order in the South during a period of traumatic change initiated by another branch of the federal government. The response of the Eisenhower administration to the southern violence ignited by the *Brown* decision offers little support for those historians who have sought recently to cast its civil rights record in a more positive light.[2] Not until faced with a direct challenge to the supremacy of the Constitution did Eisenhower act, and by then the only alternative to anarchy was military force.

The crisis in Little Rock, Arkansas, which the president confronted in September 1957 had been building since the *Brown* decision three years earlier. Few white southerners accepted the Supreme Court's desegregation ruling. An American Institute of Public Opinion poll conducted in 1956 found 80 percent of them opposed to *Brown* and only 16 percent favoring it. The white South drew together in a determined effort to preserve the traditional racial caste system from this outside threat.[3]

Although exhibiting intolerance toward anyone who favored expanding the civil rights of blacks, most white southerners disclaimed the resort to violence. A 1956 opinion poll conducted in Guilford County, North Carolina, disclosed that 75 percent of the whites there opposed using force to prevent desegregation of the public schools. Their position was the same as that articulated by the prominent individuals who dominated the White Citizens Councils, the largest and most influential organizations seeking to prevent implementation of the *Brown* decision.[4]

As Roy Wilkins of the NAACP observed, however, "Those organized elements which . . . preached defiance of the courts while piously disclaiming violence, . . . created [a] climate in which mobs . . . felt free to act." By challenging the law of the land as interpreted by the Supreme Court, southern governors, policemen, sheriffs, and judges only made the situation worse. "Self-styled respectable citizens, banded together for a campaign of resistance to the decision of the nation's highest court," Wilkins noted, gave "the green light to gangsters."[5]

In the wake of *Brown,* the South experienced a revival of the Ku Klux Klan. According to the FBI, the Klan had been "pretty much defunct . . . in the early 1950s." In August 1955, however, Eldon Edwards, an Atlanta automobile assembly plant worker, launched the U.S. Klans, Knights of the Ku Klux Klan, Inc. His organization grew quickly, establishing active branches in Georgia, Alabama, South Carolina, and Florida. Less vigorous Klan groups emerged in North Carolina, Louisiana, Tennessee, and Arkansas. Although estimates of KKK strength in the late 1950s vary widely, total membership probably never exceeded 50,000 and was more likely less than half that. Most white southerners continued to frown on the Klan, and many of the region's politicians, editors, and community leaders publicly attacked it. Nevertheless, by May 1957 klansmen had managed to stage public meetings of impressive size in the Carolinas, Georgia, Tennessee, Alabama, Louisiana, and Texas.[6] And, as the Southern Regional Council pointed out, the real significance of the Klan "lay in the ability of small membership to create disturbances, violence, and fear."[7]

Between January 1, 1955, and January 1, 1959, the eleven states of the old Confederacy experienced 210 recorded incidents of intimidation attributable to the increased racial tensions generated by the *Brown* decision. These ranged from Klan rallies and cross burnings to death threats. Klansmen appear to have been responsible for a substantial proportion of the 225 incidents of anti–civil rights violence which occurred in the South during this same period. That total included six murders (all of the victims were black) as well as twenty-nine assaults with firearms (eighteen on blacks and eleven on whites) and forty-four beatings. During the period 1955–1958, ninety southern homes suffered damage from anti–civil rights violence, sixty from explosives, fifteen from gunfire, eight from arson, and seven from stoning. Bombers targeted six schools, seven churches, seven Jewish temples and community centers, a YWCA, and an auditorium. Arsonists burned two schools and a church, and seventeen towns and cities were threatened by mob action.[8]

Much of this violence arose out of efforts to halt the advancing tide of school desegregation. During the first eight months after the *Brown* decision, relative calm prevailed throughout the South. Although Hoxie, Arkansas, experienced substantial turmoil during the summer and fall of 1955, most of the conflict there was verbal and economic rather than physical. Serious trouble began in February 1956 when a young black woman, Autherine Lucy, attempted to enter the University of Alabama under a federal court order. A mob roamed Tuscaloosa for several days, burning crosses, waving Confederate flags, and attacking cars driven by blacks. University officials soon removed Lucy from the campus and eventually expelled her. The following September, mobs in Texas turned back two blacks who tried to enter Texarkana Junior College and prevented black students from enrolling in Mansfield's high school.[9]

The most serious outbreak of anti–school desegregation violence that fall occurred at Clinton, Tennessee. On the Saturday before blacks were to enter the local high school under a federal court order, Frederick John Kasper, the executive secretary of the Seaboard White Citizens Council, arrived in town from Washington, D.C. Preaching extralegal resistance to the *Brown* decision, he immediately began organizing opposition to desegregation of the Clinton schools. Although jailed several times over the next few days, Kasper harangued crowds whenever he was free. Segregationists from elsewhere in Tennessee, and even from other states, poured into Clinton. The community became so agitated that police had to use tear gas to keep an angry mob of two thousand persons from storming the courthouse, while the crowds which surrounded the high school grew steadily larger and more violent. State troopers and National Guardsmen eventually quelled the disorders in Clinton and nearby Oliver Springs, but violence flared again in late September when someone dynamited a black home. In mid-October 125 carloads of hooded klansmen paraded through town. Continuing physical harassment forced the black students to withdraw from Clinton High in early December of that year. When a white Baptist minister attempted to lead six of them back, he was severely beaten, prompting the principal to close the school for five days. It reopened with its new black students again in attendance, but for nearly a year dynamite blasts continued to protest their presence.[10]

In Nashville, too, John Kasper ignited passions with his special brand of inflammatory rhetoric. The trouble there included rock and bottle throwing, tire slashing by a mob of about five hundred whites, and an explosion that wrecked one wing of the desegregating Hattie Cotton Elementary School. During September 1957 desegregation also led to the beating of a female student in Charlotte, North Carolina, and a black minister in Birmingham, Alabama. That fall's most highly publicized violence occurred in Little Rock, Arkansas, where a mob of angry whites threatened to break through police lines and drag newly admitted Negro students out of Central High School. The black youths escaped harm only because authorities removed them from the building. Less fortunate were a black newspaperman and three *Life* magazine employees, who were beaten by the crowd.[11]

Not all of the racial violence which followed the *Brown* decision resulted directly from efforts to keep black students out of white schools. For example, in February 1956 someone murdered Dr. Thomas Brewer, a local NAACP leader in Columbus, Georgia, and the following May the New Hope M.B. Church in Cleveland, Mississippi, which had ties to the NAACP, burned mysteriously. There does not appear to have been any direct connection between these incidents and integration. Nor was resistance to *Brown* a direct cause of the trouble which the Klan sometimes created for dissident white newspaper editors, whom it regarded as inadequately committed to segregation. Indeed, a good deal of the violence which followed the Supreme Court's 1954 decision had nothing at all to do with school integration. The desegregation of public transportation was the cause of much of what occurred in Montgomery, Alabama, and

Tallahassee, Florida, as well as of a cross burning on the lawn of a federal district judge in New Orleans. [12]

Blacks who attempted to exercise the right to vote also became targets of the sort of terrorism which grew increasingly common after the *Brown* decision. Sometimes, as in Liberty County, Florida, where flaming crosses appeared in front of the homes of two of the twelve Negro residents who dared to register, white night riders simply tried to frighten blacks out of participating in the political process. Elsewhere, as in Humphreys County, Mississippi, opponents of Negro voting supplemented economic coercion with violence. During 1955 they murdered Reverend George Lee, the first black to register there, and wounded George Counts, president of the local NAACP branch. [13]

Although black voting represented a direct challenge to white supremacy, in the tense atmosphere created by the *Brown* decision much smaller threats to the status quo also excited violent reaction. Between July 23, 1956, and February 1, 1957, for example, Koinonia, an interracial religious community near Americus, Georgia, suffered an arson, two dynamitings, and three shootings. Even more inexplicable was an April 1956 assault on popular black singer Nat King Cole at the Birmingham Municipal Auditorium. [14]

Almost as pointless were the random attacks on blacks carried out by Alabama klansmen the following year. These included the kidnapping and beating of James Henry Brock near Prattville and a raid on two homes in Maplesville. The victims of these attacks do not appear to have had any involvement in civil rights activity. Judge (his name, not his title) Henry clearly had none. The five klansmen who kidnapped, beat, and emasculated him simply selected a black victim at random. One of their number merely wanted to prove he was worthy of promotion to Assistant Exalted Cyclops. [15]

It was perhaps inevitable that in a racial climate which could produce such vicious acts of violence, lynching would again rear its ugly head. The South, which had not had a lynching since 1951, experienced three in 1955. [16] The most publicized took the life of Emmett Till, a fourteen-year-old black boy from Chicago who was found floating face down in the Tallahatchie River after he allegedly whistled at a Mississippi white woman.

The Till lynching, like so many in the past, went unpunished. Mis-

sissippi authorities brought the woman's husband and his half-brother to
trial for murder, and the state attorney general sent an assistant to Greenwood to help prosecute the case, but an all-white jury took just over an
hour to acquit the defendants. A Leflore County grand jury refused even to
indict them for kidnapping.[17]

The Till case was not the only one in which the criminal justice system
of a southern state failed to punish the perpetrators of racist violence. A
Tennessee jury found John Kasper not guilty of sedition. Alabamians
cheered as jurors in their state acquitted two men accused of an anti–civil
rights bombing in Montgomery. Indeed, during the period 1955–1957
southern juries freed the white defendants in all but one of fourteen widely
publicized cases involving the rights of blacks.[18]

Often perpetrators of racial violence avoided even indictment. For example, in 1955 an all-white grand jury in Brookhaven, Mississippi, adjourned without charging anyone in the courthouse square slaying of
black political activist Lamar Smith.[19] In the George Lee murder case, the
Belzoni, Mississippi, sheriff did not even make an arrest. According to
him, the shotgun pellets found in Lee's jaw and neck "could have been
fillings from his teeth."[20]

Sometimes the guilty did not escape punishment. In Birmingham the
klansmen who had castrated Judge Henry were convicted of mayhem and
received twenty-year sentences from Judge Alta King.[21] "There is no excuse for such a crime," King told one defendant. "You deserve more."[22]
Southern justice also punished the attack on Nat King Cole with a fine
and jailed Miami Seaboard Citizens Council members for burning a cross
on a black's lawn.[23]

Even when they punished the perpetrators of racist violence, however,
authorities in the South often displayed a lack of sympathy for the black
victims of their crimes. In August 1957 seventeen Wells, South Carolina,
men, who just wanted to beat up a Negro for the fun of it, attacked a
sixty-year-old farmhand with pop bottles and a pocket knife. The leader of
this mob received a $50 fine for disorderly conduct. The same magistrate
who assessed that mild penalty charged the black victim, who had had the
temerity to defend himself, with assault and battery.[24]

Far from cracking down on the racial violence that followed *Brown,*
some southern authorities aided and abetted it. During the Autherine
Lucy riots at the University of Alabama, Tuscaloosa Police Chief W. C.
Rayfield announced that his department did not plan to make any arrests;

it limited its role to redirecting traffic. When asked if Miami peace officers would protect the black children entering schools that were being integrated in that city, the assistant police chief replied, "If they ask for trouble, they needn't come to us for guards."[25] The Texas Rangers that Governor Allen Shivers sent into Texarkana adopted a similar position, and in Mansfield, Texas, Shivers restored order by urging the school board to transfer black students out of the district. Treating victims as perpetrators, he instructed the Rangers to arrest anyone, these children included, who represented a threat to peace.[26] As Alexander F. Miller of the Anti-Defamation League of B'Nai B'Rith pointed out in March 1958, one cause of the disorder plaguing school desegregation was "a feeling that the authority of the law will tolerate or at least wink at mob excesses."[27]

It is true that some high ranking officials in the South, among them the governors of Alabama, Florida, and North Carolina, issued statements criticizing disorder and calling for strict enforcement of the law. Attorneys general from southern and border states even endorsed a declaration of opposition to the Klan explicitly condemning its commitment to violence. It is also true that Governor Frank Clement of Tennessee dispatched thirty-nine state patrol cars, and later 644 National Guardsmen, equipped with tanks and armored personnel carriers, to Clinton and sent troops into Oliver Springs as well. The Anderson County sheriff supported his efforts by recruiting special deputies to keep the peace after the Guard withdrew. On the other hand, Shivers, under the guise of meeting his "constitutional responsibility for maintaining law and order in Texas," resegregated the Mansfield schools.[28]

The Texas governor denied he was defying federal authority, but he had used the Rangers to thwart implementation of a desegregation order from a federal court. In his defense, one should note that there was a genuine need for someone to do something about the disorder in places such as Mansfield, and that Washington had done almost nothing. Although federal court orders had triggered the violence in the South, the national government insisted that controlling it was a state responsibility. Washington clung to this position despite the fact that southern authorities repeatedly failed to protect blacks from violent interference with the exercise of rights supposedly guaranteed them by the federal Constitution.

For this the president was largely responsible. Dwight Eisenhower provided the nation with little leadership in the civil rights area. He had what one of his own aides has characterized as a "basic insensitivity" to the whole issue. Although revolted by individual acts of bigotry and fond of those blacks he knew personally, Ike cared little about the problems of Negroes in general. He promoted desegregation where federal jurisdiction was uncontested: in the armed forces, the federal bureaucracy, and the District of Columbia. But the president was a gradualist with a narrow view of the authority and responsibilities of the national government, and he disagreed with the *Brown* decision. Insisting that "coercive law" was "powerless to bring about complete compliance" where "the great mass of public opinion is in bitter opposition," he advocated reliance on patience and persuasion and thought southerners should be given sufficient time to adjust their feelings to the new social situation that the Supreme Court had mandated. He supported neither extensive legislation nor the use of federal police methods.[29]

Although Eisenhower personally deplored the anti–civil rights violence which burst forth in the South, he did not believe the executive branch of the national government should do anything about it. Keeping order and preventing rioting, Ike argued, were the states' responsibilities, and the national government could act only if they were unable to handle a crisis themselves. When violence erupted in the South, local government had acted promptly to bring it under control, the president insisted. The example he cited was Mansfield. Reminded that Governor Shivers had pacified that community by thwarting implementation of a federal court order, Eisenhower nevertheless persisted in denying that the executive branch of the national government had a role to play in such situations. He even claimed that, besides keeping the peace, states had a concurrent responsibility to ensure compliance with federal court orders. If violence kept them from meeting this responsibility, the judiciary was the branch of the national government that would have to deal with the problem, by issuing contempt citations.[30]

The caution and conservatism which characterized the president also afflicted his Department of Justice. Its line lawyers were not the reason, for they consistently wished to enforce the criminal civil rights statutes more vigorously than their superiors would allow. Nor was Eisenhower's attorney general, Herbert Brownell, responsible. A product of the eastern, or liberal, wing of the Republican party, Brownell was a former five-term state legislator who had served Thomas E. Dewey as his campaign manager during a successful run for the governorship of New York and two failed bids for the presidency. Brownell had also directed the prenomination campaign for Eisenhower in 1952. Although a "strong integrationist," he worried that racial tensions might cause the South to explode into widespread civil disorders, and he tried to ensure that the federal government would have standby policies for dealing with such a crisis. The attorney general also believed his department should take steps to ensure that people could actually exercise the rights which the Constitution promised them. Brownell urged all U.S. attorneys to be on the alert for violations of sections 241 and 242, and pressed the Civil Rights Section of the Criminal Division to go as far as its resources and existing law would permit.[31]

That unit vowed to do what the attorney general wanted, committing itself in mid-1955 "to investigate allegations of civil rights offenses and vigorously to prosecute violations in those instances where the facts demonstrate that local law enforcement cannot or will not protect the constitutional rights of the citizens."[32] Unfortunately, the Civil Rights Section's performance failed to match its promises. Part of the problem was a shortage of manpower. As of October 1955 the section could muster only eight attorneys, three of whom had to devote some or all of their time to election law, labor, and corruption cases. The job of actually prosecuting civil rights violations fell to local United States attorneys, who were generally natives of the areas they served and often sympathized with the defendants.[33]

Civil Rights suffered from a lack of nerve as well as a shortage of manpower. The restrictive interpretations which the courts had placed on sections 241 and 242 necessitated a certain caution in using them. Perhaps because of disappointments suffered when it intensified enforcement of those laws during the first two years of the Eisenhower administration, however, the Civil Rights Section adopted, in the post-*Brown* period, a more conservative prosecution policy than the state of the law required. The section's chief from 1951 to 1957, A. B. Caldwell, was a native of Arkansas whose father had once served as the librarian of that state's supreme court. After moving over to Civil Rights from the Criminal Division's Appeals and Research Section, Caldwell considerably improved the efficiency of his new organization. He did not change its established policies, for the Civil Rights Section had learned the hard way that in the South convictions, and even indictments, were difficult to obtain. Unwilling to risk the embarrassment of defeat in court, the section became, as even Caldwell later admitted, excessively cautious.[34]

In a 1956 memorandum Caldwell's immediate superior, Warren Olney III, assistant attorney general in charge of the Criminal Division, rationalized inaction. He argued that the real purpose of the civil rights statutes was not prosecution but persuasion. Those who violated them were often "the leaders or prominent citizens of a community who are merely misguided and uninformed as to the federal constitutional guarantees of citizenship." Consequently, in enforcing these laws the objective should not be jailing violators, but rather encouraging them to begin applying state law impartially. Then, there would be "no need to invoke the civil rights statute."[35]

Yet even in such places as Montgomery, Alabama, where the local authorities clearly were not providing security for blacks seeking to exercise their constitutional rights, the Justice Department refused to act. When Dr. Martin Luther King, Jr., pleaded for the federal government to do something about the situation in that city, Olney declined. "Notwithstanding our deep aversion to violent acts of the sort you describe," he wrote King, "the primary responsibility for the maintenance of law and order is lodged in state and local authorities." Olney added a reminder that "the Federal Government has no general police power."[36]

The exaggerated deference to states' rights that his letter reflected fostered an inertia which continued even after Congress in 1957 elevated the Civil Rights Section to division status within the Department of Justice. The man Eisenhower placed in charge of the new and larger organization, W. Wilson White, was a former U.S. attorney for the Eastern District of Pennsylvania who, at the time of his appointment, was serving as head of the Justice Department's Office of Legal Counsel. White was neither a resolute leader nor an innovator, and he believed the American public would not countenance a substantial expansion of federal activity in the civil rights field. Furthermore, he was convinced that problems in the South could not be solved by substituting national for local law enforcement. William Rogers, who succeeded Brownell as attorney general in November 1957, shared White's views.[37]

Even before Rogers and White took office, the Justice Department had come under pressure to increase its efforts to combat unpunished racial violence in the South. It received thousands of letters from all over the country demanding federal intervention in the George Lee and Gus Counts shootings, as well as in the Emmett Till lynching. The FBI conducted preliminary investigations into all three incidents. "No prosecutive action was taken, however, because," in each case, the Justice Department concluded, "the facts and circumstances amounted only to violations of state law."[38]

This explanation for inaction failed to satisfy black Americans, who felt particular outrage at the federal government's failure to move against Till's lynchers. That case had become the subject of "unceasing publicity in the press, and . . . numerous Sunday sermons," wrote E. Frederic Morrow, the former NAACP field secretary who, as administrative officer for the Special Projects Group at the White House, was the only black man on Eisenhower's staff. Morrow saw these expressions of discontent as "indications that we are on the verge of a dangerous racial conflagration in the Southern section of the country." He urged "some kind of statement from the White House that will indicate the Administration is aware of, and condemns with vigor, any kind of racist activity."[39] To that point the president had not even bothered to answer a telegram from Till's mother urging him to see that justice was done in Mississippi and to halt the violence there. Although the attorney general did confer with black leaders in December 1955 about the situation in that state, they remained convinced that the Eisenhower administration had abandoned southern Negroes "to the mercy of state governments that have manifested their intention to violate all laws, human and Divine, as long as it results in 'keeping the Negro in his place.' "[40]

The way the administration responded to violent interference with court-ordered school desegregation reinforced such opinions. In June 1955 the Justice Department instructed local U.S. attorneys not to have integration disturbances investigated as possible violations of the civil rights statutes. The FBI did monitor such incidents, but only in its capacity as an intelligence gathering agency. Even when University of Alabama officials begged the attorney general to send federal marshals to their troubled campus during the Autherine Lucy riots, Justice declined to act. The president considered the use of federal troops to preserve order at the university, and the administration made some preliminary preparations for such a move. Solicitor General Lee Rankin even drafted a report on the use of the army to quell a 1943 race riot in Detroit. Brownell cautioned the president not to reveal that the employment of troops had been considered.[41] In a February 1956 news conference Eisenhower, while deploring the violence at Alabama, expressed "hope that we would avoid any interference" in the situation there. This was his answer to a black reporter who had suggested that what was going on amounted to "a violation of Federal law and order."[42]

That is the way the judiciary viewed the attempted intimidation of members of the Hoxie, Arkansas, school board. The board had moved to desegregate voluntarily. Both a United States district court and the Court of Appeals for the Eighth Circuit took the position that officials attempting to implement the *Brown* decision, even if not under a judicial order to do so, had a federal right to proceed without interference. The district court enjoined a number of named defendants, and also anyone acting in concert with them, from intimidating, threatening, or attempting to harm the members of the board and from interfering with the operation of the Hoxie schools. The court of appeals upheld its action.[43]

There should have been no need for the courts to protect Hoxie's desegregation with an injunction. Those attempting to thwart it were, Caldwell and Federal District Judge Albert L. Reeves agreed, participants in a conspiracy which violated section 241. Yet the Justice Department made no move to prosecute them, despite an urgent request for federal help from Roy Pennix, the attorney for the school district. Brownell authorized the FBI to conduct numerous interrogations in the Hoxie area, apparently hoping this would deter those trying to intimidate the board. Caldwell became convinced that unless the federal government went further and gave local school officials some affirmative protection, they might have to reinstitute segregation. He proposed that Justice take some of the heat off these officials by announcing that failure to go forward with desegregation might subject them to prosecution, but Rogers, then deputy attorney general, would not permit the department to take even this limited initiative. Only when the school board itself went into federal court seeking a restraining order was any legal action taken against its militant adversaries. Caldwell gave Pennix confidential advice on the conduct of this litigation, and other government lawyers also provided him with behind-the-scenes help. Eventually, the Justice Department formally entered the case as *amicus curiae,* but it never did take the initiative or publicly assume any responsibility for preventing violence in Hoxie.[44]

Nor did the department provide leadership where violence threatened to prevent the carrying out of federal court orders. Despite the clear defiance of national authority which occurred in Mansfield, Texas, and despite an explicit request from an NAACP lawyer for federal intervention there, the department did no more than study the situation. The Clinton,

Tennessee, school board begged Washington for assistance, but Brownell responded that primary responsibility for maintaining order rested with state and local authorities. Justice left it to the board and the principal to ask a federal judge for an injunction restraining John Kasper and others from obstructing desegregation. At the invitation of the federal district court, the local U.S. attorney did participate in the resulting contempt hearing and appeal, but Washington remained uninvolved. Despite school board complaints about the department's failure to enforce the injunction, it was not until after the beating of a white minister who was trying to help black students enter the school that Brownell finally announced the federal government would prosecute persons who forcefully interfered with the integration of Clinton High. U.S. marshals then received orders to round up troublemakers, and on December 5, 1956, the Justice Department for the first time asserted its own authority to halt interference with a desegregation order, when the U.S. attorney asked the judge to have sixteen persons arrested for criminal contempt. Despite the conviction of five of those troublemakers, a member of the school board accused Brownell's department of complete indifference to Clinton's plight. The national government should assume responsibility for policing desegregation, he argued, so as to protect those communities which were trying to obey federal law.[45]

Eisenhower disagreed. Apparently he shared the views of conservative columnist David Lawrence, who contended that only state police power could be used to control disorder outside a desegregating school. Justifying federal inaction in Texarkana, the president argued that until a court found someone in contempt the Justice Department did not belong in such situations. As late as November 1958 the department continued to adhere to that policy. It did not respond to telephone appeals from Mayor Ben West of Nashville for help in preserving law and order during court-ordered desegregation in his city, but instead left local school officials to deal with rioting by seeking an injunction from a federal district court.[46]

The department and the White House commonly insisted that limitations on federal jurisdiction kept the national government from doing more to combat anti–civil rights violence, but they made little effort to expand their legal authority. Pressure for legislation began to build outside the administration, however, and by July 1955 the House Judiciary Committee had before it seven antilynching bills and an equal number of proposals to broaden and strengthen sections 241 and 242. According to the committee's chairman, Emanuel Celler (D-N.Y.), with the exception of certain aspects of the antilynching bills, none of these measures (two of which he had authored) raised any legitimate constitutional questions. Representative James Roosevelt (D-Calif.) argued with equal fervor that the failure of southern states to punish crimes such as the George Lee killing and the bomb murder of a Florida NAACP leader and his wife proved such legislation was necessary. The Justice Department apparently disagreed, for it failed to endorse any civil rights bills during 1955. When Brownell declined to appear before Celler's subcommittee, the Brooklyn legislator publicly noted the inconsistency between the attorney general's reluctance to cooperate with Congress and his claims that his department's inaction was due to weak laws.[47]

Although apparently uncooperative, the Eisenhower administration was not uninterested in civil rights. The Till case had convinced Brownell that the attorney general needed more power to protect the constitutional rights of United States citizens. It also disturbed Maxwell Rabb, a White House aide who had assumed responsibility for minority affairs because no one else in Eisenhower's inner circle seemed to want the job. On December 19, 1955, Rabb gathered together a number of concerned federal officials (including many of the small number of blacks with important positions in the administration) to discuss mob violence in Mississippi. He also spearheaded efforts to get Eisenhower to address the civil rights issue in his January 1956 State of the Union message. Although Republican legislative leaders had reservations about pushing legislation in this field, outrages such as the acquittals in the Till case and the failure of local authorities even to make an arrest for the Lamar Smith murder had overcome much of the president's previous reluctance to request it.[48]

With Eisenhower preparing to announce in his State of the Union message that the administration would soon submit a civil rights bill to Congress, the Justice Department set out to write one over New Year's weekend of 1956. On January 5 Brownell assembled a number of his top subordinates for a conference on the subject. This group (which included Rogers, Olney, and Caldwell) gave scant consideration to an antilynching bill.[49] The attorney general later told Eisenhower that this was because such a law "would entail a drastic redistribution of powers between the federal and state governments, and even if . . . constitutional . . . would be unwise."[50] Although the Office of Legal Counsel did object that the proposal failed to satisfy the state action requirement, the main reason for its elimination was the lack of a lynching anywhere in the country for more than six years. Not even representatives of the Civil Rights Section, which had drafted an antilynching proposal at Brownell's request, could see much need for such legislation.[51]

The section pressed more strongly proposals for amending sections 241 and 242. These were among the first ideas Caldwell and his associates had advanced when Brownell asked them for legislative recommendations. Like many of the bills already introduced in Congress, theirs would have corrected a defect in section 242, which the Supreme Court had pointed out in *Screws,* by adding to that statute a list of all the rights it protected. The Civil Rights Section also wanted to ease the specific intent requirement and to increase the maximum penalty for violations resulting in death to twenty years in prison and a $10,000 fine. In addition, it wanted both sections 241 and 242 altered so as to authorize the attorney general to enforce them with suits for injunctive, declaratory, or other civil relief. To Brownell and his subordinates, civil remedies appeared preferable to criminal sanctions, in part because some of them could be used for prophylactic purposes, but even more because their employment seemed less likely to provoke conflicts between the national government and state and local authorities.[52]

The language authorizing enforcement of sections 241 and 242 through civil litigation disappeared from the legislation after interested persons in the Deputy Attorney General's Office, the Office of Legal Counsel, the FBI, and the Criminal Division read and commented on the bill. The concept of suits by the attorney general to protect constitutional rights was, however, incorporated into suggested amendments to two other statutes. Refining and redrafting within the Justice Department produced, by February 24, 1956, a measure which also provided for several significant changes in section 241. The most important of these would make it applicable to individual misconduct as well as to conspiracies, punishing such violations, if they resulted in death or maiming, with up to twenty years in prison and a $10,000 fine. In addition, the draft bill contained provisions designed to ensure that section 241 could not be interpreted as protecting only rights arising out of the relationship between the individual and the federal government and to make punishable all "persons," rather than merely all "citizens," who violated it.[53]

After a meeting in the deputy attorney general's office in early March, the proposed changes to section 242 were stricken. Apparently, the reason was a desire to eliminate anything that might have an inflammatory effect on Capitol Hill, although the Appeals and Research Section had objected earlier that the list of rights which would be protected was vague and amorphous. By the time the legislation reached Congress, the proposals for strengthening section 241 also had disappeared. They were among the items Brownell included in a draft of the administration's civil rights recommendations, which he circulated to other members of the cabinet on March 7. Although J. Edgar Hoover maintained that any additional federal action to counter violent white resistance in the South would be detrimental to social peace there, the suggested changes in section 241 survived both cabinet criticism and the scrutiny of presidential aide Gerald Morgan, who discussed the bill with Justice Department officials a week later. But the Republican leader in the Senate, William F. Knowland, did not think they could pass. At a cabinet meeting on March 23, Brownell revealed that doubts existed about the desirability of the proposed changes in section 241. Some of these may have been his own. The attorney general indicated he preferred safeguarding constitutional rights with civil suits, which could head off threatened violations, rather than with prosecutions under criminal statutes, which could be initiated only after the harm had been done. Eisenhower shared this preference. The proposed amendments to section 241 encountered vigorous opposition from Health, Education, and Welfare Secretary Marion Folsom, a Georgian. He and Secretary of Defense Charles E. Wilson suggested referring them to the Civil Rights Commission, which the proposed legislation would create. The president, who remained concerned that his program would be viewed in the South as an extension of federal power, concluded the discussion by asking Brownell to confer with him later about the matter. By the time he and the attorney general met the following day, Brownell had deleted all mention of section 241 from the Justice Department's proposed civil rights message to Congress. Eisenhower gave this version his complete approval.[54]

The administration's stripped-down legislative package provided only for the creation of a civil rights division within the Department of Justice and an independent Civil Rights Commission. But in the message which he sent with it to Capitol Hill on April 9, 1956, Brownell suggested that Congress might, on its own, consider amending 42 U.S.C. section 1985 (which authorized civil suits against persons conspiring to prevent officers from performing their duties, to obstruct justice, or to deprive others of the equal protection of the laws), to permit the attorney general to initiate litigation under that law.[55]

When he finally appeared before the House Judiciary Committee on April 10 to testify about the bills which had been pending before it since 1955, Brownell not only endorsed legislation for that purpose but also gave qualified support to revision of section 241. While expressing a preference for civil over criminal remedies and indicating doubts about whether this was the time to be changing this law, the attorney general conceded that the statute suffered from serious defects. If Congress was determined to amend section 241, Brownell said, he had some suggestions; the attorney general then proceeded to lay out the very recommendations made earlier by the Civil Rights Section. Asked about the use of section 241 against lynchers, he said, "Whenever mob violence is involved, that certainly comes within the federal authority, and we believe that the laws, if they are defective in any way, should be strengthened so that there is clear authority on the part of the Department of Justice to act." Two weeks later Brownell took a similar position before the Senate Judiciary Committee. He was probably acting with at least the silent approval of the president, who apparently was willing to have adopted parts of the Justice Department's civil rights program that he did not want his administration viewed as actively promoting.[56]

After the attorney general's ambiguous performances on Capitol Hill, the Eisenhower administration made no further effort to secure enactment of legislation strengthening sections 241 and 242. For a time, however, it did back a bill authorizing the attorney general to file civil suits to prevent racist violence. Indeed, the president explicitly endorsed this concept in his 1957 State of the Union message.[57]

Eventually, the Eisenhower administration abandoned the fight to obtain even this sort of protection for those whose efforts to exercise their constitutional rights placed them in physical danger. Southerners claimed that Title III of an administration-backed House bill, which authorized the attorney general to sue for damages or injunctive relief under section 1985, was designed to force school integration. The bill passed the House 286 to 121; in the Senate, however, Richard Russell of Georgia, who was organizing southern efforts to defeat the entire measure, launched a vigorous attack on this portion of the bill. He claimed that because of the provisions of another statute (42 U.S.C. section 1993) the president could send troops into the South to enforce Title III. Although Brownell considered this a rather farfetched possibility, he readily agreed to legislative action which would preclude it, and the Senate voted 90 to 0 to repeal section 1993. Southerners continued to attack Part III anyhow. Sentiment for striking it from the bill had already become quite strong when, during a July 17, 1957, press conference, Eisenhower badly undercut the efforts of the provision's supporters and his own endorsement of a day earlier by revealing that he was confused about what Title III would do and suggesting that he himself had doubts about it. One week later the Senate voted 52 to 38 to delete from the bill authorization for the attorney general to file civil actions for violations of section 1985. The Justice Department formulated a compromise proposal under which he could do this at the request of local authorities, but the president, bothered by the way Part III had inflamed Congress and convinced by legislative leaders that any attempt to restore it might endanger the entire bill, agreed to drop the whole idea.[58]

In its final form the Civil Rights Act of 1957 protected from physical abuse and other forms of coercion only persons attempting to exercise the right to vote for candidates in federal elections; the attorney general could institute civil suits on their behalf.[59] The elimination of Part III, NAACP lobbyist Clarence Mitchell warned, would act as a "signal for hoodlums and prejudiced public officials to continue and increase their present campaign to nullify the constitutional rights of colored citizens in the South."[60] Soon Mitchell's superior, Roy Wilkins, was able to cite Little Rock as dramatic evidence of the need for the sort of protection the new law failed to provide.[61]

What happened at Little Rock in the fall of 1957 demonstrated dramatically the folly of the Eisenhower administration in refusing to accept responsibility for preventing violent interference with implementation of the *Brown* decision. On May 24, 1955, the Little Rock school board had adopted a plan under which gradual integration would begin in September 1957. Black children, alleging this program was inadequate, unsuccessfully challenged it in the United States District Court for the Eastern District of Arkansas. After ruling against them, the court retained jurisdiction in the case.[62]

Thus, it was integration under federal court supervision which precipitated the crisis that developed as the opening of school approached. About August 20, 1957, Arkansas's governor, Orval Faubus, telephoned the Justice Department in an effort to ask Brownell what Washington would do to preserve order in Little Rock. "After all," he observed later, "it was the federal government's court order. It wasn't a state order." Unable to reach Brownell, Faubus had to settle for talking with Deputy Attorney General Rogers, who told him there was very little the Justice Department could do.[63]

Rogers did offer to send a representative to confer with the governor. The man selected for that mission was Arkansas native A. B. Caldwell. Caldwell was already familiar with the situation, for he had visited Little Rock in June, after the lawyer for the school district came to Washington warning of trouble in the fall and seeking assistance from the Justice Department. At that time Caldwell had found both Superintendent Virgil Blossom and the members of the board "greatly concerned about the possibility of violence," when school started in September. He had also found school officials reluctant to institute legal proceedings against the Capital Citizens Council and other groups and individuals threatening to disrupt the planned September integration of Central High School. After his return to Washington, Caldwell had prepared a memorandum for Olney in which he discussed the possibility of the department itself initiating legal action, by prosecuting these troublemakers under section 241. The memorandum concluded there was not yet sufficient evidence to justify even a full-scale investigation.[64]

Now, meeting with Faubus on August 28, Caldwell tried to focus the discussion on section 241 and other legal means which might be used to deal with the Little Rock problem. He found the governor "not so much interested in the application of the law as he was in explaining to the Department what he planned to do." Faubus insisted that the situation was much worse now than it had been a month earlier, primarily because of an inflammatory speech Governor Marvin Griffin of Georgia had delivered in Little Rock on August 22. Claiming to be gravely concerned that violence might erupt when school opened, Faubus told Caldwell he had arranged to have a suit filed in Pulaski Chancery Court, seeking a temporary injunction to halt desegregation.[65]

Actually, as Judge Ronald L. Davies concluded after having the FBI thoroughly investigate the situation, there was very little danger of substantial violence in Little Rock. Blossom told the Bureau that school officials had heard rumors about possible trouble, but that neither they nor the police had been able to confirm them. The investigation as a whole developed "no evidence specifically supporting indication of possible vio-

lence," and, in fact, revealed an absence of even serious threats of disturbance. Faubus himself acknowledged during testimony in the chancery
court that he had no specific information that opponents of integration
would resort to force to prevent it.[66]

Although the governor lacked any real evidence of impending violence,
he may have moved to halt desegregation at Central High School out of
genuine fear that it would lead to disorder. During his meeting with
Caldwell, Faubus emphasized that his reason for initiating litigation in
chancery court was a belief that this was the only way to avoid bloodshed.
Two members of the Arkansas Public Service Commission who attended
an August 30 staff meeting in Faubus's office at which the Little Rock
situation was discussed found him very concerned that violence would
result if black students enrolled at Central High. Even Representative
Brooks Hays, whose moderate views on integration later cost him his seat
in Congress, believes the governor was sincere.[67]

To be sure, Faubus did not, as Superintendant Blossom requested, publicly declare that he would maintain order and permit no interference with
integration. Rather than have the state ensure peaceful desegregation, he
tried to dump this unpopular task on the Justice Department. Even
though Faubus behaved irresponsibly, and even if his motivation was as
political as Caldwell and former Arkansas Governor Sidney McMath insisted, he still had a point in arguing that the federal government ought
to assume responsibility for the peaceful implementation of its own court
decisions. Both Faubus and Hays thought Washington could have sent
United States marshals to maintain order in Little Rock, and they considered the Justice Department's failure to do this, in the governor's words,
"an absolute default" of what was "clearly its responsibility." "They wanted
to wait until someone was killed," he lamented later.[68]

Certainly, the inaction of the national government gave Faubus a good
excuse for seeking to delay the entry of black students into Central High
School. "The peace and order of the community," he contended, "is para-
mount to integration."[69] Predictably, Chancellor Murray O. Reed, a jurist
Faubus himself had appointed to the bench, found his argument per-
suasive. On August 29 Reed granted a temporary injunction restraining
the school board from implementing its desegregation plan.[70]

Judge Davies promptly nullified Reed's injunction, and on September 2
Faubus, still claiming he was acting to prevent violence, ordered elements
of the Arkansas National Guard to active duty and dispatched them to

Central High School. There they turned back black students who tried to enter the building. Although a Guard officer insisted the troops were necessary to keep the peace, Faubus's orders made it clear that their real mission was to maintain segregation.[71]

Judge Davies would not let them do that. Faubus insisted that what was at stake in Little Rock was "whether the head of a sovereign state can exercise his constitutional powers and discretion in maintaining peace and order."[72] He could not, Davies informed the governor on September 20, at least if that meant interfering with the right of eligible black students to attend Central High. His duty was to preserve constitutional rights, not to deny them. The judge enjoined Faubus and National Guard leaders from further obstructing the attendance of the black students.[73]

The governor responded by withdrawing his troops and, disclaiming any further responsibility for maintaining order in Little Rock, flew off to a southern governor's conference. With the soldiers gone, Police Chief Marvin Potts believed that his 175-man force could not maintain order at Central High. His officers did not even attempt to patrol the grounds. Acting on instructions from the school board, Blossom tried without success to persuade Judge Davies to send federal marshals to the school. Little Rock Mayor Woodrow Wilson Mann, whose police were not trained for riot control, tried to persuade the Justice Department to ask the judge to do this, but Brownell refused. Blossom and Mann, seemingly with some reluctance, sought help from Henry Lindsey, director of the Arkansas State Police. Lindsey sent in a limited number of troopers, but the riotous mob of one thousand persons that assembled outside Central High School on Monday, September 23, was more than they and the city police could handle. The black students managed to enter the building, but after three hours the mayor and local officials had to remove them.[74]

Thus far, as both Blossom and Faubus noted later, the federal government had done nothing to support local efforts to enforce a decree issued by one of its own courts.[75] On September 24 its protracted inaction ended with a show of military force. The president federalized the Arkansas National Guard and ordered elements of the 101st Airborne Division into Little Rock. Eisenhower took this step most reluctantly. As recently as July 17 he had told reporters, "I can't imagine any set of circumstances that would ever induce me to send Federal troops . . . into any area to enforce the orders of a Federal court."[76] The president had hoped Little Rock and Arkansas authorities would bring the situation under control.

"If the use of local police powers had been sufficient," he emphasized in an address to the nation on the evening of the twenty-fourth, "our traditional method of leaving the problems in those hands would have been pursued."[77]

What the president failed to mention was that in the past leaving the control of anti-integration violence to state and local authorities had enabled them to exploit it to keep blacks from exercising their constitutional rights. Faubus remembered Mansfield, Texas, and regarded it as a precedent for his own actions at Little Rock. To an angry president, however, his conduct was too flagrant to overlook. Although reluctant to push school desegregation, Eisenhower had consistently stated that he would honor his oath to defend the Constitution and that he considered himself bound by the Supreme Court's interpretation of it. Eisenhower had personally discussed the Little Rock situation with Faubus during a September 14 meeting at his Newport, Rhode Island, summer White House arranged by Congressman Hays. At this conference and in the behind-the-scenes negotiations which preceded it the president had stressed that the federal government did not want to interfere with the governor's responsibility to preserve law and order in his state. Eisenhower's chief of staff, Sherman Adams, told Hays, who was acting as an intermediary, that if Faubus would assure the White House that he would use his full civilian power to control the "violent ones" and take over enforcement of the desegregation order, no federal troops would be sent to Little Rock. The governor insisted on preserving law and order by delaying integration. He later claimed that Eisenhower seemed sympathetic to this idea until Brownell told him it was legally impossible. Actually, Ike seems to have been trying to suggest to Faubus how he could preserve the peace and still comply with the court order. The president proposed that Faubus simply change his instructions to the National Guard, leaving it at Central High, but directing the soldiers to allow black students into the school. The meeting ended with Eisenhower convinced that the governor would soon revoke his original orders to the Guardsmen. The statement that Faubus issued after the conference, although ambiguous, did provide grounds for optimism.[78]

Instead of adopting the president's suggestion, Faubus used his troops to maintain segregation. When enjoined by Judge Davies from doing that, he withdrew them from the scene, allowing rioting to engulf Central High on September 23. Blossom called the Justice Department, begging for federal help, while Hays relayed to Adams a plea from Mayor Mann and Chief Potts for soldiers.[79] The next day the mayor, who already had conversed by telephone with Justice Department officials and White House aide Maxwell Rabb, telegraphed a formal request to the president that "in the interest of humanity, law and order" he "provide federal troops within several hours."[80]

Eisenhower did not believe he could use the army to preserve law and order, but he found it possible to distinguish between doing that and protecting the black students at Central High. On orders from Brownell, Justice Department lawyers already had prepared a memorandum arguing that the president was authorized to send troops to Little Rock by Title 10, sections 332 and 333 of the U.S. Code, which empowered him to use the military to remove obstructions to the authority of the United States and to put down violence which hindered the execution of federal law. Advised by Brownell that he had the power to do what Mann had requested, a reluctant Eisenhower federalized the Arkansas National Guard and ordered paratroopers into Little Rock.[81] The reason is clear. As his onetime speechwriter Emmett John Hughes has observed, "The President, so slow to take firm federal action in support of civil rights, could and would respond with dispatch to a public challenge to presidential and constitutional authority."[82] Although reluctant to accept responsibility for preventing violence from frustrating implementation of the *Brown* decision, Eisenhower could not tolerate what he viewed as a challenge to national supremacy. "When a State, by seeking to frustrate the orders of a Federal Court, encourages mobs of extremists to flout the orders of a Federal Court, and when a State refuses to utilize its police powers to protect against mobs persons who are peaceably exercising their rights under the Constitution as defined in such court orders," he told Georgia's Senator Richard Russell, "the oath of office of the President requires that he take action to give that protection." Failure to act, Eisenhower added, "would be tantamount to acquiescence in anarchy and the dissolution of the union."[83]

Disturbed by this confrontation between the president and one of their number, four southern governors met with Eisenhower on October 1 in an effort to work out a compromise. After consulting by telephone with Faubus, they told the president he was prepared to assume full responsibility for maintaining law and order in Little Rock and ensuring that orders of the federal courts would not be obstructed. Eisenhower announced that as soon as the governor made a public declaration to this effect he would order the Guard returned to state control, and soon thereafter he would withdraw all federal troops. Faubus double-crossed the White House by announcing only that he himself would refrain from obstructing court orders, saying nothing about preventing others from doing so. The governor refused to guarantee the safety of the black students, so the paratroopers remained at Central High.[84]

Although Faubus branded them "occupation troops" and insisted that Washington was using "naked force" to reduce the states to "mere subdivisions of an all powerful national government," a Gallup poll found 64 percent of Americans believed Eisenhower had done the right thing.[85] Apparently the nation was as unwilling as the president to tolerate the anarchic consequences of allowing state authorities to default on their responsibility for controlling mob violence intended to thwart school desegregation.

Certainly, that is how many federal judges felt. In February 1958 the Little Rock school board, pointing to the turmoil which its efforts to integrate Central High had inspired, requested permission to delay desegregation. The district court agreed to its request. The court of appeals, however, noting that to do this would invite militants everywhere to adopt violent and unlawful means of fighting school desegregation, reversed the ruling. That court also chided the board for failing to seek injunctive relief against troublemakers, as school officials in Clinton and Hoxie had done.[86] Its decision received the unanimous endorsement of the Supreme Court, which announced that law and order were not going to be preserved by depriving black children of their constitutional rights.[87]

By the time the high tribunal handed down its ruling in September 1958, the federal officials whose inaction had induced the Little Rock crisis were finally beginning to accept some responsibility for ensuring that school desegregation would proceed peacefully. The previous autumn, after visiting the troubled Arkansas city, Civil Rights Section attorney St. John Barrett had recommended that the Justice Department initiate some sort of legal action before the troops were withdrawn from Central High. Otherwise, he contended, persons in other areas might conclude they could safely interfere with the effectuation of court integration orders. Although both Superintendent Blossom and the local U.S. attorney wanted federal prosecutions of the agitators who had incited the violence on September 22–23, Rogers, who had become attorney general on November 7, 1957, rejected Barrett's suggestion. By the fall of 1958 the soldiers were gone and Eisenhower and White House spokesmen were again emphasizing that it was state and local governments which had constitutional responsibility for maintaining law and order and ensuring that force and violence did not deprive black students of their rights.[88]

Rogers probably shared this preference for reliance on local institutions of criminal justice. A close friend of Vice-President Richard Nixon, the youngest member of the Eisenhower cabinet had spent five years as an assistant district attorney in New York County before coming to Washington to serve as counsel to a Senate committee.[89] During an August 27, 1958, address to an American Bar Association convention in Los Angeles he stressed local responsibility for preserving order and ensuring that violence did not deprive blacks of their rights. But Rogers also declared that if a state failed to meet its responsibilities in this area the executive branch of the federal government would "support and insure the carrying out of the final decision of the Federal court."[90] In Arkansas, where the governor had already demonstrated he could not be counted on to do his duty, the Justice Department took action to ensure that desegregation would be peaceful. Anxious to avoid having to use troops again, it began recruiting deputy marshals from various communities in northeast Arkansas for possible use at Central High.[91] On September 11, 1958, Rogers wrote to school board president Wayne Upton, urging him, if the Supreme Court ordered desegregation resumed, to seek an injunction forbidding interference with it. The attorney general also dispatched a letter to City Manager Dean Dauley, informing him of the steps the department was taking and suggesting that responsible officials do some advance planning to prevent violence. Rogers took care to assure Dauley that it was "not the purpose of the marshals to assume, substitute for, or in any other way intrude upon the primary responsibility of the state and its subdivisions to maintain peace and order."[92] After the Supreme Court ruled, Justice dispatched about 150 men to Little Rock. They never did more than train, for by closing the schools to prevent integration from resuming Faubus deprived them of a mission.[93] The fact that they had been sent at all, however, suggested the Justice Department had learned something from the Little Rock crisis.

Certainly, it had needed an education. The *Brown* decision, which represented an obvious threat to white supremacy, had ignited the sort of violent reaction always provoked by challenges to the South's racial caste system. Although some southern officials acted decisively to bring this violence under control, others condoned and even encouraged it. Their failure to maintain law and order necessitated that the federal government assume responsibility for doing so. Like the klansmen of Reconstruction days, those causing the wave of violence that washed over the South after *Brown* were trying to deprive blacks of rights guaranteed to them by the United States Constitution. In leaving the job of combating these troublemakers to unreliable state authorities, the Eisenhower administration evaded an obligation. It also courted disaster. Little Rock was the price the nation paid for the failure of the president and the Justice Department to assume responsibility for controlling disorder ignited by the federal government itself. Now, finally, the Eisenhower administration was beginning to do that. Unfortunately, anti–civil rights violence was accelerating far faster than the efforts of the national government to combat it. Washington's reluctance to become involved and its hesitancy to take prophylactic measures to protect constitutional rights would persist well into the presidency of Lyndon Johnson. So would the sort of uncontrolled racist violence that inadequate federal action invited.

The Attack on Bombing

Dynamite punctuated the narrative of southern social change in the late 1950s. Unlike the terrorists of an earlier era, who had resorted to rope and faggot to maintain white supremacy, the violent bigots of the Eisenhower era made explosives their weapon of choice. Many public officials saw the wave of bombings which swept the South as a problem that transcended state boundaries and, consequently, required a federal solution. In 1960, despite a lack of leadership from the Eisenhower administration, Congress provided one.

Bombing first became a serious problem during the black boycott of Montgomery's segregated bus system. On January 30, 1956, someone dynamited the home of Reverend Martin Luther King, Jr., the young Baptist minister from Atlanta who had become the leader of that movement and who would go on to win a Nobel Peace Prize as the head of the Southern Christian Leadership Conference (SCLC). Bombers also targeted the houses of two other clergymen associated with the boycott. After the Supreme Court voided Montgomery's bus segregation ordinance and blacks ended their boycott, the city experienced the worst outburst of violence the South had seen since the *Brown* decision. Terrorist acts compelled city officials to curtail bus service and then to suspend it entirely. This spasm of violence featured explosions which wrecked four Baptist churches, the homes of two ministers linked to the boycott, a filling station, a cab stand, and—for the second time—the King home.[1]

Like that home, public schools were favorite targets of racist bombers. Nine educational institutions located in Tennessee, Florida, North Carolina, Louisiana, and Virginia had come under attack by January 1959. Some of these were black schools, but those which suffered the greatest damage were white institutions attempting to desegregate. When Little

Rock's Central High School finally reopened on an integrated basis in September 1959, bombers reacted by attacking property belonging to both the school district and the city government.[2]

Explosions also protested the arrival of blacks moving into previously all-white neighborhoods, particularly in the Birmingham–Bessemer area of Alabama, where the Fountain Heights section earned the nickname "Dynamite Hill." The Birmingham–Bessemer area also produced two bombings of black churches. With many Negro ministers assuming leadership roles in the movement for racial justice and opening their chapels to civil rights meetings, those buildings became priority targets for dynamiters. When integration of Montgomery buses got underway in January 1957, bombs inflicted $60,000 worth of damage to that community's black churches in a single night.[3]

Explosions also jolted other southern religious institutions. "The attention of the general public and particularly of the Jewish community has been aroused by a recent outbreak of anti-Semitic violence," the American Jewish Congress observed in October 1958. It was reacting to the dynamiting of the Hebrew Benevolent Congregation in Atlanta.[4] Anti-Semites also attacked Jewish facilities in Birmingham, Nashville, Tennessee, Jacksonville, Florida, and Charlotte and Gastonia, North Carolina.[5]

These bombings shocked most white southerners. As a Montgomery resident noted, the January 1957 incidents in that city had "turned a lot of people's stomachs." Southern newspapers editorialized against the bombings. In Arkansas, Orval Faubus expressed his "unqualified disapproval" of the practice. The *Miami News* apparently spoke for at least the southern white elite when it wrote that "whether you believe in Integration or Segregation, certainly you do not believe the Negro should be bombed in the night. Or the Jew. Or the Catholic."[6]

White southerners even sent some dynamiters to jail. A leader of the Capital Citizens Council drew a three-year sentence for the Little Rock bombings (although Governor Faubus pardoned him after six months). A Charlotte, North Carolina, jury convicted three klansmen implicated in the bombing of a black elementary school, and the state supreme court ruled that all must serve prison terms. Its counterpart in Tennessee upheld the jailing of a man for conspiring to dynamite Clinton High.[7]

Some southern bombers did evade punishment. A Georgia jury acquitted a man accused of the Atlanta temple bombing. An Alabama one freed two individuals charged with dynamiting churches and homes in Montgomery, despite the fact that the evidence against them included a signed confession. In Birmingham, even when bombers pleaded guilty, all they received was one year's probation.[8]

Nevertheless, most public officials in the South do seem to have made a sincere effort to stamp out the epidemic of dynamiting that was plaguing their region. In South Carolina the attorney general, the governor, and the chairmen of the judiciary committees in both houses of the legislature all pressed for tougher laws against bombing and bomb threats. Tennessee Governor Frank Clement and Alabama Governor James Folsom both offered rewards for information leading to the arrest of bombers. So did Montgomery's mayor and city commissioners.[9]

Perhaps the best evidence of how serious southern officials were about halting the terroristic use of explosives was their creation of the Southern Conference on Bombing. Initiated by Jacksonville Mayor Haydon Burns after dynamite ripped a black high school and a Jewish community center in his city, the SCB began with a meeting of seventy delegates in May 1958. The founders included ten mayors and law enforcement officers from twenty-one southern communities. Out of their discussions emerged a twenty-eight city intelligence network headed by the assistant chief of the Jacksonville police force. Its mission was to halt racial bombings and bring to justice those responsible for them.[10]

The creation of the SCB reflected not only southern determination to suppress dynamiting but also a widely held belief that those who practiced this form of terrorism were part of a far-reaching conspiracy. Mayor Burns detected a common pattern in the Jacksonville, Nashville, and Montgomery bombings, while columnists Drew Pearson and Pat Watters insisted that a single gang of fanatics was responsible for explosions in several states. A spokesman for the Anti-Defamation League of B'Nai B'Rith joined Congressman Kenneth Keating (R-N.Y.) in blaming a multistate conspiracy for dynamitings of synagogues and Jewish community centers.[11]

Although southern officials made substantial efforts to combat bombing, the fact that the problem was widely perceived as interstate in scope suggested the desirability of a federal solution. Many people, among them Chairman Emanuel Celler of the House Judiciary Committee and Senators Jacob Javits (R-N.Y.) and Clifford Case (R-N.J.), urged the FBI to investigate the dynamitings. Deputy Attorney General Lawrence Walsh insisted in an April 1958 letter to Celler that there was no statutory basis on which the Bureau could act; bombing buildings was not a federal crime. Primary responsibility for investigating such offenses, Walsh argued, should remain with the communities directly involved.[12]

While also stressing the limited reach of federal jurisdiction, the White House did acknowledge that the national government could "interfere" if "invited to do so by local authorities." Southern officials wanted help from the FBI, and J. Edgar Hoover, who considered coordination among various levels of government crucial in curbing the terroristic use of explosives, was happy to provide it. By October he had ordered his agents to work closely with local officials who wanted their help. The FBI offered state and local lawmen full use of its laboratories and identification facilities and provided them with expert assistance. The Bureau also searched vigorously for any evidence that a federal law had been violated. Such a violation would, of course, justify it in assuming an even larger role in individual cases.[13] In a December 1958 speech to the Anti-Defamation League, Attorney General Rogers reported, "The Department of Justice, through the FBI, is lending every possible assistance in an all-out effort to apprehend the guilty parties."[14]

Unlike Rogers, the American Jewish Congress did not think the Bureau was doing everything it could, even under existing law. Furthermore, it saw a need for congressional legislation which would expand federal jurisdiction. Northern Republicans—ranging from the chairman of a county committee in Pennsylvania to Senator Javits and Congressman Keating—also demanded congressional action. Such southern officials as Mayor Burns and the attorney general of North Carolina joined in the call for federal legislation against bombing.[15]

The Eisenhower administration eventually responded to such demands, although not decisively enough to satisfy many blacks. The president reacted with outrage to the Atlanta temple bombing, and his insistence that the FBI give him a full report on that incident probably explains much of the enthusiasm for helping local authorities track down dynamiters which the Bureau began to display in October 1958. But the president failed to respond to a 1957 request (made by King and other black leaders just after the Montgomery bombing orgy) that he give a major speech in a southern city denouncing disorder.[16] When the president's lone black aide, E. Frederic Morrow, visited friends in New York, they "literally gave me hell for the Administration's apparent indifference to the plight of defenseless Negroes in the South."[17] Nearly two years later Morrow, deeply disturbed by continuing racial strife and bombings, lamented, "No leadership seems to be emerging."[18]

Rather than taking charge of the search for a solution to the problem of racial violence, the Eisenhower administration acted only when pressure from important interest groups became too powerful to ignore. Among the organizations demanding federal legislation against bombing were the American Jewish Congress, the Anti-Defamation League, and the Jewish War Veterans. Their endorsements carried weight, for the White House was worried about how large and influential Jewish groups might react if nothing were done. The NAACP, the American Civil Liberties Union, the American Veterans Committee, and the AFL-CIO also pressed for legislation.[19]

The sort of law they wanted had a good deal of support on Capitol Hill. By June 1958 four Democratic congressmen from outside the South— Celler of New York, James Roosevelt of California, Peter Rodino of New Jersey, and Martha Griffiths of Michigan—had introduced bombing bills in the House. So had one southerner, J. Carlton Loser (D-Tenn.). Two months later Celler, who chaired the powerful House Judiciary Committee, and one of that body's leading Republican members, Kenneth Keating, announced that they intended to cosponsor legislation making it a federal crime to transport or possess dynamite intended for use against religious, educational, charitable, or civic buildings. Keating, who believed the "interstate nature of the plots" necessitated federal intervention, said he would "support . . . any measure designed to bring . . . to justice" the perpetrators of "bombings of Negro schools and Jewish synagogues."[20] After winning election to the Senate that November, he joined his New York colleague, Senator Javits, who had been sponsoring a similar bill, on a tour of Atlanta, Birmingham, and Jacksonville. They found law enforcement officials in those cities favorably disposed toward expanding the federal role in the war against bombing. Indeed, in Birmingham the police commissioner told them the explosions there appeared to be the work of an interstate conspiracy and complained about the refusal of the FBI to intervene. The reason the Bureau had given him was lack of federal jurisdiction. Keating and Javits proposed to remove that constraint by securing enactment of a statute proscribing interstate flight to avoid prosecution for destroying a building.[21]

While they were seeking cosponsors for their legislation, two Democratic senators were also lining up support for a bombing bill. One of these was John F. Kennedy of Massachusetts. Kennedy was worried about holding onto the black vote in what he expected to be a close race for reelection in 1958 and, already eyeing his party's 1960 presidential nomination, needed to do something for civil rights that would not hurt him in the South the way his earlier public endorsement of the *Brown* decision had. In May 1958, at the request of the Anti-Defamation League, he introduced a bill to make a federal crime of the importation or interstate transportation of explosives intended for use in violation of the law of any state or territory or the illegal possession of explosives which had moved in interstate or foreign commerce. Four months later Kennedy submitted a more specific version, which would also criminalize false bomb threats. At about the same time he began discussions with North Carolina conservative Sam Ervin, a member of the Judiciary Committee and a well-known champion of states' rights. Eventually, Kennedy's staff persuaded Ervin to cosponsor the revised bill. The price which the North Carolinian exacted for his support was that the measure be broadened so it would apply to the use of explosives in labor disputes and would also make criminal interstate flight to avoid prosecution for a bombing.[22] Ervin insisted that "the bill ought to contain a provision making it clear Congress does not intend to occupy the field to the exclusion of existing state laws."[23] The Kennedy-Ervin bill, a blend of ideas from a northern liberal who supported integration and a southern conservative who opposed it, attracted the support of a wide range of other senators. The two men cemented their alliance in Demember 1958 and sought cosponsors for their legislation. By January 13, 1959, they had thirty-five. Eventually, a total of forty-five senators attached their names to the Kennedy-Ervin bill, to the Javits-Keating measure, or to both.[24]

Kennedy was understandably confident of success, and the *Charlotte Observer,* published in Ervin's home state, agreed that enactment of a law to curb racist bombing was now a virtual certainty. Only when it had become all but inevitable did the Eisenhower administration come forward with a proposal of its own. As late as June 1958, when a House Judiciary subcommittee held hearings on a number of bombing bills and resolutions, the Justice Department did not even bother to respond to a request from its chairman, Congressman Edwin Willis (D-La.), for comments on them.[25] By December 15 Justice had decided no more than that it "probably" would recommend legislation "giving the FBI some limited jurisdiction in bombing occurrences."[26] Attorney General Rogers was convinced that the situation required drastic action, but the Civil Rights Division recommended a go-slow policy. Its head, Assistant Attorney General Wilson White, contending a federal law might inflame the situation while giving local officials an excuse to relax their own efforts, urged more study of the problem.[27]

The administration finally sent a proposal to Capitol Hill on February 5, 1959. It was an extremely modest one. Eisenhower recommended making interstate flight to escape prosecution for destroying an educational or religious facility, or to avoid testifying about a bombing, a federal crime. When Attorney General Rogers appeared before House and Senate committees, he praised the steps that state and local authorities had already taken to combat bombing. Legislation was needed, Rogers said, to make clear to terrorists that their activities were a matter of serious national concern and to provide "a solid jurisdictional basis" on which the FBI could proceed to investigate bombings and to apprehend those responsible for them. He emphasized, however, that the Bureau was not a national police force and would not supersede local law enforcement agencies. What was proposed, the attorney general assured legislators, was to make "Federal action . . . a supplement to, but not a substitute for, State and local action."[28]

In addition to its fugitive bomber proposal, the administration also sent to Congress a recommendation for legislation designed to deal with future crises of the Little Rock variety. In his message the president proposed making it a crime to use or threaten to use force to obstruct court orders in school desegregation cases. By now the administration realized, as Rogers acknowledged, that "if the state is unable or unwilling to act effectively, it is to the Federal Government that the country looks for prompt and decisive action in the face of such a challenge." Both he and the president argued that the courts could not control such situations with their power to punish for contempt. As Rogers explained, that authority could be used only against those to whom judicial decrees were specifically directed and persons acting in concert with them. Desegregation orders ordinarily named members of school boards, so the contempt power was of little value in dealing with mobs working to thwart integration. A judge could enjoin individual troublemakers, but he could do this only after mobs had formed and given him some reason to restrain the conduct of their members, and he could punish rioters only for subsequent acts violating his injunction. Consequently, it was nearly impossible to control disturbances with the contempt power.[29]

The administration's proposals for combating anti–civil rights violence did not go far enough to satisfy many members of Congress. Black Congressman William L. Dawson (D-Ill.) engaged in a heated exchange with William McCulloch (R-Ohio), the House sponsor of the president's bill, over what he viewed as the inadequacies of the measure's bombing provisions. Any use of explosives for the purpose of denying a class or group of persons their constitutional rights should be a federal offense, Dawson insisted. The Kennedy-Ervin bill did not go that far, but by predicating federal jurisdiction on either interstate flight or interstate transportation of explosives it provided for FBI intervention in a far larger number of cases than did the Justice Department's proposal. Ervin, a former judge and an authority on the Constitution, insisted that his measure did not invade the police powers of state and local governments, and even Senate Majority Leader Lyndon Johnson (D-Tex.) based the bombing section of his own rather conservative civil rights bill on this interstate shipment rationale. Both Johnson's measure and the Kennedy-Ervin one also went beyond the Justice Department's proposals in protecting charitable and civic, as well as educational and religious, buildings.[30]

What upset civil rights proponents far more than the limited scope of the administration's bombing recommendation was the fact that its bill included nothing like the Part III which the Senate had deleted from the 1957 legislation. Congressman Celler and NAACP Executive Secretary Roy Wilkins both expressed disappointment that such a provision had not been included, as did Joseph L. Rauh, Jr., vice-chairman of the Americans for Democratic Action and counsel for the Leadership Conference on Civil Rights. Rauh considered Part III an "indispensable element" of any adequate legislation. Spokesmen for the American Civil Liberties Union, the Anti-Defamation League, the American Veterans Committee, the AFL-CIO, and the United Auto Workers also endorsed the Part III concept. Actually, the Justice Department itself had proposed that the administration request authorization for the attorney general to initiate suits for injunctive or declaratory relief in civil rights cases where the circumstances were such that if the aggrieved individual brought the action himself he would run a serious risk of reprisal. That proposal was deleted from the president's recommendations during a White House meeting on February 3, 1959, probably because House Republican leader Charles Halleck of Indiana objected to it as divisive and possibly applicable to labor disputes.[31]

Eisenhower insisted that his administration must offer some "moderate" and "constructive" civil rights proposals, but as Vice-President Richard Nixon pointed out, extending federal power and responsibility was contrary to Republican tradition. Not even the Mack Charles Parker lynching could overcome this GOP reluctance to have the national government assume a large role in combating racist violence. On April 24, 1959, a mob abducted Parker, a black man accused of raping a white woman, from the jail in Poplarville, Mississippi, where he was awaiting trial. Ten days later state highway patrolmen and FBI agents pulled his body from the Pearl River near Bogalusa, Louisiana.

The Bureau had entered the case at the request of Mississippi Governor J. P. Coleman, who asked for its help as soon as he learned of the victim's disappearance. Besides locating Parker's body and identifying it from fingerprints, the FBI determined precisely how the lynching had been carried out and how many of the men were responsible for it. The Bureau even obtained confessions from some members of the mob. Although federal agents had broken the case, the federal government did not prosecute it. The FBI had acted on the basis of a rebuttable presumption in the Lindbergh Act that a missing kidnap victim had been carried across a state line. When searchers found Parker's body on the Mississippi side of the Pearl River, prosecution under that statute became impossible. Since the FBI had learned that a deputy sheriff was involved in the lynching (at least to the extent of having left Parker unprotected so the mob could seize him), a federal prosecution under section 242 might have been possible. Because Coleman seemed sincere in his desire to combat violence against blacks, Rogers decided instead to turn over to him a summary of the evidence the FBI had developed.[32]

The governor announced he would give this information to the next regular session of the Pear River County grand jury, but District Attorney Vernon Broom refused to present it to that body. Without the Bureau's report, the state had no case against the mob members. The grand jury called no FBI witnesses and apparently did not even consider the Parker lynching.[33]

Rogers, himself a former prosecutor, reacted angrily to what he considered a calculated miscarriage of justice. The attorney general even told the press that the Justice Department was studying the need for a new criminal statute in the civil rights field. The existence of such a law probably would not have affected the outcome of the Parker case, for when Justice sought section 242 indictments from a federal grand jury in Mississippi, it too refused to return them. Although the Poplarville affair showed that racial prejudice could keep any judicial system from dispensing true justice, many people saw it as evidence of the need for a national law against racially motivated violence.[34] Roy Wilkins fired off telegrams to the chairmen of the House and Senate Judiciary committees, labeling the lynching a "tragic demonstration of the need for strong federal civil rights legislation to protect the lives and rights of American citizens in areas where state and local authorities are either unable or unwilling to do so."[35] Local NAACP branches in Chicago and Boston also cited the Parker case as evidence of the need for congressional action. So did Representative Charles Vanik (D-Ohio).[36]

Vanik's House colleague, Emanuel Celler, introduced an antilynching bill and vowed to a Brooklyn woman concerned about the Poplarville killing that he would do all in his power to get it passed. Congressman John Dingell (D-Mich.) also lobbied the White House on behalf of such legislation. Senator Philip Hart (D-Mich.) likewise introduced a bill on the subject, for which he recruited John Kennedy and Hubert Humphrey (D-Minn.) as cosponsors. Another Democratic senator, Richard L. Neuberger of Oregon, also offered an antilynching measure, as did Republicans Javits and Keating. Others endorsing such legislation included Senator Frank Lausch (D-Ohio) and four black members of the House.[37]

Despite Rogers's personal outrage and the fact that the Parker killing had generated strong congressional support for an antilynching bill, the Eisenhower administration declined to endorse the idea. Following the attorney general's blast at the Poplarville grand jury and his public statement that Justice was studying the matter, Congressman Dingell wrote to the president seeking his support for this type of legislation. Nearly three weeks passed. Then the White House, with the concurrence of the Justice Department, dispatched an evasive reply which expressed hope that the legislative proposals already submitted by the president would be enacted.[38]

Those, of course, had nothing to do with lynching. They included no Part III, and in the opinion of many ardent champions of civil rights (such as Wilkins, the American Jewish Congress, the American Veterans Committee, and the U.S. section of the Women's International League for Peace and Freedom), even the bombing recommendation was inadequate.[39]

Congress proved generally receptive to the views of those who wanted more decisive action. Only with respect to Part III did it do what the executive wanted. A House Judiciary subcommittee reported a bill that would have given the attorney general the power, under some circumstances, to seek injunctions against individuals who deprived other persons of the equal protection of the laws, but the full committee, over the objections of liberal Republicans John V. Lindsay of New York and William T. Cahill of New Jersey, deleted this provision. On the House floor James Quigley (D-Pa.) argued strongly for Part III, and Celler tried to get it restored to the bill. Edwin Willis of Louisiana got Celler's amendment excluded from consideration as not germane. In the Senate, Javits offered a Part III proposal limited to school desegregation cases, while Pat McNamara (D-Mich.) sought support for the broader version. They had the support of liberal Democrats, but Republican Leader Everett Dirksen opposed them. Each saw his proposal tabled.[40]

Although unable to add a Part III to the bill, liberals did manage to get interference with court orders in school desegregation cases made a federal crime. Governor Ernest Hollings of South Carolina, insisting that the people of his state believed "not only in States rights but in States responsibilities," and that no mob violence would be permitted there, attacked this part of the bill (called Title I) as an unnecessary attempt "on [the] part of the Federal Government to take over the police powers of the States."[41] Although Arkansas Attorney General Bruce Bennett viewed the provision in much the same way, opponents generally challenged it on other grounds. Most often heard from southerners was the charge that Title I, which proscribed threats, as well as actual force, employed to interfere with school desegregation orders, violated First Amendment guarantees of freedom of expression. Representative John Dowdy (D-Tex.) tried to amend Title I to provide that it should never be interpreted as preventing any person from advocating that "forced integration" was undesirable, but he lost on a voice vote.[42]

More effective were complaints that this provision improperly singled out one class of federal court orders—those in school desegregation cases—for special treatment. The House Judiciary Committee's southern minority used this as an argument for the elimination of Title I, and

Representative John J. Flynt, Jr., of Georgia offered an amendment to delete it from the bill. He had the support of Harold B. McSween (D-La.), who contended that if such a law were needed for desegregation cases it should apply generally to all types of court orders, judgments, and decrees. The House rejected Flynt's amendment on a voice vote and altered the administration's Title I only by reducing the offense it created from a felony to a misdemeanor.[43]

The Senate, on the other hand, did broaden that provision to include all court orders. It substituted for the House's Title I a slightly modified version of an amendment introduced by Ohio's Frank Lausch on March 10, 1960. The Lausch proposal provided that anyone who by force interfered with the execution of *any* federal court order, judgment, or decree should be liable to a fine of up to $1,000 and imprisonment for up to a year. Richard Russell and Arkansas's John McClellan both endorsed the Lausch amendment. Much of the opposition came from liberals, apparently concerned about its potential impact on organized labor. Handicapped by Attorney General Rogers's admission that he could live with Lausch's proposal, its opponents suffered two crushing defeats, losing an early test of strength 65 to 19 and going down to a 68 to 20 defeat on a vote to substitute it for the House's version of Title I.[44]

Congress broadened not only Title I but also the antibombing segment of the administration's bill, known as Title II. Initially, the idea of a federal law to combat attacks on buildings met with a great deal of opposition from southerners, who resisted it as an unnecessary and undesirable intrusion into local responsibility for law enforcement. During congressional hearings in the spring of 1959 Senator Holland, Governor Hollings, Lieutenant Governor Carroll Gartin of Mississippi, the attorneys general of Mississippi, South Carolina, and Arkansas, and the assistant attorney general of Florida all testified that the southern states were themselves taking adequate steps to combat bombing and that federal intervention was unnecessary. Senators J. Strom Thurmond (D-S.C.) and John Sparkman (D-Ala.), as well as the attorney general of North Carolina and the assistant attorney general of Florida, condemned Title II as an undesirable step toward centralization of responsibility for crime control. "If you . . . put the Federal Government step by step progressively into the field of law enforcement," argued Assistant Attorney General Ralph Odum of Florida, "you are going to weaken the whole structure of law enforcement in this country." Testifying before the Senate Judiciary Committee, Rogers assured those who shared Odom's concerns that Washington had no desire to supplant the states, but only sought to help them if they wanted assistance.[45]

Perhaps southerners believed him. At any rate, by the spring of 1960 their opposition to the legislation had cooled considerably. One reason was probably the seriousness of the bombing problem. Georgia's segregationist Senator Herman Talmadge, in whose state the Atlanta temple bombing had occurred, declared that he had "nothing but contempt" for the demented individuals who destroyed buildings with explosives, and endorsed the idea of criminalizing interstate flight to avoid prosecution for bombing. Also significant was the fact that southern law enforcement personnel had established for themselves the interstate dimensions of the bombing problem. The Atlanta police department had a squad of men surveilling a group that committed bombings all over the Deep South. To combat terrorism on this scale, federal assistance was essential.[46]

Congressmen Frank Smith (D-Miss.) and Overton Brooks (D-La.) nevertheless continued to resist it, condemning even the administration's modest proposal as an unwarranted intrusion into an area of state responsibility. Although Senator James Eastland (D-Miss.) insisted that congressional legislation of any type was unnecessary, the most common complaint heard from those southern legislators who still opposed Title II was that a bombing provision was out of place in a civil rights bill. That was an opinion they shared with some liberals from outside the South, such as Javits and Senator Thomas Hennings (D-Mo.).[47]

Although doubts persisted about whether this was the best bill with which to attack bombing, there was widespread agreement that Congress had to do something, and indeed that it ought to do more than the administration had recommended. In two significant ways the House broadened the legislation sent to it by the executive branch. After a subcommittee had approved the administration's recommendation that interstate flight to avoid prosecution for destroying educational and religious structures, or to avoid testifying, be made a federal offense, the full Judiciary Committee extended the coverage of this provision to all buildings, and to other types of real and personal property as well.[48]

On the floor Representative William C. Cramer (R-Fla.) offered an amendment punishing flight from state prosecution for making a bomb threat or communicating false information about a bombing. Ironically, it was a northern liberal, Judiciary Committee Chairman Celler, who objected to this proposal as extending federal jurisdiction too far. He argued that the states should make greater use of their own powers and not depend so much on the FBI. Cramer, although a southern conservative, was troubled by bomb threats which a Florida junior college had received when Eleanor Roosevelt spoke there. He argued that Congress must demonstrate "that Americans, that southerners, do not condone such acts and are determined to punish those responsible." His proposal, he insisted, would not bring the FBI too far into state crime prosecution. His colleagues supported him, adopting the amendment by a vote of 130 to 90. The Justice Department did not want responsibility for two hundred bomb threats per month, most of which were hoaxes, but Deputy Attorney General Walsh conceded it could live with the Cramer amendment. After he did so, the Senate also approved it.[49]

The upper chamber also went along with the House on broadening the legislation to cover buildings other than schools and places of worship. Before the bill which ultimately became law reached the Senate, Barry Goldwater (R-Ariz.), with the support of John J. Williams (R-Del.), Carl Mundt (R-S.Dak.), and Carl Curtis (R-Nebr.) had offered (as an amendment to a similar civil rights measure sponsored by Senator Dirksen) a proposal to punish also those who fled after destroying businesses, dwellings, and vehicles. Conservatives seem to have been trying to reshape Title II into something which could be used against labor union violence. When Holland endorsed the Goldwater amendment, however, he cited as his reason a bomb attack on the home of a Florida NAACP leader. North Carolina's Ervin also supported Goldwater, arguing, "This amendment would bring the power of the Federal Government into a field which rightly belongs to [it] . . . under the interstate and foreign commerce clause." Although Dirksen did not want his measure saddled with the Arizona conservative's proposed addition, the Senate adopted the amendment 85 to 1.[50]

By an even more overwhelming margin it also made criminal the interstate transportation of explosives intended for use in bombings. On March 14, 1960, while the Senate was considering the Dirksen measure, Keating offered an amendment which would make it a federal offense to import or transport in interstate commerce any explosive with the knowledge or intent that it be used to damage or destroy any real or personal property used for educational, religious, charitable, residential, or business purposes. He also proposed including in the law a rebuttable presumption that any explosives used for such purposes or possessed in a manner which evinced intent to so employ them had been transported in violation of the law's provisions. Keating argued that Dirksen's measure, which embodied the administration's proposals, was inadequate because it did not permit the FBI to move against bombers until they had accomplished their objective and because it excluded from federal prosecution those who never fled the jurisdiction where they committed their crimes. Noting that some of the many bombings the nation had experienced since the end of 1955 had occurred outside the South, he insisted this was not a sectional problem. Besides, said Keating, when he and Javits visited the South, officials there had made it clear they wanted federal help. Two Florida congressmen had testified in favor of antibombing legislation, and Representatives Loser of Tennessee and Willis of Louisiana were pushing for its enactment.[51]

John Sherman Cooper (R-Ky.) supported Keating. So did Ervin, but he objected to several features of the New Yorker's amendment, including its creation of a rebuttable presumption. Keating won him over on that issue, but altered his proposal in accordance with some of Ervin's other suggestions. As modified, it passed 87 to 0. Later, when the House bill came before the Senate, Keating asked to substitute his measure for its more limited antibombing title, and his colleagues agreed.[52] The bill then returned to the House, where the Rules Committee recommended acceptance of the changes which the Senate had made. On April 21, 1960, the lower chamber agreed to them by a vote of 288 to 95.[53]

Although the bill which emerged from Congress went considerably beyond what he had requested, Eisenhower nevertheless signed it into law, noting as he did so its potential for deterring obstruction of school desegregation orders and the bombing of schools, churches, and other structures. Title I of the statute that became known as the Civil Rights Act of 1960 made the actual or attempted use of threats or force to interfere with the exercise of rights or the performance of duties under a federal court order, judgment, or decree punishable by a fine of up to $1,000, imprisonment for up to one year, or both. Although making the conduct it proscribed only a misdemeanor, this provision nevertheless gave the national government a weapon that could be employed against those who resorted to mob action to thwart school desegregation. The law's Title II created three new federal offenses: 1) fleeing across a state line to avoid prosecution or confinement under state law for bombing a building used for religious, educational, or other purposes; 2) transporting explosives in interstate or foreign commerce with the intent that they be employed to damage or destroy such a structure; and 3) using the mails, telephone, telegraph, or "other instrument of commerce" to make a bomb threat. The penalties for the third of these crimes were the same as those imposed by Title I. So were the ones for transporting explosives. If a violation of those provisions resulted in injury to someone, however, the maximums rose to ten years and a $10,000 fine, and if it caused death, then either life imprisonment or capital punishment might be imposed. Flight to avoid prosecution or confinement was made punishable by a fine of up to $5,000, a prison sentence of up to five years, or both.[54]

Thus, the new law was a tough one, which significantly expanded the capacity of the national government to combat anti–civil rights violence. Yet it represented a rather minimal federal intrusion into law enforcement in the southern states. The flight section, after all, merely enabled the FBI to assist states in enforcing their own laws against bombing. The transportation-of-explosives and bomb-threat provisions were qualified by a subsection which declared that neither should ever be interpreted as occupying the field in which it operated to the exclusion of the laws of any state.[55] These features, along with the seriousness of the bombing problem and its obviously interstate character, probably account for the willingness of so many southern senators and representatives, whose predecessors had fought doggedly against an antilynching law, to support this federal legislation against racist violence.

Once the new statute was on the books, the Civil Rights Division tried to claim credit for its enactment, bragging that "with minor exceptions every provision of the Civil Rights Act of 1960 was conceived of and drafted by the Department of Justice."[56] With respect to its antiviolence provisions, that simply was not true. In this area the Eisenhower administration had followed rather than led.[57]

Its handling of a deteriorating situation in the South had been a case of too little too late. Confronted with violent resistance to the *Brown* decision, the administration had failed to assume any responsibility for the problem until the open defiance of Governor Faubus made a mockery of its reliance on the states, confronted the nation with a genuine constitutional crisis, and virtually compelled the president to use military force to restore order. Faced with an epidemic of racist bombings, the Eisenhower administration moved reluctantly toward an expansion of federal authority which even many white southerners regarded as essential. Such constitutional conservatism, persisting beyond 1960, would prove even more inadequate in the decade of turmoil that lay ahead.

Crisis Management in the Kennedy Administration

The enactment of federal bombing legislation was a minor political event in a year better remembered for the election of John F. Kennedy to the presidency. On Kennedy's "New Frontier" the Justice Department, headed by the president's younger brother Robert, often resembled the cavalry in a western movie, riding into southern trouble spots to save beleaguered victims of racist violence. Unfortunately, its dramatic rescues were only further examples of the sort of crisis management that Eisenhower had pioneered at Little Rock. Although more sympathetic to the civil rights movement than its predecessor, the Kennedy administration manifested a similar reluctance to see the national government assume responsibility for protecting the victims of violent resistance to racial change. Only when no other option remained would the federal cavalry ride South to the rescue.

When John Kennedy took office in 1961, southern racial violence remained a serious problem. Passage of the Civil Rights Act of 1960 had not halted racially motivated bombings. Most of those in late 1960 and early 1961 (in such cities as Atlanta, Chattanooga, and Nashville) seem to have been products of white determination to preserve traditional racial patterns in housing. Taking advantage of the 1960 law, the FBI frequently assisted in the investigation of these dynamitings. After apprehending three white men alleged to have attempted to bomb Arkansas's Philander Smith College for Negroes, however, the Bureau turned them over to the state for prosecution. The reason, it said, was a lack of evidence to prove interstate transportation of the explosives. [1]

Bombing was not the only form of violence to which white terrorists resorted. Klansmen extolled the value of baseball bats, ax handles, and shotguns for keeping blacks in their place. Even whites suspected of sympathy with the civil rights movement received savage beatings. In an ominous preview of an impending crisis, when two black students enrolled at the University of Georgia under a federal court order in January 1961, rioting engulfed the campus.[2]

Controlling such racial violence, the new president and his Justice Department insisted, was a state responsibility. Quickly forgotten was the fact that Kennedy had been elected on a platform calling for enactment of Title III. Democrats had adopted that plank after representatives of the Student Nonviolent Coordinating Committee (SNCC), an organization of college-age civil rights activists spawned by the sit-in movement that had swept the South in 1960, urged them to endorse increased federal protection for blacks seeking to vote or otherwise exercise their civil rights. It was not so much SNCC's urging as confusion in the Kennedy ranks that caused the party to take a strong stand on the racial issue. Robert had instructed members of the platform committee pledged to his brother to stand firm for a plank written by Harris Wofford, Tom Hughes, and Adam Chayes and sponsored by Chester Boles, not realizing that its authors had planned on the committee watering down their version.[3]

Arthur Schlesinger, Jr., a historian and former Kennedy White House aide, claims the candidate himself insisted on the plank which was adopted, but the fact of the matter is that the new president entered office without much of a commitment to the reform of American race relations. Kennedy disliked discrimination and as a congressman and senator he had consistently supported civil rights legislation. He was not, however, particularly knowledgeable in this area. Nor did Kennedy feel any real sense of urgency about civil rights. He was conscious of the moral dimension of the issue, but tended to view it as primarily a political problem. Although normally adopting a moderate posture, intended to appeal to blacks without alienating southern whites, during the 1960 campaign Kennedy briefly cast caution aside, calling to reassure the wife of Dr. Martin Luther King, Jr., after Georgia authorities jailed the civil rights leader. That dramatic gesture enabled him to realize a campaign objective by capturing about 70 percent of the black vote.[4]

Although those ballots were Kennedy's margin of victory over Republican Richard Nixon, his administration failed to mount a vigorous effort on behalf of civil rights. He did appoint more blacks to top federal jobs than any previous president had, but, convinced that the 87th Congress would never enact civil rights legislation anyhow, Kennedy disappointed liberals by failing to introduce any. The Southern Regional Council sent the new president a report urging action by the executive branch to combat the violence, reprisals, and intimidation surrounding school desegregation, but instead of implementing its suggestions, he called on southern communities to solve the problem themselves.[5]

Although the president was ultimately responsible for his administration's civil rights policies, the man charged with their execution was his brother. The new attorney general was a lawyer of limited experience, most of it as a staff counsel for Senate committees that specialized in investigating communism and labor racketeering. Yet he had been an opponent of segregation at least since his student days at the University of Virginia Law School. Robert Kennedy managed to hide his racial views well enough that such southern senators as James Eastland, Sam Ervin, and John McClellan enthusiastically supported his nomination to head the Justice Department. A few months after taking office the new attorney general made it clear where he stood. In a May 1961 Law Day address at the riot-torn University of Georgia, he endorsed the Supreme Court's school desegregation decision, condemned violence, and expressed determination to ensure that judicial orders were enforced.[6]

Robert Kennedy also invigorated a rather moribund Civil Rights Division. Between December 1961 and December 1963 it expanded by approximately 60 percent. In addition, as one lawyer recalled later, there was a new emphasis on action. Civil Rights Division attorneys abandoned their Washington offices for the field, heading South to enforce voting rights legislation.[7]

While bringing new vigor to the Justice Department's civil rights work, Robert Kennedy also brought caution, especially where violence was concerned. For him, this was a political problem. Although sincerely committed to civil rights, "Bobby" was even more committed to his brother. If the national government assumed responsibility for southern law enforcement, "Jack" would surely suffer politically. Contrary to what Alabama Governor John Patterson claimed later, the attorney general understood the concept of dual sovereignty and accepted the limitations it imposed on federal power. Indeed, he welcomed them, for they provided a convenient rationalization for avoiding action likely to harm his brother in the South.[8] Asked about the national government's failure to combat anti–civil rights violence in Alabama and Mississippi, the attorney general responded that eventually the situation in those states would work itself out. "Now maybe its going to take a decade; and maybe a lot of people are going to be killed in the meantime; and I think that's unfortunate," he said. "But in the long run I think it's for the health of the country and the stability of this system; and it's the best way to proceed."[9]

This seemingly callous comment reflected the constitutional philosophy of the man the Kennedys chose to head the Civil Rights Division: Burke Marshall. A brilliant graduate of the Yale Law School who came to the Justice Department from the prestigious Washington law firm of Covington and Burling, Marshall impressed even his adversaries as an extremely knowledgeable attorney, but his specialty was antitrust, not race relations. Although he had assisted behind the scenes with the drafting of the voting provisions of the 1960 Civil Rights Act, Marshall lacked public identification with the struggle for racial equality. This did not bother Robert Kennedy, who wanted a man interested in doing what was best for the president as well as for blacks. Besides, since nominees to head the Civil Rights Division had often encountered southern opposition in the Senate, Marshall's lack of a relevant record might actually be an asset.[10] It must have seemed odd, however, to hear the man about to become the government's top civil rights lawyer tell a Senate committee during confirmation hearings, "I have really had no experience in that field."[11]

Rather than expertise in race relations law, Marshall brought to his new Justice Department post a deep commitment to federalism, particularly in the field of law enforcement. He recognized that in the South sheriffs and police officers frequently tolerated, and even participated in, interference with the exercise of constitutional rights by blacks and their supporters. But Marshall did not believe the solution to this problem lay in having the national government assume responsibility for protecting the targets of anti–civil rights violence. The Justice Department's tiny force of United States marshals (which had pacified New Orleans during school desegregation there in 1960) was far too small to prevent trouble throughout the South. Only by creating a national police force could the federal government physically protect all the potential victims of racist terrorism. Congress, Marshall was sure, would never authorize such an organization. Even had it been willing to do so, he would not have recommended such a step, for any president backed by a national police force would be a threat to liberty.[12] As late as 1965, when the situation in the South had become

much worse than it was when he took office, Marshall still insisted that
the trouble there did not warrant "departure from this historic pattern of
limited federal power."[13]

In his opinion, "Problems of protection [had to be] the responsibility of
local law enforcement agencies."[14] If these proved reluctant to meet their
obligations in this area, Washington should endeavor to persuade them to
do their duty. If that approach failed, federal courts might, on occasion,
order local authorities to protect persons engaged in lawful civil rights
activities. But under the federal system there was really no substitute for
local law enforcement. The long-run solution to the problem of unpunished anti–civil rights violence lay not in injunctions but rather in
changes effected through the political process, which would encourage
authorities in the South to do a better job of protecting those they did not
like.[15] Ultimately, the federal government had no choice but to rely on
southern institutions, because "they are going to be there when we leave."
In the short run that often meant leaving persons involved in the burgeon-
ing civil rights movement exposed to attack, but Marshall believed their
plight was the result of a temporary breakdown in southern law enforcement which would last for only a few years. Like Robert Kennedy, he
thought "we ought to live through it."[16]

Marshall's federalism was not the "apology for the existing social order"
that Victor Navasky has charged. As assistant attorney general, he did a
great deal to force unwanted change upon a reluctant South. Even
Thurgood Marshall, the former NAACP attorney destined to become the
first black justice on the Supreme Court, agreed with his basic proposition
that the federal government was not a policing authority. But the inaction
and deference to state and local officials which Burke Marshall's constitutional philosophy required did accord nicely with the political needs of the
Kennedy brothers. Robert echoed Marshall's views with apparent sincerity, but acknowledged that even if the Constitution had not been written in such a way as to preclude massive federal intervention in southern
law enforcement, he would still have regarded it as unwise. The alleged
"constitutional impotence" of the national government probably did not
cause the attorney general and his top civil rights aide nearly as much
distress as Schlesinger insists, nor bother President Kennedy nearly as
much as Marshall and his brother claimed.[17] When confronted with demands for remedial action to correct the inadequacies of southern law

enforcement, the White House readily pleaded that "the role of the Federal Government in our constitutional system . . . is limited."[18]

Many Justice Department lawyers agreed. Marshall felt confidence in, and retained, most of the attorneys who had served under Harold Tyler, the last man to head Eisenhower's Civil Rights Division. Among them was John Doar, a Republican named by Tyler as his top assistant in July 1960. Doar, a graduate of Princeton University and the law school of the University of California at Berkeley, came to the Justice Department from a small-town family law practice in New Richmond, Wisconsin. He accepted a job offer from Tyler because he liked trial work and, in his words, "had some clear ideas about civil rights in this country." Although Doar came to be regarded by people in the civil rights movement as more committed to their cause than the somewhat distant and detached Marshall, he shared with his new boss a conviction that there were strong constitutional limitations on what the federal government could do in the field of criminal law enforcement. Like Marshall, Doar insisted the Justice Department was not a police force that could protect civil rights activists from harm throughout the South.[19]

Such views were not confined to the Civil Rights Division. They seem to have been shared by most members of the ad hoc team, drawn from throughout the Justice Department, which rallied around Robert Kennedy during major racial crises. This group included Deputy Attorney General Byron White and Nicholas Katzenbach, who first headed the Office of Legal Counsel and then took over White's job when he was elevated to the Supreme Court in 1962. Also included was Assistant Deputy Attorney General Joseph Dolan. Other members were assistant attorneys general Norbet Schlei (Office of Legal Counsel), Louis Oberdorfer (Tax Division), Ramsey Clark (Lands Division), and John Douglas (Civil Division), Public Information Officer Edwin Guthman, and Kennedy's administrative assistant, John Nolan. Some of these men, such as Katzenbach, a former law professor, openly endorsed Marshall's views on the requirements of federalism. The only Justice Department leader who seems to have disagreed at all with them was Clark.[20]

Not surprisingly, the Kennedy Justice Department tended to downplay prosecution and to emphasize negotiation. It would not even file a civil suit without "first discussing the matter with state and local authorities." Proper respect for the federal system, Marshall and the attorney general believed, required them to maximize opportunities for local self-correction of civil rights problems. Kennedy urged state officials to use their own police forces to ensure that the laws were enforced equitably and to keep mob violence from interfering with the carrying out of court orders, so that the employment of federal marshals or troops would not be necessary.[21]

Only rarely did the Justice Department attack official or private violence with a criminal prosecution, and never did it do so unless the state in which the trouble arose had failed to act. Despite the demands of lawyers associated with the civil rights movement for vigorous use of sections 241 and 242, the number of cases brought under those laws increased only slightly from what it had been during Eisenhower's presidency. The Justice Department sometimes attributed its failure to bring more civil rights prosecutions to the difficulty of persuading southern grand juries to indict and southern trial juries to convict. Yet, as William Taylor, staff director for the Civil Rights Commission, pointed out, because section 242 was a misdemeanor statute, prosecutions under it could be initiated without an indictment. A simple information filed by a federal prosecutor would suffice. Not until 1963 did the division resort to this procedure. Many civil rights lawyers insisted that fear of failure should not deter the government from bringing cases, because even an unsuccessful prosecution could educate the public and induce caution on the part of potential violators. The Civil Rights Commission also criticized the division for giving too much weight to the likelihood of obtaining a conviction. Not until 1964 or 1965, however, did its policy change. Although attributing his division's inertia to the cautious attitudes of the two men who headed its criminal section, A. B. Caldwell and John Murphy, Marshall acknowledged that he himself did not emphasize the use of sections 241 and 242.[22]

What the assistant attorney general did stress was voting rights litigation. Through civil suits, he believed, the Justice Department could win the franchise for southern blacks. Although insisting that the federal government lacked the authority to protect them against violence, Robert Kennedy was equally sure it could do something about voting. Once blacks gained political rights, he, Marshall, and the president were convinced, southern officials would have to become more responsive to their wishes. The problem of unpunished racial violence would then solve itself. "No one could argue against that as a general principle," Thurgood

Marshall observed. "But in the meantime Negroes were being killed and denied their rights."[23] As far as he was concerned, the states could not protect their right to protest racial discrimination, and the federal government would have to do so.

Violent southern reaction against the Freedom Rides soon made the same point, and forced the Kennedy administration to retreat temporarily from its constitutional principles. The crisis which compelled it to take that step was one product of a developing trend within the civil rights movement away from litigation and towards direct action. The Eisenhower administration had generally confronted violence that resulted from attacks on passive black victims by whites bent on keeping them from enjoying the benefits of judicially mandated desegregation. These situations demanded little more from the federal government than determination to prevent forceful interference with the implementation of court orders. Now, civil rights activists became instigators, challenging segregation nonviolently, but in ways likely to provoke violent resistance by whites. Furthermore, they often acted without bothering to obtain explicit judicial sanction for particular undertakings. Keeping violence from interfering with the exercise of constitutional rights in the South became a much more complex and difficult task than it once had been.

The new administration was slow to recognize the changing nature of the situation confronting Washington, for the first of the direct action tactics to attain widespread popularity created no law enforcement crisis. The sit-ins had begun on February 1, 1960, when four black students from North Carolina A&T seated themselves at the segregated lunch counter of a Woolworth's store in Greensboro and demanded equal service. Their quiet defiance ignited a movement which swept across the South like a prairie fire, touching more than one hundred cities within a year. When the Kennedys entered office, black students, assisted by some white integrationists, were still sitting-in, attempting to pressure commercial establishments and public facilities into altering their racial policies. The new administration elected to take no independent action to protect the rights of these demonstrators.[24]

Two things enabled it to get away with that decision. One was the relatively low level of violence associated with the early sit-ins. Jacksonville, Florida, experienced three days of turmoil, which featured Klan attacks on demonstrators and resulted in the shooting death of a black bystander. Racial rioting also erupted in Portsmouth, Virginia, and Chat-

tanooga, Tennessee, and there were violent incidents associated with sit-
ins and similar demonstrations in Atlanta, New Orleans, Nashville,
Houston, Columbia and Rock Hill, South Carolina, and Jackson and
Biloxi, Mississippi. "Yet," as historian/political scientist Howard Zinn
observed from the perspective of deep personal involvement in the civil
rights movement, "considering the number of people involved in demonstrations and the intense psychological tremors accompanying this sudden
attack by long-quiescent Negroes on the old way of life, violence was
minimal."[25]

The restraint displayed by the demonstrators themselves was one of the
major reasons for this. Another important factor was the performance of
southern law enforcement. There were reports about police in New Orleans, Rock Hill, and Jacksonville failing to provide protesters with adequate protection. Generally, though, law enforcement personnel endeavored to preserve the peace. Often, their way of protecting demonstrators
was to use arrest as a means of removing them from dangerous situations,
but this was by no means always the case. In Chattanooga and Richmond
the police concentrated on controlling white hoodlums, and in Winston-
Salem, Durham, and Greensboro municipal officials sought to prevent
disorder by desegregating their communities as quickly as possible.[26]

Unfortunately for the Kennedy administration, Alabama officials behaved far less responsibly during the Freedom Rides. The rides were an
initiative of the Congress of Racial Equality (CORE), whose recently in-
stalled national director, James Farmer, and his staff were looking for a
dramatic nonviolent action that could advance the southern protest movement, and also the status and funding of their organization. Farmer, a
longtime Christian pacifist, was the son of a professor at black Wiley
College in Texas and a graduate of the Howard Divinity School. In 1942
he and several other members of the Fellowship of Reconciliation had
founded CORE. Five years later the new organization sent an interracial
group into the South to test compliance with a recent Supreme Court
decision forbidding the segregation of interstate buses. On February 1,
1961, one of Farmer's aides suggested that the same tactic might be employed again, this time to test compliance with the Court's 1959 ruling
requiring the integration of terminal facilities used by interstate carriers.
The new national director considered this "a capital idea." On May 4 two
integrated groups of civil rights activists boarded buses in Washington,

D.C., bound for the Deep South, one traveling Trailways and the other going Greyhound.[27]

On the Greyhound bus was a black seminary student, John Lewis. He left Washington "prepared for the possibility of some acts of violence," but was "shocked and couldn't believe the type of violence and reaction" he and his fellow Freedom Riders actually encountered.[28] All went well until they reached Rock Hill, South Carolina. There several young white men confronted Lewis when he sought to enter a whites-only waiting room. Although he informed them that the Supreme Court had affirmed his right to be there, they attacked him, knocking the young black man to the ground. When Lewis's white companion, Albert Bigelow, an ex-navy captain, tried to protect him, he too was beaten.[29]

Following the trouble in South Carolina, the Freedom Ride progressed peacefully across Georgia. On May 14 the Greyhound bus reached Anniston, Alabama, where a black college student had been beaten in January for using the supposedly desegregated waiting room of the local railroad station. A mob of 100 to 150 whites, armed with clubs, chains, and blackjacks, greeted the bus, breaking its windows and slashing its tires. When the Greyhound drove off, the mob followed. Six miles out of town the driver had to pull over because of a flat tire. As Bigelow recalled later, "They surrounded us again, yelling and smashing windows, brandishing clubs, chains, and pipes." Someone threw a fire bomb inside the bus, and as the Freedom Riders fled from the flames several of them were beaten.[30]

About an hour later another mob greeted the Trailways group in Anniston. Eight white hoodlums boarded their bus and forced the driver to order the black Freedom Riders to move to the back. When they refused, the toughs attacked them. Two white Freedom Riders, James Peck and Professor Walter Bergman, tried to intervene, only to be kicked and beaten. Bergman received a crushing blow to the skull which nearly killed him. In Birmingham "a mob lined up on the sidewalk only a few feet from the [bus station] loading platform. Most of them were young. . . . All had hate showing on their faces."[31] They tore into the Freedom Riders, badly injuring nine people. Peck received wounds which required fifty-three stitches.[32]

While angry racists mobbed the Freedom Riders, Alabama law enforcement stood idle. In Rock Hill the police had come promptly to the rescue of Lewis and Bigelow, and only because the two men declined to press charges were the hoodlums who beat them not arrested.[33] In Anniston, on the other hand, "no police were in sight." The only officer present while the Greyhound bus was under attack "did nothing to stop the vandalism, but fraternized with the mob."[34] Only belatedly did other policemen, who had been standing by elsewhere, appear on the scene and disperse the crowd. When the Freedom Riders reached Birmingham, "although the police had advance warning of the possibility of violence, no police were present." The Birmingham superintendent of police, Eugene "Bull" Connor, later stated that he had been shorthanded because it was Mother's Day.[35] Actually, Birmingham police officials had promised the Ku Klux Klan fifteen minutes during which to attack the Freedom Riders "with absolutely no intervention from any police officer whatsoever."[36] Not all Alabama law enforcement personnel collaborated with the Klan or stood idle while it ran amok. A courageous plainclothesman from the Department of Public Safety, Eli L. Cowling, who was on the Greyhound bus, risked his life at Anniston to defend its passengers, blocking the stairwell, drawing his gun, and singlehandedly keeping the mob from getting aboard.[37] His performance was the exception, however.

Little else justified federal faith that state and local authorities could be trusted to protect the Freedom Riders. Determined not to usurp any law enforcement responsibility, the FBI, although informed three weeks in advance, by an informant within the Ku Klux Klan, about the Birmingham attack, did nothing to prevent it. When the informant, Gary Thomas Rowe, asked agents what the Bureau was going to do to protect the Freedom Riders, they responded that the FBI was an investigative agency whose job was merely to gather information. Rowe received assurances that the Klan would not be permitted to beat up the Freedom Riders, but apparently the Bureau expected local authorities to prevent this. Although he told agents that the Birmingham police were cooperating closely with the Klan, the FBI passed to them information it had obtained on the Freedom Riders' itinerary and schedule.[38]

The Bureau had no monopoly on wishful thinking. With President Kennedy about to leave for summit meetings in Europe, his brother wanted desperately to avoid an ugly domestic incident. The attorney general and his advisors recognized that the Freedom Riders had a clear right to travel from state to state and concluded that there was no point in trying to talk them out of exercising it. Hence, Edwin Guthman would recall later, "Bob and his associates thought the best course of action would be for local authorities to guarantee the riders' safety."[39]

With that aim in mind, the attorney general telephoned Governor John Patterson of Alabama on May 15. He sought assurances that the governor would protect the Freedom Riders, but Patterson, more interested in preserving segregation than in providing a police escort for persons he regarded as troublemakers, equivocated. After leading Kennedy to believe he was going to protect the Riders, the governor issued a statement saying he would not be responsible for their safety.[40] Then Patterson disappeared—according to Guthman, "undercutting an intensive effort by the Administration to convince Alabama authorities that it was in their own interest—as well as the national interest—to accept responsibility for the safety of citizens travelling interstate and permit the Freedom Ride to proceed without violence."[41]

Meanwhile, although the Birmingham police were now keeping crowds away from the bus station, the situation there had become so threatening that the Freedom Riders decided to abandon their bus trip and fly on to New Orleans. They were soon replaced by SNCC members from Nashville. Determined to prove that violence could not defeat the drive for black equality, these students decided to complete the original journey. Upon arriving in Birmingham, they too confronted a mob. When no bus driver would transport the group to Montgomery, the police took them into protective custody. They were treated well in jail, but the next morning Connor drove the would-be Freedom Riders to the Tennessee line and dumped them off along the highway. Undeterred, they obtained a car and returned to Birmingham.[42]

Confronted with an increasingly volatile situation in that city and a total abdication of responsibility by Governor Patterson, the Kennedy administration had little choice but to consider federal action to protect the federal right of interstate travel. The president desperately wanted to avoid another Little Rock, for he had criticized Eisenhower's handling of that situation and a repetition of it would embarrass him in his forthcoming meeting with Soviet leader Nikita Khrushchev. Besides, the idea of using troops against American citizens was distasteful to him. Byron White and several other Justice Department attorneys searched for alternatives. Finally, White recommended deputizing Border Patrolmen, prison guards, and Treasury Department alcohol and tobacco agents to assist the small force of United States marshals which had been receiving riot training since Little Rock. Marshall added a proposal that the government seek an injunction forbidding the Klan from interfering with interstate travel and ordering police in Alabama to protect persons exercising that right. He, White, and the Kennedys agreed that before anything else was done, another attempt should be made to persuade Patterson to do his duty. This time the president himself would try.[43]

The governor was still avoiding phone calls, so Kennedy had to settle for a conversation with Lieutenant Governor Albert Boutwell. Eventually, the president received word through an intermediary that Alabama's elusive leader would confer with a personal representative of the president, and the Justice Department's John Seigenthaler flew to Montgomery in that capacity. He informed Patterson that the federal government was willing to provide marshals and any other assistance necessary to keep commerce moving, but the governor insisted that was not necessary.[44] Patterson said "he wanted to assure the President and the federal government that he had the means, the ability, and the will to preserve law and order and to protect all individuals in the State of Alabama."[45] On the basis of these assurances, and others which Robert Kennedy received from Floyd Mann, the head of the Alabama Highway Patrol, twenty-one student Freedom Riders left Birmingham for Montgomery on May 20.[46]

Mann's troopers escorted their bus to the outskirts of Montgomery, then passed responsibility for protecting the group to the local police commissioner, L. B. Sullivan. The FBI already had told the city police the Freedom Riders were coming, and fifteen minutes before the bus pulled in they assured the Bureau there would be no violence. At the same time a member of the department was telling a reporter that the police would not lift a finger to protect the Freedom Riders. No officers were present when the bus arrived, but a mob of a thousand white racists was. John Doar, describing the scene by telephone to Robert Kennedy, reported, "Oh, there are fists, punching. . . . There are no cops. It's terrible. It's terrible. There's not a cop in sight." Eventually, Floyd Mann appeared on the scene with his troopers. He fired a warning shot into the air, making it clear to the crowd that there would be no killing that day. By the time the mob dispersed, however, a number of people had been injured, among them John Seigenthaler.[47]

While receiving a blow-by-blow account of the rioting that felled Seigenthaler, Robert Kennedy tried again to call Patterson. The governor was "out of town." With even Republicans, such as Pennsylvania Senator Hugh Scott, urging that federal power be utilized in Montgomery, the Kennedy administration made what Marshall characterized later as a "constitutional" decision. The attorney general told White to get his marshals moving. The president, exercising authority vested in him by Title 10, section 333, of the United States Code, made an official finding that law and order had broken down in the Montgomery area and ordered his brother to take whatever steps were necessary to restore it. He did this despite a belated and almost ludicrous telephone call from Patterson, who tried to excuse the Montgomery Police Department by saying it was too small to handle such a large mob, but at the same time insisted that Alabamians needed no outside help to control the situation. By the next morning they had it anyhow: a force of around four hundred federal marshals had assembled at nearby Maxwell Air Force Base, charged with assisting state and local authorities in the protection of persons and vehicles.[48]

In the meantime, Doar had rented a car and driven fifty miles to ask a sympathetic federal district judge, Frank Johnson, to enjoin those responsible for the violence. The same day Doar filed his complaint, Johnson, a Republican Eisenhower appointee who as a U.S. attorney had vigorously prosecuted white landowners for holding blacks in involuntary servitude, issued a temporary restraining order. On June 2, after a five-day hearing, the judge granted a preliminary injunction forbidding three Klan organizations and several Klan leaders from conspiring to interfere with interstate travel, from threatening, intimidating, or committing acts of violence against interstate passengers or the bus companies, and from "obstructing, impeding, or interfering with the free movement of interstate commerce in and through the State of Alabama." Furthermore, Johnson ordered Sullivan and the members of the Montgomery police force to cease "failing or refusing to provide protection" for persons traveling through their city in interstate commerce.[49]

By the time he issued this injunction, it was obvious that many of those responsible for maintaining law and order in Alabama needed judicial prodding. On Sunday, May 21, White had met with Patterson, Mann, and the Alabama attorney general, McDonald Gallion. He made an imposing representative of federal authority. "Whizzer" White, who stood six feet two and weighed a trim 190 pounds, had been an All-American back at the University of Colorado and the 1938 Rookie of the Year in the

National Football League. As formidable intellectually as he was physically, he had also been a Rhodes Scholar, a top student at the Yale Law
School, and a clerk for Supreme Court Chief Justice Fred Vinson. Although the deputy attorney general assured the Alabama officials with
whom he met that the federal government wanted to "work with state and
local law enforcement officials," their meeting was an acrimonious one.
Governor Patterson demanded to know what law the Justice Department
had relied upon in sending marshals to Alabama and insisted that what it
should be doing was talking the Freedom Riders out of coming. Patterson
urged White to supply him with information from FBI files on what he
claimed were the Communist connections of these civil rights activists.
He also asked for federal help in gathering evidence that could be used to
prosecute them in the state courts. Gallion claimed that the Freedom
Riders were violating an injunction which an Alabama judge had issued
against CORE and wanted the marshals to arrest them for contempt.
Although White continued to insist that the federal government was interested only in maintaining the integrity of the interstate bus system and
in protecting "any other federally guaranteed rights . . . deprivation of
which is threatened by violence," Patterson blasted Washington for supporting and encouraging outside agitators. The governor even threatened
to arrest the marshals, claiming their presence constituted an encroach-
ment on the rights of the citizens of Alabama.

In an agitated summary of the state's position, he declared:

> We have adequate forces to enforce the law. We don't need any as-
> sistance from the federal government to do it. We have not asked for
> any assistance. We don't want the assistance of the federal government
> . . . , and we don't believe that the United States has any legal or
> constitutional right to come in here with federal marshals and do what
> they are proposing to do, and I think that your presence . . . will only
> further complicate and aggravate the situation and worsent [sic] federal-
> state relations.[50]

On the same day that Patterson delivered this tirade he also telegraphed
Robert Kennedy, making several of the same points he had made to
White. The governor also assured the attorney general that Alabama's law
enforcement personnel were prepared to maintain law and order.[51]

They got a chance to prove it that evening. When 1,500 blacks assembled at a Montgomery Baptist church to honor the Freedom Riders

(who slipped into the building in disguise) and to hear speeches by Martin Luther King, Jr., his SCLC aides Wyatt Tee Walker and Ralph David Abernathy, and CORE leader James Farmer, a white mob gathered in a park across the street. The police did nothing. White ordered one hundred of his marshals into action, and using nightsticks and tear gas they engaged the rock and bottle throwing mob as it tried to advance on the church. In Washington the attorney general debated whether to send in troops. The necessary presidential proclamation had been drafted the previous evening, and soldiers were on alert. Kennedy walked to the telephone to order them into action, but Burke Marshall urged him to wait five or ten minutes more. In the nick of time the omnipresent Floyd Mann charged to the rescue, leading a squad of state troopers into the fray and helping the marshals drive the mob back from the church.[52]

Now, at last, Patterson acted. Apprised of the skirmish at the church, the governor declared martial law around 2:00 A.M. Adjutant General Henry Graham led National Guard troops onto the scene, and they dispersed the mob.[53]

Once Alabama authorities took the necessary action to bring the situation in Montgomery under control, the Justice Department quickly reduced the federal presence there. After White and Robert Kennedy conferred with Graham and Mann, the Justice Department decided to withdraw its marshals to Maxwell Air Force Base, leaving protection of the church to the National Guard. Dr. King, who did not believe Alabama soldiers would protect his people, called the attorney general to protest. To his surprise, Graham's Guardsmen escorted the besieged blacks safely home.[54]

Back in Washington, Senator Javits introduced a resolution commending the president for his handling of the Alabama crisis. Although southern objections and Senate rules kept it from being brought to a vote, his colleague Joseph Clark (D-Pa.) was sure the measure had the support of at least eighty senators. On the other hand, many spokesmen for the South complained bitterly about the continued presence of six hundred marshals in Alabama. A former governor of that state, Jim Folsom, disgusted with the irresponsibility of his successor, urged the Justice Department to keep its men on hand as long as trouble continued, but Orval Faubus and Arkansas Congressmen Wilbur Mills and E. C. Gathings, along with the Montgomery and Alabama Chambers of Commerce, demanded the removal of these "armed federal forces."[55]

At the other extreme stood liberal Representative Lester Holtzman (D-N.Y.), who urged the president "to send federal troops into the state in an all out effort to restore law and order."[56] Such action did not seem necessary to Robert Kennedy. Alabama authorities had finally demonstrated they had the will, as well as the capacity, to keep the peace, and he "wanted nothing better than to give them the chance."[57] On May 24 the attorney general issued a statement in which he declared, "Our obligation is to protect interstate travellers and maintain law and order only when local authorities are unwilling or unable to do so."[58]

By then the Freedom Riders had departed Montgomery for Jackson, Mississippi. James Farmer, who had joined them on the buses, was "scared spitless," for they were protected only by Mann's troopers and the Alabama and Mississippi National Guards. Awaiting them was Governor Ross Barnett, who was no more anxious to have these "agitators" in his state than Patterson had been, and a state attorney general who told Burke Marshall he would not advise the governor to provide the Freedom Riders with police protection.[59] Barnett also insisted that he did "not want any police aid from Washington, either marshals or federal troops."[60] Although Robert Kennedy feared the Freedom Riders might be killed in Mississippi, he complied with the governor's wishes. After "much soul searching in the White House and the Justice Department," the administration decided that marshals would not accompany the Freedom Riders to Jackson.[61] According to Marshall, "It was decided that our responsibility was, despite all the reports, to try to make the state of Mississippi bear the responsibility for law and order."[62] With this objective in mind, Kennedy held more than thirty conversations with Senator James Eastland over a period of several days. The Mississippi segregationist agreed to assume responsibility for the safety of the Freedom Riders, provided they could be arrested for breach of the peace if they tried to integrate the terminal facilities in Jackson. On this basis, Barnett, anxious himself to avoid violence, agreed to provide them with an escort. For the alleged purposes of preserving the peace and saving lives, the same attorney general who had moved so decisively to safeguard the federal right of interstate travel in Montgomery accepted a deal which allowed its exercise to be thwarted in Mississippi. Although prepared to dispatch troops if Barnett failed to keep his word, Kennedy actually did no more than closely monitor the progress of the Freedom Riders as they rolled toward jail in Jackson.[63]

On May 26, 1961, twenty-seven of them were convicted there after brief trials. As other would-be Freedom Riders, answering a call for reenforcements put out by Farmer, poured into Jackson, they too were apprehended by the police. By the end of the summer, the arrest total had climbed past three hundred. When the NAACP Legal Defense and Education Fund made an unsuccessful effort to enjoin the Jackson prosecutions, the Justice Department supported it with an amicus curiae brief in the Supreme Court. More than that, Justice would not do. If the Jackson police were kept from arresting demonstrators, Kennedy and Marshall feared, they might abdicate their peacekeeping responsibilities. For these federal officials, ensuring that local authorities would preserve order took precedence over desegregation. Their top priority was avoiding the need for marshals and saving the national government from policing responsibilities. As they saw it, the demonstrators could always vindicate the right to integrated travel by appealing their convictions through the judicial system. What Kennedy and Marshall ignored was the heavy financial burden which the bail, fines, court costs, and legal expenses arising out of the Jackson prosecutions imposed on CORE, and indeed on the entire civil rights movement. The resulting shortage of money impeded assertion of the right to travel elsewhere in the South.[64]

That was not a major concern of the Kennedy administration. On May 24 the attorney general, still more worried about the embarrassment the Freedom Riders were causing his brother than about the principle for which they were fighting, had issued a statement asking for a "cooling off period." He repeated this request in a telephone conversation with Martin Luther King. Although Kennedy claimed during a press conference on June 15 that the Justice Department would insist on the Riders' right to protection from violent interference, they continued to face uncontrolled mobs.[65] Not long after Kennedy spoke, a group of Freedom Riders bound for Jackson encountered a hostile crowd in Montgomery. As in May, the police made no effort to disperse the crowd.[66] The same thing happened in July at the Shreveport, Louisiana, bus station and in November at the one in McComb, Mississippi. The Justice Department's response to the McComb incident demonstrated how little had really changed as a result of the May crisis in Alabama.[67] "The question," as Marshall saw it, "was who was going to maintain order."[68] The federal government had some marshals across the line in Louisiana it could have employed for that purpose. Rather than sending them to McComb, Marshall negotiated with the mayor. That official issued a statement indicating his commitment to enforcing the law and added some special deputies to his police force, who brought the mob at the bus station under control.[69]

As in Jackson, however, reliance on local authorities meant sacrificing constitutional rights to preserve order. A few weeks later the same mayor who had cracked down on white violence at the bus station obtained a preliminary injunction from segregationist Federal District Judge Harold Cox. On grounds that the Congress of Racial Equality intended to provoke breaches of the peace, Cox forbade CORE from encouraging, sponsoring, or financing black utilization of McComb's terminal facilities. Not until May of 1963 did the Fifth Circuit Court of Appeals overrule him.[70]

It is ironic that Governor Patterson should have accused the Justice Department of "encouraging a wave of lawlessness throughout the nation and encouraging a disregard and disrespect for law and order among certain elements."[71] He was referring, of course, to civil rights activists, but actually those most emboldened by the policies of the Kennedy administration were southern city officials. When Freedom Riders, returning home from Jackson in August, stopped off in Monroe, North Carolina, to participate in civil rights picketing there, Ku Klux Klansmen and other hoodlums harassed and molested them. The blacks sometimes fought back. The police occasionally intervened, but when they did they arrested only blacks. The demonstrators requested protection from the federal government, but it was not forthcoming; the North Carolina governor's office had guaranteed Washington that the state would step in if local authorities could not handle the situation. On August 27 rioting erupted, and when local civil rights activists sought protection from the police they were arrested. Fearful blacks then armed themselves for self-defense. The whole affair ended with the prosecution of several Negroes for the alleged kidnapping of a white couple they may only have been trying to rescue from a mob. Patterson, who urged Attorney General Kennedy not to send marshals to Monroe, "but to leave North Carolina alone and let them handle their own domestic matters," got what he wanted. The results were not encouraging.[72]

Monroe illustrated how little actually had changed as a result of the dramatic events in Alabama. During the crisis there, Justice Department leaders had reluctantly concluded that the federal government could not avoid acting. Hence, they had used marshals, sought an injunction, and even prosecuted nine Anniston residents on charges of willfully burning an interstate bus. This assumption by the national government of responsibility for police functions normally belonging to the states resulted, in Marshall's opinion, in a temporary and localized alteration of the federal system. Given the extreme nature of the situation, that was "constitutionally permitted." The sort of measures employed in Alabama could be utilized elsewhere only under equally compelling circumstances, however. After May 1961 Kennedy administration policy was to protect targets of anti–civil rights violence only when all attempts at persuasion had failed and local law enforcement had utterly abdicated its responsibility for the maintenance of order.[73]

The administration demonstrated this again during the fall of 1962 when the efforts of Mississippi authorities to prevent the enrollment of a black man, James Meredith, at the state university in Oxford spawned bloody rioting on the Ole Miss campus. Reacting to that crisis, the Kennedy administration, to the dismay of Governor Barnett, once again departed massively from its basic policy of "letting the states take care of their own problems."[74] The reason was that, like the Eisenhower administration at Little Rock, it had to act in order to ensure that a federal court would be obeyed and the integrity of the judicial system preserved. Those were issues which had to be faced after September 10, 1962. On that date Supreme Court Justice Hugo L. Black overturned a stay of a Fifth Circuit order for Meredith's admission, clearing the way for Federal District Judge Sidney Mize to order the immediate enrollment of the would-be student, who had been trying to gain admission to Ole Miss since January 1961. Rather than obey the federal courts, Barnett called upon Mississippi officials and a statewide television audience to join him in defying the judiciary. His defiance confronted the national government with a problem that by September 15 was consuming practically all of the time of the top half-dozen men in the Justice Department.[75]

"What I was trying to avoid basically," the attorney general recalled later, "was having to send troops and . . . having a federal presence in Mississippi."[76] Using soldiers there would involve the same political risks as sending them to Alabama, and besides, Kennedy found the idea of employing troops against their own countrymen revolting. As a result of the success the Justice Department had achieved with marshals during the Freedom Rides, its leadership concluded that this was the solution to all major civil rights crises. Even before Justice Black issued his order, it began augmenting its small force by deputizing Border Patrolmen and prison guards. By early September, although inadequately trained, these "deputies" were standing by for duty in Mississippi.[77]

The Kennedy administration hoped to avoid sending them there by resolving the Ole Miss crisis through informal negotiations. Justice Department officials conferred with Mississippi business leaders, as well as with the governor and with Lieutenant Governor Paul Johnson. On September 15 the attorney general placed the first of a number of telephone calls to Barnett. His objective was to turn the governor and his state away from what Burke Marshall regarded as a "course of actual insurrection."[78]

While attempting to reason with state officials, the Justice Department left to them the preservation of law and order. Former Alabama Governor James Folsom advised a different course, suggesting to President Kennedy that he federalize the Mississippi National Guard, command its members to stay home, and then dispatch guardsmen from other states to the Ole Miss campus. The resolution of the Freedom Rides crisis had persuaded administration officials, however, that southern governors could be relied upon to keep the peace. Robert Kennedy, Marshall, and Katzenbach decided to proceed on the assumption that Barnett, Colonel T. B. Birdsong, the head of the Mississippi Highway Patrol, and other Mississippi officials would protect Meredith from harm and maintain order.[79]

What they forgot was that during the Freedom Rides state officials had preserved the peace by sacrificing black rights. That was all Barnett was prepared to do now. In a telegram and two telephone conversations with Robert Kennedy on September 25, the governor insisted repeatedly that Mississippi authorities would prevent violence. That same day Barnett directed all sheriffs and other law enforcement officers to do whatever was necessary to protect peace and security. Unfortunately, this directive also announced that in order to prevent violence and breach of the peace, the governor was interposing the police powers of the state. What that meant became apparent if one read the proclamation he had issued the previous day, which declared liable to summary arrest and confinement any representative of the national government who tried to arrest or fine a Mississippi employee for one of his official acts (such as excluding Meredith from Ole Miss). The governor intended to preserve order and segregation by interjecting the authority of the state between the national government and the citizens from whom it was demanding obedience.[80] "We are going to fight this thing," he told the attorney general.[81] In a third September 25 conversation with Kennedy, Barnett hedged his promise to prevent violence, saying if Meredith showed up for classes at Oxford he could not guarantee things would remain peaceful.[82]

The attorney general was unwilling to keep Meredith away. Pledging allegiance to the Constitution and laws of the United States and to the principle of national supremacy, he told Barnett on September 24 and 25 that he intended to enforce the orders of the federal courts. But Kennedy shrank from using federal force to ensure that the enrollment of Meredith would be peaceful. Indeed, he declined even to put pressure on the governor by telling him troops were being alerted for duty in Mississippi. Long after the Ole Miss crisis ended, Kennedy still insisted that committing soldiers before rioting engulfed the campus would have been worse than continuing to rely on Barnett's assurances.[83]

He was wrong about that. Far from preserving the peace, the man Kennedy came to recognize as a rogue and a weakling precipitated a riot. Barnett, a graduate of the Ole Miss law school, had twice run unsuccessfully for the governorship before finally capturing it in 1959. He entered office in 1960 pledging a strong segregationist stance. Barnett was a former chairman of Mississippi's State Sovereignty Commission, an organization established in 1956 to prevent desegregation, and as governor he supplied state funds to the Association of Citizens Councils. It was his desire to keep Ole Miss all-white. If he could not do that, then at least Barnett wanted to avoid the blame for integrating the university. To protect his standing with segregationist constituents, he sought to arrange a charade that would convey the picture of a sovereign state and its courageous governor being ground under by overwhelming federal force. On the morning of September 26 Tom Watkins, a Jackson attorney, Barnett advisor, and informal representative of the state, telephoned Burke Marshall. Later that day Meredith, who had been turned away from the Ole Miss campus on September 20, was to make a second effort to register there, accompanied by John Doar and Chief U.S. Marshal James McShane. Watkins advised Marshall that if the federal party made a show of force Mississippi authorities would then step aside and let the black student enter. But the actors failed to follow his script. In Oxford a small army of state troopers under the command of Lieutenant Governor Johnson confronted Meredith and his companions. When McShane tried to shove Johnson aside, the lieutenant governor would not budge. Meredith and his federal escort had to withdraw. The next day Watkins called

Marshall to say the show of force had not been big enough and to promise that if a larger group of marshals would confront Barnett with drawn revolvers the governor would step aside and allow Meredith to enter the university. The governor would also make sure that law and order were preserved. Still intent on avoiding the use of troops and keeping law enforcement in the hands of Mississippi authorities, the attorney general agreed to this dangerous farce. Meredith headed for Oxford again, accompanied by twenty-five marshals.[84]

While their thirteen-car caravan was on the road, Kennedy had several conversations with Barnett and Johnson. They told him a mob had assembled at Ole Miss and predicted people would be killed if Meredith entered the campus. Concerned about the ability of Mississippi authorities to control the situation, the attorney general ordered the federal convoy to return to Memphis. That decision was a wise one, for Barnett had created an explosive situation in Oxford. A month earlier Benjamin Muse had surveyed the situation there for the Southern Regional Council and had predicted violence would occur only if outsiders precipitated it. Now the governor himself had summoned "an army of helmeted, club-carrying sheriffs and state highway patrolmen" in from out of town. It had come not to maintain order but to participate in Barnett's battle with federal authority, apparently unaware that this was supposed to be a sham engagement.[85]

Clearly looking for a real fight, hordes of wild-eyed civilians poured into Oxford, swelling the ranks of angry students and townspeople. Beginning on the twenty-seventh, calls went out all over the South from a telephone at the state's Ole Miss command post in Alumni Hall, summoning militant racists affiliated with groups such as the Ku Klux Klan and the National States Rights party to mobilize for the defense of Mississippi sovereignty. Barnett did not place these calls himself, and he was appalled when he began to receive telegrams promising help from the recipients. After the Fifth Circuit Court of Appeals found the governor in contempt on the twenty-eighth and gave him five days in which to purge himself, he and his executive assistant, Hugh Boren, made an effort to persuade these outsiders to stay away. It was too late. Cars filled with gun-toting volunteers streamed into Oxford anyhow.[86]

Although unwilling to admit his own responsibility for the situation that was developing there, Barnett did recognize that it was becoming dangerously explosive. He wanted to avert violence, but, unfortunately, protecting his political position remained a higher priority. Barnett proposed another charade: while he manned the battle lines in Oxford, Meredith would register secretly in Jackson. The attorney general and the president demanded and got from a reluctant governor assurances that he would maintain order, both in the Mississippi capital and on the campus, where Meredith would begin classes a day later. The deal they struck soon fell apart. The next morning Barnett called Robert Kennedy at home to say he could not go through with it. Furious, the attorney general threatened that his brother, who was to appear on national television that evening, would reveal that the governor had made an agreement for the secret registration of Meredith. Fearful of what such a revelation would do to his standing with diehard segregationists, a whining Barnett begged Kennedy to keep the aborted deal a secret. He even offered to let them bring Meredith to the campus that very day. During a subsequent telephone conversation between Marshall and Watkins, it was agreed that the black student would register in Oxford that afternoon.[87]

Although Watkins assured Marshall that state police would maintain order while Meredith registered, the president was not convinced. He had himself talked three times with Barnett the previous day.[88] President Kennedy also had sent the governor a telegram in which he demanded an explicit commitment that Mississippi police officials would "cooperate in maintaining law and order by preventing violence in connection with federal enforcement of the court orders."[89] Unable to obtain what he regarded as "satisfactory assurances that law and order could or would be maintained in Oxford . . . during the coming week," the president had federalized units of the Mississippi National Guard.[90] Just after midnight on September 30 he reluctantly signed an executive order and proclamation which made it legally possible for him to use the armed forces to enforce law and maintain order in Mississippi. Later, army troops moved to standby positions in Memphis.[91]

The president's reluctance to rely on the state of Mississippi proved fully justified. Barnett did call on his constituents to do everything in their power to preserve the peace, but, typically, the governor combined this with an inflammatory assertion that he had been forced to bow to the "oppressive power" of the United States government. Although claiming to have 180 highway patrolmen, 200 to 300 soldiers, and numerous sheriffs on the campus, Barnett indicated to Robert Kennedy that he doubted whether this force could maintain order.[92]

In fact, it failed not only to preserve the peace but even to protect the federal marshals dispatched to Ole Miss to ensure Meredith's safety and prevent interference with his registration. The federal government took care to coordinate with Colonel Birdsong, whose highway patrolmen actually led its men onto the campus. Justice Department leaders believed that Birdsong, because he was a law enforcement professional like Floyd Mann in Alabama, would prevent violence, regardless of the political consequences. He probably would have done so had George Yarbrough, president pro tem of the Mississippi Senate (who arrived at Ole Miss around 7:00 P.M., armed with a proclamation designating him as the governor's personal representative), not effectively displaced Birdsong from command of his own troopers. Yarbrough ordered the highway patrol to withdraw from the campus. Katzenbach, in charge of the Justice Department party on the scene, objected. The deputy attorney general, a product of Princeton and the Yale Law School, and like his predecessor, Byron White, a former Rhodes scholar, had joined the government after teaching law at both Yale and the University of Chicago. The former professor sought to educate Yarbrough about the folly of his intended course of action, trying to convince him that withdrawing the troopers would incite violence and produce disastrous consequences. Adamant, Yarbrough would agree only to delay the withdrawal.[93]

While he and Katzenbach argued, the crowd on the campus grew larger and uglier. Although peppered with thrown objects, the marshals remained passive, relying on the highway patrol to control the mob. Some troopers tried to protect them, but others, sympathetic to the crowd, either stood idle or egged it on. One of them told some rioters to "give them hell." Around 7:30 the highway patrol radio broadcast instructions to withdraw from the campus. During the confused period which followed the issuance of this order, many troopers left their stations. At least some of them returned a few moments later. Although their milling around had enabled the crowd to press menacingly close to the marshals, they apparently were trying to push it back when, at 7:58 P.M., the marshals opened fire on the mob with tear gas. Some troopers were hit in the back with gas canisters. Even those who had tried to do their job became enraged at the marshals, and by 10:00 the highway patrol, claiming its masks did not provide adequate protection against the type of gas being used, had withdrawn from the scene and was on its way out of Oxford.[94]

Its departure left about three hundred marshals and a number of Justice Department attorneys besieged in and around the Ole Miss administration building, known as the Lyceum. The mob continued to pelt them with bricks and chunks of wood and concrete. About 9:00 P.M. they came under sporadic rifle and shotgun fire. The shooting intensified as more of the armed militants who were flocking into Oxford to "stand with Ross" arrived on the scene. Twenty-eight marshals received gunshot wounds, and 150 suffered injuries serious enough to require medical attention. A bystander and a French newsman were killed in the rioting. Three times the besieged men almost ran out of tear gas. Fearful, the marshals requested permission to use their own guns. Katzenbach refused to authorize them to return fire, and so did President Kennedy, who, along with the top leadership of the Justice Department, was in telephonic contact with the Lyceum.[95]

The shooting did force the president and his advisors to take the one step they had tried desperately to avoid. Around 8:00 P.M. the president began a televised address on the Ole Miss crisis by pointing out that Meredith had been taken onto the campus without the use of the National Guard or other troops. Within two hours Katzenbach told the attorney general sadly that they had better send in the army. At the White House, where the Kennedys and Marshall were huddled, the president, terribly concerned about the safety of Meredith and the marshals, issued the marching orders. About midnight Captain Murry Falkner, a nephew of novelist William Faulkner, his arm broken and blood streaming from a wound, led a 55-man contingent of Mississippi National Guardsmen up to the besieged Lyceum. Four and a half hours later a rather disorganized force of United States Army regulars arrived from Memphis.[96]

Six months later there were still nearly three hundred soldiers in Oxford. Before he and his brother could remove them, the attorney general informed Barnett, they had to have from him "and other officials of the state . . . adequate assurance by deed and word that you will accept and carry out the basic responsibility of the State for maintaining law and order . . . [including] responsibility for the personal safety of James Meredith." The governor and his subordinates remained reluctant to do all that keeping the peace required. Besides, Barnett and other segregationist politicians found the presence of federal troops in their state politically useful, and many Oxford business people welcomed the security they provided. So John F. Kennedy continued to preside over what Mississippians rightly regarded as a military occupation.[97]

Although reminiscent of Reconstruction, his actions found favor even with some white southerners. South Carolina's Senator Strom Thurmond, Congressman Joe B. Waggoner of Louisiana, and the Alabama congressional delegation communicated their displeasure to the president, but others, among them Governors Farris Bryant of Florida and Terry Sanford of North Carolina, praised Kennedy's handling of the situation. Like law school deans and professors throughout the country, Senator Allen Ellender (D-La.) recognized that what had been at stake at Ole Miss was preservation of the rule of law. Even leading Mississippi businessmen reacted to the crisis there by adopting a resolution stressing the importance of maintaining law and order.[98]

Influential industrialists, business leaders, and educators in South Carolina agreed—and managed to persuade potential troublemakers that law and order must be preserved at all costs. Consequently, in January 1963 Clemson University managed to admit its first black student without the slightest disturbance. The determination of local civic and business leaders, and even the attorney general of the state, to prevent violence and maintain the rule of law also helped to bring about the peaceful desegregation, later that year, of the University of Alabama.[99]

Another factor was also important there: the firmness of the federal government. The president still preferred to rely on local law enforcement. He knew the police forces of the state of Alabama and the city of Tuscaloosa were capable of preserving the peace on the university campus, and he hoped that those with constitutional responsibilities for maintaining law and order would do their duty. Certainly, the administration had no more desire to use troops at the University of Alabama than it had at Ole Miss, but the situation there was potentially very dangerous. Like Barnett, Alabama Governor George Wallace was an outspoken segregationist. Born in the small Alabama community of Clio in 1919, he had graduated from the University of Alabama Law School in 1942, then spent three years as an enlisted man in the Army Air Force. After World War II, Wallace served for six years in the Alabama legislature (1947–1953) and for five more as a state judge (1953–1958) before winning the governorship in 1962. After taking office, he frequently expressed hostility toward federal authority and made statements that encouraged violence. When Robert Kennedy met with him in the spring of 1963, Kennedy made clear not only the administration's commitment to enforcing court orders requiring desegregation but also its willingness to use "all the force behind the federal government . . . for that purpose." The Ole Miss rioting had revealed that the use of large numbers of marshals in such situations was pointless, because they could not maintain order without the assistance of local law enforcement agencies. This time, if the situation demanded more than the small number of men needed to implement the court order, the Kennedys would send in troops.[100]

The president of the University of Alabama, Dr. Frank Rose, did not want soldiers, asking instead for FBI agents. Wallace, on the other hand, hoped the federal government would use troops. Then he could impress segregationists by making a show of defiance without risking the sort of violence which the state's clergymen, educators, businessmen, labor leaders, and editors (prodded by the Justice Department) had informed him they would not tolerate. Wallace called out five hundred National Guardsmen, but he assured the president they would be used only in the event they were "needed to maintain law and order and preserve the peace." Meanwhile, his handpicked highway patrol chief, Al Lingo, had called the Grand Dragon of the KKK to tell him that any known klansmen seen in Tuscaloosa during the coming confrontation would be immediately arrested. On June 11, 1963, Wallace and Katzenbach acted out a little drama for the television cameras: the deputy attorney general escorted two black students up to the building where they were supposed to register, and the governor blocked the doorway. Katzenbach read a presidential proclamation ordering Wallace to cease his interference with the implementation of a court order, and the governor responded with one denouncing the allegedly unconstitutional intrusion of the federal government into Alabama affairs. Then, marshals and Justice Department lawyers escorted the black students to their dormitories while the president federalized the Alabama National Guard. Four hours later Brigadier General Henry V. Graham led the Dixie Division onto the campus. After returning General Graham's salute and scolding the national government briefly, Wallace withdrew.[101]

Having bowed to federal authority, he then attempted to abdicate state responsibilities. On June 12 the Alabama Highway Patrol's participation in security arrangements at the university slackened noticeably. Wallace insisted that having created the situation in Tuscaloosa and usurped powers reserved to the states, the national government was now responsible for maintaining order and protecting the black students. The president did not agree. "Responsibility for the maintenance of law and order on the campus of the University of Alabama continues to rest with local and state authorities," Kennedy insisted. After conferences on the matter, state troopers stayed on duty in the Tuscaloosa area, and Wallace ordered one hundred of them to patrol the campus to prevent disorders. When some renegade National Guardsmen set off bombs near the university and in a black residential neighborhood, state authorities prosecuted them. [102]

By then, a black student had registered without incident at the University of Alabama's extension center in Huntsville. Desegregation proceeded peacefully there, and the troops standing by at Redstone Arsenal were never used. The reason was that Wallace stayed away, blaming his failure to make another stand for segregation on the president. [103]

Besides preventing violence on two campuses, federal firmness also produced positive results in several Alabama school districts that desegregated in September 1963. Judge Johnson issued a temporary restraining order which enjoined Wallace from failing to keep the peace in and around the affected schools. When the governor threw the marshals who attempted to serve the restraining order off the capitol grounds, President Kennedy responded firmly. He issued a proclamation commanding all persons engaged in the unlawful obstruction of justice and all those banding together to interfere with the execution of federal law in Alabama to cease and disperse. The president also federalized the Alabama National Guard. Twenty black students then entered formerly all-white schools in Tuskegee, Mobile, and Birmingham. There were "moderate sized disorders" in the latter city, but the local police did an effective job of controlling them. Explaining his failure to stop school desegregation, Wallace told reporters: "I can't fight bayonets with my bare hands." [104]

His words highlighted the value of prompt military intervention. From the tragic events at Ole Miss, the Kennedy administration had learned the hard lesson that the time to send in troops was before the irresponsible conduct of segregationist state officials could create a violent situation which threatened the enforcement of a federal court order. It had failed to draw from that crisis the broader lesson that a firm commitment by the national government to the suppression of all disorder intended to interfere with the exercise of constitutional rights was necessary to halt the escalation of violence and intimidation in the South. After the Ole Miss riot, an ad hoc Subcabinet Group on Civil Rights discussed what might be done about this problem. The recent crisis had reinforced the Justice Department's belief that if the federal government attempted to exercise any control over the administration of justice vast problems would inevitably result. Although Mississippi juries acquitted the Ole Miss rioters, the department remained committed to local control of criminal justice.[105]

When a second black man entered the University of Mississippi in the fall of 1963, Governor Barnett insisted that Washington should assume responsibility for his safety. It refused. "I consider this a gross and irrational error," the student wrote the Justice Department. "In the absence of federal protection, my life is in grave danger."[106] According to the NAACP, there existed a "clear and present danger" to the lives, well-being, and property of all blacks in Mississippi identified as leaders of the effort to end discrimination. It begged the president to have the federal government "invoke every means at its disposal to ensure the safety of those . . . exposed to reprisals by reason of their activity in behalf of racial justice."[107]

By mid-1963 there were many such persons, not only in Mississippi but also in Birmingham, Alabama. During the winter of 1962–1963 the SCLC and its Birmingham affiliate, led by Reverend Fred Shuttlesworth, mapped strategy for a spring offensive against discrimination in that rigidly segregated city.[108] Martin Luther King expected it to meet violent resistance. "In my judgment," he told those attending one planning session, "some of the people sitting here today will not come back alive from this campaign."[109] Yet King believed that only by exposing the violence inherent in segregation could the civil rights movement arouse the public sufficiently to force the federal government to take corrective action.[110]

Birmingham did not disappoint him. A community with a history of racist violence, where the Klan encountered no interference from the authorities, it had experienced eighteen racially motivated bombings between 1957 and 1963. Once the SCLC campaign got under way, the already high level of racist violence rose dramatically. A black newspaper reported twenty bombings, shootings, and beatings between March and September of 1963.[111]

Private citizens perpetrated some of this violence, but law enforcement officers were responsible for much of it. In the past, Birmingham policemen had conspired with the Ku Klux Klan and had encouraged its members to commit acts of terrorism. Surprisingly, when King's demonstrations began, both the police department and the sheriff's office asked klansmen not to interfere. They wanted to handle the situation themselves. That hardly meant safety for the demonstrators. The head of Birmingham's all-white police force, Eugene "Bull" Connor, was such an outrageously reactionary bigot that he had managed to alienate even the city's white power structure. After someone dynamited Shuttlesworth's Bethel Baptist Church in December 1962, Connor brought police dogs into the black community to drive back the large crowd that gathered to protest the bombing. Both a federal grand jury and a citizens' committee had accused his department of brutality. During the first few days of King's demonstrations the Birmingham police displayed restraint, making arrests decorously and going to court for an injunction against protest activity. Beginning on May 3, however, their emphasis shifted to physically repulsing demonstrators. While white bystanders threw bricks and rocks, police dogs bit several blacks. Nightsticks and high pressure hoses injured others. [112]

SCLC leaders reacted to this police brutality with expressions of joy. "We've got a movement," they exclaimed happily. [113] The conduct of the Birmingham police provoked the sort of public outrage that King had hoped for. "The misuse of law enforcement agencies and their power in Birmingham is a matter of grave concern to all right-thinking people," Los Angeles Mayor Sam Yorty declared. [114] Pressure for federal action mounted. Senator Javits and Representative John Gilbert (D-N.Y.) prodded the White House to charge those responsible for the brutality with violation of section 242, and in Birmingham so many civil rights complaints were filed (some of them lacking adequate legal foundation) that Attorney General Kennedy became concerned about the amount of time and money his department was expending on them. Some people demanded more from the federal government than just criminal prosecutions. Javits and retired black baseball star Jackie Robinson were among those urging the president to send troops to Birmingham. The senator suggested that sections 332 and 333 of Title 10 of the United States Code (on which Kennedy had relied in sending soldiers to Ole Miss) might provide him with the authority to do this. [115]

The Kennedy administration pleaded powerlessness. Although Burke Marshall and Joe Dolan went to Birmingham in an effort to mediate the underlying dispute over segregation, federal action against violence at first extended little beyond FBI participation in the investigation of some bombings. Indeed, despite the authority provided by the Civil Rights Act of 1960, the Bureau was even slow to begin probing the dynamitings which had plagued Birmingham since the late 1950s. Although providing local authorities with some assistance earlier, the FBI did not undertake a bombing investigation of its own until street demonstrations led to civil violence in the spring of 1963. On May 11, following a Ku Klux Klan rally in a Birmingham park, someone dynamited the home of King's brother, Reverend A. D. King. Then bombers attacked the A. G. Gaston Motel, used as a headquarters by the civil rights movement. The seething rage of Birmingham blacks, angry about police brutality and frustrated by the professed inability of the federal government to do anything about it, exploded in a major riot. That was enough to invigorate the FBI.[116]

It also inspired the president to make a dramatic gesture. The following evening Kennedy told a national television audience: "This Government will do whatever must be done to preserve order, to protect the lives of its citizens, and to uphold the law of the land."[117] He had instructed the secretary of defense, the president said, to alert units of the armed forces trained for riot control duty and to dispatch some of them to bases near Birmingham. In addition, he had directed that the preliminary steps required before the Alabama National Guard could be called into federal service be taken immediately. While three thousand soldiers moved toward Birmingham, Governor Wallace protested what he characterized as an intrusion upon the right of a city and state to handle their own domestic affairs. Pointing out that neither he nor the Alabama legislature had asked the federal government for military assistance, Wallace requested that Kennedy withdraw the armed forces immediately. He also demanded to know "under what authority you would send federal troops into this state?"[118] The president, whose Ole Miss experience had made him reluctant to accept assurances that state police could maintain order, replied that "Federal troops would be sent to Birmingham, if necessary, under the authority of Title 10, Section 333, Paragraph 1 of the United States Code relating to the suppression of domestic violence."[119] Unimpressed, the Alabama legislature commended Wallace for challenging Kennedy's "racist" violation of state sovereignty. It joined the Birmingham city council in urging the president to withdraw the soldiers.[120]

Their outrage was premature, for as Kennedy pointed out to Wallace, no "final action" had yet been taken with respect to Birmingham; the federal troops were merely standing by. The president continued to hope that the citizens of Birmingham would conduct themselves in such a manner as to make outside intervention unnecessary. He received assurances from the Alabama House delegation, as well as from Wallace, that local and state law enforcement personnel could and would keep the peace. [121] On May 18 the president got a chance to question the governor about Birmingham when the two men found themselves together on a helicopter flight from Muscle Shoals to Huntsville. According to Pierre Salinger, Kennedy's press secretary, "Wallace replied that his main interest was in maintaining law and order and that the situation was quiet." The governor told Kennedy there were about one thousand city and state peace officers in Birmingham and expressed confidence that this force could keep the peace. [122]

Although pressing Wallace to resolve the racial crisis in that city, the president never did send federal troops there. He withheld them even after Birmingham exploded in rioting following the bombing of the black 16th Street Baptist Church on September 15, 1963. That blast killed four young girls who had been attending Sunday school. "I feel like blowing the whole town up," raged the embittered grandfather of one of the victims. That afternoon and evening angry blacks battled with police, set fire to white businesses, and pelted firemen with rocks and bricks. Not even shotguns and a six-wheeled riot tank could control them. [123]

"Unless some immediate steps are taken by the Federal Government to restore a sense of confidence in the protection of life, limb and property . . . ," King informed the president, "we shall see in Birmingham and Alabama the worst racial holocaust the nation has ever seen." [124] Blacks were arming for self-defense, and even whites felt insecure. Roy Wilkins wired the White House, urging that the fullest possible use be made of the 1960 bombing statute. Others demanded sterner federal action. One hundred and fifty of Birmingham's black business and professional people proposed that the army take over the city. King and Shuttlesworth also begged for troops. So did James Baldwin, Bayard Rustin, and five other black spokesmen who met with the president at the White House on June 8. [125]

Despite their entreaties, Kennedy declined to commit soldiers to Birmingham. He did express "a deep sense of outrage and grief," did again send Marshall and Dolan (along with John Nolan) to Alabama, and did promise that the FBI would "lend every assistance" in tracking down those responsible for the bombing. For Alabama's Senator John Sparkman that was enough. He urged Kennedy not to deploy the troops waiting in the wings at Fort McClellan and at Maxwell Air Force Base. The president's brother and Marshall also opposed sending in the military. The solution to Birmingham's problems, the attorney general argued, lay in the local community and in the hearts and minds of its people. Military occupation of the city, he and other administration leaders reasoned, could not be a long-range solution to racial tensions there. It could only exacerbate them and make the lot of Birmingham blacks worse. The president did say that Washington would not hesitate to use federal force if state law enforcement machinery actually broke down or sided with the mob.[126] "But given this country's reliance on state and local law enforcement rather than Federal police," Anthony Lewis told readers of the *New York Times,* "it would be a long step for Federal troops to take over the basic job of protecting life and property in an entire city."[127]

It was a step the Kennedys never took. Instead, the president sent Kenneth Royall, a former secretary of the army, and Colonel Earl "Red" Blaik, the retired West Point football coach, to Birmingham as his personal mediators. James Baldwin branded Kennedy's action an "insult to the Negro race." "We ask for Federal troops," a Washington black observed bitterly, "and we get two retired officers."[128] Upon their arrival in Birmingham, Royall and Blaik found a city gripped by fear and foreboding and terrorized by telephone threats of further bombings. Both blacks and whites were frightened.[129] In a report which they prepared for the president, the two men noted that in meeting after meeting blacks had begged them for immediate protection. "Physical protection and restoration of law and order transcend all other interests in the community," they stated.[130] Royall and Blaik were to deliver their final report to the president on November 25, but they were unable to do so. On November 22 Kennedy was assassinated in Dallas.[131]

At the time of his death the administration was still insisting that the way to deal with violence in places such as Birmingham was to outlaw the racial segregation which inspired it. "We abandoned the solution, really, of trying to give people protection," Robert Kennedy recalled later.[132] Instead, the administration reacted to the May bombings and rioting in Birmingham by moving at last to honor John Kennedy's 1960 campaign pledge to enact major civil rights legislation. That seemed to be the moderate course, the one best suited both to preventing the black revolution from turning violent and to keeping the president ahead of the mounting pressure for federal action.[133]

The administration introduced a bill which did not address directly either the problem of violence perpetrated by repressive police or the issue of that committed by private mobs. Under pressure from civil rights lobbyists, Judiciary Committee Chairman Emanuel Celler and other liberals got a House subcommittee to recommend a measure which included a provision authorizing the attorney general to seek injunctions restraining the denial of any right, privilege, or immunity secured by the Constitution or federal law. Jacob Javits joined in this effort to revive the old Title III of 1957, introducing a bill of his own in the Senate. The objective of civil rights groups supporting these initiatives was to provide protection for peaceful demonstrators.[134]

As late as August 3, 1963, the Leadership Conference on Civil Rights believed that the president would support them, but in the end the administration took a strong stand against Title III. To Burke Marshall, it was a "desperate measure," an understandable and even inevitable reaction to the sort of abuses of state and local power the nation had witnessed in Birmingham, but, nevertheless, an unwise and even dangerous proposal. In the first place, the measure approved by the House subcommittee did not authorize the attorney general to enjoin only attacks on black protest; it would give him the power to seek injunctive protection for all kinds of constitutional rights, ranging from the free exercise of religion to the possession and use of property. Because the attorney general would have to decide when to invoke such a law, it would force him to decide which rights deserved governmental protection and which persons should be assisted in exercising them. It would turn him into a censor. Even if it were limited to the protection of civil rights demonstrations, Marshall reasoned, Title III would still force attorneys general to decide which to protect and which not to. They lacked the wisdom that task required. Besides, Title III could not be effective unless there were a national police force to provide physical security for those demonstrators to whom it extended judicial protection, and he still considered that unthinkable.[135]

When Robert Kennedy appeared before an executive session of the House Judiciary Committee on October 15, 1963, he echoed many of Marshall's concerns. Among the reasons the attorney general found the proposed Title III objectionable was that it would involve the federal courts in making decisions about when, where, and how people might protest, matters traditionally left to local officials. "One result might be that state and local authorities would abdicate their law enforcement responsibilities, thereby creating a vacuum in authority which could be filled only by federal force," Kennedy said. That would necessitate the creation of a national police force—a step he too insisted would be "abhorrent to our federal system." Furthermore, Title III could not provide real security for civil rights protesters, because it would be completely ineffective against sporadic acts of violence such as bombings and spontaneous acts of brutality by individual police officers. The way to protect demonstrators was to correct the injustices in voting, education, and access to public accommodations that forced them to expose themselves to danger in the streets. [136]

Under pressure from the attorney general, the full Judiciary Committee rejected the bill approved by its subcommittee and recommended passage of one unencumbered by Title III. The administration's stance drew criticism both from the Leadership Conference on Civil Rights and from Senator Javits, who pointed out that rejection of Title III left the federal government with only one means of responding to the sort of anarchy which had engulfed Little Rock and Ole Miss: military force. [137]

Resort to that was, of course, precisely what the Kennedy adminstration had spent three years trying to avoid. Its focus had been consistently on means rather than ends. Instead of attacking the problem of anti–civil rights violence, it had concentrated on minimizing the federal response to major manifestations of that phenomenon. To their credit, the Kennedy brothers and Burke Marshall had kept mob violence from thwarting judicial enforcement of the Constitution. On the other hand, they had not made it safe to exercise constitutional rights in the South. Victories in a series of confrontations with irresponsible southern officials willing to sacrifice law and order to preserve segregation had proved the administration's courage and its skill at crisis management. These victories, however, had added nothing to the security of those champions of racial change victimized by violence and intimidation in small skirmishes far from the great battlefields of Montgomery, Birmingham, and Ole Miss. They too needed federal protection. From the crisis managers of the Kennedy administration they received only noble words about federalism.

The Problem of Protection

For the Kennedy administration, the civil rights movement posed a difficult and frustrating problem. The more aggressive the movement became and the more it insisted on challenging discrimination with direct action rather than litigation, the more violent were the reactions that it triggered. Escalating violence against civil rights activists exposed in often quite dramatic ways the biases that still infected southern criminal justice. It also called attention to the administration's continuing commitment to traditional federalism, which involved reliance on state and local institutions that were part of a system for maintaining white supremacy. Increasing violence against civil rights activists generated ever more insistent demands that the federal government provide them with protection. Yet the Kennedy administration spurned these calls for help, responding to them only with rhetorical hand-wringing and further obeisance to the supposed demands of federalism.

The administration's refusal to provide protection embittered the voter registration workers it had urged to place themselves at risk in Georgia and Mississippi. Embarrassed by the publicity surrounding the Freedom Rides, it had tried to direct the civil rights movement into more moderate and constructive channels. A massive campaign to register black voters in the South seemed an attractive alternative, especially because it would enhance the president's prospects for reelection in 1964. The idea also appealed to SNCC, for it thought such a campaign could be used to call attention to southern injustice. Some members of that organization met several times in Washington during June and July of 1961 with representatives of CORE, the SCLC, the NAACP, the National Urban League, and the National Student Association. These meetings led to the creation of the Voter Education Project. Set up under the auspices of the Southern Regional Council in

April 1962, VEP was financed by the Taconic and Field foundations and the Stern Family Fund, and headed by black Arkansas attorney Wiley Branton. It launched a two-and-one-half-year, $870,000 campaign to enroll black voters.[1]

The Kennedy administration was deeply involved in the process which led to VEP's creation. In 1961 Attorney General Robert Kennedy convened and participated in a June 16 meeting of the sponsoring groups, and both Burke Marshall and White House aide Harris Wofford took part in a July 28 gathering. SNCC representatives came away from these conferences convinced that the administration had promised to protect participants in the voter registration campaign, a matter of life-and-death significance to them. Unlike the government and Roy Wilkins of the NAACP, who wanted the campaign to focus on relatively safe urban areas, SNCC was determined to force a confrontation between the Justice Department and the southern power structure by plunging into some of the toughest and most unyielding rural counties in the South. Apparently, Robert Kennedy and Burke Marshall never actually went beyond quite general assurances of support.[2] Although there was no explicit discussion of the subject, however, they managed to leave Branton with the impression that "the Justice Department would take all steps necessary to protect federal or constitutional rights, [including] . . . the elementary matter of protection."[3]

The civil rights workers who invaded southwest Georgia that year soon discovered that Branton had badly misread the department's intentions. They were entering hostile territory, a section which had been a center of the slave plantation system, and where the black majority still lived in shacks and worked the land for a white minority. Few of the Afro-Americans living there dared to protest their lot or even to register to vote. Rural counties like "Terrible Terrell" and "Bad Baker" were such tough targets that before attacking them SNCC decided it would first have to build a base of operations in Albany, a city of sixty thousand and southwest Georgia's principal trading center. The "Albany Movement" began with the arrival there of SNCC field secretaries Cordell Reagan and Charles Sherrod in October 1961. Albany Police Chief Laurie Pritchett reacted to SNCC's campaign of Freedom Rides, sit-ins, and mass marches by announcing that he would not let "any Negro organization" take over his town. Pritchett's officers made hundreds of arrests. A local court sent Dr. Martin Luther King, Jr., and Reverend Ralph David Abernathy to jail, and the governor of Georgia twice dispatched the National Guard to Albany.[4]

Violence punctuated the turmoil there. By mid-summer of 1963 there had been three shooting incidents, one of which left a man dead. Two July 1962 demonstrations escalated into rock and bottle throwing by black youths. That same month a white man, Frank Nichols, struck SNCC's Ralph Allen and Joseph Pitts. Neither the local police nor the sheriff's department would arrest Nichols.[5]

Given the attitudes that permeated Albany-area law enforcement, this was hardly surprising. When C. B. King, a local black attorney, visited the Dougherty County jail to check on the condition of a white SNCC field worker who had been arrested, Sheriff Cull Campbell beat him with a heavy walking stick. Admitting he had "knocked hell out of" King, the sheriff justified his action by saying, "I'm a white man and he's a damn nigger." Peace officers roughed up civil rights activists, and during the summer of 1963 Pritchett initiated a campaign of deliberate brutality in which police kicked and beat demonstrators and allowed white prisoners to attack the protesters they arrested. The Justice Department sent FBI agents and attorneys to Albany as observers, but they did virtually nothing to halt the violence.[6]

The confrontation continued to escalate, not only in the city but in the surrounding rural counties as well. According to SNCC, during the period April 21, 1962, to December 8, 1963, there were shooting incidents in Terrell, Sumter, and Lee counties. In Sasser a police officer told four SNCC voter registration workers he would put them in the cemetery if they did not leave town immediately, then fired on them when they departed too slowly for his tastes. Private citizens assaulted voter registration workers in Terrell and Sumter counties, while law enforcement personnel beat civil rights activists (among them the pregnant Mrs. Marion King) in those two counties as well as in Mitchell County. Houses used by the movement also came under attack. During a three-week period in August and September of 1962 three churches in Lee and Terrell counties "used for SNCC's voter registration campaign meetings" burned to the ground. James Farmer of CORE and Charles McDew of SNCC both called upon the federal government to halt what McDew characterized as "the Nazi-like reign of terror in Southwest Georgia."[7]

The FBI quietly investigated many of the violent incidents that occurred in the area. The Justice Department's most visible response to the turmoil in southwest Georgia, however, was the August 1963 indictment of nine leaders of the Albany Movement for conspiring to obstruct justice by picketing a store belonging to a white juror who had helped acquit a sheriff accused of shooting and beating a black man. That same month in Americus, Georgia, where SNCC workers had been beaten on the streets, state authorities lodged capital charges of inciting insurrection against three of them and a CORE activist. Small wonder that an atmosphere of intimidation surrounded the voter registration effort, or that frightened civil rights workers wondered openly what had become of the federal government that was supposed to protect them.[8]

National authority was equally invisible in Mississippi. There the voter registration effort began during the summer of 1961 when SNCC's Robert Moses, responding to a request from a local NAACP leader, came to McComb. A former Harlem schoolteacher with a Harvard master's degree in philosophy, Moses was determined to make that town a base of operations in desolate and violent south Mississippi. He and the little band of black and white civil rights workers who followed him into the state endured constant intimidation. Although the principal techniques employed against them were abuse of power and misuse of the criminal justice system, hostile white Mississippians also resorted to force. Between Moses's arrival and the end of 1963, SNCC recorded sixty-two incidents of racist violence in Mississippi, many of them clearly directed against its voter registration campaign.[9]

The most serious trouble occurred in Amite, Walthall, Sunflower, Leflore, and Rankin counties. When Moses tried to lead some blacks to the Amite County courthouse in Liberty on August 22, 1961, to register them to vote, Billy Caston, a cousin of the sheriff, attacked and beat him. Two weeks later Travis Britt, another SNCC worker, who had gone to Liberty with Moses, received a severe beating on the courthouse lawn. On September 25, during a confrontation at a cotton gin, E. H. Hurst, a white state representative, shot and killed Herbert Lee, a black Amite County resident who had been helping Moses with his voter registration work. Fearing for his own life, a black witness, Louis Allen, told a coroner's inquest that Hurst had acted in self-defense. When Allen finally admitted several years later that he had lied, someone silenced him permanently with a shotgun. Such violence and intimidation accomplished its objective, frightening Amite County blacks into giving up their efforts to register to vote and temporarily derailing the campaign to help them do so. The violence around Liberty produced echoes in nearby McComb, where whites attacked three SNCC workers during a march by black students, staged in part to protest the Lee killing. [10]

Meanwhile, John Hardy had led nine SNCC workers into the Walthall County seat of Tylertown. On September 7, 1961, as Hardy was leaving the office of John Q. Wood, the registrar of voters, Wood pistol-whipped him, shouting as he did so, "Get out of here you damned son-of-a-bitch and don't come back."[11] During 1962 Fannie Lou Hamer, a forty-four-year-old black woman who had been inspired to political activism by SNCC and would go on to national prominence as the leader of the Mississippi Freedom Democratic party, had to leave the Indianola area after shots were fired into a house where she was staying. There were also shooting incidents in Harmony and Ruleville during 1962 (the latter resulting in serious injury to two girls), as well as firebombings in Biloxi and Columbus. [12]

The following year the Greenwood area became the center of violent resistance to the voter registration campaign. On February 28, 1963, some white men in a Buick opened fire on Moses, SNCC's Jimmy Travis, and Randolph Blackwell of VEP while they were driving from Greenwood to Greenville, wounding Travis in the shoulder and neck. Sam Block and three companions barely escaped injury two weeks later when shotgun pellets slammed into the parked car in which they were seated outside the Greenwood SNCC office. On the night of March 23 fire gutted the office itself. [13]

Although the Greenwood city administration condemned this violence, the police department harassed the victims instead of protecting them. Its performance was typical. Mississippi peace officers commonly stood by while white citizens attacked civil rights workers, and as SNCC's Ivanhoe Donaldson reported in late 1963, "In many ways, both Negroes in the various communities, and SNCC field workers were harassed and intimidated by local police." Leflore County authorities did arrest three suspects in the Jimmy Travis shooting. When whites attacked three civil rights workers in McComb, however, officers took the victims into custody. An all-white judicial system did no more to control violence against the voter registration campaign than did the police. A coroner's jury accepted E. H. Hurst's contention that he had killed Herbert Lee in self-defense, and a six-man jury in a justice-of-the-peace court, ignoring the testimony of the victim and two eyewitnesses, found Billy Caston not guilty of assaulting Bob Moses. [14]

In April 1963 Aaron Henry, president of the Mississippi State Conference of the NAACP, begged the White House for "protection of the workers in the voter registration movement." He was not alone. SNCC bombarded the national government with demands for protection, calling for federal intervention in such southwest Georgia trouble spots as Terrell County, as well as for help in McComb and Greenwood, Mississippi. SNCC Chairman Charles McDew also asked for a federal investigation of the Jimmy Travis shooting. Executive Secretary James Forman went even further, urging the president to dispatch troops to Greenwood. Field secretaries Samuel Block and Willie Peacock seconded that demand and added a request for soldiers in the town of Belzoni. [15]

In sending insistent telegrams to the Justice Department and the president, SNCC was, of course, seeking publicity as well as protection. The wire services, which would not disseminate stories about the voter registration campaign itself, or even about the often violent repression it encountered, did regard telegrams to top government officials as newsworthy. Consequently, SNCC sent these and then issued press releases about them in a conscious effort to arouse public support for the movement. It hoped to force the national government to intervene against what Forman characterized as the "wave of terror" sweeping over the South. Only if Washington did this, SNCC leaders were convinced, would there be any chance of registering black voters in places such as Leflore County, Mississippi. In Greenwood, Moses launched demonstrations designed to precipitate federal intervention. [16]

SNCC was not the only organization pushing for this. By October 1962 the NAACP was also urging the administration to send troops to Mississippi. VEP, CORE, and the Southern Conference Education Fund also demanded action. So did individual civil rights leaders, such as A. Phillip Randolph. [17] "We earnestly urge you," Martin Luther King wrote Robert Kennedy in March 1963, ". . . to take whatever steps that are necessary to safeguard the lives and property of voter registration workers and those who apply." [18] Organizations ranging from the Communist party through Americans for Democratic Action, the Fort Washington–Manhattanville Reformed Democrats, and the AFL-CIO to the Undergraduate Council at Dartmouth College added their voices to the chorus demanding that the

national government protect voter registration workers.[19] "Federal protection is essential for these people," United Auto Workers President Walter Reuther informed John Kennedy. The reason was that they were "being
denied any protection by local and state authorities."[20] One measure of
how many people shared Reuther's feelings is the sixty telegrams received
by the White House during the period March 27–March 29, 1963, demanding that it do something about the situation in Greenwood. Many
called for the use of federal troops.[21]

The government's response to these demands for protection was meager. The FBI, which, according to Robert Kennedy, "hadn't done a
helluva lot" in the civil rights area previously, did increase its investigations by nearly 50 percent between 1960 and 1963. The Bureau checked
out alleged violations of the various federal laws to protect black voting,
and between 1961 and 1963 it investigated numerous intimidation cases.
The FBI also conducted inquiries into a number of incidents of anti–civil
rights violence, among them the wounding of Jimmy Travis, the shotgun
attack on Samuel Block and his companions, and the church burnings
around Albany, Georgia.[22] It made few arrests, however, and its performance was, in the opinion of John Doar and his onetime assistant Dorothy
Landsberg, "far from adequate."[23]

Burke Marshall considered the FBI's conduct of civil rights investigations utterly incompetent. In fairness to the Bureau, jurisdictional squab-
bles, for which the Civil Rights Division was at least partly responsible,
hampered its performance. Furthermore, because the FBI was badly un-
derstaffed in the South, it had to depend for much of its information about
violent episodes on such "indirect sources" as cooperative ministers and
teachers. On the other hand, J. Edgar Hoover made no effort to rectify
this situation by shifting manpower resources from communism and organized crime to civil rights. Nor did the attorney general ever order him to
do so.[24] The FBI's investigations remained inadequate, and consequently,
as Nicholas Katzenbach noted later, "neither the [Justice] Department
nor the Bureau fully appreciated the significance or indeed the genesis of
the repeated acts of violence and bloodshed being committed ever more
frequently throughout the South on blacks and civil rights workers."[25]

The FBI also defined its role too narrowly. If some act of anti–civil
rights violence happened to violate a federal statute, the Bureau would
investigate, but generally only after being specifically and formally asked
to do so by the Civil Rights Division. The FBI did almost nothing to

prevent future trouble. If warned in advance by an informant that a Klan group was planning some act of terrorism, the Bureau would simply pass the information along to the Civil Rights Division and to local law enforcement. With the police in many southern communities themselves harassing and intimidating civil rights workers, such "help" was often worse than useless. Even when violence took place in their presence, FBI agents would not intervene. The FBI ignored the fact that if the perpetrators were peace officers, what they were doing probably violated section 242, as well as the fact that if preplanned, their violent deeds might be overt acts furthering a conspiracy punishable under section 241. The Bureau insisted that its men lacked the authority to do more than stand by snapping pictures and taking notes. Hoover did not want his agents making arrests in these situations, and his nominal superiors in the Justice Department were afraid to order him to have them do so. Katzenbach feared that if they did, agents would just avoid locations where anti–civil rights violence was likely to occur, thus depriving the government of the evidence they were now collecting.[26]

Although Hoover attributed the Bureau's passivity to a lack of "authority to give personal protection to anyone," this was not the real reason for the FBI's failure to take decisive action.[27] The director, who had grown up in Washington when the capital was still a southern city, was at worst a racist and at best had little sympathy for the civil rights movement and no desire to promote its objectives.[28] When questioned by reporters in 1964 about the Bureau's policies, he informed them it was "not a police agency" and did not "guard anybody." Said Hoover, "We simply can't wet nurse everybody who goes down to try to reform or re-educate the Negro population of the South."[29] Many of the FBI's resident agents in the South were southerners who shared the director's racial attitudes and his lack of enthusiasm for the civil rights movement.[30]

Their prejudices and the institutional needs of the FBI impelled the Bureau in the same direction. It depended heavily on cooperation and assistance from police and sheriff's departments throughout the country. Most of the stolen car cases for which the FBI took credit, for example, were actually handed over to it by local law enforcement agencies. The Bureau was understandably reluctant to disrupt its relationships with southern police departments by pressing too hard on civil rights matters. While their superiors pressured agents to go easy on local law enforcement, Hoover argued that his agency should combat racial violence only by training southern police to cope with it themselves.[31] "I have been one of those states' righters all my life," the director told reporters.[32]

Dr. Martin Luther King, Jr., did not share Hoover's enthusiasm for FBI cooperation with southern law enforcement. In November 1962 King complained that agents in Albany, Georgia, were constantly in the company of members of the local police force. "One of the great problems we face with the FBI in the South is that the agents are white Southerners who have been influenced by the mores of the community," he told the press. King added that FBI men who agreed with segregation could not honestly and objectively investigate it. Since only one of the five agents assigned to the Albany FBI office was a native southerner, there was an element of distortion in King's allegations, but it was hardly great enough to justify Hoover's charge, made two years later, that King was a "notorious liar." Although inaccurate in some of its details, the picture that King sketched of an FBI too closely aligned with southern law enforcement was fundamentally accurate.[33]

Despite the fact that President Kennedy sympathized with the voter registration workers, the Bureau's policies differed more in degree than in kind from those of the Justice Department. Over one weekend in July 1962 the president bombarded Marshall with telephone calls asking if there was not something that could be done about Albany. During a press conference on September 13 of that year he condemned the recent church burnings and shootings in the South as "cowardly" and "outrageous." Those involved in the voter registration effort, Kennedy added, deserved protection from the United States government as well as from state and local authorities. Yet, according to Branton, "The Justice Department never provided protection at any time." Before leading SNCC field workers into southwest Mississippi, Bob Moses wrote to John Doar to ask about federal intentions should lawlessness occur there. He received assurances that the government would vigorously enforce federal laws proscribing intimidation, threats, and coercion against would-be voters, but in fact the Justice Department did not do so.[34]

Sam Block, Lawrence Guyot, and Lavaughn Brown learned the hard way how reluctant federal officials were to protect those involved in the voter registration campaign. On August 16, 1962, they telephoned Marshall from inside the Greenwood SNCC office, where they were besieged by armed whites who appeared to have the support of the police. The assistant attorney general told them he could do nothing—until after a crime had been committed. Marshall did telephone an FBI agent, but it was several hours before he arrived on the scene. Rather than trying to protect voter registration workers, the Justice Department negotiated with state and local authorities, seeking to persuade them to halt the violence and to let blacks vote. The leadership of the department too readily accepted the assurances of southern public officials, such as Governor Ernest Vandiver of Georgia and Mayor Asa D. Kelley, Jr., of Albany, that they could preserve law and order without help from the national government.[35]

Justice too rarely brought federal criminal prosecutions against those responsible for the violence. Not until June 1964 was anyone arrested in the South on a complaint alleging violation of section 241. During the Kennedy years the Civil Rights Division did initiate a number of section 242 prosecutions, but most of these were ordinary police brutality cases. For example, the Justice Department prosecuted a deputy sheriff in Mansfield, Louisiana, for blackjacking a handcuffed black prisoner, and two Atlanta police officers for beating a Negro they were arresting. Although neither indictments nor convictions for police brutality were easy to obtain in the South, the Civil Rights Division was clearly committed to using the power of the national government to combat this form of violence. In March 1962 Marshall proposed to Congress legislation which would have explicitly made it a federal crime to inflict summary punishment on a prisoner or to use force to extract a confession from him. It would also have substantially increased the penalties for such conduct.[36]

Although moving vigorously against interracial police brutality in the South, the Civil Rights Division appeared reluctant to bring federal criminal prosecutions in those areas where the voter registration campaign had sparked violent resistance. The reason may well have been that success seemed unlikely. Although John Doar and other government lawyers considered the Hurst case unwinnable, the Justice Department nevertheless took the matter to a federal grand jury in Mississippi in October 1961. It refused to return an indictment. Federal prosecutors had enough evidence concerning Registrar John Q. Wood's attack on John Hardy at Tylertown, Mississippi, to prove a case against him, but because a jury seemed unlikely to convict, Doar elected not to prosecute. In Greenwood the FBI investigated shootings, but when suspects were arrested, federal authorities allowed the state to prosecute them on felonious assault charges. Not until early 1963, after the Southern Regional Council had severely criticized the national government for its inaction in Albany, Georgia, did the Justice Department make any use of criminal prosecutions there. On January 3 it charged (using an information filed by a prosecutor rather than a grand jury indictment) Terrell County Deputy Sheriff D. E. Short with four counts of violating section 242 by threatening voter registration workers and firing a pistol at them. In addition, on January 24 Civil Rights Division lawyers presented to a federal grand jury three cases arising out of the violence in southwest Georgia. One was based on the caning of C. B. King, another on a church burning, and the third on an attack on an FBI agent. The division seems to have moved when it did in order that Attorney General Kennedy could declare, in a report submitted to the president the same day (and obviously intended for public consumption), that the Justice Department had acted to the limit of its authority in Albany and that "although no violation of federal law was found in most cases, prosecutive steps were taken where appropriate." Since the grand jury refused to indict in any of the three cases presented to it, and since a trial jury took only twenty minutes to acquit Deputy Short, the reluctance of the department to resort sooner to criminal prosecution is understandable.[37]

Less understandable is the minimal use it made of civil litigation to combat violent attacks on the voter registration campaign. In his March 1963 report to the president, Attorney General Kennedy asserted that the Justice Department had filed seven suits against "attempts at intimidation, verbal, economic, and physical." Generally, however, such actions, brought under 42 U.S.C. § 1971 (b)—a part of the Civil Rights Act of 1957—were aimed at enjoining economic coercion rather than violence. The Justice Department attacked with civil litigation such forms of intimidation as the boycott of a black farmer by local merchants and the firing of a black teacher by a board of education. It refused to seek a broad injunction against the sort of interference with constitutional rights that was occurring in Albany, insisting the government had no evidence that the police were not providing adequate protection there. In Mississippi the Civil Rights Division did ask a federal district court for a temporary restraining order after John Hardy was beaten and arrested in Walthall County. Although originally requesting very broad relief against an alleged conspiracy to deprive that county's black residents of the right to vote, however, the government appealed only the district judge's refusal to restrain a state prosecution of Hardy. In a suit against the city of Greenwood, the Justice Department sought, among other things, to enjoin municipal officials from failing to provide reasonable protection for those engaging in voter registration activities. However, it dropped its request for a temporary restraining order when local authorities promised to release some arrested demonstrators and maintain order in the future.[38]

To those left exposed to violent southern racism, such halfhearted efforts seemed utterly inadequate. Nor did they appear sufficient to many supporters of the civil rights movement. Bent on calling attention to the problems of harassment and violence, and on pressuring the national government into doing more about those problems, CORE summoned into existence a Commission of Inquiry into the Administration of Justice in the Freedom Struggle. Chaired by former first lady Eleanor Roosevelt, with Socialist party leader Norman Thomas as its vice-chairman, the commission included such liberal luminaries as Nuremberg prosecutor Telford Taylor, psychologist Dr. Kenneth Clark, ACLU official Roger Baldwin, and Americans for Democratic Action spokesman Joseph L. Rauh, Jr.[39]

After James Farmer carefully informed Marshall about its plans, the commission staged public hearings in Washington on May 25–26, 1962. A parade of witnesses trooped before it to render distressingly repetitious accounts of intimidation, violence, and police brutality. Bigelow and Peck told about being beaten during the Freedom Rides. C. B. King was there to report on what had happened in Albany, and Bob Moses to describe the situation in Mississippi. Some of the witnesses were prominent figures in the civil rights movement, such as Farmer. Others were obscure young activists. Their testimony was a parade of horribles.[40]

The commission also heard a good deal of criticism of the Justice Department and the FBI. A Civil Rights Division lawyer who attended the hearings reported to Marshall:

> The Federal Bureau of Investigation was roundly criticized by many of the witnesses, and this critical attitude was also evinced by the questions of several members of the [commission]. The general tenor of these criticisms was that the Special Agents were not interested at all in civil rights cases, were perfunctory in their investigations, did not pursue all available leads, and in several cases were outspokenly critical of those engaged in direct action in the Freedom Struggle.[41]

Although testimony about the FBI was especially vitriolic, the rest of the Justice Department did not escape criticism. There were complaints about how seldom police brutality prosecutions were brought in cases where the victims were civil rights activists. The department also came under attack for failing to protect witnesses brave enough to testify before state agencies or courts. Representative William Fitz Ryan (D-N.Y.) complained that the Justice Department and the attorney general had yet to demonstrate they were "determined to take action in civil rights cases." They were not, he felt, using all the power they had. Ryan dismissed the difficulty of obtaining convictions from southern juries as insufficient reason for failing to prosecute under sections 241 and 242. Louisville attorney Louis Lusky also thought the Justice Department could do more. He commended the Civil Rights Division as a "vigorous" and "energetic" agency which was "enforcing the law . . . fully," but suggested that it make greater use of the means employed during the Freedom Rides. When southern police failed to enforce state criminal laws against private citizens who resorted to threats and violence, Lusky argued, the Justice Department should respond with federal marshals and with injunctions forbidding them to withhold protection.[42]

Neither his testimony nor that of the other witnesses before the Commission of Inquiry had much effect. It shocked Mrs. Roosevelt and Thomas, but the press and the electronic media largely ignored the hearings. Numerous members of Congress, liberals as well as conservatives, declined Mrs. Roosevelt's invitation to attend, and Burke Marshall informed Farmer he could not be present either. All the assistant attorney general did was dispatch a lawyer from the Civil Rights Division to monitor the proceedings.[43]

Although CORE insisted that its hearings had made a positive impact on the Justice Department, they produced no apparent change in government policy. Five months later representatives of a number of civil rights organizations tried again to persuade Attorney General Kennedy to intervene in the South on behalf of peaceful demonstrators. They failed. In November 1962 Dr. Martin Luther King, Jr., warned the president that if the federal government did not take decisive action soon, blacks might turn to retaliatory violence to protect themselves.[44]

The Mississippi Advisory Committee of the Civil Rights Commission agreed with King that Washington was not providing threatened blacks with all the protection that it should. In a pamphlet published in January 1963 the committee condemned as unwisely narrow and limited the Justice Department's interpretation of the functions of its Civil Rights Division. Three months later the Civil Rights Commission itself took the unusual step of issuing an interim report describing the perilous state of constitutional rights in Mississippi.[45] It called upon the president to "strengthen his Administration's efforts to suppress existing lawlessness and provide federal protection to citizens in the exercise of their basic constitutional rights."[46] Both the White House and the Civil Rights Division responded quite defensively to the commission's report, but they did not alter course. As far as the Kennedy administration was concerned, providing "ordinary police protection" remained a state and local responsibility.[47]

Administration policy would have been far more credible had not those responsible for administering criminal justice in many parts of the South persisted so obviously in failing to enforce the law in cases involving civil rights activists. The wave of violence about which witnesses before the Commission of Inquiry had complained rolled on largely unchecked until President Kennedy's death. During 1963 ten persons died in circumstances directly related to racial protests, and there were at least thirty-five bombings in the South. In July of that year someone fired a high-powered rifle into the SNCC headquarters in Albany, Georgia, and in December the homes of local blacks who had aided voter registration workers in nearby Dawson and in Sumter County, Georgia, came under attack. Intimidation and violence were also serious problems in Mississippi.[48] "We members and field secretaries of SNCC . . . realize that it is very dangerous to even work in Mississippi on Voter Registration," Sam Block reported in September. "It could [cost] any of us our lives."[49] There was danger in Alabama too. In June a white man beat Reverend Bernard LaFayette, who was doing voter registration work in Selma, and on October 7, during "Freedom Day" demonstrations in that city, state police officers battered two SNCC members. During 1963 CORE voter registration projects met violent resistance in both north Florida and Louisiana. When that organization and the Voters League launched marches in Plaquemine, Louisiana, in June to dramatize a variety of demands, police attacked the demonstrators with tear gas, fire hoses, billy clubs, and electric cattle prods. James Farmer had to flee, protected by an armed escort and hidden in a hearse. In the same area someone bombed a Catholic school that had integrated briefly. At Danville, Virginia, police attacked demonstrators with clubs and fire hoses, and in Lexington, North Carolina, two thousand whites fell upon the fifty black participants in an NAACP meeting.

The blacks defended themselves with guns, killing one white man and wounding another.[50]

That blacks should have resorted to self-help was hardly surprising, for official efforts to control such racist violence remained generally inadequate. In places such as Tallahassee, Florida, and Greenwood, Mississippi, men employed to enforce the law looked the other way while whites violated it by harassing and even shooting at civil rights workers. Often, rather than arresting the perpetrators of racist violence, southern policemen took the victims into custody. For example, after someone fire-bombed and shot up the house of Hartman Trumbow, one of the first blacks to register to vote in Holmes County, Mississippi, the sheriff arrested Trumbow and three SNCC workers for arson and also lodged "interfering with an investigation" charges against Bob Moses. After four whites pushed a black student through the window of a drugstore in Talladega, Alabama, police arrested the victim for inciting a riot and breaking and entering. A *Washington Post* correspondent covering an April 1963 conference on the civil rights movement, attended by police executives from all of the southern states except Louisiana and Mississippi, did report that those responsible for law enforcement in the South now seemed to be concentrating on doing their jobs impartially. And a few months later police in Emporia, Virginia, offered some support for his conclusion when they arrested American Nazi party leader George Lincoln Rockwell on a charge of inciting whites to acts of violence and war against blacks. In many other communities, however, racism still distorted police performance.[51]

Sometimes law enforcement personnel themselves committed acts of racist violence. In Gadsden, Alabama, state troopers pummeled SNCC field secretary Lindy McNair, whom they had arrested for driving with an out-of-state license. A local CORE member received worse treatment, being stripped naked and burned with a cigar, as well as beaten. In Winona, Mississippi, jail officers used fists, nightsticks, and leather weapons on six or seven civil rights workers (among them Fannie Lou Hamer) apprehended for sitting in at a bus terminal. The NAACP accused Danville, Virginia, police of beating children as young as two years old.[52]

Southern courts were little better at protecting civil rights activists than were southern peace officers. As late as 1963 they remained almost totally white institutions. Sitting in segregated courtrooms, white judges and white juries dispensed racially biased justice. In Danville, pistol-packing Judge Archibald Aiken, guarded by a platoon of state troopers and local policemen, combated disorder by enjoining nonviolent demonstrations. Nearly 150 protesters went to jail for violating his injunction. Like Aiken, many southern judges seemed to view themselves "less as impartial umpires and dispensers of justice than as defenders of white supremacy."[53]

Others were scrupulously fair, and southern state courts did produce a few convictions of whites for acts of violence against blacks. Some of these were for ordinary interpersonal violence having no obvious connection with the civil rights movement. A Georgia jury, for example, convicted a white bartender of manslaughter for shooting to death a black man who swore at him after their cars collided. Other cases had definite civil rights overtones. In Columbia, South Carolina, a white man received thirty days on the county work gang for slapping a fifteen-year-old black girl who had refused to move to the rear of a bus. A Virginia court found a white sawmill worker guilty of assaulting the executive secretary of that state's NAACP unit while the victim was engaged in a dispute with a restaurant owner who had refused to serve him. The judge fined the defendant $25, although the normal penalty for assault was only $10.[54]

But these were exceptional cases. From the beginning of the sit-in demonstrations in 1960 through the spring of 1965, at least twenty-six blacks and white civil rights workers died at the hands of southern racists. Only one of the killers (who received a ten-year sentence for manslaughter after shooting a black woman to death during 1964 demonstrations in Jacksonville, Florida) went to prison. All of the others avoided punishment because they were either not arrested, not indicted, or not convicted.[55]

During 1963 several spectacular anti–civil rights murders went unpunished. The bloodiest of these crimes was the bombing of Birmingham's 16th Street Baptist Church on September 15. That crime deeply disturbed many white residents, who contributed $100,000 to a reward fund, and the city council pledged to put the "total strength" of the municipality behind the effort to capture and punish the perpetrators. Alabama Attorney General Richmond Flowers vowed to prosecute the case personally and said he would ask for the death penalty. Nevertheless, those responsible for the killing of four little black girls went free. The FBI entered the case under the 1960 bombing statute and committed a total of 231 agents to the investigation. It checked out more than eight thousand suspects and subjected major white hate groups to harassing surveillance. By September 29 the Bureau, Birmingham police, and the Jefferson County Sheriff's Department had identified a small group of klansmen who were probably responsible for the bombing. But before the FBI could obtain a confession or the evidence necessary to prosecute these suspects, Governor Wallace, after meeting with Al Lingo, the head of the Alabama Highway Patrol, dramatically announced that the state expected to break the case. A few hours later Lingo's men arrested two individuals a klansman had told them the Bureau was planning to apprehend. The highway patrol subsequently charged R. E. Chambliss, Charles Cagel, and a third suspect, John W. Hall, with illegal possession of dynamite—a misdemeanor. All three were convicted of this trivial offense in a City Recorder's Court and sentenced to a $100 fine and 180 days in jail. In the opinion of furious city, county, and federal authorities (among them J. Edgar Hoover), the premature action of the state police, by revealing to those responsible for the crime how much the FBI probably knew about them, seriously impaired the chances of building a case against the perpetrators. Reportedly, the conspirators met and the leader threatened the others with death if they talked. There were no further arrests and no prosecutions on major charges.[56]

The Justice Department was sure the state police had deliberately sabotaged its case in order to protect the Klan. Writer George McMillan thought Lingo's organization was guilty merely of bowing to pressure from a governor determined to best the federal government in a race to catch the bombers.[57] Whatever the motives of the state police, the consequences of their actions were disastrous. Fred Shuttlesworth had good reason for asking, "Is this the best the Nation can expect of the combined forces of the Federal, State and Local law agencies?"[58]

What followed the murder of William Moore was equally disillusioning. Moore, a white mailman, a CORE member, and a former mental patient, set out on a "Freedom Walk" from Washington, D.C., to Jackson, Mississippi, where he hoped to deliver a plea for civil rights to Governor Ross Barnett. He wore a sandwich board sign protesting segregation. On April 24, 1963, when Moore was forty miles from Anniston, Alabama, someone gunned him down. President Kennedy labeled the killing an outrageous crime, and Clarence Mitchell, a black state legislator from Baltimore, urged the federal government to aid in finding Moore's murderer. FBI ballistics tests soon identified a .22-caliber weapon belonging to Floyd Simpson, a grocer who had conversed with the victim on the day he died, as the murder weapon, but an Etowah County grand jury refused to indict Simpson. Furthermore, when an interracial group of CORE and SNCC members tried to complete Moore's walk, whites threw stones and bottles at them as they moved south from Chattanooga. At the Alabama line, Lingo's state police, acting on his orders, arrested the marchers, in the process repeatedly shocking one of them with an electric cattle prod. State officers insisted that they would go on looking for the "real" killer, but they made no arrests. Insisting that the federal government lacked jurisdiction, United States Attorney Mason Weaver said he had no intention of prosecuting Simpson.[59]

So Moore's murderer remained at large, along with the killer of Medgar Evers. Evers, Mississippi field secretary for the NAACP, was shot to death at 12:30 A.M. on June 12, 1963, as he stepped from his car in the driveway of his Jackson home. The slaying enraged local blacks, who demonstrated and then rioted. A major civil disturbance, which erupted when a number of blacks broke away from a mourning parade and surged toward Jackson's main business district, ended only when John Doar, standing alone in the middle of Farish Street, managed to persuade the rioters to disperse. The Evers killing angered John Kennedy too. The president observed that he was beginning to think Congressman Thaddeus Stevens, the scourge of the South during Reconstruction, had been right about that part of the country and about how to deal with its white inhabitants.[60]

Kennedy's outburst was not entirely fair to the city of Jackson, which did offer a $5,000 reward for information leading to the arrest and conviction of Evers's killer. On the other hand, the outcome of the case provided more than ample justification for distrusting white southerners. Robert Kennedy placed the full investigative resources of the Justice Department at the disposal of Jackson police, and by June 23 the FBI had a suspect in custody. He was Byron De La Beckwith, a Greenwood fertilizer salesman known as both an outspoken racist and a gun collector. A day later the Bureau turned Beckwith over to Mississippi authorities for prosecution on murder charges.[61]

At his trial, said the *Pittsburgh Courier,* an "entire trouble-torn state with its swirling human pool of hate mongers and racists, led by Gov. Ross Barnett, [would face] a challenge as to whether or not it [would] allow men to get away with murder."[62] Mississippi failed the test. On July 2 a Hinds County grand jury, which included one black member, indicted Beckwith, but at his February 1964 trial an all-white jury failed to reach a verdict. The FBI had traced the telescopic sight on the .30/.06 rifle found near the murder scene to Beckwith and had identified a fingerprint on the weapon as his. The jury also heard testimony from two cab drivers who said they had been asked by the defendant where Evers lived, and from a woman who testified that she had seen his car parked near the victim's home at about the time of the shooting. The only weakness in the state's case was its inability, because of the mangled condition of the slug, to prove conclusively that the fatal shot had been fired from the .30/.06 rifle. Nevertheless, when the judge declared a mistrial after twelve hours of deliberations, six or seven jurors were still voting not guilty. The only thing Beckwith and many other Mississippians found surprising about this was that the jurors had not all favored acquittal. The prosecution, urged on by civic and business leaders, who felt the time had come to repudiate the unwritten law that any white man could inflict violent discipline on any black, retried the defendant the following April. Again the jury was all-white. The evidence presented was the same, and so was the outcome. The only difference was that this time eight jurors stood firm for acquittal. In a sad commentary on Mississippi justice, the victim's brother, Charles, found it "encouraging" that any of them had voted guilty.[63]

Most black leaders had little hope for southern justice. They insisted that only federal action could save others from the fate of Medgar Evers. Speaking for the NAACP, Aaron Henry and Clarence Mitchell (the organization's lobbyist and father of the Maryland legislator of the same name) urged Congress to enact legislation that would protect civil rights workers in Mississippi from snipers and law enforcement officials.[64] "Let's not wait until more deaths have resulted before recognizing that law and order have broken down in Jackson and that the Federal presence is necessary now," the director of the American Negro Leadership Conference on Africa wrote the attorney general.[65] His words echoed those of Congressman Charles Diggs (D-Mich.), who less than two weeks before the Evers killing had asked the president whether it would take a death in Mississippi to make him realize that stronger national action was needed there. Diggs considered it urgent that Kennedy deploy federal troops and National Guardsmen to protect black citizens attempting to exercise their constitutional rights. A. Phillip Randolph agreed with him about the need for Washington to act, urging that FBI agents, marshals, and, if necessary, soldiers, be sent to Greenwood.[66] Wiley Branton too was "very concerned about the failure of the federal government to protect the people who have sought to register and vote and who are working actively to get others to register."[67]

Such concerns were not limited to blacks, nor were those who expressed them worried only about Mississippi. All ten chairmen of the August 1963 March on Washington, a group which included such prominent white liberals as United Auto Workers President Walter Reuther, called on President Kennedy to provide federal protection to Alabama blacks. Shad Polier, chairman of the American Jewish Congress's Governing Council, criticized the failure of the Justice Department to prosecute local law enforcement officials in Albany, Georgia, while the New Jersey State Branch of the Women's International League for Peace and Freedom urged the federal government to "assert its overall authority and take appropriate action" in the William Moore case.[68]

The most incessant and insistent demands for federal protection came from the two civil rights organizations that were bearing the brunt of southern violence. CORE begged the Justice Department to send marshals to Plaquemine, Louisiana, and asked the president to protect peaceful marchers in Brownsville, Tennessee.[69] "The federal government," James Farmer told the attorney general, "must act to protect its citizens."[70] SNCC expressed similar sentiments. It pressed for the federal government to intervene at Selma and in Mississippi and protested the inadequacy of the government's response to its pleas for help.[71]

SNCC did more than just complain. In January 1963 Bob Moses, six other student activists, and William L. Higgs, a white Jackson lawyer, filed a class action suit against the attorney general and FBI Director Hoover. The plaintiffs alleged that Mississippi law enforcement officers and private citizens were harassing, threatening, intimidating, attacking, and unconstitutionally jailing them and other persons in their position. Higgs, who acted as attorney for the group, and his co-counsel William Kunstler asked the United States District Court for the District of Columbia for a declaratory judgment affirming that plaintiffs and other members of their class were entitled to have marshals and FBI agents protect their constitutional rights and making it clear that those federal law enforcement officers were legally required to safeguard both their rights and their persons. The SNCC group also requested a writ of mandamus directing Hoover and Kennedy to have their agents arrest, imprison, and institute criminal proceedings against those state and local police officials and civilians in Mississippi responsible for depriving them of their rights.[72] On

July 2 of that year Judge Luther W. Youngdahl dismissed their complaint
for failure to state a claim on the basis of which relief could be granted.[73]
He had no choice, the judge contended, for the plaintiffs were seeking
remedies which his court lacked the power to grant. They wanted him to
force executive officers to perform acts which were clearly matters of discretion, lying within areas of responsibility assigned to them rather than
to the judiciary. Youngdahl also ruled that the plaintiffs had failed to
allege the existence of a justiciable controversy which would support an
action under the Declaratory Judgment Act. There was no disagreement
between the parties concerning the scope of the defendants' authority, he
reasoned, merely a dispute over the wisdom of their failure to use it.

According to Judge Youngdahl, the Justice Department had a legal
right to refrain from protecting civil rights workers. For the most part the
department's leaders continued to insist that this was the wisest course for
the government to follow. The rise in the number of police brutality complaints which accompanied the increase in demonstrations during the
summer of 1963 did have some effect on Marshall's thinking. On September 18 the Justice Department filed a seven-count information in Oxford, Mississippi, charging the police chief, the sheriff, and three other
law enforcement officers in the town of Winona with violating section 242
by beating Fannie Lou Hamer and her companions. The same day Marshall advised Robert Kennedy that he was thinking about bringing a
broader police brutality case in Plaquemine, Louisiana. He continued to
stress, however, that the legal authority of the national government was
limited. Marshall remained convinced that there was no workable way for
Washington to protect all of the civil rights workers in Mississippi, let
alone throughout the South. Those who sought protection from the Justice Department were likely to be advised that the FBI would inform local
authorities about their problem.[74]

Responding to a December 1963 letter from a political science professor
at Ole Miss, Marshall commented almost plaintively:

> The point about protection is the most difficult and frustrating we
> have to live with under the federal system. I say over and over again—
> hundreds of times a year—that we do not have a national police force,
> and cannot provide protection in a physical sense for everyone who is
> disliked because of the exercise of his constitutional rights. The
> marshals we have used are taken from duty in the service of papers and

the like in many states. At most I can round up maybe 100, for short term duty. They are not police officers. They are not hired for that and we have no budget for it. Congress would never grant one.

In any event, if we learned anything in 1963, it is that no one can be fully protected.

There is no substitute under the federal system for the failure of local law enforcement responsibility.[75]

Such fatalism and resignation, no matter how realistic or how respectful of American constitutional traditions, could never find favor among civil rights workers under siege in the South. In a telegram every bit as plaintive as Marshall's letter, SNCC's John Lewis asked the attorney general: "Just what do you expect Negroes to do to defend themselves against vicious onslaughts from whites with clubs and sticks or dynamite and guns?"[76] It was a question which demanded a better answer than the Kennedy administration had provided.

That Bloody Freedom Summer

Born in an act of violence, the administration of President Lyndon B. Johnson almost immediately confronted a violent problem. Although the crisis management of the Kennedy years had kept major race riots from thwarting judicial enforcement of the Constitution, persistent attacks on voter registration workers and random acts of racist terrorism increasingly threatened constitutional rights. Intensifying as 1964 progressed, by mid-summer these would push some parts of the South to the edge of anarchy. Two brutal murders—one in Georgia, the other in Mississippi— would make it politically impossible for the national government any longer to stand on the sidelines waiting for local authorities to act.

Those killings changed federal policy in ways few people could have anticipated in the months just after the Kennedy assassination elevated Lyndon Johnson to the presidency. A former member of both houses of Congress, who had served as Senate majority leader in the 1950s, Johnson was from Texas and was distrusted by liberals. In the 1930s he had vigorously resisted enactment of an antilynching law. Punishing murder, Johnson then insisted, was a state responsibility. Well into the 1950s, after moving up to the Senate, "LBJ" continued to oppose civil rights legislation. His motives were political, for Texas probably would not have elected him had he done otherwise. In his personal outlook Johnson was never fully in step with southern traditions. He came from a county in the central Texas hill country outside Austin which had few black residents and little stake in the South's racial caste system. Mississippi's Paul Johnson considered him a westerner. Lacking deeply held prejudices, LBJ readily changed his position when elevation to Democratic leadership in the Senate and presidential ambitions necessitated that he adopt a stance more acceptable to a national constituency. Johnson helped secure enactment of the 1957 and 1960 civil rights acts. As vice-president, although having little influence on Kennedy administration policy, he did gain an increased awareness of the urgency of the black problem as both a political and a moral issue.[1] Then came the assassination. "When I sat in the Oval Office after President Kennedy died and reflected on civil rights," Johnson recalled later, "there was no question in my mind as to what I would do."[2] He pushed to enactment the legislation his predecessor had introduced in 1963 and amazed civil rights leaders and ordinary black people by becoming a champion of their cause.[3]

Despite Johnson's surprisingly vigorous support of legislative efforts to promote racial equality, federal policy on southern racist violence remained largely unchanged. The new president seems to have wanted terrorism stopped,[4] but as two reporters for the *New York Herald Tribune* observed, "Like his predecessors Mr. Johnson recognizes the rights reserved to the states to uphold law and order." Johnson considered himself "duty bound to respect that right barring a breakdown in local law enforcement or defiance of federal jurisdiction."[5] So, of course, did Robert Kennedy, who remained at the Justice Department for several months, and Burke Marshall, who stayed on as assistant attorney general until a year after the assassination, and whose philosophy of federalism continued to influence department policy even after his departure. During the early months of the Johnson presidency, Justice continued to emphasize the importance of local responsibility for law enforcement and to stress the futility of federal prosecutions in the South.[6]

Events in 1964 severely tested this commitment to nonintervention. On July 2 of that year Johnson signed the most sweeping civil rights law in the nation's history. Despite intense southern opposition, it had passed Congress with overwhelming bipartisan support. The most-discussed provision of the Civil Rights Act of 1964 was Title II, which declared that all persons were entitled to the full and equal enjoyment of places of public accommodation, such as hotels, motels, restaurants, and movie theaters, "without segregation on the ground of race, color, religion, or national origin." This was only one of ten titles in a 28-page law which also empowered the attorney general to file suits to desegregate public facilities other than schools and, on complaint, to initiate litigation to compel educational institutions to comply with the *Brown* decision. The act authorized the commissioner of education to provide technical assistance to local school boards that were trying to desegregate, and expanded the investigative authority of the Civil Rights Commission. One title outlawed discrimination in employment, and another provided for the cutting off of federal financial assistance to programs that discriminated. The act also contained a number of provisions intended to make enforcement of black voting rights more effective. Nothing in it directly enhanced the power of the federal government to combat racist violence, but Title X did create a Community Relations Service which it charged with assisting places such as Birmingham to resolve "disputes, disagreements and difficulties" caused by racial discrimination. When he signed the new law, the president expressed hope that it would "bring peace to our land."[7]

That was not to be. Spurred by the highly visible work of civil rights activists and the triumphant march of the civil rights bill through Congress, the Ku Klux Klan had mobilized for a counteroffensive. As late as January 1964 it had been a badly weakened movement.[8] By May the Anti-Defamation League was reporting, "There has been a significant resurgence of the Klan throughout the South."[9] Such established groups as the United Klans of America gained strength, but particularly ominous was the rapid rise of the White Knights of the Ku Klux Klan, a violence-prone Mississippi organization that broke off from the Louisiana-based Original Knights of the Ku Klux Klan in December 1963 and thereafter enjoyed great recruiting success among poor and uneducated whites in a state which was rapidly becoming the principal battleground of the civil rights struggle. By October the Klan also had acquired new life in the Carolinas, Tennessee, Louisiana, and Georgia. It had grown particularly potent in Alabama and some parts of Florida.[10]

In Florida, Klan strength was greatest around Jacksonville and St. Augustine. By the middle of 1964 those communities were awash in racist violence. On February 16 someone bombed a black home in Jacksonville. The FBI arrested six klansmen, but all-white juries refused to convict any of them. Only the one who pleaded guilty suffered any punishment. In late March blacks took the offensive. Reacting against police efforts to break up civil rights demonstrations, they attacked both law enforcement personnel and white civilians. Bombs damaged numerous buildings, including the mayor's office. White men were wounded by gunfire and slashed with razor blades, and a black woman was shot to death. By April 19 the situation in Jacksonville had become so menacing that the president of the local and state NAACP organizations, Richard H. Pearson, felt compelled to beg both Governor Farris Bryant and President Johnson to take action to avert a race war.[11]

As bad as things became in Jacksonville, they were worse in St. Augustine. The first permanent European settlement in the United States had a deplorable civil rights record and a history of racially motivated shootings and beatings. Sporadic protests began there in 1962, and the following year Dr. Robert Hayling, a dentist and NAACP leader, launched almost daily demonstrations. Police beat and jailed the protesters, and someone fired four shotgun blasts into Hayling's home. The homes of two black families who had enrolled their children in white schools also came under attack, as did some Negro nightclubs. Vowing not to die like Medgar Evers, Hayling publicly rejected nonviolence, and he and three companions set out to spy on a Ku Klux Klan rally. Klansmen captured the four and savagely beat them. A judge dismissed charges against three of the assailants, and a jury acquitted the fourth. On the other hand, Hayling and two of his companions were convicted of assault. The dentist received a sixty-day jail sentence and a $100 fine. By November 5, 1963, according to Burke Marshall, the situation in St. Augustine had become abominable.[12]

It soon grew worse. Hayling and other St. Augustine black leaders asked the SCLC to launch a major desegregation drive in their city, and Dr. Martin Luther King, Jr., agreed to do so. St. Augustine was preparing to celebrate its 400th anniversary in 1965, and King did not want federal funds used to finance a segregated birthday party. Also, the quadracentennial gave St. Augustine symbolic significance. Demonstrations there would attract attention and might generate the sort of publicity that could pressure Congress into passing the civil rights bill. By exposing the savagery of the Klan, the protesters might also compel the Justice Department to begin protecting blacks and civil rights workers. King sent several of his top aides to St. Augustine in early 1964, and during Easter week the first wave of demonstrators arrived. Led by the mother of the governor of Massachusetts, this group included several prominent women and clergymen from the Boston area and a number of college students.[13]

The arrival of these outsiders angered local whites, sowing the seeds of further violence. In May, Hosea Williams secured King's permission to conduct night marches to St. Augustine's historic slave market. On the evening of May 28, as a column of four hundred black demonstrators circled that symbolically significant objective, a mob of about fifty whites attacked them with fists, clubs, knives, iron pipes, and bicycle chains.

March leader Andrew Young was kicked unconscious. That same night someone shot an SCLC staff member, and a cottage rented for King's use was hit by gunfire. The local police chief, Virgil Stuart, and the St. John's County sheriff, L. O. Davis, reacted by banning all night marches and forcibly blocking those who tried to defy this order. On June 9 Federal District Judge Bryan Simpson voided their decree, but when blacks marched that night, angry whites again attacked them. The following evening the police had to use tear gas to scatter a rock-throwing mob swollen by visiting thugs from outside the area. [14]

Police protection was not something black protesters were used to receiving in St. Augustine, for in that city law enforcement personnel generally cooperated closely with the Klan. Both Chief Stuart and Sheriff Davis opposed the efforts of the civil rights movement, and numerous policemen were suspected of being klansmen. So were many of the several hundred local white men Davis deputized to help control the demonstrations. Indeed, Hoss Manucy, who headed a Klan front called the Ancient City Hunting Club, spent most of his time in and around the sheriff's office. [15]

Thus, it is hardly surprising that civil rights leaders felt they needed help from the federal government. On May 29 King wired President Johnson, stating, "All semblance of law and order has broken down in St. Augustine." He called on Johnson "as President of our nation to use the influence of your high office to immediately provide federal protection through the Department of Justice for the members of the Negro community who seek redress of their grievances under the First Amendment." [16] The SCLC leader wired Attorney General Kennedy, telling him "naked violence" was defeating law and order in St. Augustine. Fearful of what might happen to King there, his father telephoned the Justice Department on June 9. The national board of the SCLC and the organization's executive director, Wyatt Tee Walker, both complained to the White House about the federal government's failure to protect their leader. Meanwhile, King and Hayling were condemning the conduct of the St. Augustine police and urging Johnson to intervene in a situation which they characterized as "the most complete breakdown of law and order since Oxford, Mississippi." [17]

Despite pleas for federal intervention, the president and the Justice Department left peace-keeping in St. Augustine to state authorities. After King's first telegram on May 29, Marshall did call the FBI, but only to

ask for current intelligence on the situation. Meanwhile, Lee White, associate counsel to the president, telephoned Governor Bryant. White, a
lawyer from Nebraska, had joined the White House staff during the Kennedy administration after previous service as an assistant to both John
Kennedy, who was then in the Senate, and his father, Joseph P. Kennedy,
who at the time was a member of the Hoover Commission. Despite his
ties to the Kennedy family, White remained on the presidential staff after
the assassination, as associate special counsel from 1963 to 1965 and special counsel to the president in 1965 and 1966. Under Johnson, White
functioned as the principal White House advisor on racial matters. When
White contacted Bryant, the governor assured him that the Florida state
police and National Guard could handle the situation in St. Augustine.[18]
By June 9, however, the city was again slipping into chaos. White and
Marshall still thought the proper response was to talk to Bryant, expressing concern and offering "to be of any proper help." Neither man believed
"there was any basis on which federal marshals or federal troops could be
used."[19]

White received assurances that state personnel adequate to maintain
order had been sent to St. Augustine. Two hundred troopers moved into
the city, and on June 15 Bryant transferred law enforcement authority
there from local officials to the state police. Although one SCLC leader
complained that the troopers did little to protect black demonstrators,
both Walker and King were satisfied with their performance. Klan violence flickered out—temporarily.[20]

On June 18, when black protesters invaded a segregated motel swim-
ming pool, St. Augustine exploded again. Two days later Bryant issued an
order banning demonstrations, but it failed to halt the violence. On June
22 and again on June 25 whites attacked black bathers on the beach, and a
Klan-led mob set upon participants in a march staged in defiance of
Bryant's order. Two nights later armed bands of whites and blacks roamed
through the city, shooting at homes and cars.[21] Besides failing to quell
the violence, Bryant's order conflicted with the one issued earlier by Judge
Simpson. Contending he would "do or permit nothing which will erode
in any way the power of the state generally to carry out its responsibility
for maintaining law and order," the governor refused to appear in federal
district court in Jacksonville to show cause why he should not be held in
contempt.[22]

Several other state and local officials did take the stand there, testifying that it was impossible to keep white mobs from assaulting civil rights activists in St. Augustine and that there was a clear and present danger of killing in the streets. Nevertheless, White and Marshall remained opposed to sending in the federal marshals King wanted, let alone the troops Andrew Young requested. Fortunately for the national government, Dr. King, believing the St. Augustine campaign had reached a hopeless stalemate, was seeking a graceful way to jettison a potential embarrassment. When Bryant established an emergency biracial committee to open negotiations between white and black leaders, King seized upon this opportunity to call off demonstrations. St. Augustine remained tense, but the sort of mass disorder that had produced demands for federal intervention abated.[23]

In Louisiana, on the other hand, the pattern of threats, intimidation, violence, and police harassment established in 1963 persisted throughout 1964 and into 1965. The civil rights movement there was the target of harassment, ranging from cross burnings to murder, which seriously impaired CORE voter registration efforts. In West Feliciana Parish, whites resorted to gunfire and arson until blacks began arming and threatening to retaliate. In Jonesboro, where klansmen burned crosses and marched through the black section of town behind a sheriff's patrol car, terrorism kept potential black voters from going to the courthouse to sign up with a registrar who was under a court order not to discriminate against them. In Bogalusa, which reportedly had the South's largest per capita concentration of klansmen, the KKK forced the cancellation of a speech by a noted racial moderate, former Congressman Brooks Hays. Its members also burned crosses and flogged both black residents and CORE workers.[24]

The targets of their violence and intimidation received little help from policemen or sheriff's deputies, who demonstrated a persistent unwillingness to maintain law and order.[25] A Harvard Law School student who served as a civil rights volunteer in Louisiana during the summer of 1964 found that "private violence is sanctioned and often encouraged by local law enforcement officials."[26] CORE activists reported numerous incidents in which police personnel stood by while hostile whites attacked civil rights workers.[27] In Bogalusa a mob formed to lynch CORE's Bill Yates and Steve Miller. Deputy Sheriff Doyle Holiday and Chief of Police Claxton Knight offered to escort Yates and Miller out of town, but when they refused to go, declared, "We have got better things to do than protect people who are not wanted here."[28] Although Ronnie Moore and

Mike Lesser called both the Jonesboro police chief and the local sheriff after three carloads of whites chased them at speeds of up to 105 miles per hour, the two civil rights workers got no response until they contacted the FBI.[29]

The Bureau investigated incidents of violence and intimidation in Louisiana, but CORE wanted the national government to do more than that, for it was convinced that only federal protection could end racist terrorism there. In a July 1964 telegram to Attorney General Kennedy, Moore pleaded, "Your intervention essential to prevent bloodshed and uphold basic rights of all citizens."[30]

Georgia and Alabama also provided evidence of a need for federal action. Four days after the Civil Rights Act went into effect a white mob forcibly removed some Negroes from a Selma theater they were attempting to integrate. Local police officers declined to protect the victims. Indeed, some of them may have participated in attacks on blacks waiting outside the theater. During the first days the Civil Rights Act was in operation, there were also beatings and riots in Americus, Georgia. There too the police not only failed to defend the black victims but actually participated in some of the attacks. Alabama state troopers even refused to protect journalists covering a civil rights demonstration.[31]

Even where police behavior was not so irresponsible, there were scattered incidents of racist violence and intimidation during the summer of 1964. Whites threatened blacks in both Arkansas and North Carolina. In the former state there were beatings, and in the latter robed and armed members of the KKK sought to frighten blacks by riding through their communities on "intimidation raids."[32]

While Arkansas and North Carolina were experiencing a few scattered incidents of violence and intimidation, Mississippi was suffering through a summer of rampant terrorism. The disorder there, which did more than anything else to heighten demands for federal intervention in southern law enforcement, was a reaction to the Mississippi Summer Project of the Council of Federated Organizations. Formed in 1962, COFO was an umbrella organization that, theoretically, united all the national civil rights groups working in Mississippi, although SCLC participation was slight and the NAACP's contribution did not extend much beyond the services of its state leader, Dr. Aaron Henry, who also acted as president of COFO. SNCC, whose Bob Moses functioned as program director for the umbrella organization, and CORE, whose David Dennis occupied its number two administrative post, dominated COFO. The driving force behind the Mississippi Summer Project was SNCC. Except in the one congressional district where CORE had a program, it supplied most of the manpower. The project's objective, according to Moses, was to make white America aware of conditions in Mississippi by bringing some of its own children face to face with them. COFO recruited more than five hundred white college students to assist in registering black voters and to man "freedom schools" and community centers which would provide instruction in government, remedial reading, humanities, and other scholastic and vocational subjects. Augmenting this group were as many as 150 law students and a group of attorneys organized by the National Lawyers Guild, who had volunteered to provide legal assistance to COFO workers. About one hundred clergymen also participated.[33]

By invading Mississippi with this civil rights army, SNCC hoped to provoke a confrontation between state and federal authorities which would force the national government to do something about the intimidation and violence that were stymieing civil rights work there.[34] In December 1963 John Lewis declared that SNCC intended to create a crisis so massive "the federal Government will have to take over the state."[35] The way to do this was to put white students in danger and, perhaps, even get some of them killed. SNCC insisted that it was not inviting violence and did not want any, but leaders of the organization recognized that nothing else would bring about massive federal intervention. They were shrewd enough to realize that, in order to capture the country's attention and force Washington to act, someone would have to die. Bitter experience had convinced SNCC activists that the nation and its leaders cared more about white lives than black ones. Dennis concluded (somewhat coldly, he admitted) that the death of a white college student would maximize the attention focused on the situation in Mississippi. So COFO deliberately recruited students from the best colleges, youth who were often also the children of influential whites, and thrust them into positions of extreme danger in the most violent of southern states.[36]

This tactic did not at once produce the desired results. Justice Department officials were deeply concerned about the explosive situation they saw developing in Mississippi. The Civil Rights Division alerted the FBI, as well as borrowing the Organized Crime Unit from the attorney general to gather intelligence. Justice persuaded influential journalists to write stories highlighting the impending crisis, and even contacted state political leaders to encourage them to do something about it. But in an April 1964 speech at Boston College, Deputy Attorney General Katzenbach warned civil rights workers not to expect the national government to guard them; they would have to depend on state and local authorities for protection.[37]

John Doar conveyed the same message to the student volunteers COFO assembled for a one-week orientation at the Western College for Women in Oxford, Ohio. The federal government could not guarantee their safety, he told them, and they should guide their conduct accordingly. His words made even more ominous the other warnings the volunteers received. Veteran civil rights workers told them to expect arrest, verbal abuse, and physical attack. James Forman warned the white students they might be killed. Frightened, some returned home.[38]

Those who pressed on to Mississippi found precisely what they had been warned to expect. SNCC's Cleveland Sellers remembered that summer later as "the longest nightmare I ever had."[39] News of an impending invasion by civil rights workers had thrown Mississippi's white population into a panic. "The Summer Freedom Project has aroused fears in some quarters comparable to the ancient terror of a slave uprising," Southern Regional Council Director Benjamin Muse reported. The mayor of Jackson purchased an armored car and stocked it with shotguns and tear gas, while in counties throughout the state peace officers practiced riot-control tactics. Moderate sentiment had increased somewhat in Mississippi since the Ole Miss riots in 1962, and Muse considered Paul Johnson, who was now the governor, a vast improvement over Ross Barnett. On the other hand, the Klan and similar white vigilante groups were growing rapidly in soil fertilized by racial tensions. The White Knights were committed to resist to the very end, and thousands of Mississippi whites stood ready to attack blacks at any provocation. By as early as January 1964 a number of political leaders in the state were predicting violence and bloodshed.[40]

They were prescient. Even before the COFO volunteers arrived, the state experienced a rash of killings, beatings, and threats. Between early January and mid-May there were nearly forty "Klan type" incidents, ranging from cross burnings, through beatings, to murder. Force and intimidation were especially common in the Klan-infested southwestern corner of the state, where five blacks were reported to have died in civil rights related killings during a six-month period. The violence in that area was "shocking even by Mississippi standards," Moses and Henry observed.

There was also disorder in the Delta. After the May dynamiting of the *Laurel Leader-Call,* a voice of moderation on racial issues, the like-minded *Delta Democrat-Times* predicted that if those with the power to crush the "killers, arsonists, and dynamiters" did not do so soon, blood would flow in Mississippi.[41]

The authorities failed to act, and the Freedom Summer proved to be bloody indeed. By the time the COFO summer project officially ended on August 16, three civil rights workers had been killed. At least four other persons had been shot and wounded and fifty-two beaten or injured in some other way. In addition, thirteen black churches had been destroyed by fire and seventeen buildings of various types, along with ten automobiles, had been damaged by arson or bombs.[42]

The worst violence occurred in McComb. Between June 22 and September 23 seventeen bombings rocked that community.[43] In addition, four churches burned, two blacks were flogged, and four whites (two of them civil rights workers and the others merely sympathizers) were beaten. After seeing his barbershop dynamited, a cross burned on his lawn, and his family threatened, local NAACP leader C. C. Bryant took to guarding his house at night with a shotgun.[44] "How much more violence [is] to be tolerated before intervention?" the parents of a young civil rights worker injured in a McComb bombing asked the president.[45]

Events in other Mississippi communities raised the same question. Between June 16 and August 24, 1964, Greenwood experienced four beatings, one bomb threat, and a shooting. In Hattiesburg three civil rights workers and a rabbi suffered beatings, some youths who tried to integrate a drive-in were "roughed up," and there was a shooting incident. At Canton a firebombing punctuated a chorus of gunfire. Even Jackson, regarded as relatively careful about protecting civil rights workers, experienced numerous violent incidents, including several shootings. Two whites armed with billy clubs beat a volunteer at a major downtown intersection, and a voter registration worker was attacked with a baseball bat outside the COFO office.[46]

Perpetrators of such crimes had little to fear from the law. The state did make some efforts to prevent violence. For one thing, Governor Johnson infiltrated the Klan as well as COFO with informers. The son of former Mississippi governor Paul B. Johnson, Sr., he had served in the Marine Corps during World War II and as an assistant United States attorney from 1948 to 1951. During his governorship Johnson emphasized improving law enforcement. Opposed to disorder as well as integration, he strengthened the highway patrol, with the objective of employing it to control the Klan. The legislature supported his efforts with a criminal syndicalism law designed for use in suppressing militant racist organizations. Even those state political leaders who deplored the outrages of white vigilantes, however, remained convinced that the best way to prevent trouble was by "keeping the Negroes from giving provocation."[47]

The outlook of the sheriffs, who provided what passed for law enforcement in most of predominantly rural Mississippi, was far less enlightened. Many of them, and many of their deputies as well, were reputed to be members of the Klan and similar organizations. As these peace officers saw it, their job was to control Negroes, not to protect them from white attackers. Many city policemen shared this outlook. Those in McComb reacted to the bombings there by charging blacks with criminal syndicalism.[48] Nor were Mississippi law enforcement personnel willing to arrest persons who attacked white civil rights workers. After beating COFO volunteer Steve Miller so badly that he suffered amnesia, a Gulfport white man walked up to a policeman and announced: "I got me one." The officer did nothing.[49] In the opinion of the Southern Regional Council, the crimes of violence perpetrated against the civil rights movement in Mississippi during the summer of 1964 could not have been committed in the number and with the frequency they were "without the indulgence, and in too many cases the cooperation," of local peace officers. Although there were some of these who conscientiously served the law, the council observed, that type was "not numerous."[50]

Indeed, in Mississippi, law enforcement personnel often participated in violent attacks on civil rights activists. When five SNCC members were stopped by a state policeman in Clarksdale, the officer dragged James Black from the car and pummeled him until he acknowledged being a "nigger." Numerous civil rights workers suffered beatings in Jackson's Hinds County Jail. In Winona the sheriff, the chief of police, and a state trooper all participated in assaults on black activists. They even turned one of their victims over to a group of citizens who administered a second beating. Civil rights workers complained that Mississippi jailers often allowed white prisoners to attack them and sometimes even offered bribes to induce such assaults.[51] The state's need, Benjamin Muse pointed out during the summer of 1964, was "not for more policemen, but for . . . a reorientation of law enforcement."[52]

Mississippi's judicial system needed reorientating too. It was, according to Charles Evers of the NAACP, "a disgrace to the nation." He made this harsh evaluation after nine men arrested for sixteen bombings in the McComb area escaped punishment. They pleaded guilty, but Judge W. H. Watkins, saying the defendants had been "unduly provoked," gave all of them probation. Even J. Edgar Hoover considered his action "scandalous." In Laurel another judge repeatedly dismissed the charges against, or found not guilty, local whites charged with beating or threatening blacks or civil rights workers. Mississippi prosecutors also subverted justice. After two Madison County COFO workers filed an assault complaint against a gas station owner, the county attorney got the trial delayed until the victims had to return to school, knowing that with no complaining witnesses present the court would have to dismiss the charges.[53] The ultimate security for perpetrators of racist violence was the jury system. In May 1964 a Mississippi district attorney wrote confidently to Robert Kennedy, "You cannot whip us as long as we have the right of a jury trial."[54]

Such attitudes help to explain why the national government found itself under mounting pressure to intervene in Mississippi. Many demands for federal protection came, of course, from the civil rights organizations supporting the Summer Project. During the early months of 1964 Evers of the NAACP, Farmer and Dennis of CORE, and Lewis and Moses of SNCC all contacted officials in Washington, seeking help with the volatile and dangerous situation in Mississippi created by the combination of terroristic violence and inadequate law enforcement. In March COFO filed a report with the Mississippi Advisory Committee of the Civil Rights Commission in which it argued that the rights and lives of black Mississippians had to be protected.[55]

The following month Bob Moses launched an organized campaign to persuade Washington to do this. It included asking the Mississippi Advisory Committee to put pressure on the Justice Department.[56] In an April 6 memorandum Moses took a different tack. Reflecting the emphasis of Professor Howard Zinn, a historian/political scientist close to the SNCC leadership, who stressed the importance of presidential action to protect constitutional rights in the South, Moses wrote: "The President must be made to understand that this responsibility rests with him, and him alone, and that neither he nor the American people can afford to jeopardize the lives of the people who will be working in Mississippi this summer." He proposed that civil rights leaders seek a meeting with Johnson.[57] On May 25 Moses, Henry, and Dennis wrote to the White House, requesting that the president meet with a COFO delegation "to discuss preparations for the summer." When they received no response, Moses wrote again, asking for the stationing of federal marshals, FBI agents, and Justice Department lawyers in key areas of Mississippi, "or even, in the event of a complete breakdown of law, sending in Federal troops."[58] Lee White advised the president not to see the COFO delegation. He considered it "nearly incredible that these people who are voluntarily sticking their head [sic] into the lion's mouth would ask for somebody to come down and shoot the lion."[59]

The Justice Department was not much more responsive to the movement's pleas for help. In early June, Farmer tried vainly to obtain an appointment with Attorney General Robert Kennedy. The best he could do was a meeting with Marshall and some representatives of the FBI. This conference yielded only disconcertingly inconclusive results.[60]

Although repeatedly rebuffed by officials in Washington, the movement's requests for federal protection enjoyed widespread support. Mothers and fathers of student volunteers formed a Parents Emergency Committee for Federal Protection of Students in the Mississippi Summer Project and also asked to see the president. They wanted assurances that Johnson would not allow their children's lives to be put needlessly in jeopardy. A woman whose husband had been beaten by the police in Mississippi wrote Burke Marshall that in view of the continued failure of state and local authorities to meet their law enforcement responsibilities she could not understand how the national government could remain inactive. The White House received petitions from hundreds of persons around the country who expressed concern for the safety of the student volunteers and called upon the president to give them federal protection.[61] In addition, Johnson heard from a group of about forty Boston-area clergymen and professors and their spouses, among them such prominent figures as Mark DeWolfe Howe, Leonard Levy, Robert Coles, Oscar Handlin, and Arthur Schlesinger, Sr. They pointed out that in the past federal intervention had come only after direct challenges to the implementation of court orders and in the presence of threats of force and violence. "We believe that it is both possible and politically desirable for the Administration to take preventive or deterrent action in this instance," they wrote.[62]

In an effort to persuade Washington to dispatch a "peace-keeping force" to Mississippi, and also for the purpose of focusing national attention on the situation there, COFO staged a repetition of the Roosevelt Commission hearings at the National Theater in Washington on June 8. A panel consisting of Coles, authors Paul Goodman and Joseph Heller, journalist Murray Kempton, sociologist Graham Skyes, New York Family Court Judge Justine Polier, educator Harold Taylor, and social worker Noel Day heard testimony from the parents of student volunteers and from black Mississippians who had experienced intimidation, violence, and police brutality. Witnesses described the failure of law enforcement personnel to help persons whose rights had been violated and told of the participation of peace officers in anti–civil rights violence. The panel also heard testimony about crimes that had gone unprosecuted and about prejudice and hostility in the Mississippi courts. The federal government received criticism too, with witnesses complaining about the unresponsiveness of both the FBI and the Department of Justice.[63] After the hearings the panel wrote to President Johnson, asking him to send sufficient federal marshals to Mississippi to protect the constitutional rights of citizens. Panel members also wanted the Justice Department instructed to "take the initiative in enforcing provisions of the Constitution."[64]

Those invited to attend the hearings included members of Congress. COFO also held a briefing for interested senators and representatives at which it supplied them with a legal memorandum outlining the statutory authority of the federal government in civil rights matters and the laws that empowered Washington to employ marshals, FBI agents, and troops to enforce the Constitution in the South. COFO announced that its Mississippi office would telephone details of all incidents to Washington immediately. The organization's legal advisors would then determine under what statutes the federal government was empowered to act and relay this information to congressional offices, so that they could in turn contact the Justice Department to demand immediate action. COFO requested that in the meantime members of Congress urge Justice to assign marshals to areas where it had projects, to set up branch offices in Mississippi cities, and to warn state and local officials that the Constitution was going to be enforced. COFO also asked legislators to urge President Johnson to meet with leaders of the Summer Project and to make immediate use of his authority under 10 U.S.C. section 332 to employ federal troops and/or the Mississippi National Guard to enforce the laws of the United States and "suppress rebellion." How successful COFO was in enlisting congressional support is unclear, but at least some of those it contacted did enlist in its campaign. [65]

Despite such support, COFO's call for massive federal intervention went largely unanswered. The White House was clearly worried about the impending crisis in Mississippi, but its principal concern seemed to be having answers for reporters who might question Johnson about what action the national government could and would take. Well into June, demands for federal intervention, and even requests to discuss the situation with the president, went unanswered. [66]

The Justice Department was only slightly more responsive than the White House. After visiting Mississippi at the beginning of June, Marshall did recommend using some gentle persuasion to get the FBI more actively involved in the struggle against racist violence. He proposed encouraging the Bureau to develop techniques for identifying terrorists and prodding it to investigate their connections with law enforcement officials. His most concrete suggestion was that the FBI be urged to employ against Klan-type organizations the sort of infiltration tactics it had used against Communist groups. Kennedy accepted Marshall's recommendations and passed them along to the White House, adding a proposal that Johnson ask the Bureau to report to him by the end of June on what it had learned about the membership, leadership, and plans of the Klan and similar groups. [67]

Despite considering "the situation in Mississippi to be very dangerous," the attorney general urged no other innovations. [68] The Justice Department remained committed to the principle that "problems of enforcement are the responsibility of local law enforcement agencies." [69] On July 1 Deputy Attorney General Katzenbach sent the president a memorandum in which he argued against any fundamental change in federal policy. Katzenbach conceded that the twenty-seven professors from prestigious northeastern law schools, led by Mark deWolfe Howe of Harvard, who had asserted recently that the president possessed the legal authority to take protective action in Mississippi, were correct. There was available, he acknowledged, a great deal of information with which the government could establish that there had been the sort of complete breakdown of state law enforcement which would make it possible for the president, under the authority of sections 332 and 333, to use troops to enforce the Fourteenth Amendment. "But in view of the extreme seriousness of the

use of those sections, I believe that the government should have more
evidence than it presently has of the inability of State and local officials to
maintain law and order—as a matter of wisdom as well as law." Nor did
Katzenbach favor sending marshals to Mississippi. Here again, the problems were "more practical than legal." The marshal service was neither
large enough nor well enough trained to assume broad-scale responsibility
for maintaining order. Furthermore, the presence of federal law enforcement personnel would "aggravate the emotions of the populace." White
Mississippians would blame them for the actions of the civil rights workers they were protecting. More important, the use of marshals would
alienate local peace officers, who might then abdicate their own responsibilities. In Katzenbach's opinion,

> Once local law enforcement ceases to function in any sizeable area, the
> number of personnel required to maintain control without the actual
> use of weapons exceeds the manpower resources of every branch of the
> federal service except the military. It is essential, therefore, to encour-
> age State and local law enforcement agencies to carry out their respon-
> sibilities and, if at all possible, to avoid using federal personnel in such
> a way so as [sic] to provide an excuse for abandonment of responsibilities
> by such agencies.[70]

Justice Department priorities remained essentially what they had been
throughout the tenure of Burke Marshall and Robert Kennedy. In mid-
June, Jim Peck, who had suffered a severe beating while the national
government relied on local authorities to protect the Freedom Riders,
asked Marshall, "Does somebody have to be killed before the Federal government intercedes?"[71]

The answer, unfortunately, was yes. Among those who would have to
die were three participants in the Mississippi Summer Project. Michael
"Mickey" Schwerner, a twenty-four-year-old graduate of Cornell and an
experienced settlement house worker, came to Meridian, along with his
wife Rita, in early 1964 to set up a voter education center for CORE.
There he met and enlisted the assistance of James Chaney, a twenty-one-
year-old black high school dropout who worked as a plasterer and who was
also active in CORE. Together, the Schwerners and Chaney reached out to
the black youth of Meridian, and with the aid of high school students,
Mickey and James began canvassing for potential voters. Their project
experienced some petty harassment (such as threatening telephone calls,

periodic shutting off of utility service, and eviction from its headquarters), and Mickey was arrested once for blocking a crosswalk during a demonstration. But it encountered no violence. The local "power structure," which loathed the Klan, had ordered the police not to harm the Schwerners and to see to it that no klansmen did either. Thus, the environment into which Mickey and Chaney brought Andrew Goodman seemed relatively safe. Goodman, a twenty-year-old student at Queens College, was the son of a New York building contractor and a SNCC member. Like Schwerner, he was Jewish. Goodman met Chaney and the Schwerners at the Oxford, Ohio, training center where they had gone to pick up volunteers for the Meridian project. Early on the morning of June 20 the three young men bid what was supposed to be a temporary farewell to Rita, who planned to join them later in Mississippi, and drove south to die together.[72]

Before leaving Oxford they had received word of some trouble in Longdale, a black community about forty miles northeast of Meridian in Neshoba County. On May 31 the Schwerners had held a civil rights meeting there in the Mount Zion Methodist Church, where they hoped to set up a freedom school. On the night of June 16 klansmen attacked members of the Mount Zion congregation, and someone burned down the church. Upon arriving in Meridian on the evening of June 20 Schwerner learned some of the details of what had happened at Longdale. He also heard that the National Lawyer's Guild's Committee for Legal Assistance in the South wanted someone to locate witnesses its attorneys could interview. Schwerner resolved to go to Neshoba County the following day. Chaney and Goodman decided to accompany him.[73]

On Sunday, June 21, the three of them drove to Longdale, where they talked with several black residents and examined the pile of ashes that had once been the Mount Zion church. On their return journey, at about 4:30 P.M., Neshoba County Deputy Sheriff Cecil Ray Price stopped their station wagon, claiming they had been speeding. With the assistance of two highway patrolmen, Price took the three civil rights workers to the county jail in Philadelphia. There Chaney, the driver, was booked for speeding and the other two were held for investigation. A few minutes after 10:00 P.M., Price told all three of them they could go if Chaney would post a $20 cash bond. He did, and a little after 10:30 the three young men drove out of Philadelphia in the station wagon. They never reached Meridian.[74]

Even before their release, worried civil rights workers, told to expect them back by 4:00 P.M., had begun making inquiries. Beginning at 5:30 P.M. telephone calls went out from COFO offices in Meridian and Jackson to law enforcement agencies in the Philadelphia area. Neshoba County Sheriff Lawrence Rainey did not answer his telephone, and the city police, the highway patrol, and someone at the jail all denied knowing the whereabouts of the missing men. At 10:00 P.M. law student Sherman Kaplan called FBI agent H. F. Helgeson in Jackson, and about a half hour later COFO telephoned a Justice Department lawyer, Frank Schwelb. Although both men were contacted again during the evening, neither proved particularly helpful. When Robert Weil of the Jackson COFO office asked Schwelb for an investigation, he got a lecture on the limits of FBI jurisdiction and authority.[75]

By the next day, the federal government was becoming a good deal more helpful. Ron Carver of the Atlanta SNCC office called John Doar in Washington, and at 6:00 A.M. Doar assured him he had invested the FBI with the power to look into the matter. Hoover delayed until noon, but then ordered the Bureau office in Memphis to make a search. Prodded by the federal government, the Mississippi Highway Patrol and the Neshoba County Sheriff's Department also began looking for the missing station wagon. When James Farmer called the White House late in the morning, Lee White assured him he would be in touch with the Justice Department and that everything possible was being done. That was not quite true. Not until 6:20 P.M. did Attorney General Kennedy and his aides determine that the time had come for the federal government to go all out, treating the disappearance of the three civil rights workers as a kidnapping and employing the procedures and techniques normally used in abduction cases. Doar relayed this decision to the FBI. The next morning Inspector Joseph Sullivan arrived in Meridian from New Orleans with five agents to take charge of the search. The Bureau eventually committed 150 men to the case. To one Philadelphia resident, it seemed that the FBI was everywhere.[76]

Neshoba County resented the Bureau's presence, and that of other outsiders as well. Philadelphia residents threatened reporters from the *New York Times* and *Newsweek* and beat one from the *Detroit News*. Someone hit a law student over the head with a heavy chain. When an integrated team of attorneys from the Committee for Legal Assistance in the South, which included the wife of Michigan Congressman Charles Diggs, went to Philadelphia to interview Sheriff Rainey, a mob of more than one hundred persons surrounded the group outside the courthouse. Rainey and some other Neshoba County residents insisted the three civil rights workers really were not missing at all, but were perpetrating a hoax to embarrass their community.[77]

The implausibility of that theory became apparent on the afternoon of June 23 when the FBI, aided by a tip from a citizen, located the burned-out hulk of the station wagon in Bogue Chitto Swamp about thirteen miles from Philadelphia. Hoover now dispatched Assistant Director Al Rosen to Philadelphia to take over the investigation. Rosen flew south in a presidential aircraft. By now the White House as well as the Bureau and the Justice Department was under intense pressure from members of Congress, the press, the public, and parents of Mississippi volunteers to break the case. Aided by fifty highway patrolmen and a contingent of sailors from a nearby naval air station, the FBI searched the swamp. It found nothing.[78]

Not until August 4 did the Bureau finally locate the missing civil rights workers. By then they were dead. On July 31 a paid informant, whose identity was so secret the FBI would not reveal it to Justice Department lawyers or even the attorney general, told Inspector Sullivan that the missing men were buried under an earthen dam on the Olen Burrage farm. With the aid of a helicopter, agents located the dam the next day, but it took until the fourth for them to get a search warrant and gather together the heavy earth-moving equipment needed to tear it down. After a full day of digging with a bulldozer and hand spades, a search party unearthed the badly decomposed remains of Schwerner, Chaney, and Goodman. All three had been shot. In addition, Chaney's skull, his right forearm, and several of his ribs had been shattered. A pathologist who examined the black victim's body at his mother's request concluded he had been beaten severely with a blunt instrument or a chain, a conclusion which squared with an account of the killing Governor Johnson obtained from acquaintances in the Klan. They told him a klansman, aroused by the fact that Chaney "was acting pretty smart aleck and talking pretty big," had struck him with a trace chain.[79]

While the FBI was searching for Chaney and his companions, another black man died a violent death in Georgia. Lemuel Penn, director of adult and vocational education for the District of Columbia Public Schools, was a lieutenant colonel in the army reserve. After completing two weeks of annual training at Fort Benning, near Columbus, Georgia, he and two other black officers set out to drive home to Washington on July 10. In the early hours of the following morning, while passing through the college town of Athens in the northeastern part of the state, they aroused the interest of three members of the local Klan klavern, who saw their out-of-state license plates. Having heard rumors that Martin Luther King intended to make Georgia a testing ground for the Civil Rights Act, the klansmen concluded that these "out of town niggers" might stir up trouble in their community. They followed them out of Athens, and on a bridge across the Broad River near the village of Colbert pulled alongside the black officers' car. Two of the klansmen opened fire with shotguns, and a load of buckshot slammed into Penn's head, killing him instantly.[80]

His murder, along with the disappearance of Chaney, Goodman, and Schwerner, generated tremendous pressure for the sort of federal intervention in southern law enforcement the Justice Department had resisted for years. The White House received telegrams from all over the country about the Penn killing. A night letter from a number of St. Louis residents demanded "federal protection for the lives of Negro and white citizens of the south, especially in Georgia and Mississippi." Its authors told the president his duty was clear.[81] Johnson, who sent a personal representative to Penn's funeral, apparently agreed. In a letter of condolence to the slain man's widow, the president assured her that "the Federal Government . . . will do everything possible to apprehend those responsible for the heinous crime which took your husband from you and your children."[82]

Because Penn was an army officer traveling under military orders, there were obvious grounds for federal intervention in his case, but it was the highly publicized Neshoba County incident which generated the greatest pressures for the national government to assume a more active role in the South. As soon as word spread about the disappearance of the three civil rights workers, supporters of the missing men began planning demonstrations at the Justice Department and the White House. They also asked for appointments with top government officials. The parents of Schwerner and Goodman flew to Washington, where they talked with Nicholas Katzenbach and met briefly with Robert Kennedy. Congressmen William Fitz Ryan (D-N.Y.) and Ogden Reid (R-N.Y.), who represented the districts in which the Goodmans lived and Mickey Schwerner had resided, called the White House, asking if the parents could also see the president. At first Johnson said no, but after Lee White pointed out what the Republican *New York Herald Tribune,* owned by Reid's family, could do with his refusal, the president changed his mind. Johnson assured the weeping mothers and fathers that the government would use every resource at its disposal to solve the mystery. On June 29 he met with Rita Schwerner, and in July he met with Chaney's mother, who came to the White House escorted by James Farmer.[83]

Apparently, the renowned Johnson "treatment" was less than completely effective with relatives of the Neshoba County victims. After her visit Rita Schwerner held a press conference at which she criticized the president for refusing to commit five thousand men to the search for her husband. During July and August her mother, Mickey's father, and Goodman's parents all wrote to the White House, pressing for action in the Neshoba County case and for a greater effort by the national government to control violence in Mississippi. It was essential, Nathan Schwerner asserted, "that a police power be exercised by the Federal government."[84]

Mothers and fathers of other Mississippi volunteers also pressured Washington. Thirteen of them from all over the country, billing themselves as the Parents Emergency Committee, met with White and Katzenbach on June 24. Citing views expressed by Mark DeWolfe Howe and other legal authorities, they disputed Robert Kennedy's contention that the Constitution prohibited any sort of federal police force in Mississippi. The response they received was "most disheartening." Nevertheless, COFO urged parents of volunteers to use their influence "to pressure President Johnson and Attorney General Kennedy into a commitment to protect workers *before* violence occurs." It suggested they ask that marshals be stationed throughout the South and that the Justice Department and the FBI provide full and immediate help. COFO also suggested that parents seek to persuade newspapers and radio and television stations in their communities of the need for federal protection. Relatives of the volunteers responded, bombarding the White House, the Justice Department, and members of Congress with calls for action and using COFO-supplied information to point out to the president that he did have the authority necessary to safeguard the rights and safety of their loved ones. In the opinion of Wiley Branton, the parents of white student volunteers "helped to create a kind of pressure to which the Justice Department reacted politically."[85] While continuing to insist that law enforcement was a state and local responsibility and that the federal government had no authority to provide police protection, Justice offered parents assurances that "all persons who intimidate, harass, or harm civil rights workers in violation of federal law will be prosecuted to the full extent of the law."[86]

Mothers and fathers were not the only persons insisting that the national government do more. After visiting Philadelphia, SNCC's John Lewis urged that protection be provided for civil rights workers in each of Mississippi's eighty-two counties.[87] Following the discovery of the bodies of Schwerner, Chaney, and Goodman, he declared, "The federal government can no longer afford to remain aloof while unprotected students . . . try to ensure constitutional rights that never should have been denied."[88] Lewis communicated the same message to President Johnson. CORE delivered it to the government as a whole, picketing federal buildings in several northern cities and the Justice Department in Washington. With the assistance of Congressman Jonathan Bingham (D-N.Y.), a COFO delegation consisting of Bob Moses, Lawrence Guyot, and James Forman managed to obtain a meeting with Marshall, Doar, and Arthur Schlesinger, Jr. They were not pleased with the attitude of the assistant attorney general, who expressed unwillingness to become involved in a "guerilla war" by arresting a Mississippi sheriff.[89]

COFO, on the other hand, was anxious for combat with Mississippi peace officers. On July 10 it filed suit in the U.S. District Court for the Southern District of Mississippi against Lawrence Rainey, all other sheriffs and deputies in the state, the head of the Mississippi Highway Patrol, the Ku Klux Klan, and the White Citizens Councils. The plaintiffs in this action alleged the existence of a conspiracy to commit terroristic acts intended to hinder or prevent the exercise of constitutionally protected rights. They also charged that such acts already had been committed, and requested an injunction restraining the defendants and the groups they represented from using force against themselves and other persons in their position. COFO also wanted a federal commissioner appointed in every Mississippi county to ensure the safety of black residents and student volunteers. In addition, the plaintiffs' attorney, William Kunstler, asked the Justice Department to protect all of those involved in the presentation of the case.[90]

Although Judge Sidney Mize dismissed the COFO suit, pressure for federal intervention continued to build from other directions. The Southern Regional Council published a pamphlet in which it argued that if Mississippi, its political subdivisions, and its people continued to shirk their law enforcement responsibilities, the national government had an inescapable duty to act. The NAACP took an even harder line. Responding to what it characterized as the "states rights murders" of the three civil rights workers, five hundred delegates to its national convention staged a protest demonstration at the Department of Justice. On June 26 the convention adopted a resolution calling on the federal government to exercise its power under Article IV, section 4, of the Constitution to ensure to every state a republican form of government by displacing Governor Johnson and his subordinates and taking over completely the administration of Mississippi. Because of the NAACP's importance and its reputation for moderation, the White House took very seriously this "most severe and drastic" recommendation.[91]

Although extreme, the NAACP proposal reflected a widespread belief that the time had come for the national government to treat the disease afflicting Mississippi. Hundreds of petitioning citizens from New York, New Jersey, Michigan, and the state of Washington communicated that message to the White House. A Louis Harris poll reiterated it, disclosing that although two out of three Americans opposed the Summer Project, 71 percent of the population thought the president should send troops to Mississippi if the shooting and killing there continued.[92] "Now it is perfectly true," an Illinois man wrote the president, "that the constitution relegates the enforcement of law and order to the states, but the federal government still has the right, and more important, the Duty to step in . . . when a state cannot—or will not—enforce its own law and order, or when it manifestly violates the rights guaranteed by the constitution."[93]

Numerous newspapers expressed similar sentiments. The *New York Times,* for example, endorsed federal intervention, if this were necessary to prevent intimidation and violence from depriving blacks of their constitutional rights, and also supported the use of whatever force was needed to make such intervention effective. Predictably, such black newspapers as the *Baltimore Afro-American* and the *Atlanta Daily World* demanded vigorous action by the national government to uphold law and order in Mississippi. Even such moderate white-owned southern papers as the *Atlanta Constitution* and the *Arkansas Gazette* agreed that if state and local officials continued to default on their responsibility to guarantee personal security, federal authorities would have to assume a much larger law enforcement role.[94]

On Capitol Hill a bipartisan array of northern liberals echoed the press and the public. Four days after Goodman, Schwerner, and Chaney disappeared, New York's Republican senators, Jacob Javits and Kenneth Keating, called on the president to send federal marshals to Mississippi. Somewhat later, Congressmen Robert Ellsworth (R-Kans.) and Donald Rumsfeld (R-Ill.) contacted the White House to express their concern about constituents who were serving as student volunteers and to urge federal action to prevent further violence in Mississippi. The most insistent member of Congress was William F. Ryan (D-N.Y.), who bombarded the White House with stacks of petitions and in early October 1964 released an open letter to the president in which he and seventeen other congressmen from Johnson's own party called for "massive federal assistance to put a halt to further violence in connection with civil rights activities in Mississippi."[95] LBJ read this communication "with deep interest." Responding defensively to the Ryan letter, Lee White enumerated the many things which, he said, the federal government had done since the previous July to combat racial violence in Mississippi.[96]

The list was lengthy, for the Penn killing and the Neshoba County disappearances had spurred long quiescent Washington into action. By July 14 top FBI officials were acknowledging "the need for expanding our coverage of Klan and Klan type organizations" and instructing field agents "to step up [their] informant program in such" groups.[97] With both Katzenbach and the president displaying great interest in the Penn case, the Bureau made a massive commitment to tracking down the killers of the black reserve officer. On July 12 J. Edgar Hoover dispatched Assistant Director Joseph Casper, who happened to be vacationing in Myrtle Beach, South Carolina, to Athens, Georgia. Hoover instructed Casper to "bear down completely and thoroughly in this case so that it may be promptly resolved."[98] To assist him with the investigation, the Bureau detailed experienced agents from offices in northern cities such as Washington, New York, and Newark, being careful to ensure that the men selected were not former police officers and had no relatives in Georgia government or law enforcement. By the beginning of August the FBI had fifty-three agents looking for Penn's killers and had expended over 14,500 man-hours on the case. A few days later one of the men involved in the shooting confessed, identifying the others. On August 6 Hoover and Attorney General Kennedy announced the arrests of four members of Clarke County Klavern 244 of the United Klans of America: Herbert Guest, thirty-seven, a gun-collecting garage owner with a first-grade education; Joseph Howard Sims, forty-one, a machinist and the Kladd (sergeant at arms) of the Athens Klan; Cecil William Myers, twenty-five, a textile worker who generally went about with a pistol strapped to his hip; and James S. Lackey, twenty-nine, a gas station attendant and the man from whom the FBI had extracted the admissions that broke the case.[99]

Although the Bureau's quick success in Georgia was impressive, the vast expansion of its role in Mississippi was even more dramatic. The reason for the change was presidential pressure. Lyndon Johnson took an intense personal interest in the disappearance of Schwerner, Chaney, and Goodman. To him, the three missing civil rights workers symbolized "the whole racial issue brought together in a specific situation."[100] The president followed the case closely, personally questioning FBI officials about the progress of the investigation and ordering it intensified after the discovery of the bodies. Johnson sensed that the explosive situation in Mississippi was building toward an ominous climax which could heighten racial tensions across the country and endanger his chances of winning a term of his own in the 1964 elections. The president wanted action—and he wanted it immediately.[101]

On the evening of June 23, 1964, the day searchers located the burned-out hulk of the station wagon the three civil rights workers had been driving, Johnson summoned Kennedy, Katzenbach, and Marshall—but not J. Edgar Hoover—to a meeting at the White House. Five hours of discussion produced a decision to send Allen Dulles, retired head of the Central Intelligence Agency, to Mississippi as the president's personal representative. His assignment was to discuss law enforcement problems with Governor Johnson and selected private citizens. Before departing for Jackson, Dulles was careful to meet with Hoover and assure him of his intention to do nothing that might create an impression of direct involvement in the Neshoba County investigation. Nevertheless, implicit in his mission were both presidential criticism of the FBI and a threat to the director's bureaucratic "turf."[102]

Accompanied by John Doar, Dulles arrived in Jackson on June 24. He discussed what might be done to strengthen law enforcement in Mississippi with both Governor Johnson and Colonel Birdsong of the Department of Public Safety and also dined with fifteen public officials and business leaders. The former CIA head offered assurances that "full-scale" federal intervention was not imminent. On the other hand, at a meeting with civil rights leaders the following day he indicated the national government was prepared, if necessary, to use troops to control the "friction" in Mississippi. Benjamin Muse, with whom Dulles also talked on June 25, told him that outside journalists considered federal military intervention inevitable. According to Muse, the state's business and political leaders expected outrages against blacks to continue until a cathartic convulsion jolted Mississippians to their senses. [103]

Dulles returned to Washington convinced that an expanded federal presence in Mississippi was essential. During a two-hour meeting at the White House on June 26 he acknowledged that primary responsibility for the suppression of terroristic activities should remain with state and local authorities. He even suggested enhancing their effectiveness by increasing cooperation between the president and Governor Johnson. But Dulles also told LBJ and Justice Department leaders that direct federal action was needed. Muse had explained to him that because of its longtime involvement in combating communism the FBI was popular in Mississippi. Its agents, he believed, would inspire less resentment than any other element of national authority which might be deployed there. Hence, Dulles recommended that the Bureau commit more men to Mississippi and assume some responsibility for deterring racist terrorism. Doar and Katzenbach agreed with him. By now, even Robert Kennedy recognized that what Dulles proposed was the only viable alternative to sending troops. [104]

The president shared the attorney general's reluctance to resort to military force, and the White House carefully avoided promising federal police protection for civil rights workers. With the ACLU joining other groups in criticizing the administration's failure to act, however, Johnson instructed Hoover to send fifty more agents to Mississippi. On June 29 Robert Colby Nelson of the *Christian Science Monitor* observed, "The past week's events in Mississippi have spurred the federal government toward a new role in the prevention of racial strife." Its involvement continued to grow. One of Dulles's suggestions was that the FBI, which had no field office between Memphis and New Orleans, open one in Mississippi. With political pressure on him mounting, Hoover ordered his aides to study the idea. Then, on July 10, he dramatically flew to Jackson to open a field office there. State and city officials were honored guests at the ceremonies, and the director stressed in his remarks that the key to keeping the peace remained their observance and enforcement of the law. The opening of the Jackson office, he assured Governor Johnson, represented no intrusion into

Mississippi's jurisdiction. Hoover offered FBI training for the state's highway patrolmen and obtained promises of cooperation from Mississippi
Attorney General Joe Patterson. Although the director's words sounded
somewhat like echoes from the past, he and the Bureau had, however
reluctantly, altered course. While in Mississippi, Hoover met with
Charles Evers, Medgar's brother. When Evers expressed fear for his own
life, the director told him to keep in touch with Roy K. Moore, the agent
who would be in charge of the new field office. Hoover also publicly
denounced violent resistance to the civil rights laws. [105]

Not long after he returned to Washington, the FBI launched a major
attack on the Ku Klux Klan. On July 30 the Bureau transferred responsibility for monitoring the activities of klansmen from its General Investigative Division to its Domestic Intelligence Division. At the same time,
Hoover authorized Domestic Intelligence to apply counterintelligence and
disruptive tactics to the Klan and similar white hate groups. William
Sullivan, the assistant director who headed that unit, committed it to
destroying the KKK, using penetration techniques employed earlier
against the Communist party. By August 27 his office had developed a
recommendation for a "hard-hitting" program to disrupt seventeen Klan
organizations and nine other white hate groups, all but three of them in
the South. [106] On September 2 Hoover ordered implementation of this
Counterintelligence Program (COINTELPRO). Its purpose, he declared,
was "to expose, disrupt and otherwise neutralize the activities of the various Klans and hate organizations, their leadership and adherents." [107] The
focus of this COINTELPRO was the KKK's violence-prone "action
groups." [108] A year after launching it Hoover informed the attorney general, "We . . . are seizing every opportunity to disrupt the activities of
Klan organizations." [109]

Besides harassing these groups, the FBI penetrated them with informants who kept it apprised of their plans and activities. During the first
year of the COINTELPRO, the Bureau recruited 774 spies. During that
period about 70 percent of all newly enrolled klansmen were FBI informants. The Bureau penetrated every one of the fourteen Klan organizations then in existence, and in at least half of the units spies won election
to top-level leadership positions. By 1965 over 15 percent of the Ku Klux
Klan was working for the FBI. Information supplied by an army of informants enabled the Bureau to track down those responsible for such acts of
anti–civil rights violence as the burning and bombing of more than twenty

homes in the McComb area. Sometimes it even enabled the FBI "to forestall violence in certain racially explosive areas."[110]

The Bureau was finally doing something to make Mississippi safer for its black residents and for student volunteers from the North. Hoover continued to insist that the FBI was not a police force and that it would not protect civil rights workers. But as the *St. Louis Post-Dispatch* observed, the mere presence of more than 150 agents in the state tended to discourage murder, arson, beatings, and shootings. Occasionally, the Bureau would provide civil rights workers with a more active form of protection. In Philadelphia, Mississippi, for example, two agents patrolled the black community at night, guarding a COFO office which klansmen had threatened to bomb or burn. When a policeman in the same town refused to apprehend armed whites who showed up outside a black youth center looking for a fight, FBI Inspector Joseph Sullivan berated and shook the officer. Although the policeman still made no arrests, nightriding did abate in Philadelphia. Sometimes Hoover's men even unobtrusively protected the director's nemesis, Martin Luther King, Jr.[111] In December 1964 a onetime Justice Department critic of the FBI declared: "There was once a legitimate basis for bitching, but along with the rest of the country, the bureau is now accepting its responsibility in civil rights—and doing a hell of a job in Mississippi."[112]

Indeed, during the last half of 1964 the FBI did far more than the Justice Department. Even after the disappearance of Schwerner, Chaney, and Goodman, Katzenbach continued to oppose the use of troops, or even marshals, in Mississippi,[113] and Burke Marshall continued to respond to letters asking that something be done to ensure the safety of the student volunteers there with assertions that "the Federal Government has no authority to provide ordinary police protection."[114] The Justice Department was troubled enough, however, to increase the number of attorneys it assigned to Mississippi and to consider opening branch offices of the Civil Rights Division in Jackson and McComb.[115] It was also beginning to think seriously about criminal prosecutions. In the same July 1 memorandum in which he argued against the use of federal personnel to keep the peace in Mississippi, Katzenbach suggested that "vigorous investigation and prosecution where federal crimes are involved [might] serve in conjunction with state police action" to forestall a complete breakdown of law and order.[116] While insisting that the federal government could not provide protection, Katzenbach's assistant, Joseph Dolan, promised, "All persons who intimidate, harass, or harm civil rights workers in violation of federal law will be prosecuted to the full extent of the law." Even Burke Marshall, although still dubious about the chances for success before hostile southern juries, came around to endorsing prosecution of racial murders and other violations of civil rights. Even if unsuccessful, he concluded, these could improve the law enforcement climate in the South.[117]

This subtle change of attitude within the Justice Department was important, for in Mississippi, as in Georgia, the invigorated investigative efforts of the FBI produced arrests in a major civil rights killing. When President Johnson ordered additional agents into the state in June, he vowed to keep them there as long as necessary. That proved to be quite a while, since apprehending those responsible for the Philadelphia murders took six months. By late September of 1964 the Bureau was rapidly building up a network of informants within the White Knights of the Ku Klux Klan, the principal terrorist group in the area. Information obtained from carefully recruited spies pointed agents to two Meridian truck drivers who had rather suddenly moved out of the area. By early November the FBI had located James Jordan in Gulfport, Mississippi, and Doyle Barnette in Cullen, Louisiana, and had obtained signed statements from the two men in which they admitted participation in the abduction/murders and identified the other persons involved. The Bureau did not move against those Jordan and Barnette linked to the killings for nearly a month, probably because it was still gathering corroborating evidence. Delmer Dennis, a recently recruited informant whom the leader of the White Knights, Imperial Wizard Sam Holloway Bowers, fortuitously selected as one of his top aides, was supplying the FBI with a good deal of information. Then suddenly, just before Thanksgiving, the Bureau announced that it knew who the killers were. The reason for this dramatic gesture seems to be that civil rights leaders, angered that Hoover had told some reporters Dr. Martin Luther King, Jr., was "the most notorious liar in the country," were demanding that the president fire the director.[118]

Nine days later, on December 4, the FBI made nineteen arrests in the Philadelphia case. Among those it took into custody were the Neshoba County sheriff, Lawrence Rainey; his deputy, Cecil Ray Price; and a Philadelphia policeman, Otha Neal Burkes. Arrested along with them were six other Neshoba County residents and eight Meridian klansmen, as well as Jordan and Barnette.[119]

The FBI had provided the Justice Department and the White House with the perfect response, not only to questions about when the killers of Chaney, Schwerner, and Goodman would be apprehended, but also to complaints about the federal government's failure to combat violence in Mississippi.[120] Both the Bureau and the new Johnson administration had come a long way in one short year. Prodded by the president, the FBI, for so long unwilling to do anything to protect civil rights activists, had now launched an ongoing program to disrupt and destroy the terrorist organization responsible for the worst of the violence against them. Propelled by events during the Freedom Summer, at least one federal agency had moved beyond the sort of temporary crisis management that had characterized the national government's response to disorders such as those at Little Rock and Ole Miss. The Justice Department still clung to the assumptions about federalism that had limited its role since 1954, but pressure from the president and an outraged public was also moving it toward a more activist posture. The bombing, burning, and bloodshed that convulsed parts of the South during the summer of 1964, and the persistent failure of local authorities to control this violence, had rendered a policy of avoiding substantial federal intervention in southern law enforcement no longer tenable. After the Bureau made its arrests in the Philadelphia case, the *Arkansas Gazette* observed: "The sovereign state of Mississippi was manifestly unwilling or incapable of solving the crimes, so . . . the FBI had to do the job."[121] Its editorial comment capsulized the lesson of 1964: if states refused to control and punish anti–civil rights violence, the federal government would have to step in and do it for them.

The *Price* and *Guest* Cases

After the FBI apprehended her husband's killers, Rita Schwerner reminded a reporter, "Arrests in themselves are nothing unless you can get convictions."[1] Obtaining justice in southern courts remained virtually impossible, as a jury had recently demonstrated by acquitting the killers of Lemuel Penn. Despite its preference for reliance on local institutions, the Justice Department had to face the fact that in the South these institutions simply were not working. Nor could it ignore the swelling chorus of nonsouthern voices demanding the punishment of racist killers. The Civil Rights Division decided it had no choice but to initiate federal prosecutions against the slayers of Chaney, Goodman, and Schwerner, and against the killers of Lemuel Penn as well, but the cases it brought soon foundered on the inadequacies of existing law. Fortunately for the Justice Department, the Supreme Court shared the spreading belief that the national government must do something about anti–civil rights violence. It rescued the Georgia and Mississippi prosecutions—and in the process went a long way toward giving the national government the legal capacity to deal with the situation in the South.

Of particular importance was the Court's decision in *United States v. Guest,*[2] a legal monument to the shortcomings of both Georgia justice and long-standing Justice Department policies. Nine days after the FBI made its arrests in the Penn case, the United States attorney for the Middle District of Georgia, Floyd Buford, announced that if a state grand jury would indict the suspects, federal authorities were prepared to turn them over to Georgia for trial.[3] Buford had wanted the national government to try the klansmen first, for he considered "this case with its national importance and nationwide attention it has received an excellent vehicle for prosecution under section 241."[4] In addition, the U.S. attorney had grave

doubts about the competence of the local prosecutor, Solicitor General
Clete Johnson of Georgia's Northern Judicial Circuit, whom he regarded
as too inexperienced to be trusted with such an important case. Buford
informed St. John Barrett of the Civil Rights Division that he had no
confidence in Johnson and asked him to relay his reservations to Burke
Marshall, but Marshall and the Justice Department were determined to
defer to prosecution by local authorities.[5]

Buford therefore publicly promised that the federal government would
"cooperate and assist the state officials in every way possible in the state
prosecution."[6] The FBI agreed to make the results of its investigation
available to Clete Johnson, and on August 15, 1964, supplied him with a
synopsis of a 1,360-page report it had prepared. While the Bureau assisted Johnson, Buford took steps to ensure that the local prosecutor
would not botch the case. The U.S. attorney told Johnson bluntly that he
would be a fool to try it himself and encouraged him to request the appointment of a well-qualified special assistant to help him. As a result of
Buford's initiative, Governor Carl Sanders designated Jeff Wayne, a veteran criminal lawyer from nearby Hall County and the solicitor general of
the Northeast Judicial Circuit, to act as a special prosecutor in the case.
Wayne, who enjoyed a reputation as an aggressive prosecutor, soon asked
the FBI to provide an agent to sit at the counsel table during the trial to
assist the prosecution in preparing its witnesses. The Bureau readily as-
sented to this request. It also agreed to check out the ninety-six individuals on the petit jury list and to provide four agents to testify before
the Madison County grand jury.[7]

That body assembled on August 25 in a courthouse situated squarely in
the center of the main road through the tiny county seat of Danielsville, a
farming village of 363 souls nestled amidst poultry, dairy, grain, and
soybean farms in the rolling hills of northeast Georgia. After deliberating
for less than four hours, the grand jury returned murder indictments
against Cecil Myers, Joseph Howard Sims, and James S. Lackey.[8] It acted
on the basis of evidence which seemed more than adequate to convict the
three klansmen. On August 6 Lackey had confessed to the FBI, laying out
the story of how Penn had died and implicating Myers and Sims. According to his statement, early on the morning of July 11 he and the other two
defendants had followed a white Chevrolet out of Athens. In the vicinity
of the Madison County community of Colbert, Sims had announced he
was "going to kill me a nigger." At the urging of his companions, Lackey,

the driver, had drawn abreast of the Chevrolet. "When I was alongside the negroes' car, both Myers and Sims fired shotguns into the negroes' car," Lackey admitted.[9]

His confession left no doubt about how Penn had died, or about who was responsible for his murder. Nevertheless, the killers escaped conviction. Lackey's attorney, John Williford, persuaded Judge Kelly Skelton to sever his client's case from those of the other defendants, but the prosecution was still able to use the statement against Sims and Myers. Johnson and Wayne managed, with the testimony of eight witnesses, to convince Skelton that the Penn killing was the product of a conspiracy, and thus to receive Lackey's statement into evidence against Sims and Myers as an admission of their coconspirator. The prosecution attempted to corroborate his confession with testimony from Herbert Guest, the other Athens klansman arrested by the FBI. Guest proved to be an extremely uncooperative witness, repudiating a signed statement he had given to the Bureau earlier. This statement revealed that Guest had seen Sims armed with a shotgun soon after the murder, that the defendants had discussed details of the killing, and that they had admitted their responsibility for it. The prosecution also produced two other witnesses who had been in Guest's garage when Sims and Myers returned from shooting Penn. The rest of the state's evidence, which included the testimony of the victim's traveling companions, added little to its proof. Nevertheless, the prosecution's case was a strong one.[10]

Certainly, it should have been more than adequate to overcome the rather feeble defense presented by James Hudson, a top Athens criminal lawyer, and James Darsey, a former Justice Department attorney who had once prosecuted Japanese war criminals. Taking advantage of a unique Georgia procedural rule, they put Sims and Myers on the stand to make unsworn statements about which they could not be cross-examined. Beyond these self-serving assertions of innocence, the defense could offer little but the testimony of two witnesses who claimed to have seen the defendants in an all-night restaurant in Athens at the time of the murder. Since one of these witnesses had actually spent most of the night in question across the street and the other admittedly had focused his attention on chain reading a pile of newspapers, they failed to provide the defendants with a really convincing alibi.[11]

Nevertheless, on September 4, after deliberating for only a little over three hours, an all-white jury acquitted both Sims and Myers. The verdict was in part the result of what Buford saw as "hostility toward the Federal government resulting from the passage of the Civil Rights Act of 1964, and Federal involvement in civil rights problems in the South generally."[12] The FBI's Atlanta Field Office thought the acquittals reflected community disagreement with the principle of intervention by the national government "in a purely local matter." There were disturbing indications that the verdict was also a product of racism. The trial had taken place in a segregated courtroom, and when Penn's companions, Major Charles E. Brown and Colonel John D. Howard, testified in their officers' uniforms, white jurors, some of them former privates and corporals, evinced obvious displeasure.[13] During his closing argument, defense attorney Darsey "hammered at the racial issue."[14] He accused the White House and the Justice Department of unleashing a horde of FBI agents on Madison County with instructions not to "come back until you bring us white meat." When they could obtain this in no other way, he charged, these "carpetbaggers" had brought a sham case.[15] Darsey, his face red with anger, urged the jury to "never let it be said that a Madison County jury converted the electric chair into a sacrificial altar to satisfy the appetite of the clamoring mob."[16] This was the right way to appeal to what he five times reminded its members was an "Anglo-Saxon jury." Two-thirds of the jurors either belonged to or sympathized with the Ku Klux Klan, and those who did not may well have feared recrimination from racist neighbors if they had voted guilty. Only one member of the jury hesitated even briefly before voting to acquit. The swift acquittal of Sims and Myers convinced Johnson there was no point in even bringing Lackey to trial.[17]

Justice Department lawyers considered the Madison County verdicts an obvious miscarriage of justice, and Buford believed the federal government was now obliged to pursue prosecution of the defendants. Surprisingly, so did officials in Washington. The Civil Rights Division, along with the Criminal Division, gave reports of the Penn case a detailed review, and by September 15 it had prepared a rough draft of an indictment.[18] Civil Rights, after years of inertia in the face of mounting racist violence, chose this moment to act, Marshall explained later, because the case involved a murder. Hence, even though Georgia already had tried the accused, the Justice Department had to prosecute them too. He did not believe that "a state prosecution should be a bar . . . to subsequent federal prosecution."[19] Nor did John Doar. In his opinion, if circumstances made effective state prosecution impossible, then subsequent

federal action was appropriate. Doar and Marshall were unwilling to trust
a United States attorney who was a southerner with a case of this type. So,
with the presidential contest between Lyndon Johnson and Senator Barry
Goldwater, a conservative Republican opponent of federal action in the
civil rights field, approaching a conclusion, they sent St. John Barrett
down from Washington to take charge of the prosecution.[20]

On October 16, 1964, prodded by Barrett, a federal grand jury in the
Middle District of Georgia returned indictments charging Sims, Myers,
Lackey, Guest, and two other Athens klansmen, Denver Willis Phillips
and George Hampton Turner, with violation of section 241. These defendants were accused of conspiring to deprive blacks of their rights to full
and equal enjoyment of places of public accommodation, to the equal
utilization without discrimination of facilities owned, operated, or managed by the state of Georgia or its political subdivisions, to the full and
equal use of the public streets in the Athens area on the same terms as
white persons, to travel freely to and from Georgia, and to use the highways and other facilities of interstate commerce within the state, as well as
to deprive them of "other rights exercised and enjoyed by white citizens in
the vicinity of Athens, Georgia."[21]

The indictment did not, of course, charge the Athens klansmen with
murder. That was still not a federal offense. The Penn killing did have
what Marshall regarded as a "federal aspect": the fact that the victim had
been traveling interstate. If Lemuel Penn had been a Georgia resident, the
jurisdictional basis for a federal prosecution would have been difficult, if
not impossible, to establish, he believed.[22] Because the victim was passing through the state on his way home to the District of Columbia, Civil
Rights Division lawyers believed they could reach his killers with section
241. As they saw it, "The right to travel interstate was clearly a federally
protected right."[23] Other knowledgeable observers were not so sure.[24]
Furthermore, as the United States Commission on Civil Rights pointed
out, "Standing alone, proof that the defendants shot Penn would probably
be legally insufficient to permit a jury to find [them] guilty of [the al-
leged] conspiracy."[25] After years of withholding federal protection from
civil rights activists, at least in part because of uncertainty about the scope
of section 241,[26] the Justice Department had charged into a case to which
that law did not clearly apply, seeking to transmute a murder into a crime
the national government could prosecute. Its reasons were emotional and
political.

That became obvious when it also launched a federal prosecution in Mississippi. Two and one-half months before the FBI made arrests for the Neshoba County killings, the Justice Department already had eight lawyers, led by Robert Owen of the Civil Rights Division, working on the case. Despite Burke Marshall's reluctance to displace state criminal justice, he decided national policy required that this be done in Philadelphia, Mississippi. The nature and enormity of the crime and the "atmosphere" surrounding it all influenced his thinking. So too did the "enormous" public pressure for conviction and punishment of those responsible for the killings. Also impossible to ignore was the personal interest the president had taken in the case. It was, in Johnson's opinion, of tremendous symbolic significance. The White House wanted to demonstrate that when the "law of the land" was violated, "appropriate action" would follow. Marshall later claimed to have been convinced from the very beginning that the federal government must prosecute those responsible for the Neshoba County murders.[27]

Perhaps he held such convictions, but it did not become evident for many months that the Justice Department intended to assume exclusive responsibility for this prosecution. At about the time the Georgia jury was acquitting Sims and Myers, FBI officials, led by Inspector Sullivan, were urging Mississippi authorities to file state charges in the Mississippi case. According to Governor Paul Johnson, "They had hit a stone wall and . . . they . . . wanted [me] to have the state arrest the suspects in order to put pressure on them to talk."[28] Probably, Johnson's analysis of the Bureau's motives was correct, for not until November did the FBI obtain the two confessions that enabled it to break the case. As of September, its agents still lacked sufficient evidence to obtain indictments. Nevertheless, Sullivan wanted to convene a federal grand jury, believing that by threatening some law enforcement officials and other persons with indictment for unlawful beatings and arrests and for conspiring to keep civil rights workers out of Neshoba County he could frighten them into talking about the murder. Acting Attorney General Katzenbach and the president thought this tactic was worth trying.[29] Sullivan seems to have thought that state arrests could supplement it, helping to intimidate some klansmen into informing on others. Governor Johnson refused to cooperate. "I told [the FBI] we did not have a case that would stand up, [and] that there was no sense in making the arrest unless the case could hold," he recalled later.[30]

According to Johnson, he was looking at the matter as a lawyer. Although unwilling to act precipitously, he was as determined as anyone else to see the killers convicted. The "law was going to be enforced," the governor claimed. But the Justice Department did not really trust Mississippi officials to bring an honest prosecution. Besides, any state case would have to be brought in the county where the crime occurred. Information the government had obtained implicating Philadelphia and Neshoba County law enforcement personnel in the plot to kill Schwerner, Chaney, and Goodman made the idea of letting local authorities handle this case seem "absolutely absurd" to Civil Rights Division lawyer David Norman.[31]

Just how ludicrous it really was became apparent in late September. Bent on sending a message to the Klan, to those Neshoba County lawmen involved with it, and to the entire Philadelphia community, Inspector Sullivan persuaded the Civil Rights Division to ask U.S. District Judge Harold Cox to convene a federal grand jury in Biloxi. The FBI was prepared to provide it with a 3,278-page report detailing civil rights violations in the Philadelphia area. The Bureau soon received a tip that an effort would be made to force the FBI to reveal the evidence it had gathered and to disclose the identities of its potential witnesses. Three days before the Biloxi hearings a state grand jury in Neshoba County subpoenaed Sullivan, Special Agent in Charge Ray Moore, and four other agents. At Burke Marshall's request, Sullivan advised County Attorney Raymond Jones that the Bureau personnel under subpoena could not comply because they were needed in Biloxi. Undeterred, Mississippi Circuit Judge O. H. Barnett (a cousin of the former governor) instructed the Neshoba County grand jury to seek whatever evidence the FBI had gathered in the case. Insisting that it was "time for the government to put up or shut up," he fired off telegrams to both J. Edgar Hoover and Acting Attorney General Katzenbach, requesting that they instruct all agents having information about the murders to appear and testify.[32]

Premature disclosure of its evidence, the FBI believed, would seriously impair the investigation and also endanger its informants within the White Knights. Confronted with what appeared to be a calculated effort to thwart apprehension and prosecution of the killers, the federal government refused to cooperate with the Mississippi criminal justice system. Hoover informed Judge Barnett that Katzenbach had instructed him not to let his agents appear before the Neshoba County grand jury "at this time" or to disclose to it any information obtained by the FBI's investigation. The acting attorney general also advised Moore that in his opinion disclosing to anyone other than the federal grand jurors what the Bureau had found would "be inimical to the public interest." Moore managed to work out an agreement with Jones and Barnett under which no FBI personnel would have to testify, but an attorney, Howard Shapiro of the Civil Division, would appear before the grand jury as a representative of the Justice Department. Shapiro read a statement from Katzenbach promising that at an appropriate time in the future the department would make evidence and testimony available to state and local authorities. On September 30 the grand jury adjourned without returning a single indictment, issuing a blistering report excoriating the FBI for its refusal to cooperate. Two days later its federal counterpart in Biloxi, apparently impressed by the mass of evidence presented to it by Robert Owen, overcame the racist attitudes of some of its members and returned secret indictments charging five present and former Philadelphia and Neshoba County peace officers with police brutality.[33]

These September events suggested a state prosecution was a highly impractical idea. Nevertheless, discussions concerning which government should arrest and try the killers continued until two days before the FBI rounded up the suspects in the case. On December 2 Sullivan and Moore met twice with Governor Johnson and Mississippi Attorney General Joe Patterson. William H. Johnson, the Neshoba County prosecutor, also participated in the second of these meetings. Neither state officials nor the representatives of the federal government thought it likely that indictments, let alone convictions, could be obtained in Neshoba County. District Attorney Johnson insisted that a successful prosecution was possible there, but Patterson pointed out that even if he were right about this, the fact that the local grand jury was no longer sitting posed a serious problem. In Mississippi, grand jury terms were prescribed by statute, so another one could not be convened for some time. If the state made arrests prior to presentation of the case to a grand jury, it would have to take the accused before a justice of the peace or other committing magistrate for arraignment and a preliminary hearing. There, it would have to disclose much of its case, including the identities of informant witnesses, who would then face retaliation by the Klan. Because of the problems posed by state procedure, the governor and the Mississippi attorney general urged simultaneous action by state authorities and the national government.

Prosecutor Johnson eventually endorsed this idea. The second meeting concluded with an agreement that the FBI would arrest the suspects on civil rights charges and they would then immediately be served with murder warrants. This arrangement, which had Katzenbach's approval, was contingent on the outcome of state research to be conducted the following morning. On the afternoon of December 3 Mississippi officials informed Inspector Sullivan that they had decided not to file charges in the case at the present time. Although the reason given was the results of the research, Governor Johnson earlier had evinced considerable reluctance to let it appear that he had been pressured into acting by Martin Luther King, who had issued a statement saying that arrests would be made within a few days. The Civil Rights Division had been making preparations to go ahead on its own if the state refused to cooperate. Marshall, who was now enthusiastic about prosecuting the Neshoba County case, and Katzenbach authorized the apprehension of nineteen men on section 241 charges and two for misprision of a felony.[34]

Mississippi never prosecuted anyone for the Philadelphia murders. Both District Attorney Johnson and the Neshoba County grand jury blamed the FBI for this. The Bureau's refusal to turn over needed evidence was the reason for their inaction, they insisted.[35]

For a time it appeared that the federal government might also fail to punish the Mississippi killings. On the morning of December 10, 1964, nineteen of the accused klansmen (all but James Jordan and Doyle Barnette, who had not yet been brought to that city) assembled in the small courtroom of the Meridian federal building for a preliminary hearing. In attendance were many civil rights workers and local blacks, among them Chaney's mother. On the bench sat United States Commissioner Esther Carter. Because Carter was not a lawyer, Chief Judge Sidney Mize had sent along his law clerk, Thomas Stennis, to advise her. His presence did not keep the commissioner from rendering an erroneous ruling which temporarily derailed the federal prosecution.[36]

The government's first witness was FBI agent Henry Rask, who testified that he had obtained a signed confession from Horace Doyle Barnette. Civil Rights Division lawyer Robert Owen then attempted to introduce the confession and have Rask discuss its contents. Defense attorneys promptly objected that the government was trying to use hearsay evidence and demanded to see the confession. To Owen's utter dismay, Commissioner Carter sustained their objection, although she did decline to turn the confession over to them. Since her task in this preliminary hearing was merely to determine whether there was probable cause sufficient to justify sending the case to a grand jury, and since the Supreme Court had ruled more than eight years earlier that a grand jury might consider hearsay evidence, Owen knew she was wrong. The acceptance of signed confessions in proceedings such as this was routine. Nevertheless, he could not persuade Commissioner Carter to change her mind. After checking with Katzenbach in Washington, Owen announced that the government would produce no further evidence at this preliminary hearing. Instead, it would request the immediate convening of a grand jury. Carter responded by dismissing all charges against the defendants.[37]

"Jesus, Jesus no!" screamed a black woman as she fell to the pavement outside the courthouse. James Farmer also expressed surprise and shock at Carter's ruling. Some southern newspapers joined the Justice Department in denouncing what the *Nashville Banner* branded a "disillusioning" and "insufferable" decision.[38]

Katzenbach, who apparently agreed with that assessment, asked U.S. District Judge Harold Cox to reconvene the federal grand jury which had indicted Philadelphia and Neshoba County lawmen for police brutality. It assembled in Jackson on January 11, 1965. The grand jurors bore a heavy burden, Greenville's *Delta Democrat-Times* pointed out, for if they returned indictments in this case, many of their fellow white Mississippians would regard them as traitors. After meeting for four days the grand jury decided that those allegedly responsible for the Philadelphia murders would have to stand trial, but it did so by a majority of only one vote. It indicted eighteen men on felony charges of violating section 241 by conspiring to deprive Schwerner, Goodman, and Chaney of federally secured rights. It also returned a four-count misdemeanor indictment which accused the same defendants of acting under color of law to deprive each murdered man of his constitutional right to be immune from punishment without due process of law and of his right to be secure in his person while in the custody of the state of Mississippi, both violations of section 242, as well as of conspiring to deprive the victims of these rights.[39]

The next morning, as a bitter north wind whipped snow flurries across the eastern Mississippi landscape, federal marshals swept through Neshoba and Lauderdale counties, picking up sixteen of the accused. Horace Doyle Barnette was arrested in Shreveport, Louisiana, and Jordan surrendered voluntarily to the FBI in Atlanta. Commissioner Esther Carter soon released the defendants on $5,000 bonds. This time, she could do no more.[40]

Judge Cox had greater power. Although a Kennedy appointee, he was a native Mississippian and a close friend of segregationist Senator James Eastland. His appointment to the bench had inspired vehement protest from Roy Wilkins, who soon had plenty of evidence to support his negative assessment. Cox enjoined CORE from encouraging desegregation of the McComb bus terminal. He also consistently opposed the Justice Department's voter registration efforts in Mississippi, complaining bitterly about the amount of time he had to waste "fooling around" with these "lousy cases." A few months earlier Cox had demanded that the department prosecute for perjury some of its own witnesses in civil rights litigation. When it refused to do so, he held U.S. Attorney Robert Hauberg in contempt.[41]

On February 24, 1965, Cox struck again, dismissing the felony charges against all of the defendants except Jordan, whose case had been transferred to Atlanta.[42] The section 241 indictment, he contended, was void under the decision of the Fifth Circuit Court of Appeals in *United States v. Williams,* which the Supreme Court had affirmed. According to Cox, *Williams* had established that section 241 applied only to interference with rights which arose from the relationship between the victim and the national government. It was intended to protect rights which were federally created, not those, such as the right not to be deprived of liberty or life without due process of law, which were merely federally guaranteed. Thus, "The indictment surely states a heinous crime against the State of Mississippi, but not a crime against the United States."[43]

Besides dismissing the more serious charge facing all of the defendants, Cox also eliminated most of the misdemeanor counts against all but three of them. As he saw it, only Sheriff Rainey, Deputy Sheriff Price, and Philadelphia Police Officer Richard Willis were capable of acting under color of law to deprive Schwerner, Goodman, and Chaney of federally created rights in violation of section 242. Because the other defendants were private citizens, it was not possible for them to act under color of law. Cox dismissed the three substantive counts in the second indictment against all of the accused except the three lawmen. However, the judge reasoned that while private citizens could not personally violate section 242, they were capable of entering into a conspiracy with peace officers having as its object the violation of that statute. Consequently, Cox let the conspiracy count stand against all defendants. Under his rulings, all of the klansmen would come to trial, but most on a single minor charge, and not even Rainey, Price, and Willis for any offense that carried a maximum sentence of more than one year in prison. Justice, it seemed, had been mocked again in Mississippi. The *Baltimore Afro-American* editorialized bitterly that Cox had done "grave violence to the kind of justice the vast majority of Americans believe in."[44]

He was not the only jurist to thwart the federal government's new attack on racist violence. Judge William Bootle of the Middle District of Georgia also caused problems. Bootle was not a judicial obstructionist like Cox, willing to defy the Constitution and exploit the powers of his office to preserve white supremacy. In January 1961 he had ordered two black students admitted to the previously all-white University of Georgia. When officials of that institution suspended them, claiming campus rioting made this necessary, Bootle ordered the black youths readmitted, and when Governor Ernest Vandiver attempted to close the university to prevent its integration, he swiftly issued a restraining order preventing him from doing so.[45] Despite having sustained the government's position in earlier civil rights litigation, Bootle on December 29, 1964, dismissed the federal indictment in the Lemuel Penn case.[46] The Justice Department was not surprised. Nor was the *Washington Post*. Although it had bitterly condemned Georgia justice for its failure to punish the killers of a District of Columbia resident, the *Post* declined to criticize Judge Bootle because it considered his decision a "certainly not unreasonable" example of "judicial restraint."[47]

The ruling accorded with Supreme Court precedent. Civil Rights Division lawyers had brought this case realizing the law was against them, but hoping they could persuade the court to change it. For Bootle to have ruled in their favor would, they recognized, have required him to anticipate a change of position by the high tribunal. Although innovative lower court judges sometimes did that, his conservative ruling was proper and what the Civil Rights Division itself expected.[48]

Bootle seems to have believed that in bringing this case the federal government had exceeded its constitutional authority.[49] The reason he gave for his ruling, however, was that section 241, as interpreted by the Supreme Court, did not punish the sort of conduct in which the six klansmen allegedly had engaged. That law was not as sweeping as a literal reading would seem to indicate, he said. It punished only those who conspired to injure, oppress, threaten, or intimidate a citizen seeking to exercise one of that limited class of rights which were peculiar attributes of national citizenship. Section 241, Bootle asserted (citing and quoting at length from the *Williams* opinions of the Court of Appeals and the Supreme Court), "was never intended by the Congress to embrace, and therefore does not embrace, Fourteenth Amendment rights."[50] Since several sections of the indictment appeared to be directed at a conspiracy to deprive blacks of rights guaranteed by the Equal Protection Clause of the Fourteenth Amendment, his analysis knocked the props from under much of it. The government contended that the right of equal access to places of public accommodation stemmed from Title II of the 1964 Civil Rights Act. No part of the indictment could rest on that statutory foundation, Bootle insisted, because Title II spoke of a right to use such facilities "without discrimination or segregation on the ground of race, color, religion, or national origin," and the government had omitted this vital language from its allegations.[51] Besides, the legislative history of the 1964 act made it clear that Congress had intended to subject violators only to the penalties for which that law itself provided. Thus, conspiring to deprive someone of the rights and privileges it created could not be a violation of section 241. Nor could conspiring to interfere with interstate travel, for the right to move freely from one state to another (which had existed before the Constitution) was not an attribute of national citizenship. Bootle's interpretation of section 241 rather drastically restricted its scope. To read the statute any more broadly, however, and particularly to hold that it protected the exercise of "other rights enjoyed by white citizens in the vicinity of Athens, Georgia," would, he believed, render it unconstitutionally vague and indefinite.

What concerned Bootle even more than the potential due-process problems which section 241 posed was the vast expansion of federal criminal jurisdiction which this indictment seemed to involve. It was, he observed, "common knowledge that two of the defendants . . . have already been prosecuted in the Superior Court of Madison County, Georgia for the murder of Lemuel A. Penn and by a jury found not guilty." Important as it was that "the defendants be tried where not already tried" and, if convicted after a fair trial, appropriately punished, it was "equally important that this court not usurp jurisdiction where it has none."[52]

The government did not have to accept Bootle's refusal to try the case, for the Criminal Appeals Act made possible speedy review of his decision by the Supreme Court. Within two weeks after Bootle dismissed the indictment, Burke Marshall addressed a lengthy memorandum to Solicitor General Archibald Cox, urging Cox to carry *Guest* to the high tribunal. "In our view it is important that this case be appealed to the Supreme Court," Marshall wrote. "Terrorism . . . not only represents a device increasingly used to maintain white supremacy in certain deep South areas, but it is also a matter of fundamental concern to the national conscience." The federal government, he argued, simply could not "confess its inability to deal with these outbreaks." Since section 241 was an important weapon in its limited statutory arsenal, the Justice Department had to know whether the Court considered that law "adequate for the control of this type of terrorism."[53]

Marshall was candid enough to acknowledge that the *Guest* case posed numerous legal problems. Among them were the constitutional difficulties associated with that portion of the indictment alleging conspiracy to interfere with a supposed right of interstate travel. In the opinion of Louis F. Claiborne, a member of Cox's staff, this was a charge that was " 'phony' on its face." Although there was agreement within the Solicitor General's Office that Bootle's ruling should be appealed, both Claiborne and Ralph Spritzer, first assistant to the solicitor general, recommended that the government abandon this "contrived claim." Claiborne also believed there should be no appeal from the district court's dismissal of that portion of the indictment predicated on Title II, for he agreed with Bootle's assessment of the legislative history of the Civil Rights Act. Spritzer, on the other hand, favored basing the government's claim of denial of federal rights, and thus its entire appeal, on the 1964 law. To him the rest of the indictment seemed "untenable."[54]

The difficulty with it was its application of section 241 to a conspiracy to interfere with Fourteenth Amendment rights. As Bootle had pointed out, in *United States v. Williams* four members of the Supreme Court had taken the position that such rights were not within the purview of the statute. Because Justice Frankfurter's opinion did not represent the views of a majority of the Court, one could argue that it was not a binding precedent, and Spritzer agreed with Marshall that the high tribunal would probably decide the issue the other way now. As he noted, however, "The present case goes well beyond the situation presented in Williams." There the defendants were charged with acting under color of state law. Here the indictment contained "no suggestions that the state was in any way implicated in the acts which the defendants, as private persons, directed against Negroes." Because the Supreme Court had long taken the position that the Fourteenth Amendment did not empower Congress to reach purely private action, Spritzer regarded as untenable those portions of the indictment dependent on it.[55]

The Civil Rights Division conceded this was "the most difficult part of [the] case." Marshall thought it was possible for Fourteenth Amendment purposes, however, to draw a tenable distinction between the deprivation of rights on the one hand and interference with them on the other; only a state, as the grantor of a right or privilege, could "deprive" a person of it, but a private individual could "interfere" with the exercise of such a right or privilege once it became vested. "It would seem that Congress, at a minimum, has the power, under section 5 of the fourteenth amendment, to protect fourteenth amendment rights against interference by private parties," he contended. That was what Congress had done in enacting section 241, and the indictment could be upheld on that basis. Although the Court might disagree, Marshall believed, "the effort to sustain our position should be made."[56]

The Civil Rights Division wanted to appeal on this issue because it realized that at stake in *Guest* was something more than just the future of the Georgia prosecution. Given the limited scope of section 241, as interpreted by the Supreme Court, and given also a judicial construction of this statute which required the government to prove that the purpose of any alleged conspiracy had been to interfere with the free exercise of one of the small group of rights that section 241 had been held to protect, the existing law was an unsatisfactory weapon with which to combat terroristic violence in the South. New legislative authority could not be sought, the Civil Rights Division was convinced, unless existing judicial remedies were first exhausted. Furthermore, until the Supreme Court decided the issue of constitutional power to legislate posed by *Guest,* the constitutionality of any new legislation designed to solve the problem of southern racial violence would be impossible to determine.[57]

The arguments pressed by the Civil Rights Division eventually prevailed. Despite the reservations of his staff, the solicitor general appealed almost all aspects of Bootle's ruling, jettisoning only that portion of the indictment charging conspiracy to interfere with the enjoyment of "other rights exercised and enjoyed by white citizens in the vicinity of Athens, Georgia."[58] It was not until March 29, however, that the government filed a jurisdictional statement with the Court, asking it to hear the case. In the interim, Judge Cox had handed down his rulings in the Mississippi case, now known formally as *United States v. Price*. Doar had no doubt that the Neshoba County killings involved sufficient state action to make those indictments valid.[59] The White House had been offering the Mississippi prosecution as proof of "the strong desire of the federal administration . . . to insure that there is law and order."[60] Aware of the political importance of the case, the Justice Department asked the Supreme Court for expedited consideration of Cox's rulings. "This case, as members of the Court and indeed the entire country are aware, is one of extraordinary gravity and intrinsic importance," government lawyers emphasized in a motion which they filed on March 9. "The public interest requires prompt disposition of all charges."[61] Despite their prodding, the Court refused to expedite the case.[62] Apparently, only after suffering this setback did Justice Department leaders make the final decision to appeal *Guest*, a case which posed more difficult issues than did *Price*. Perhaps, had the Court been willing to reverse Judge Cox promptly and allow the national government to get on with a prosecution which much of the nation was demanding, the Justice Department would have let Bootle's decision stand and settled temporarily for the relatively modest broadening of sections 241 and 242 potentially attainable in the Mississippi case. Forced to wait many months for any help at all from the Court, at a time when the public and the president were expressing outrage over further racist killings spawned by resistance to King's voting rights campaign around Selma, Alabama, and were pressing the department to develop legislation that could curb anti–civil rights violence, it eschewed the safe approach. Rather than seeking to expand federal power to punish racial violence by small increments that would not require the Court to make drastic, and therefore potentially embarrassing, departures from precedent, it elected to appeal both *Price* and *Guest*.[63]

The Justice Department was now convinced that terrorism, intimidation, and reprisal directed at blacks attempting to exercise "their federal constitutional and statutory rights" were "national concerns properly evoking national action."[64] In order to determine as quickly as possible what the federal government could do about them, the department elected to establish in a single round of litigation both the outer limits of its authority under sections 241 and 242 and whether the political branches had the constitutional power to correct the deficiencies of those Reconstruction laws. In their request for review of *Guest,* government lawyers included a pointed reminder that "until this Court definitively resolves the constitutional and statutory questions now presented, neither the executive nor Congress can determine the need for remedies or the appropriate solution."[65]

The Court agreed to hear both cases,[66] and Thurgood Marshall argued them for the government on November 9, 1965. After pressuring Archibald Cox into giving up the post of solicitor general to return to the Harvard Law School faculty, President Johnson had named the former NAACP attorney as his replacement, making him the highest ranking black man in federal legal service. By revealing nearly two months in advance that Marshall would argue *Price* and *Guest,* the administration underscored how important it considered those cases. "Emotionally caught up in the issue," Cox prepared several pages of suggestions for his successor's oral argument. Perhaps employing some of these, Marshall urged the Court to uphold the power of the federal government to punish "lynch mob murder."[67]

The focus of his argument, as well as of the briefs filed by all parties in both cases, was section 241. That law, H. C. "Mike" Watkins, a Meridian attorney representing the defendants in the Mississippi case, insisted, was never intended to protect the right to be free from racial violence. Watkins and the other nine lawyers who signed the appellees' brief in *Price* denied that the Constitution guaranteed Americans security from assault, murder, oppression, or other forms of interference by their fellow citizens. Such security was a natural right, and responsibility for assuring it rested with the states, they claimed. The Fourteenth Amendment did not safeguard it. Nor was it protected by section 241, which applied only to federal rights.[68] Like these Mississippi attorneys, James Hudson, representing five of the Georgia defendants, claimed section 241 punished only persons acting under state authority. He hammered home the point that there were "no controlling Supreme Court decisions holding" that "a conspiracy to deny other persons rights and privileges secured by the fourteenth amendment" violated this law.[69] Charles Bloch, a Macon lawyer appointed to represent Lackey, set forth arguments similar to Hudson's. Both insisted, among other things, that there was no federally guaranteed right of interstate travel and, consequently, that section 241 could not reach a conspiracy to interfere with it.[70]

Justice Department lawyers responded that this law did protect the

right to pass freely from state to state and also the right to use the instru-
mentalities of interstate commerce, because both of those rights arose
directly from the relationship between individual citizens and the federal
government itself. The solicitor general and his colleagues also disputed
the proposition that section 241 did not protect Fourteenth Amendment
rights. *Williams* had not resolved this issue against them, they claimed,
because in that case the Court had divided evenly on the question. The
Justice Department's *Price* brief asserted that "the language of the statute,
its context, and its legislative history" established that section 241 applied to rights guaranteed by the Due Process Clause.[71]

Government lawyers also labored to persuade the justices that section
241 reached private conspiracies to interfere with rights flowing from the
Equal Protection Clause. Rather than frontally assaulting the Court's past
construction of that clause, they endeavored to square their argument with
the traditional interpretation. In its *Guest* brief, the Justice Department
argued that, appearances to the contrary notwithstanding, there was state
action in the case. The Equal Protection Clause, the government contended, required states to make available to all their citizens what they made
available to some of them. It also demanded that they ensure all potential
beneficiaries of what they provided actually could enjoy it. What the Equal
Protection Clause did, the government argued, was to impose upon the
states an affirmative obligation to take action against private conspiracies
directed at depriving some class among their citizens of the use of public
facilities and sanction federal intervention if they violated that affirmative
duty. Section 241, passed by Congress in the exercise of the power given it
by section 5 of the Fourteenth Amendment to enforce the amendment's
other provisions by appropriate legislation, was an example of such intervention. Private individuals were subject to punishment under it for conspiring to interfere with the use of public facilities by others, "not because
they themselves violate the Constitution, but because they effectively perpetuate or cause a denial of equal protection by the State."[72]

The government also insisted that section 241 could be used against
those who conspired to deprive others of rights created by Title II of the
Civil Rights Act. It vigorously disputed the contention of Hudson and
Bloch that in 1964 Congress had explicitly excluded those rights from the
protection of the 1870 conspiracy statute. The Justice Department also
challenged the contention of counsel for the Mississippi klansmen that the

Supreme Court lacked jurisdiction to hear a direct appeal from Judge Cox's ruling dismissing the section 242 charges against the fifteen private citizens among their clients. The essence of the defense attorneys' argument was that these civilians were incapable of acting under color of law and, consequently, could have been properly charged only with aiding and abetting the three peace officer defendants. Since the indictment did not allege that offense (or even contain words that might somehow bring private persons under section 242), its allegations were insufficient. The Supreme Court was not empowered to hear direct appeals from dismissals of indictments on grounds of inadequacy; hence, it lacked jurisdiction.[73] The government responded to this argument by contending that "when the private members of the mob knowingly linked hands with the officers to carry out a common plan to deprive Schwerner, Goodman, and Chaney of their constitutional rights, they lost their claim to be treated as mere private citizens" and became "amenable to the statute as persons acting under color of law." In the alternative, the fifteen defendants in question had been "properly indicted as aiders and abettors."[74]

The Supreme Court did not find it necessary to accept that proposition in order to reverse Judge Cox's ruling. "Private persons, jointly engaged with state officials in the prohibited action, are acting 'under color' of law for purposes of the statute," it concluded in an opinion handed down on March 28, 1966.[75] Speaking for the Court, Justice Abe Fortas noted that the detention and calculated release of Chaney, Goodman, and Schwerner by a peace officer had made possible the "brutal joint adventure" which claimed the lives of the three civil rights workers. "Those who took advantage of participation by state officers in accomplishment of the foul purpose alleged," he concluded, "must suffer the consequences of that participation."[76]

Although accepting the Justice Department's interpretation of the "under color of law" language in section 242, the Supreme Court declined to endorse the government's contention that section 241 protected rights created by Title II of the 1964 Civil Rights Act. On the same day that it decided *Price,* the Court, speaking through Justice Potter Stewart in the *Guest* case, announced it lacked jurisdiction to decide that issue. Judge Bootle's dismissal of the relevant portion of the Georgia indictment, Stewart maintained, had been based, at least alternatively, "upon his determination that this paragraph was defective as a matter of pleading." Therefore, settled procedures under the Criminal Appeals Act precluded the Supreme Court from reviewing his decision. Stewart seemed to be straining hard to avoid deciding a difficult issue.[77]

The reason was probably a desire to avoid conflict with Congress over whether it had removed Title II from the protection of section 241. The Court took a more forthright position on the issue of whether the 1870 statute secured the right of interstate travel against interference by private conspiracies. In *Guest,* all of the justices but John Marshall Harlan agreed that it did.[78]

The far more crucial questions posed by both cases were whether section 241 protected Fourteenth Amendment rights and, if it did, against whom it safeguarded them. In his *Price* opinion, Justice Fortas maintained that Judge Cox was wrong in assuming *Williams* had held that the 1870 law did not apply to such rights. Pointing out, as had the government, that only a minority of the justices participating in that case had taken this position, he asserted the question remained open. Fortas then answered it, announcing that section 241 did indeed apply to "rights or privileges protected by the Fourteenth Amendment."[79] Stewart resolved the same issue in *Guest* by simply citing *Price.*[80]

While saying what section 241 protected, Fortas avoided providing a complete answer to the question of who might be prosecuted under it. His reason for doing so was the state action doctrine. Fortas appeared to concede the continued validity of that hoary concept.[81] It posed no problem in this case, he insisted, because "We are here concerned with allegations which squarely and indisputably involve state action."[82] "Whatever the ultimate coverage of the section may be," Fortas was sure it extended "to conspiracies otherwise within the scope of the section, participated in by officials alone or in collaboration with private persons."[83] Thus, *Price* did not "raise fundamental questions of federal-state relationships."[84]

Guest did because none of the defendants in that case was an employee of a state or one of its political subdivisions. In order to hold the *Guest* indictment valid, Stewart would have to repudiate the state action doctrine—or so it seemed. By being more than a little disingenuous, he managed to reverse Bootle without taking that seemingly unavoidable step. Stewart purported to find that, "contrary to the argument of the litigants, the indictment in fact contains an express allegation of state involvement sufficient at least to require the denial of a motion to dismiss." The straw to which he clung so desperately was the accusation that

the defendants had sought to accomplish the objective of their conspiracy
in part " 'by causing the arrest of Negroes by means of false reports that
such Negroes had committed criminal acts.' " This allegation, Stewart
argued, was broad enough to cover charges of active connivance with
agents of the state or of official discrimination.[85] His opinion, which depended on a construction of the indictment in conflict with that of the
district court,[86] rested on assumptions that bore little relation to the facts
of the case. It had about it a fairy-tale quality. Furthermore, it disposed of
this facet of the litigation without saying anything about whether the
Justice Department could punish private racial violence under section 241
or what power Congress had to enact new legislation for that purpose.

Nevertheless, one commentator was soon writing, "*Guest* abolished the
requirement that action attributable to the state must be found as a condition precedent to the application of federal statutes which implement the
fourteenth amendment," and another was asserting that a majority of the
Supreme Court had held that section 5 gave Congress the power to protect
from private interference a right to equal utilization of public facilities.[87]
These interpretations rested not on anything Stewart had written, but on
a pair of concurring opinions in *Guest,* which between them expressed the
views of two-thirds of the Court. In one of these Justice William Brennan,
writing also for Chief Justice Earl Warren and Associate Justice William
O. Douglas, argued that section 241 was designed to punish entirely
private conspiracies to interfere with the right of equal utilization of state
facilities. According to Brennan, section 5 of the Fourteenth Amendment
empowered Congress "to enact laws punishing *all* conspiracies to interfere
with the exercise of Fourteenth Amendment rights, whether or not state
officers or others acting under the color of state law are implicated in the
conspiracy."[88] As Brennan saw it, Congress had used that authority in
enacting section 241. He at least implied it could have gone even further,
punishing not only conspiracies but also nonconspiratorial private conduct
interfering with the right to equal utilization of state facilities.[89] Justice
Tom Clark, the author of the second concurring opinion, gave no hint that
he accepted the latter idea (although Brennan was sure Clark agreed with
him), and he took no position on whether section 241 represented an
exercise of congressional power to pass "appropriate legislation" implementing the Fourteenth Amendment. But along with Justices Fortas and
Hugo Black, he did echo Brennan on the subject of the extent of congressional power, saying there could "be no doubt that the specific language of

§5 empowers Congress to enact laws punishing all conspiracies—with or without state action—that interfere with Fourteenth Amendment rights."[90] Thus, although saying nothing about the continued vitality of the state action doctrine, six justices endorsed a major departure from that principle. The noticeable differences between the two concurring opinions made it impossible to say with any degree of certainty what that departure was or to articulate with precision the legal principle for which *Guest* stood.

The ambiguity and confusion in the opinions was the result of judicial efforts to keep the Supreme Court from getting in the way of congressional attempts to combat racist violence in the South. The justices appear to have been as outraged about the Philadelphia murders as the rest of the country, and their ruling in *Price* was unanimous. Only Stewart seems ever to have entertained doubts about how that case should be decided.[91]

Initially, there does not seem to have been much division within the Court over *Guest* either, but the draft opinion which Stewart circulated on January 26, 1966, aroused concern in the minds of Brennan and Black, who thought it could be read as placing undue limitations on congressional power. Stewart wrote that the Equal Protection Clause spoke only to states and persons acting under their authority and that section 5 empowered Congress "to effectuate and implement only those rights the Amendment itself confers."[92] He took note of the Justice Department's suggestion that "the default or neglect of the State to accord the equal protection of the laws to its inhabitants might be a predicate for congressional action under the Equal Protection Clause and §5 of the Fourteenth Amendment," but did not (since he could find no such default in this case) express any views on the validity of that theory.[93] Brennan found what his colleague had written ambiguous and the implications which might be drawn from it disturbing. To the extent that Stewart's opinion could be read as limiting the power of Congress under section 5 of the Fourteenth Amendment, he considered it inconsistent with the expansive reading the Court was giving the identically worded enforcement provision of the Fifteenth Amendment in *South Carolina v. Katzenbach*.[94] To the extent that his colleague's draft could be read as recognizing congressional authority to protect from private conspiracies blacks seeking to use desegregated public facilities, it gave rise to the question of whether section 241 represented an exercise of that power. Brennan feared Stewart had implicitly answered this question in the negative. If he had not done so, the reason had to be that section 241 applied only when there was an allegation of state default in a particular case, a proposition which itself generated a number of perplexing theoretical problems. "Given the urgent needs of the times, and the prospect for further legislation in this area, it seems imperative that these questions be resolved," Brennan wrote in a memorandum to his colleagues. He also expressed his concerns in a letter to Stewart, who was out of town at the time.[95]

When Stewart returned to Washington, he acknowledged that his colleague's concerns were well founded. The two passages concerning congressional power were, he wrote other members of the Court, pure dicta which did not belong in the opinion. Consequently, he was deleting them. Although Stewart did this, Brennan, who already had started to work on an opinion of his own, apparently remained concerned about the negative implications which might be drawn from the remainder of what Stewart had written. On March 11 he circulated among his colleagues a formal expression of his own views. Twelve days later he sent them a second version, which carried Justice Douglas's name as well as his own. After making a few additional minor changes, Brennan also secured Warren's endorsement.[96]

Tom Clark, meanwhile, continued fully to support the Stewart opinion. After reading the first version of it, he had written its author, "This is fine with me."[97] Clark also expressed approval of the revised draft deleting references to congressional power. What concerned him (and apparently Fortas as well) was not anything Stewart had written, but rather Brennan's assertion that the Court's official spokesman had by implication accepted the appellees' contention that Congress lacked constitutional authority to punish private conspiracies aimed at interference with Fourteenth Amendment rights. Rather than risk having those who read the Brennan opinion conclude that a majority of the Supreme Court would reject future legislation of this type, Clark and Fortas, along with Black, elected to make a very explicit—although in their minds legally unnecessary—statement of their views on the matter. Consequently, six justices wound up on record in support of an expansive reading of the Fourteenth Amendment which had contributed nothing to deciding *Guest*.[98]

The end product of the process of action and reaction initiated by Stewart's cautious and conservative opinion was, as many observers noted, the dramatic alteration of an important facet of American law. Together *Guest* and *Price* effected two changes of tremendous significance. The first was bringing Fourteenth Amendment rights within the protection of section 241, making it possible to reach with that law persons who conspired to deprive others of due process or equal protection. By taking this step, a law student remarked, the Supreme Court had finally, after ninety-six years, accorded section 241 "the scope which its sponsors apparently intended it to have and which the statutory language plainly indicates."[99] The second change the Court wrought was in the state action doctrine. Legal commentators noted that in *Guest* six justices had reached the conclusion that it was "no longer applicable to enforcement legislation."[100] If perhaps predictable, the stand taken by Brennan, Clark, and their supporters represented a dramatic departure from what at least one knowledgeable authority insisted had been the original intention of the framers of the Fourteenth Amendment.[101] Since the justices had not adopted a common position, it was unclear how far the state action doctrine had eroded and how much private conduct could now be reached by congressional legislation enacted under the authority of section 5 of the Fourteenth Amendment. It was obvious, however, that the Court had taken a bold step in order to assure Congress that it had the constitutional power to move against anti–civil rights violence.

While legal commentators emphasized the Court's removal of a major limitation on congressional power,[102] for the popular press the importance of *Guest* lay in the extent to which the decision had enhanced the capacity of the Justice Department to move against unpunished racial violence with a statute already on the books.[103] Federal prosecutors did not have to wait for Congress to act. They could put Ku Klux Klan killers on trial immediately.

EIGHT

The South on Trial

With *Price* and *Guest,* the Supreme Court removed all doubts about whether the federal government possessed the legal authority to prosecute Ku Klux Klan conspirators for anti–civil rights killings in the South. While those cases were on appeal, events in Alabama provided further evidence that the southern states could not be relied upon to control racist violence and generated further political pressure for the national government to act. Even before the Court ruled, John Doar brought Klan killers to trial in Alabama. After it upheld the *Guest* and *Price* indictments, the Civil Rights Division also tried klansmen in Georgia and Mississippi. By pressing these three prosecutions, the division placed not just the Klan but the South itself on trial. Although the national government had the authority to prosecute anti–civil rights violence, only juries composed of white southerners had the power to convict those responsible for such crimes, and history indicated they would not do so. The rest of the country wanted justice in these cases. Americans elsewhere would be watching, skeptically, to see if the white South could provide it.

The first group of southern whites to face this challenge sat as a federal jury in Alabama. During early 1965 SNCC and the SCLC mounted a major voter registration campaign in that state's black belt. It produced a violent reaction. In Dallas County, Sheriff Jim Clark, his deputies, and possemen beat, clubbed, and cattle-prodded demonstrators. In Perry County a state trooper shot and killed a young black "freedom fighter," Jimmy Lee Jackson. Escalating violence climaxed on Sunday, March 7, at the Edmund Pettis Bridge in the Dallas County seat of Selma. A crowd of black protesters led by Hosea Williams and John Lewis defied an order from Governor Wallace and attempted to march out of town along U.S. Highway 80 toward the state capitol in Montgomery. State troopers commanded by Colonel Albert Lingo, along with Clark's deputies and mounted possemen, waded into the marchers with horses, whips, clubs, cattle prods, and tear gas, injuring many of them and scattering the rest. Their brutality appalled the North, which witnessed it on television news shows.[1]

Wallace denied that Alabama lawmen had used excessive force. Indeed, he claimed that by halting a march which would have exposed the demonstrators to attack by irate whites they actually had saved black lives. The governor's comments, along with the Jackson killing and what had happened at the Edmund Pettis Bridge, made it obvious that in Alabama the authorities, far from working to control anti–civil rights violence, were themselves a major part of the problem. In Lowndes County, blacks complained with justification that those who were supposed to preserve order consistently failed "to punish the perpetrators of acts of violence," but instead "conspired . . . to deny the Negro citizens the equal protection of the laws."[2] Dr. Martin Luther King, Jr., accurately summed up the situation in Alabama when he told fellow SCLC leaders, "Official voices of the state and county governments have said by their word and deed that the Negro's quest for freedom should be crushed."[3]

Official Alabama's obvious complicity in attacks on civil rights demonstrators evoked a swelling chorus of demands for federal intervention. SNCC urged that Washington send marshals to Selma, while a University of Texas professor wanted the army employed to protect constitutional rights there. The head of the American Jewish Congress, a Unitarian minister, Chicago businessman Charles Percy, and 115 citizens of Oberlin, Ohio, all telegraphed the president, asking him to intervene in Alabama.[4] Even the General Assembly of Connecticut spoke up, adopting a resolution which urged "the federal government to use every legal means available to protect peaceful citizens of Alabama in the exercise of their rights."[5]

Although Washington prepared contingency plans for sending seven hundred soldiers to Selma, the president at first resisted the pressure for intervention. Johnson tended to be less reluctant than the Kennedys and Burke Marshall (who had resigned from the Justice Department on January 15 to return to private law practice) to use troops in a civil rights crisis. His voting rights bill was before Congress, however, and the president feared "a hasty display of federal force" might ruin chances for its passage. Besides, Wallace assured him on March 12 that Alabama was prepared to assume what Johnson considered its constitutional obligation. "As governor, I propose to take whatever steps are necessary to preserve order in this state and to protect all of the people in Alabama," Wallace informed the president. The governor added that "state authorities are completely adequate to cope with the situation." In a subsequent face-to-face meeting between the two men, he argued strongly that maintaining law and order was a state responsibility. Johnson agreed—but made it clear he had troops standing by and would use them if Alabama authorities failed to do their jobs.[6]

When they abdicated their responsibilities, he used the soldiers. On March 8, still determined to march to Montgomery, leaders of the Selma protest asked the United States District Court for the Middle District of Alabama to enjoin state and county authorities from interfering. Wallace responded by asking for an injunction against demonstrations on the public highways of Alabama. The Justice Department also intervened in the case. After initially disappointing civil rights forces by turning down their request for a temporary restraining order and forbidding them to undertake their pilgrimage until the case was resolved, Judge Frank Johnson announced on March 17 that the "plaintiffs and the members of the class they represent are entitled to police protection in the exercise of [the] constitutional right to march along U.S. Highway 80 from Selma to Montgomery."[7] Observing that Wallace, Clark, Lingo, and "the members of their respective enforcement agencies" had been trying to discourage Negroes from exercising the rights of citizenship, Judge Johnson enjoined Alabama authorities from interfering in any way with the proposed march. He also insisted that they provide adequate police protection to the participants.

Judge Johnson's injunction unmasked hypocrisy. After insisting that the maintenance of law and order should be left to the states, Wallace now demanded that the federal government protect the Selma-to-Montgomery marchers. At the governor's request the Alabama legislature passed a resolution claiming the state lacked the money to do the job. Alabama asked Washington to furnish enough marshals to ensure the safety of the demonstrators, or if the National Guard had to be used, to pay the cost of mobilizing the 6,200 troops its Department of Public Safety estimated would be needed.[8]

Confronted with an admission that the state "could not protect the marchers on its own" and "needed federal assistance," the president "gave such assistance immediately."9 Johnson called selected units of the Alabama National Guard into federal service and also sent regular army military police units to the march route to keep the peace and assist in quelling disturbances and enforcing the court order. The ultimate result of this "failure of state responsibility" was the employment of nearly 3,000 troops, 100 FBI agents, and an equal number of federal marshals to protect the demonstrators.10 The Justice Department dispatched John Doar, Ramsey Clark, and Stephen Pollak to Alabama to make sure the march would proceed peacefully. Although Montgomery authorities and state troopers agreed to assist them, the president nevertheless chided the governor, reminding him of his own earlier insistence that "responsibility for maintaining law and order in our federal system properly rests with state and local governments." Johnson expressed surprise that Wallace had asked for "federal assistance in the performance of such fundamental state duties."11

The *New York Times* and the *Washington Post* joined the president in berating Alabama for defaulting on its responsibilities. The *Montgomery Advertiser,* on the other hand, applauded a maneuver which had forced the federal government to pay for protecting a demonstration it disliked. The Columbia, South Carolina, *State,* although no lover of civil rights demonstrators, could not share the *Advertiser's* joy. By leaving the protection of the marchers to federal authorities, it said, Alabama had written "another chapter . . . in the historical transfer of power" from the states to the central government. The *Times's* assessment was similar: "Before Mr. Wallace goes on television with another of his lachrymose complaints about the extent to which the federal government is throttling the states, we hope he will look in a mirror and see who is responsible."12

While inviting an expansion of federal power, Alabama also provided the nation with additional demonstrations of the inadequacies of southern justice. One of these came in a case which began the very night the Selma-to-Montgomery march reached its triumphant conclusion. Four klansmen followed a car occupied by Mrs. Viola Liuzzo, a volunteer driver from Detroit who had been assigned to transport demonstrators back to Selma, and Leroy Moton, a young SCLC worker. After a high-speed chase, they overtook it on a deserted stretch of Highway 80 in Lowndes County. With driver Gene Thomas yelling at his companions to "Shoot the hell out of them," the other klansmen opened fire. A .38 slug ripped into Mrs. Liuzzo's brain, killing her instantly.13

She was not the first civil rights worker to die in Alabama that spring. On the night of March 8 white thugs had attacked and beaten three Unitarian ministers on the streets of Selma. One of their victims, Reverend James Reeb, received multiple skull fractures from which he died two days later. His death drew fifteen thousand persons to a memorial service at Washington's Lafayette Park. In Alabama, the legislature refused even to express sympathy to Reeb's widow. [14]

Alabama's growing reputation for bigoted butchery increased still further as a result of the killing of Jonathan Daniels on August 20. Daniels, an Episcopal seminarian from New Hampshire, and five companions, all of whom had just been released from the Lowndes County jail after serving a few days on minor charges related to the picketing of some white-owned businesses, tried to enter a grocery store in Hayneville to purchase food. Tom Coleman, a state highway department engineer and part-time deputy sheriff, cursed the civil rights workers and ordered them off the premises. He then opened fire with a shotgun. Hit in the stomach, Daniels died immediately. Father Richard Morrisroe, a Catholic priest from Chicago, fell critically wounded. [15]

Although Coleman had killed one man and badly injured another, his fellow Alabamians expected him to escape punishment. They were right. Lowndes County Solicitor Arthur Gamble refused to seek a murder indictment against the well-connected killer, whose brother was the local superintendent of schools. Gamble's inaction outraged Alabama Attorney General Richmond Flowers, a racial moderate. Flowers took over prosecution of the case, but when his office requested a postponement until Morrisroe could recover sufficiently to return from Chicago to testify, the judge abruptly terminated its participation. Coleman then stood trial for manslaughter in a proceeding well attended by klansmen and featuring defense insinuations of an immoral relationship between Daniels and a black female witness. When the jury took just under an hour and a half to find Coleman not guilty, Flowers exploded. Those who wished to kill, cripple, and destroy had now been issued a license to do so, he fumed. [16]

They probably thought they already had one. Collie Leroy Wilkins was living proof that white terrorists could kill with impunity. Less than a day after the slaying of Viola Liuzzo, the FBI had arrested Wilkins, along with his fellow klansmen Eugene Thomas and William Orville Eaton, for that crime. The Bureau had managed to apprehend them within hours of the shooting because one of its informants, Gary Thomas Rowe, was in the car with the killers when the murder occurred. Impressed, Dr. Martin Luther King, Jr., wired congratulations to his old adversary J. Edgar Hoover, praising him and his agency for their work in containing the violence and savagery that was running rampant in Alabama. [17]

Although the Bureau had arrested the alleged killers on a complaint authorized by John Doar (now acting head of the Civil Rights Division) that alleged violation of section 241, Wilkins stood trial for murder. The federal government turned him over to local authorities despite a quarrel between the FBI and Sheriff Clark and despite the Justice Department's suspicions about Circuit Solicitor Gamble. The attorney general asked the FBI to supply him with background information on Gamble, including whether or not he had connections with the Ku Klux Klan. The Bureau reported back that the Alabama prosecutor had often expressed disapproval of the Klan and its objectives. The FBI also had encouraging dealings with Governor Wallace, who told one agent he felt complete disgust at the "cowardly act" which had taken Liuzzo's life. Wallace ordered Colonel Lingo to make the full resources of the Alabama Department of Public Safety available to the FBI, instructed Gamble to cooperate fully with the Bureau, and requested that federal authorities supply state ones with any information that would justify arrests for murder. Apparently impressed with the governor's sincerity and persuaded that Gamble would prosecute the case vigorously, the national government once again deferred to a southern state. The Justice Department furnished Alabama authorities with relevant portions of FBI investigative reports, while the Bureau did records checks on potential jurors and provided prosecutors with testimony and advice. [18]

The special agent in charge at Mobile believed Gamble could successfully prosecute Mrs. Liuzzo's killers for murder in Lowndes County, but he was wrong. A state grand jury indicted Wilkins in April 1965. During his May trial the Imperial Wizard of the United Klans of America, Robert Shelton, and the Alabama Grand Dragon, Robert Creel, sat smugly in the courtroom while Imperial Klonsel Matt Murphy, boasting all the while about his commitment to white supremacy, acted as Wilkins's attorney. Murphy presented a defense which featured intimations of a sexual relationship between Mrs. Liuzzo and Leroy Moton. Despite the eyewitness testimony of FBI informant Rowe, prosecutors could not obtain a conviction. Rowe found the courtroom atmosphere "icy" and his fellow Alabamians outraged that a southerner would have infiltrated an organization dedicated to the preservation of the white race. Two jurors, one of them a member of the White Citizens Council, said after the trial they could not believe the informant because, by testifying, he had violated a Klan oath of secrecy. Although the other ten were willing to convict Wilkins of manslaughter, these two held out, hanging the jury and forcing Judge T. Werth Thagard to declare a mistrial.[19] Gamble and County Solicitor Carlton Perdue expressed determination to try Wilkins again, but Murphy declared that if they did he would "blow [the] state's case out of the water." At a post-trial press conference he "unloosed a tirade against federal intervention and the 'niggers.'"[20]

By the time Wilkins came to trial again in October of 1965, Murphy was dead, the victim of an automobile accident. His successor as defense counsel, former Birmingham Mayor Arthur Hanes (ironically a onetime FBI agent), enjoyed even greater success. This time Attorney General Flowers prosecuted the case himself, carrying all the way to the Alabama Supreme Court an unsuccessful fight to exclude from the jury anyone who considered civil rights workers inferior. Despite Flowers's efforts, the jurors who decided Wilkins's fate included six self-proclaimed white supremacists and eight present or former Citizens Council members. This jury took just one hour and forty-five minutes to acquit the defendant. White spectators cheered its verdict.[21] A disillusioned Gary Rowe considered the trial "a mockery—of the jury system, of the concept of justice, of me." Rowe left Alabama, vowing to FBI agents and government lawyers that he would never return.[22]

Even the less decisive results of the first trial had been enough to convince Montgomery liberal Virginia Durr that in Alabama "murder had become not only condoned but honored, if it was against the 'enemy.'"[23] Jack Minnis of SNCC agreed. To him, the acquittal of Wilkins proved that "it is not a punishable crime to kill a Negro or a civil rights worker in Alabama."[24] In December of 1965 another all-white jury produced further evidence to support Minnis's contention, taking less than two hours to acquit the three Selma businessmen accused of beating James Reeb to death.[25] Attempting to explain that verdict, Walter Royal Jones, Jr., a Unitarian clergyman who had attended the trial, observed, "Murder is not murder except in the community that regards it as so." The slaying of a civil rights worker lay outside the boundaries of that crime as delineated "by the community conscience" of Alabama.[26] The state certainly seemed to be one of those parts of the South where, as Jack Nelson of the

Los Angeles Times wrote in July 1965, "No matter how brutal the killing, the chance of convicting a segregationist of killing a Negro or white integrationist is almost nil."[27]

Even in the federal courts a determined prosecution could fail because, as the *Washington Post* said, "criminal charges are tried by local juries."[28] Nevertheless, John Doar insisted on bringing the killers of Viola Liuzzo to trial before twelve of their fellow Alabamians. Doar, who had moved up to replace Burke Marshall in January 1965, shared many of his predecessor's views and made no conscious effort to change the course of Civil Rights Division policy. As a general rule, he believed, the federal government should defer to good-faith state prosecutions. But Doar was concerned that American youth might become disillusioned if more were not done about the situation in the South. Even before the first of Collie Leroy Wilkins's two state trials, a federal grand jury, meeting in Montgomery in April 1965, had charged Wilkins and his two confederates with conspiring to injure, threaten, or intimidate Mrs. Liuzzo for trying to exercise federally protected rights. After Wilkins's October acquittal, Doar pushed the federal case to trial. He did so despite the fact that, with *Price* and *Guest* still pending in the Supreme Court, the legal basis of the prosecution was at best questionable. The government had to overcome defense efforts to get the indictment dismissed, or at least to delay the proceedings until after the Court ruled. Doar had never before prosecuted a criminal case, but he relished trial work far more than his predecessor and he felt strongly about this case. The new assistant attorney general went to Alabama to take personal charge of the prosecution.[29]

Despite the outcome of the two state trials, Doar had some reason to hope for success. For one thing, this case would be tried in Montgomery rather than in Lowndes County, a place where whites had long controlled a black population four times as numerous as themselves through rigorous disfranchisement and occasional lynching. Rowe found the federal grand jurors who questioned him in Montgomery far more attentive and far less hostile than the residents of Haneyville whom he had encountered during the state trials. Also, there had been at least a few recent hints that the attitudes of southern jurors were beginning to change. The Mississippi juries that had refused to convict Byron De La Beckwith for shooting Medgar Evers in 1964 reportedly had split 7–5 and 8–4 for acquittal. The *Charlotte Observer* saw "a strong ray of hope in the fact that neither of the Beckwith juries moved quickly to acquit the defendant by reason of his race." Even the earlier history of the Liuzzo case furnished some grounds for optimism. After all, in the first of Wilkins's two state trials, ten jurors had voted to convict him of first-degree manslaughter. That "a Southern jury had come so close . . . to sending a white man to prison for killing a civil rights worker" suggested to *New Republic* editor Murray Kempton "that the first time this happens cannot be far away."[30]

In fact, it was not, as Doar proved seven months later. Although in theory trying a section 241 conspiracy case, he and his co-counsel in reality prosecuted a murder. They presented witnesses to the fact that the accused, all of whom resided in the Birmingham area, had been in the vicinity of Selma on the last day of the voting rights march, and introduced evidence to link defendants Eaton and Thomas to weapons that had been fired at Mrs. Liuzzo. Leroy Moton, who was riding in the car with her, recounted his confused recollections of the evening's events. The heart of Doar's case, however, was the testimony of Gary Thomas Rowe. The FBI informant had at first declined to testify. Despite extensive efforts by the Justice Department and the Bureau to persuade him that there was some point in telling his story in court for a third time, he persisted in refusing to do so. Only after a meeting with Doar, in which the assistant attorney general informed him of his intention to try the case himself and assured him that this jury would be more fair-minded than the ones he had faced in Haneyville, did Rowe agree to testify.[31]

Once on the stand, Doar's reluctant witness more than justified the efforts expended to persuade him to appear. Rowe, who had joined the KKK for the FBI and then served as one of its "investigators," said he had known all of the defendants in the United Klans of America. On the morning before Mrs. Liuzzo was shot, he testified, he and the three klansmen had driven to Montgomery to watch the conclusion of King's voting rights march. When the day's activities ended, the four of them had proceeded to Selma, where they considered attacking a group of blacks. Then they spotted a car with a white female driver and a black male passenger. According to Rowe, Gene Thomas had announced: "We are going to get them tonight." After a chase at speeds of up to 100 miles per hour, Thomas told the others, "Get your guns out, we are going to take them." Rowe testified that Thomas handed his weapon to Wilkins, who fired two shots in the direction of the other car. Eaton also shot at it, and the vehicle veered off the road. Rowe described how Wilkins and Eaton had thrown away some shell casings later recovered by the FBI. He denied firing at the Liuzzo automobile himself, a claim which an FBI ballistics expert supported. Neil P. Shanahan, the agent in Birmingham to whom Rowe had reported regularly, confirmed some other details of his story. The defense managed to establish that the FBI had paid Rowe around $12,000, and it got him to admit that he had fought with blacks during the Birmingham Freedom Rider disorders in 1961 and been arrested during the rioting at the University of Alabama in 1963. He also acknowledged having made no effort to keep Wilkins from firing at the Liuzzo car. The defense failed, however, to cast any real doubt on his account of the murder.[32]

Handicapping its efforts to rebut Rowe's story was his description of the attempts the defendants had made on the night of the shooting to find someone who would provide them with an alibi. This testimony cast serious doubts on the veracity of two witnesses who claimed the three klansmen had been in a VFW club in Brighton, Alabama, at the time of the murder. About all the defense could add to this alibi evidence was some implausible testimony to the effect that the Klan did not advocate violence and had instructed its members not to take guns to Montgomery. Counsel for the accused sought to picture Rowe as an agent provocateur and to create the impression that he had done the shooting. The defense also tried to persuade the jury that the FBI had bribed its informant to testify against his fellow klansmen. None of the defendants took the stand. Although able to create the impression that Moton might have changed some facets of his story since the night of the shooting, the defense proved unable to mount a similarly effective attack on Rowe's testimony.[33]

Lacking sufficient evidence to rebut the prosecution's case, Arthur Hanes played on the prejudices of the jury. While cross-examining one government witness, he went out of his way to elicit the irrelevant information that the crowd which had attended the march and rally on the day before the murder had been "racially mixed." In his closing argument Hanes launched an attack on Dr. Martin Luther King, Jr., and on "organizations at work in this country to divide us, and to destroy us." He branded Rowe a Judas who "worked for pay" and characterized him as a bad father who had failed to support his children. Finally, in an apparent effort to capitalize on the jurors' presumed commitment to states' rights, Hanes asked them to "consider who brought these charges."[34]

In their own closing arguments Doar and U.S. Attorney Ben Hard-

eman argued that private citizens could not be allowed to defend segregation by taking the law into their own hands. The assistant attorney general went even further. "The rights were all on the other side," he declared. "The rights under our system were all with the Negroes that were
marching from Selma to Montgomery, whether you like it or not." The
very court in which they were sitting, Doar reminded members of the
jury, had handed down an order granting them those rights.[35]

The same judge who had issued that injunction was trying this case. In
his charge to the jury Frank Johnson echoed Doar. Pointing out that those
who participated in the Selma-to-Montgomery march had possessed both
a legal and a constitutional right to do so, he declared they were entitled
to be free from "harassment, intimidation and oppression [*sic*] whether
or not I as the Judge of the court or you as jurors agree with the ends for
which those rights were exercised." As jurors, Johnson instructed them,
their concern should not be with furthering or impeding any political or
sociological cause. They must not let their prejudices for or against the
accused, the federal government, or "any citizen against whom the defendants are alleged to have conspired" influence their verdict.[36]

In the end the jurors met his challenge to surmount their biases, but
they did so only with great difficulty. After the jury had deliberated for
most of one afternoon and part of the following morning, foreman T. H.
Kirby, a school superintendent from Lee County, informed Judge Johnson
that they were hopelessly deadlocked. Rather than declaring a mistrial,
the judge reminded the jurors of the importance of the case and the length
and expense of the trial. There was no reason to believe, he said, that
"more intelligent, impartial or competent jurors" could be found to decide this case. Ignoring Hanes's protest that this additional charge was
prejudicial to his clients, Johnson sent the jury back to deliberate
further.[37]

At 2:00 P.M. on December 3, 1965, it returned with a historic verdict:
"guilty as charged in the indictment."[38] Doar expressed pride at the way
the American system of justice had performed in this case, and President
Johnson declared: "The whole nation can take heart from the fact that
there are those in the South who believe in justice in racial matters and
who are determined not to stand for acts of violence and terror."[39] The
defendants appealed the surprising verdicts against them, but without
success. Eaton died before the Fifth Circuit Court of Appeals could decide
the case. When it did, on April 27, 1967, the court upheld the convic-

tions against his surviving codefendants.[40] "We have not the slightest doubt," the Fifth Circuit concluded, "that this evidence, . . . along with the inferences reasonably to be drawn therefrom, was quite enough to support the verdict."[41] The court ruled that participants in the Selma-to-Montgomery march had been exercising an attribute of national citizenship and rejected the contention that the indictment had failed to state an offense under section 241.

By the time the Fifth Circuit handed down its decision, another southern jury also had convicted Klan members of violating section 241. In Athens, Georgia, James Lackey, Herbert Guest, and Denver Phillips had moved successfully to have their cases severed from those of Lemuel Penn's alleged killers, Cecil Myers and Howard Sims. Myers, Sims, and the sixth defendant, George Hampton Turner, came to trial on June 28, 1966. Doar expected the Penn case to be a tough one, but he was enthusiastic that the Supreme Court had given the Justice Department the opportunity to try it. The Athens proceeding excited considerable interest because this was the first case to be tried under section 241 after the Court's *Price* and *Guest* decisions.[42]

As in the earlier state trial of Myers and Sims, the defense sought to exploit the prejudices of the white Georgians who comprised the jury and to capitalize on their hostility toward an integrationist national government. Although avoiding the wildly racist rhetoric that had spiced Darsey's closing argument in Danielsville, James Hudson, again representing the accused klansmen, did make some muted appeals to the sort of sentiments on which his former associate had played so successfully. The most notable of these was the assertion (made while defending some anti-integration picketing in which his clients had engaged) that "we have got as many rights" as the "colored people."[43] Hudson also stressed the capacity of Georgians to deal with their own problems and to punish their own wrongdoers. "We don't have to rely on the United States for everything," he told the jury.[44]

This time such appeals were far less successful than they had been in 1964. Second Assistant Attorney General St. John Barrett, who supervised preparation of the case for the Civil Rights Division, believed the government had a good chance of getting a favorable verdict from a jury, if for no other reason than because federal prosecutors were better than even the best-intentioned state ones. The outcome of the trial justified his optimism. The jury returned verdicts in the Myers-Sims-Turner trial on July

2. Judge William Bootle ordered these sealed until after Lackey, Guest, and Phillips were tried, so that the verdicts would not influence the jury hearing their case. The results of both trials were announced on July 8. Georgia jurors had acquitted four of the defendants, but they had found both Sims and Myers guilty. Judge Bootle gave each of the convicted men a ten-year sentence, the maximum allowed under section 241.[45]

U.S. Attorney Floyd Buford had justified the confidence of the Civil Rights Division, which believed he possessed sufficient commitment and competence to try this important case without Barrett, who remained in Washington during the first trial. Buford "quarterbacked" the government's efforts masterfully and labored twelve hours a day, seven days a week preparing its case. During the trials FBI agents overheard newsmen, court officials, and even defense attorneys praising his performance. Barrett called the U.S. attorney's argument in the second trial "a masterpiece."[46] After the verdicts were announced, Buford declared triumphantly, "The jury has spoken; the court has ruled; justice has been done."[47]

Despite the four acquittals, the last of these assertions was as true as the others, for the killers of Lemuel Penn were going to prison. Like its predecessor in Alabama, this was really a murder trial dressed up as a civil rights conspiracy case, and like their counterparts in Alabama, Georgia jurors had voted to convict klansmen for racial killings. They had not heard what was supposed to be the government's case. As the indictment, and particularly the initial complaint filed by the FBI, made clear, its original core was a charge of conspiracy to deprive blacks of rights created by the 1964 Civil Rights Act. When the Supreme Court refused to review Judge Bootle's dismissal of that portion of the indictment, it left the prosecution in a difficult position. The government could not prove the pipe-dream conspiracy between klansmen and police which Justice Stewart had fabricated to justify the *Guest* decision, so it was unable to try the defendants for their efforts to deprive blacks of equal access to state facilities. That left only the charge that the accused had plotted to "interfere with travel in interstate commerce." The government had to build its case around this allegation, attempting to prove it rather largely with evidence gathered for other purposes.[48]

Much of what it offered concerned the Penn killing. The government devoted about one-third of its trial time to that incident. Trying this portion of the case as if it were in fact prosecuting a murder, it included among its witnesses the doctor who performed the autopsy on Penn and an FBI firearms and ballistics expert. The prosecution seemed to agree with Hudson that "the only manifestation of this conspiracy that might tend to convict the defendants is the murder of Lemuel Penn."[49]

Certainly, that killing was about the only element of its case that seemed to have much to do with impeding interstate travel by blacks. Although Buford insisted that "the alleged agreement to keep out of state Negroes away from the Athens area" was the essence of the government's case, he acknowledged to the jury that in order to prove its existence the government would have to resort to bringing "evidence in here to you to show a broader conspiracy."[50] In presenting their case in chief, he and the three Justice Department lawyers working with him called twenty-five witnesses. Seven of these gave testimony bearing on the Penn killing. The only others who discussed anything that even arguably involved interstate travel by blacks were two Athens policemen, who described an incident in which Sims (with Myers present) had sworn at an elderly black couple with New Jersey license plates who asked for directions to Atlanta. The other government witnesses all testified about matters which, although generally tending to establish the existence of some sort of conspiracy, were local in nature. For example, Chief Edward E. Hardy and two other members of the Athens Police Department discussed the actions of several of the defendants, among them Sims, who had brandished a pistol during a Klan demonstration against black picketing of a popular drive-in restaurant on Athens's main street (which also happened to be a U.S. highway). In addition, the prosecution offered police and civilian testimony about some shooting at an apartment complex inhabited by blacks in which Myers and Guest apparently had participated. Scratching hard for evidence, it even reached beyond the date of the indictment, offering proof of an October 1965 incident in which Sims, Myers, and five other Klan members had forced a black farmer off the road and beaten him. Since the victim had been driving between two points in the same county, like most of the prosecution's evidence, this testimony, although damaging, did little to prove that the defendants had conspired to interfere with interstate travel.[51]

The prosecution was about as successful in linking the defendants to such a conspiracy as in proving its existence. This failure alone could explain the acquittals of defendants Turner and Phillips. With respect to the former, the prosecution by its own admission was able to prove little more than that he had been present at the drive-in restaurant confrontation. The government could claim to have connected Phillips only with the apartment complex shooting.[52]

The acquittals of Guest and Lackey are more difficult to explain, for the government had presented a substantial amount of evidence against each of them. The reason those defendants did not share the fate of Sims and Myers seems to be that, unlike their convicted codefendants, they had not shot Lemuel Penn. The fact that Guest and Lackey were not involved in the incident with the travelers from New Jersey might explain why they were not found guilty of involvement in a conspiracy to interfere with interstate travel. What principally distinguished the cases against them from those against Sims and Myers, however, was that neither had fired at Penn. The government failed to prove that Guest bore any responsibility at all for the killing. Lackey's confession was admitted into evidence at his trial, so the jury which acquitted him knew he had acted as a driver for the klansmen who killed the black educator. Although that made him guilty of murder under Georgia law, the fact that he did not pull a trigger probably explains why jurors found him not guilty. Certainly, the fact that Sims and Myers did shoot Penn is the reason why the jury convicted them. When the defense counsel tried to get a certified copy of the indictment and not-guilty verdict from the state trial admitted into evidence, Buford objected loudly, insisting that it would not be germain or relevant because this was a conspiracy case, not a murder trial. But the evidence that Sims and Myers were guilty of the federal crime with which they were charged was unimpressive.[53] Although Hudson was careful to remind the jury that "these boys are not being tried for killing anybody," it seems really to have been the murder of Lemuel Penn for which jurors convicted them.[54] On appeal Sims and Myers challenged the admissibility of some of the evidence the government had used to establish their responsibility for that crime, but the Fifth Circuit, ruling against them on that and other issues, affirmed the convictions.[55] For a second time a federal jury comprised of white southerners sent racist killers to jail.

Fifteen months after the Athens convictions, other jurors in Mississippi returned guilty verdicts against some of the perpetrators of the Neshoba County murders. That hearing was widely viewed as a trial, not only of the defendants but of Mississippi and its people. Federal authorities could "do no more than investigate and present a case against the accused," as the *Nashville Tennessean* pointed out. "In the end justice must be meted out by a jury of Mississippians."[56]

Convincing twelve of them to do justice would not be easy, but John Doar, again taking personal charge of a major civil rights prosecution, was eager to try. The bulk and complexity of the evidence probably made his participation necessary; but what motivated Doar to go to Mississippi himself was determination to establish that neither the law nor the U.S. Department of Justice was helpless in the face of such an outrage as the Neshoba County killings. He also wanted to prove that even a Mississippi judge and jury could be persuaded to do their duties.[57] "I am here," he announced, "because your National Government is concerned about your local law enforcement and in a conviction that local law enforcement must work if we are to preserve our liberty and freedom."[58]

Doar assumed personal responsibility for prosecuting the case only after Judge Cox had once more derailed it. On October 7, 1966, Cox, who earlier had indicated he was in no rush to try this "ordinary garden variety type law suit," again dismissed the indictments. His rationale exuded irony: the grand jury panel used in the Southern District of Mississippi did not contain an adequate number of Indians, women—and blacks. Although the government acquiesced in Cox's ruling, recognizing that the procedures employed to select the indicting grand jurors did not square with the dictates of a recent decision by the Fifth Circuit Court of Appeals, the segregationist judge came under fire from the northern press. In part this was because he refused to convene a new grand jury to take up the case unless the Justice Department would agree to have it also investigate a Head Start program run by civil rights workers. When the grand jury finally did assemble, Doar made no attempt to secure new section 242 indictments. On February 27, 1967, he got it to indict nineteen men for violation of section 241. The only changes in the lineup of defendants were the deletion of Jimmy Lee Townsend and the addition of E. G. "Hop" Barnett, a former Neshoba County sheriff, and Sam Holloway Bowers, Jr., the Imperial Wizard of the White Knights of the Ku Klux Klan.[59]

Bowers and his fellow klansmen may well have believed that the presence of Cox on the bench enhanced their chances for acquittal. Certainly, Doar and his co-counsel, Civil Rights Division lawyer Robert Owen and U.S. Attorney Robert Hauberg, were not optimistic about their chances

before him. To the surprise of both parties, Cox tried the case with scru-
pulous fairness.[60] He instructed the jury to decide it "without sympathy,
bias or prejudice" and explicitly declined "to suggest or convey in any way
or manner any intimation as to what verdict I think you should find."[61]

Spared the anticipated interference from the bench, the prosecution
proceeded to build a case against the defendants. Many of the forty-one
witnesses it produced gave testimony which was quite routine and notable
only for demonstrating that, although brought under a civil rights statute, this was really a murder case. A number of FBI employees took the
stand to do nothing more exciting than establish the chain of custody of
physical evidence or discuss ballistics tests. The government used two
agents, three dentists, and a fingerprint examiner to prove that the corpses
the Bureau had located under the earthen dam were indeed the remains of
Chaney, Goodman, and Schwerner. It also produced a series of witnesses
who explained why the victims were in the Philadelphia area and traced
their movements on the day they disappeared. None of this evidence,
except for some testimony that Deputy Price was the man who had arrested the victims and taken them to jail, linked any of the defendants to
the murders it established had taken place.[62]

The testimony of Joseph M. Hatcher, a Meridian police officer who had
been a Klan member in June 1964, did. He testified that on June 22 Edgar
Ray "Preacher" Killen had told him the three civil rights workers had been
taken care of, describing where the bodies were buried and asserting that
the victims' car had been burned. Unlike Hatcher, two of the most important witnesses Doar used to link the defendants to the murders were paid
FBI informers. Carlton Wallace Miller, also a Meridian policeman, had
joined the White Knights in March or April of 1964. He identified nine of
the defendants as klansmen and testified that both Killen and defendant
Frank Herndon had acknowledged to him assembling a group of Meridian
klansmen to go to Neshoba County on June 21, 1964. Killen had told him
what had happened to the victims, and Herndon had talked with him about
the disposal of their car. Miller also claimed that the Imperial Wizard had to
approve any "elimination" carried out by White Knights.[63]

Reverend Delmer Dennis, a Meridian minister, was also an FBI informant. Although acknowledging that Sam Bowers had never admitted to
him being involved in the abduction and slaying of the three civil rights
workers, he confirmed that White Knight murders required the approval of
the state organization, headed by the Imperial Wizard. Dennis also pro-

duced a coded message from Bowers, which revealed knowledge of the crime and a determination to cover it up. In addition, he told of gatherings attended by defendants at which the elimination of Mickey Schwerner had been discussed and the state organization's approval of that project revealed. Dennis described a Klan assembly at an abandoned gym in Neshoba County from which a group that included several of the accused had sallied forth with weapons to attack a meeting at the Mount Zion Methodist Church, an assault which a member of that congregation confirmed had taken place. Finally, Dennis linked both Deputy Price and Sheriff Rainey to the White Knights and gave testimony about statements Price had made indicating he was present when the civil rights workers were killed. Dennis, who had been an FBI informant since November 1964, made an extremely effective witness, for he had remained in the Klan until the moment he took the stand and was then serving as Province Titan, the personal administrative representative of Imperial Wizard Bowers. Adding to his credibility was the fact that the minister was a self-proclaimed segregationist. [64]

His brother Willie, a civil service employee who had served as an FBI informer for about three months, also testified for the government. He did not hurt the defendants nearly as much as one of their own, James Jordan. Jordan, who had confessed to the FBI and subsequently been paid about $8,000 by the Bureau (most of it to cover economic losses suffered when he moved out of Mississippi), denied having killed anyone himself. He admitted, however, having been part of a group of men which had driven the three civil rights workers to an unpaved road in rural Neshoba County and there shot them to death. The killers had been able to kidnap Schwerner, Goodman, and Chaney, Jordan testified, because Deputy Price had pulled their station wagon over with his patrol car. Jordan placed Price at the location of the killing, along with Horace Doyle Barnette, Jimmy Snowden, Jimmy Arledge, Billy Wayne Posey, Alton Wayne Roberts, and Jerry McGrew Sharpe. In addition, Jordan implicated Herndon, Killen, "Pete" Harris, Travis Barnette, and Bernard Aikins in the planning of the murders. He testified that Killen, Price, and Hop Barnett had issued instructions to the death squad during its mission and that he and his accomplices had received orders to return home after it was over, along with assurances that everything would be "taken care of," from a car occupied by Officer Willis and someone else. Jordan also reported that Bowers had told him in May 1964 that Schwerner should be gotten rid of, although under cross-examination he acknowledged never having heard the Imperial Wizard actually order his elimination.[65]

To confirm Jordan's account of what had transpired on the night of the murders, the prosecution introduced a confession which Horace Doyle Barnette had given to the FBI in November 1964. Judge Cox admitted it into evidence, but only after ordering Doar to block out the names of all defendants other than Jordan. That probably did not keep the jury from identifying the individuals to whom it referred, for anyone who had heard Jordan's testimony could fill in most of the blanks. The confession, which Doar read to the jury, supported his witness on all essential points but one: Jordan had claimed that when the fatal shots were fired he was down the road, waiting to direct another car to the scene; according to Barnette's statement, it was Jordan himself who gunned down Chaney. Barnette said that after begging his fellow klansmen to "save one for me," Jordan had complained bitterly that they "didn't leave me anything but a nigger."[66]

Although the government's star witness appeared to be a murderer who had told at least one large lie, its case was a strong one. That presented by the thirteen defense lawyers (a group which included every member of the Neshoba County bar but the county attorney) was not. They paraded 114 witnesses to the stand. Some of these testified about what they represented as the refusal of the FBI to cooperate with local authorities, while others attacked the reputations of the government's informer witnesses. Many attested to the good character of the accused (Imperial Wizard Bowers even managed to find two blacks to vouch for him). The defense presented numerous alibi witnesses who claimed particular defendants had been with them on June 21. Many of these, however, were close friends or relatives of the accused, and a substantial percentage failed actually to establish the whereabouts of the men for whom they testified during the crucial hours after the civil rights workers were released from the Neshoba County jail. Only one defendant, Herman Tucker, the alleged driver of the bulldozer used to bury the bodies, took the stand to testify in his own behalf.[67]

The defense sought to compensate for a weak case with appeals to the prejudices of the jury. For example, attorney Laurel G. Weir asked one prosecution witness if Schwerner had tried "to get young male Negroes to sign statements agreeing to rape a white woman once a week during the hot summer of 1964." Noting there was no apparent basis for this question in the record, Judge Cox sharply rebuked Weir. The lawyer managed, however, to get away with asking the same witness whether "colored women" had stayed in Schwerner's apartment, as well as with questioning another one concerning what the dead men had said about school integration. Three times defense counsel asked government witnesses whether Schwerner was an atheist. During their closing arguments they again sought to capitalize on the racism and Christianity of the jurors. Counsel for the accused also tried to exploit resentment toward the civil rights movement, but their favorite target was the national government. They complained about Doar and some of the prosecution's witnesses being from that city of "great confusion," Washington, D.C. The defense also appealed to state pride, insisting that Mississippi could enforce its own laws and telling jurors they did not need an attorney from the nation's capital to tell them what to do. Weir warned his listeners not to let Doar use this case to "make the federal government the power in this country."[68]

Like his opponents, U.S. Attorney Robert Hauberg played on the jurors' loyalty to Mississippi, but he did so by arguing that the Philadelphia murders had shamed their state and implying that the way to remove the stain from its reputation was to convict the killers.[69] In his own closing argument Doar defended federal intervention in this case. "When local law enforcement officials become involved as participants in violent crime and use their positions, power, and authority to accomplish this," he said, "there is very little to be hoped for except with assistance from the federal government." Doar denied that Washington was invading Mississippi. The federal government had enacted the law the defendants were accused of violating, but they were being tried in a Mississippi city before a Mississippi judge and a Mississippi jury. "The sole responsibility [for] the determination of the guilt or innocence of these men remain [sic] in the hands where it should remain," Doar emphasized, "in the hands of twelve citizens of the State of Mississippi."[70]

These twelve Mississippians responded positively to his challenge to enforce the law against perpetrators of racist violence. Judge Cox's charge to the jury was poorly organized and repetitious, but impeccably fair. After hearing it, five white men and seven white women, most of them from working-class backgrounds, deliberated for nearly ten hours over two days, then reported to the court that they could not agree upon a verdict. However, Cox refused to declare a mistrial. Instead, he delivered a "dynamite charge." Like Frank Johnson in Alabama, Judge Cox lectured the jury on the importance of the trial and the great expense both sides would incur if it had to be repeated. There was no reason to believe, he said, that the case could be tried better another time or that a better jury could be found to decide it. Cox informed the jurors that, while they did not have to reach the same verdict for all defendants, it was their duty to consult with one another and deliberate with a view to reaching agreement. Then he sent them out to talk some more. They worked well into the night and deliberated further the following day. Concerning Killen, Sharpe, and Hop Barnett, the jury remained divided, but on October 20 it returned verdicts in the cases of the other fourteen defendants.[71]

Although acquitting seven of them, these jurors convicted an equal number. To the surprise and outrage of whites in Neshoba County, they found Bowers, Price, Roberts, Posey, Arledge, Snowden, and Horace Doyle Barnette guilty. For the most part, like its counterpart in Georgia, this jury seems to have convicted on the basis of direct involvement in a killing rather than participation in some sort of conspiracy. With the exception of Bowers, all of those found guilty were among the men Jordan had placed at the murder scene. The only member of that group who escaped conviction was Jerry Sharpe, the beneficiary of a hung jury. Apparently some jurors believed the sister and brother-in-law who testified he had been in bed at their house when the killings took place. The cases against some of the other defendants were weak enough to justify acquittal. About Olan Burrage, for example, all Doar even claimed to have proved was that he owned the land on which the killers had buried the bodies. Yet the jury also refused to convict men, such as Herndon, against whom the prosecution clearly had presented sufficient proof to permit conviction for conspiracy. Its reason for including Bowers among those it found guilty was probably the testimony that he had ordered the murders, but that line of reasoning should have led also to the conviction of Killen. "Preacher" had been active in state and local politics in recent years, and perhaps that, along with his status as a part-time Baptist minister, swayed enough minds to earn him a hung jury.[72]

That the jurors had returned any guilty verdicts at all surprised many court observers, who had expected this case to end as trials of whites accused of racial killings always had in Mississippi.[73] Attorney General Joe Patterson saw the surprise outcome as vindicating his much-maligned state. "After all the criticism . . . ," he thought it "pertinent to point out that it was a Mississippi judge who presided over the federal court case, a Mississippi U.S. attorney who helped prosecute, and a Mississippi jury which convicted seven men."[74] Had he waited until December 29, Patterson would have had to acknowledge that a Mississippi jurist, while sentencing Bowers and Roberts to the maximum ten-year prison term, had imprisoned Price and Posey for only six years and Snowden and Doyle Barnette for only three.[75] Still, his was not the only sanguine assessment of the Meridian trial. The father of victim Robert Goodman found it encouraging that "the people in the South, in a civil rights case, sat in judgment of their own actions and decided they would not tolerate violation of law and order."[76] The *Jackson Daily News* thought the guilty verdicts would "discourage those bent on violence from future activity of this sort in Mississippi." In the opinion of Ralph McGill of the *Atlanta Constitution,* the Meridian jury had rendered "a landmark decision." Its verdict was, according to the *New York Times,* proof of a "quiet revolution that is taking place in Southern attitudes—a slow, still faltering but inexorable conversion to the concept that a single standard of justice must cover whites and Negroes alike."[77]

The Mississippi jury, along with those in Georgia and Alabama, had proved that white southerners could be persuaded to punish perpetrators of anti–civil rights violence. They had, however, returned their historic verdicts in federal courtrooms under prodding by federal prosecutors and federal judges. To many people, the southern states and their criminal justice systems still seemed hopelessly biased and unreliable. Even after the convictions in Meridian, civil rights groups and northern liberals continued to press for a federal solution to the problem of racist violence in the South. What was needed, they insisted, was congressional legislation.

A Federal Law

While prosecuting klansmen under section 241, the Justice Department also pressed Congress to provide it with a more satisfactory weapon for combating racist violence in the South. After reading what Justices Clark and Brennan had written in the *Guest* case, Ralph Spritzer informed his superiors in the Solicitor General's Office that the concurring opinions were intended "to make clear that there is a need for further legislation and to give assurance . . . that such legislation, if enacted, would be sustained." He added that the Justice Department should "seize the initiative immediately and unhesitatingly . . . press for congressional action."[1] Inspired by the spasm of violence and injustice that convulsed Alabama during 1965, the department already had begun preparing to do precisely that. In the spring of 1966 the Johnson administration sent to Capitol Hill legislation designed to protect blacks and civil rights workers. Its timing was not ideal. Increasingly divided over both goals and tactics, the movement that had built support for earlier civil rights bills was disintegrating. Alienated by the angry rhetoric of SNCC and CORE militants and frightened by rioting in the black ghettos of northern cities, many whites outside the South were losing the enthusiasm they had developed for the equal rights crusade. Sensitive to their changing mood and hostile to the attack on housing discrimination to which Lyndon Johnson linked his protection proposal, Congress balked. The administration had to labor until May 1968 to obtain enactment of a federal law against anti–civil rights violence.

The process which led to the adoption of that statute began during the Selma crisis in early 1965. The first and best-known legislative product of that spring's disorder in Alabama was the Voting Rights Act of 1965, which the president signed into law on August 6. It had been propelled through Congress by the violence there. The Voting Rights Act suspended the use of literacy tests and similar devices traditionally employed to exclude blacks from the southern political process in any state or part of a state in which less than 50 percent of the persons of voting age were registered or had voted in the 1964 presidential election. It also provided for the appointment of federal "examiners" to register blacks and supervise elections in states which persisted in violating the Fifteenth Amendment.[2]

Although violence against the civil rights movement was one of the major reasons for its enactment, the new law contained only two obscure sections dealing with that problem. Section 11(b) forbade anyone, whether acting under color of law "or otherwise," to intimidate, threaten, or coerce any person for voting, attempting to vote, or urging or aiding someone else to vote. Section 12(a) made violations of section 11(b) criminal offenses, punishable by a fine of up to $5,000, a prison sentence of up to five years, or both. Together, these provisions made the actual or threatened use of force against all potential black voters, and all voter registration workers as well, federal crimes. That was more than the Justice Department was trying to accomplish. The corresponding sections in the bill which it had drafted protected only persons whose right to vote was secured by some other provision of the bill. Both the testimony of Attorney General Katzenbach before congressional committees and the way the department used the law after its enactment suggest that what Justice was most interested in was safeguarding such persons from economic coercion. CORE asked for legislation that would impose federal penalties comparable to the state ones for murder on anyone who killed a would-be voter, and the Leadership Conference on Civil Rights (an umbrella organization of civil rights groups represented before the House Judiciary Committee by Roy Wilkins of the NAACP) sought to have the coverage of this part of the bill expanded to embrace all qualified voters. Neither suggested altering it to protect civil rights workers. The House Judiciary Committee rewrote the measure in a way which had that effect, despite a reminder from Representative Byron Rogers (R-Colo.) that under the state action doctrine even the Justice Department's proposal was of dubious constitutionality. The full House adopted the committee's section 11(b), and the Senate eventually agreed to it also. There was little controversy concerning this part of the bill, and few people in Congress or the administration seem to have known or cared much about it.[3]

Ku Klux Klansmen in full regalia rally around a burning cross. (*Atlanta Journal Constitution.*)

President Dwight D. Eisenhower (left) and Arkansas Governor Orval Faubus meet in Newport, Rhode Island, on September 14, 1957, to discuss violent opposition to school desegregation in Little Rock, Arkansas. (Dwight D. Eisenhower Library; UPI/Bettmann Newsphotos.)

President Eisenhower signs the Civil Rights Act of 1960 while Attorney General William Rogers (left) and Deputy Attorney General Lawrence Walsh look on. (Dwight D. Eisenhower Library.)

Attorney General Robert F. Kennedy (left) talks with his brother, President John F. Kennedy. (John F. Kennedy Library.)

Below left: John Doar replaced Burke Marshall as assistant attorney general in 1965. He prosecuted personally those accused of some of the most highly publicized anti–civil rights killings of the mid-1960s. (John Doar.)

Below right: Assistant Attorney General Burke Marshall headed the Civil Rights Division of the Department of Justice from early 1961 until early 1965. (Lyndon B. Johnson Library.)

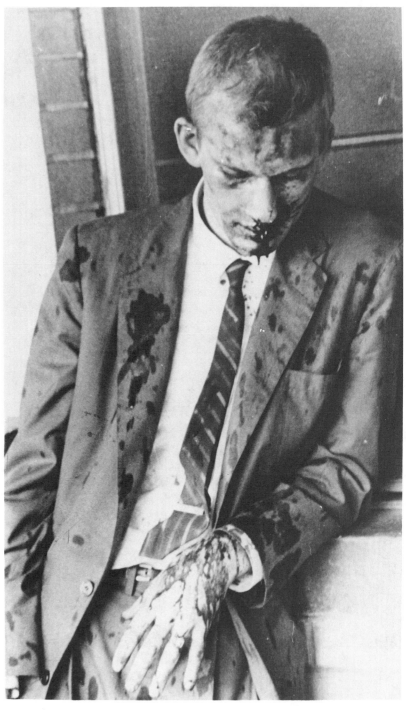

This Freedom Rider was one of those attacked by a mob of angry white racists in Montgomery, Alabama, on May 20, 1961. (AP/Wide World Photos.)

Birmingham Public Safety Commissioner Eugene "Bull" Connor's police force became notorious for its close cooperation with the Ku Klux Klan and for violent attacks on civil rights demonstrators. *(Birmingham News.)*

Government lawyers and federal marshalls escort black student James Meredith across the riot-torn campus of the University of Mississippi in September 1961. (AP/Wide World Photos.)

Dr. Martin Luther King, Jr. (center), who repeatedly called for increased federal protection of civil rights activists in the South, is shown here with Attorney General Robert F. Kennedy (left). (AP/Wide World Photos.)

This flier asked the public to assist the Federal Bureau of Investigation with the massive investigation that it launched after three civil rights workers disappeared in Mississippi in 1964.

Lieutenant Colonel Lemuel Penn's car was splattered with blood when he was shot to death by Ku Klux Klansmen near Colbert, Georgia, on July 11, 1964. (AP/Wide World Photos.)

President Lyndon B. Johnson (right) responded to Alabama Governor George C. Wallace's refusal to assume responsibility for protecting the Selma-to-Montgomery voting rights march of April 1965 by sending federal troops into Alabama. (Lyndon B. Johnson Library.)

Members of Congress watch as President Johnson signs the Civil Rights Act of 1968 which significantly expanded the authority of the federal government to punish anti–civil rights violence. (Lyndon B. Johnson Library.)

Perhaps that was because by the time section 11(b) became law the White House and the Justice Department were already moving to attack the violence problem with other legislation. The bloodshed around Selma, combined with the failure of the Alabama judicial system to punish those responsible for it, escalated demands for a new federal law against racist terrorism. Pressure for enactment of such a statute began to build during the nationwide sympathy protests that followed the killing of Reverend James Reeb. Immediately after the murder of Jonathan Daniels, spokesmen for SNCC, CORE, the SCLC, the National Urban League, the Episcopal Society for Cultural and Racial Unity, the National Catholic Conference for Interracial Justice, the Union of American Hebrew Congregations, and the National Council of Churches of Christ in America called on President Johnson to introduce "legislation to permit federal investigation and prosecution of all acts of racial violence and terror in jurisdictions which have demonstrated their unwillingness to mete out equal justice."[4] Following the acquittal of Collie Wilkins, Martin Luther King, Jr., announced that he was cutting short a European tour and returning to Atlanta to mount a campaign to make the murder of persons pursuing their constitutional rights a federal crime. The outcome of the Tom Coleman trial outraged the nation, and the Unitarians, the NAACP, and the New York Association of Trial Lawyers all reacted to it by calling for a national law punishing racially motivated killings and assaults. Newspapers as diverse as the *Baltimore Afro-American,* the *New York Times,* and the *Greensboro Daily News* endorsed such legislation.[5] "The need is clear . . . ," the *Times* editorialized in December 1965, "for a law making it a Federal crime to commit an act of violence or to threaten violence with racial purpose or effect against any person."[6]

The Johnson administration proved quite receptive to demands for the enactment of such a law. The Liuzzo murder stunned top officials of the Justice Department, and Attorney General Katzenbach became quite upset when an Alabama jury acquitted the alleged killer of Jonathan Daniels. By 1965 the department was clearly in a mood to take decisive action against racist violence. Besides prosecuting those responsible for the murder of Viola Liuzzo, it initiated contempt proceedings against the chief of police and the public safety commissioner of Bogalusa, Louisiana, for failing to protect peacefully demonstrating civil rights workers, filed criminal charges against a deputy sheriff in that parish, and obtained an injunction forbidding the Original Knights of the Ku Klux Klan from engaging in further acts of intimidation in the area. Even the FBI was moving aggressively, opening a field office in South Carolina and dramatically increasing the number of civil rights investigations it conducted, particularly in Louisiana and Mississippi. The bureau was doing what John Doar and his assistant, Dorothy Landsberg, would later characterize as "a tremendous job" of helping to contain terrorist activity. Hoping to further enhance the FBI's capabilities, President Johnson asked Congress for a hundred additional agents, to be formed into a special civil rights force.[7]

Enraged by the Liuzzo slaying, the president also requested legislation to curb anti–civil rights violence. Mrs. Liuzzo's murder appears to have affected him deeply. When he heard about it at 1:00 A.M., the president immediately called the FBI, asking for details. He telephoned the Bureau two or three more times that night and would have placed a call to the victim's husband had J. Edgar Hoover not dissuaded him. Later that day Johnson went on national television with the director to announce the arrests of Wilkins, Eaton, and Thomas. The president denounced the Klan and told the public he had directed Attorney General Katzenbach to develop legislation to bring it under control.[8]

By April 7, 1965, the Justice Department was proceeding as rapidly as possible to design "a bill for that purpose." Various divisions submitted suggestions to the deputy attorney general. Among these were proposals from the Internal Security Division, an organization normally more concerned about Communists than klansmen. It suggested requiring Klan groups to register with the government, and also proposed enactment of a law making murder, manslaughter, assault, threats of violence, and the destruction of property federal crimes when the motive behind them was the victim's involvement in activities directed toward the achievement or exercise of any one of ten enumerated rights (which ranged from voting and equal protection to freedom of religion). Internal Security also recommended proscribing both conspiracy to engage in such conduct and the organization of groups that advocated oppression or intimidation. It was proposing a breathtaking extension of federal criminal jurisdiction.[9] "From every point of view it would be preferable if prosecutions of those who engage in such conduct are carried out by state authorities pursuant to state law," one attorney in the division remarked. "The need for federal legislation has arisen only because state authorities have failed to act."[10] Hoping to fill the vacuum created by their inaction, a number of top

Justice Department officials met on April 22 in the deputy attorney general's office to review legislative proposals for dealing with the KKK, and on May 7 the president assured Governor John Volpe of Massachusetts that he intended "to send my proposals to Congress in the near future."[11]

Nearly a year passed before Johnson did what he had promised. In the interim the White House considered other ways of dealing with the problem. During October 1965 one of Johnson's top aides, George E. Reedy, suggested that the situation required a change in the South's concept of justice, which might be brought about by having former southern governors with "advanced views" on race relations confer with state and community leaders. Special Counsel to the President Joseph Califano was skeptical about this idea, but told Johnson he thought it might help to have the attorney general talk to bar association leaders about the importance of fair trials in the South. Lee White endorsed both plans.[12]

While the president pondered alternatives, the House Committee on Un-American Activities also considered what to do about the KKK. Five days after Johnson's televised attack on the Klan the committee, bowing to administration pressure, voted unanimously to undertake an investigation of the hooded order. In late October, Congressman Charles Weltner, an Atlanta Democrat who had suggested such an inquiry even before the Liuzzo killing, told the press the committee's efforts might yield "legislation to control acts of violence." His Republican colleague, John Ashbrook of Ohio, agreed. According to the *New York Times,* the Justice Department was waiting to see what the House Committee on Un-American Activities did before making specific recommendations to Congress. The committee concluded its hearings on February 24, 1966, but not until June did its chairman, Representative Edwin Willis (D-La.) introduce legislation to proscribe Klan activities. His bill resembled anti-Communist legislation with which the courts had found First Amendment problems, and Attorney General Katzenbach expressed doubts about its constitutionality. He urged that the House pass instead a measure drawn up by the administration.[13]

During the summer of 1965 its "Klan task force" in the Justice Department had studied the problem of racist violence in the South. The adequacy of laws already on the books was evaluated, and both the Civil Rights Commission and the Leadership Conference on Civil Rights made specific suggestions for legislation against racial violence. An inter-agency task force headed by John Doar unanimously concluded that such legislation was needed. Katzenbach remained reluctant to expand federal jurisdiction as far as civil rights groups desired, but while continuing to hope that southern states would prosecute crimes of violence against those working for racial equality, he now favored legislation that would give the national government somewhat more authority in this area than it possessed under existing laws. By the time the president, in his January 12, 1966, State of the Union message, called for enactment of a statute "to strengthen authority of Federal courts to try those who murder, attack, or intimidate either civil rights workers or others exercising their constitutional rights—and to increase penalties to a level equal to the nature of the crime," Justice had given the problem a good deal of thought. Two weeks after the president spoke, Ramsey Clark, the University of Chicago–trained Dallas lawyer and son of Supreme Court Justice Tom Clark, who had become deputy attorney general in 1965, ordered the Civil Rights Division to prepare a memorandum explaining each of the existing statutory provisions under which legal action might be taken against persons who interfered with or intimidated civil rights workers. Meanwhile, Harold Koffsky of the Criminal Division prepared brief and very preliminary alternative drafts of a bill. Stephen Pollak, first assistant in the Civil Rights Division, and Louis Claiborne of the solicitor general's staff expanded these into a much broader and more complex measure. After making a list of specific activities which seemed to require federal protection, they drafted legislation that would cover them all. [14]

Pollak and Claiborne were still at work when the president told a television audience on March 15 that he was asking Congress to deal with a number of racial problems, including "violence against Negroes and Civil Rights workers." They did not finish the bill for a number of weeks, although "appropriate people" in the House and Senate were standing by, ready to introduce it. The principal reason for the delay was that the Supreme Court had not yet ruled in *Price* and *Guest*. Although confident of winning those cases, the Justice Department did not think it could put a bill into final form without seeing the Court's opinions. Deputy Attorney General Clark suggested sending the rest of the administration's civil rights proposals on to Capitol Hill without the violence measure, but because Attorney General Katzenbach expected rulings by April 1, the White House decided to hold up the entire package. After reversing this decision and electing to send a message to Congress on March 28, it, in turn, scrapped those plans when the Court ruled that morning. There followed two weeks of furious drafting in the Justice Department.[15] By April 13 Katzenbach and his men had completed their work and the "legislative package [was] in shape and ready to go."[16]

Fifteen days later the president's proposals finally reached Capitol Hill. By then the Justice Department had persuaded the White House to delete some of the harsher language from the original draft of the civil rights message, which the attorney general considered "unnecessarily belligerent and inflammatory to the South."[17] Although long delayed and somewhat watered down, what Johnson sent to Congress remained a forceful appeal for the enactment of legislation *"to make our authority against civil rights violence clear and sure."* The measure he was submitting, the president told legislators, was *"designed to prohibit any interference with the exercise of fundamental rights by threats or force, by any person—whether as an individual or in a group and whether privately or officially."*[18]

Title V of his comprehensive civil rights bill specifically identified nine "protected activities": voting, use of public accommodations, public education, public services and facilities, employment, housing, jury service, use of common carriers, and participation in federally assisted programs. It proposed to guard members of minority groups against attack while they were engaging in those protected activities, as well as against violence directed at them because they had done so in the past or might do so in the future. In addition, Title V would extend federal protection to persons who urged or aided others to exercise their civil rights. It addressed the sort of terrorism that had taken Lemuel Penn's life by providing punishment for violence directed at victims selected, not because of what they themselves were doing, but for purposes of intimidating others. In addition, Title V would relieve the government of the "specific intent" burden it had been forced to shoulder in section 241 and 242 cases. The offenses created by the new law would carry penalties that varied with the seriousness of the violation, ranging upward to imprisonment for life. The administration also recommended incorporating graduated punishments into sections 241 and 242.[19]

These proposals had the predictable support of Roy Wilkins and the Anti-Defamation League. SNCC too was demanding legislation. A June 5 shotgun attack on James Meredith aroused others to join these perennial advocates of civil rights measures. Meredith was making a one-man pilgrimage from Memphis, Tennessee, to Jackson, Mississippi, attempting to encourage his fellow blacks to overcome fear and exercise their right to vote, when a gunman wounded him from ambush. The president condemned this shooting and ordered Katzenbach to spare no effort to bring the perpetrator to justice. The Board of Aldermen of Paterson, New Jersey, and the Iowa Conference of the United Church of Christ reacted to the Meredith shooting by demanding federal legislation.[20] So did AFL–CIO President George Meany. Of Johnson's proposal, he said simply, "The act must be passed."[21]

Although the Meredith shooting generated considerable support for the administration's bill, prospects for passage of the legislation were clouded. In the months that had elapsed since enactment of the Voting Rights Act, the coalition responsible for the passage of that law, and of the Civil Rights Act of 1964, had begun to crumble. The "movement" (as the loose alliance of individuals and organizations working to improve the lot of black Americans was often called) was falling apart. Its disintegration became apparent during a mass march through Mississippi which civil rights activists mounted after the Meredith shooting. Roy Wilkins of the NAACP and Whitney Young of the National Urban League hoped to use this demonstration to generate support for federal legislation against anti–civil rights violence. SNCC and CORE wanted to utilize it to denounce the Johnson administration. In early 1966 SNCC was seething with anger at the federal government because of the January 3 murder of one of its voter registration workers, Sammy Younge, who was killed by a gas station attendant in Tuskegee, Alabama, when he tried to use a whites-only rest room. The hostility of both that organization and CORE had much deeper roots, however. Disappointed by the administration's reluctance to enforce laws already on the books and convinced that white liberals would sell them out whenever it served their interests to do so, the young activists in SNCC and CORE had turned away from interracialism, integration, and nonviolence during late 1965 and early 1966. SNCC's election of Stokely Carmichael to replace John Lewis as its leader and CORE's supplanting of James Farmer with the more militant Floyd McKissick confirmed the change of temper within the two groups. Carmichael's angry call for "Black Power" during the Meredith March revealed it to the rest of the world. While not repudiating the young SNCC and CORE militants, Dr. Martin Luther King, Jr., declared that this new slogan did not mean the movement was seeking power for Negroes only. Carmichael and McKissick promptly rejected his soft interpretation of Black Power.[22]

As the movement fell into disagreement and squabbling, white support for its objectives melted away. The fiery rhetoric of militant black nationalists, such as Carmichael, was partly responsible for this. Whatever the real meaning of Black Power was (and every civil rights leader gave his own connotation to that badly overworked phrase), most whites were sure it meant Negro violence against them. Fueling their fears were the ghetto riots that burned through one large city after another during the "long hot summers" of 1964–1967. More than forty of these erupted in 1966. That was twice as many as the previous year, when a bloody conflagration in the Watts section of Los Angeles horrified white America. Although 1966 produced no riot as large as that one, black sections of Chicago, Cleveland, Dayton, Milwaukee, and San Francisco experienced civil disturbances serious enough to require the use of National Guard troops to quell them.[23] "After Watts," as Allen Matusow has written, "the legions of moderate whites who had so recently demanded justice for the meek, Christ-like demonstrators at Selma began melting away."[24] Coming as they did in the wake of the landmark civil rights legislation of 1964 and 1965, the ghetto riots looked like evidence of black ingratitude. They alienated previously sympathetic whites, whose departure from the coalition that had passed those laws was hastened by the demands the movement was now making, demands that would affect more than just the South. Its call for jobs and an end to housing discrimination threatened the interests of northern whites themselves. Burning and looting in the ghettos provided a socially acceptable rationale for expressions of antiblack sentiment inspired at least in part by other concerns.[25]

They also made politicians reluctant to support further civil rights legislation. The Johnson administration found itself caught in the middle. On the one hand, it could not do enough to satisfy the most militant members of the movement. When the White House hosted a conference on civil rights on June 1–2, 1966, SNCC refused even to show up, and many of the activists who did participate sharply criticized the federal government for—among other things—not doing more to provide protection in the South. Yet, in seeking enactment of additional civil rights legislation, the Johnson administration risked being slapped down by a white backlash. Northern politicians were beginning to win elections with calls for "law and order" that were often little more than thinly disguised appeals to racism, and neither they nor their constituents were anxious to do any more for blacks.[26]

Despite a general lack of enthusiasm for civil rights legislation on Capitol Hill, there was considerable support there for federal action against southern violence. Immediately after the president's March 1965 denunciation of the Klan, two Republican senators and twenty-one GOP House members had endorsed his call for legislation against night riders.[27] By the time Johnson sent his bill to Congress in April 1966, a bipartisan group of twenty senators, headed by Paul Douglas (D-Ill.) and Clifford Case (R-N.J.) had introduced their own measure in "response to the violence at Selma and Birmingham, the street corner and highway killings of men and women peacefully asserting their constitutional rights, and the kind of outrageous justice that has resulted in the acquittal of practically self-confessed murderers." Representatives Charles C. Diggs, Jr. (D-Mich.), and Donald M. Fraser (D-Minn.) submitted similar measures to the House.[28] Several months after the president sent his message to Congress, the House Republican Policy Committee explicitly endorsed Title V, declaring it "would require an assumption of federal responsibility that is long overdue."[29]

Unfortunately for the administration, other facets of its omnibus civil rights bill were far less popular. This was particularly true of Title IV, an open-housing provision, which one White House aide considered "extremely dangerous to pursue." It was opposed by key Republican leaders such as Senator Dirksen and Congressman McCulloch. Neither Katzenbach nor Larry O'Brien, who handled legislative liaison for the White House, had much hope even for the bill's less controversial titles. Although the white backlash had done the most to dim prospects for enacting further legislation to benefit blacks, Katzenbach and O'Brien insisted that the biggest problem confronting the administration was apathy. Participants in the June White House Conference did advocate additional civil rights legislation and call explicitly for enactment of Title V, but even among normally strong supporters of racial justice, the sort of enthusiasm that had propelled the Civil Rights Act of 1964 and the Voting Rights Act through Congress seemed to be lacking.[30]

As Katzenbach and O'Brien feared, the administration's proposals failed to gather enough momentum to become law. After holding hearings on fifty-one civil rights measures, a subcommittee of the House Judiciary Committee endorsed a substitute for the Justice Department bill. This measure included two additional titles, one of which was a Part III provision. The full committee discussed the substitute nine times, and after substantially limiting the coverage of its open housing title, voted to recommend passage.[31]

The bill it sent to the full House included a slightly altered version of the administration's civil rights violence proposal. Katzenbach had assured the committee that this provision did not diminish state and local responsibility for the maintenance of law and order and was intended only to give the federal government the capacity to deal with racist fanatics when authorities in their own communities were unwilling or unable to do so. Title V enjoyed overwhelming bipartisan support. Two Republican members of the Judiciary Committee, McCulloch of Ohio and Charles Mathias of Maryland, called it a long overdue assumption of federal responsibility. Southerners Richard H. Poff (R-Va.) and William C. Cramer (R-Fla.), while noting their unease about "any transfer of jurisdiction from the States to the Federal Government," deplored "even more the use of force and violence against any man anywhere who is lawfully pursuing some activity authorized by law." They asked only that use of Title V be restricted to situations in which there had been a "failure of State process."[32]

Although enthusiastically endorsing Title V, the Judiciary Committee made one change in it which some civil rights supporters found disturbing. Representative George W. Grider (D-Tenn.), a racial moderate from Memphis, persuaded his colleagues to insert the word "lawfully" before the list of protected activities, so that the statute would protect only those who were behaving legally when they were attacked or threatened. The reason for the adoption of this amendment, by a close 18–16 vote, was white concern about continued black unrest in the urban ghettos. Proponents of the addition claimed it was needed to prevent the new law from being used to punish policemen for actions taken to control rioting. Critics replied that potential victims of murder and assault should not lose the protection of Title V because they had committed some minor offense, such as parading without a permit.[33]

Upset by the addition of the word "lawfully," SNCC's Washington counsel branded this portion of the bill seriously deficient. Both Stokely Carmichael and Fannie Lou Hamer, evincing their growing disillusionment with white liberals, dismissed the whole civil rights bill as a useless sham. It also aroused conservative opposition. The Rules Committee refused to report the measure, and Celler had to maneuver what he considered a piece of "vital and essential legislation" onto the floor without committee approval.[34]

There, civil rights supporters from both parties managed to beat back an effort by Poff to delete the Judiciary Committee's Part III (although the House did accept an amendment somewhat restricting the circumstances under which that provision could be used).[35] Proponents of federal action against civil rights violence also managed to save Title V. Unlike Texan John Dowdy, who considered it unconstitutional class legislation, most members of the House apparently agreed with Mathias that "Title V is a badly needed and overdue reform."[36] Professing no desire to preempt any field of law enforcement, they nevertheless insisted that the unwillingness of some state and local officials to protect the exercise of federal rights made such a statute necessary. A motion by North Carolina's Whitener to delete Title V went down to defeat on a voice vote; his proposal to make only persons acting under color of law subject to punishment for violating this provision lost 35 to 52.[37]

Title V fared better than an indemnification provision pushed by the Leadership Conference on Civil Rights. On August 8 black Representative Charles Diggs (D-Mich.) offered an amendment providing for the creation of a federal board to compensate those persons suffering bodily injury or property damage because of violations of Title V. Both the subcommittee and the full Judiciary Committee had rejected this proposal earlier, but liberals from both parties endorsed it. The opposition included not only southern conservatives but also Celler and McCulloch, the chairman and ranking Republican on the committee. They were apparently worried about how much indemnification might cost and how it would be administered, and bothered by the fact that the administration had proposed nothing of this nature. The Diggs amendment appears to have been acceptable to the Justice Department, but nevertheless it lost on a voice vote.[38]

So did a motion by Don Edwards (D-Calif.) to delete the word "lawfully." Edwards proposed replacing it with a declaration that nothing in Title V should be construed as denying or impairing the authority of law enforcement officers to fulfill their duties. Dowdy nevertheless charged that the Edwards amendment would turn this bill into an authorization to riot. He issued an ominous reminder of recent civil disturbances in Chicago, Cleveland, and Omaha. Worried about the upcoming November elections and how their constituents would react to ghetto rioting and to the Black Power rhetoric of Afro-American militants, House members responded to his appeals and rejected Edwards's proposal.[39]

Urban civil disorders bothered the House more than attacks on blacks and civil rights workers in the South, as it proved by adding an antiriot provision to what was supposed to be a civil rights bill. Introduced by William Cramer (R-Fla.) as a substitute for an even more extreme proposal by Robert T. Ashmore (D-S.C.), this amendment made moving in interstate commerce to incite a riot a federal crime. Although Edwards objected that urban rioting had "nothing to do with the great peaceful non-violent civil rights movement," and William F. Ryan attempted to persuade his colleagues that they were losing sight of the real purpose of Title V, a wave of emotion swept the House. It adopted Cramer's amendment by a 389 to 25 vote. On August 9, 1966, a now radically altered "civil rights" bill survived a motion to recommit, then passed 259 to 157.[40]

Although successful in the House, it died in the Senate, killed by the chairman of the Judiciary Committee's Subcommittee on Constitutional Rights, Sam Ervin. The North Carolina Democrat had been a consistent opponent of civil rights laws, which he considered "special privileges enacted by Congress" for the benefit of racial minorities.[41] Ervin regarded the administration's 1966 proposals as both "unwise" and "unconstitutional" and vowed to "do everything within my power to see that this bill is defeated."[42] Although hostile to the measure as a whole, he purported to have some sympathy for Title V. Ervin strongly opposed indemnification, but claimed he could support legislation to make acts such as the Meredith shooting federal crimes, if (like his 1959 bombing bill) it rested on the Commerce Clause. The administration had based Title V on the Fourteenth Amendment, a constitutional provision which, Ervin insisted, authorized the federal government to punish private individuals only for aiding or abetting violations by state officials.[43]

Attorney General Katzenbach disputed the North Carolina senator when he appeared before the subcommittee on June 7, 1966. A majority of the Supreme Court had said section 5 of the Fourteenth Amendment gave Congress the power to reach "purely private misconduct," he contended. Ervin dismissed what Clark and Brennan had written in *Guest* as "gratuitous and mistaken advisory opinion[s]" which had not eliminated the state action requirement. He accused Katzenbach of misinterpreting the Fourteenth Amendment in a way which would give Congress the

power to legislate anywhere in the entire field of criminal law.[44] "Title V
would serve as a precedent for making any State crime a Federal crime and
would require a Federal police force—the opening wedge of a police
State," Ervin claimed.[45] Almost certainly, his constitutional objections
were inspired by policy considerations, but they do seem to have been
sincere. At one point Ervin proposed amending the Constitution to explicitly give Congress the power to punish threats and violence designed
to prevent the exercise of federal rights.[46]

Florida's Senator Spessard Holland supported that idea, but Katzenbach
considered such an amendment unnecessary. While admitting he would
have been requesting this legislation no matter what the Supreme Court
had said in *Guest,* the attorney general insisted the opinions in that case
had removed all doubt about the constitutionality of Title V. Senator
Edward Kennedy (D-Mass.) assured Katzenbach his "statements with regard to the majority of six in the *Guest* case" were "sufficient to assure the
Members of the Congress they can support this legislation." South Carolina's Senator Strom Thurmond disagreed, correctly pointing out that in
providing for the punishment of nonconspiratorial private offenses Title V
went beyond what Clark and Brennan had expressly endorsed. Macon,
Georgia, attorney Charles J. Bloch, one of the losing lawyers in *Guest,* and
an old ally of Ervin, who testified against the bill at his friend's request,
even employed Stewart's official opinion of the Court as support for the
proposition that Congress lacked authority to punish anything beyond the
deeds of persons acting under color of state law.[47]

Bloch's reading of *Guest* was strained at best, but the political savvy of
those opposing Title V more than compensated for the weakness of their
constitutional arguments. Although the longtime leader of southern
forces in the Senate, Georgia's Richard Russell, doubted they could stop
the administration's civil rights package, he promised a last-ditch fight
against it. Ervin and his allies on the Judiciary Committee kept the bill
bottled up until September. Civil rights supporters then attempted to
bypass them by bringing the House-passed measure directly to the Senate
floor. Southerners countered that maneuver with a filibuster. Attempts to
shut off debate failed because Senator Dirksen, opposed to the bill's open-
housing title and perhaps influenced by fellow Republican Roman Hruska
(who disliked provisions dealing with jury selection), would not support
them. Cloture efforts on September 14 and 19 obtained majorities, but
fell short of the necessary two-thirds.[48] On September 26 Ervin reported

triumphantly, "The bill is dead for this Congress and I am glad to have had a part in its demise."[49] "It would have been hard to pass the emancipation proclamation in the atmosphere prevailing this summer," White House aide Harry McPherson observed to Katzenbach.[50]

Although the administration had lost a major battle, the war was far from over. By now an escalating military conflict in Vietnam was occupying much of the president's attention, and by openly proclaiming their opposition to American involvement in that war King, SNCC, and CORE had reduced still further their already declining value as allies in the political struggle for equal rights at home. Northern cities remained volatile, and the white backlash continued to build. Nevertheless, the Johnson administration did not retreat from the civil rights fight. After its 1966 defeat, Joe Califano immediately requested the creation of an inter-agency task force on civil rights. That group, chaired by Stephen Pollak of the Civil Rights Division, recommended that Johnson again propose legislation "substantially similar to Title V." Consideration was given to splitting the 1966 bill into its component parts, but in February 1967 the president promised civil rights leaders that he would make every effort to obtain enactment of the entire omnibus measure. Early in the 90th Congress, the administration submitted to Congress a revised version of its original proposal. Like the 1966 measure, this one contained sections punishing violence and intimidation. Referring to "unfortunate instances" when "State and local law enforcement officials have failed to carry out their responsibilities," Ramsey Clark, who had become acting attorney general when Katzenbach moved to the State Department, insisted that effective federal action was needed to protect citizens in the exercise of "distinctly federal rights."[51]

Clark echoed sentiments expressed the previous June by black leaders and other prominent Americans participating in the White House Conference on Civil Rights. They had urged broad support for federal legislation that would provide greater "protection to Negroes and civil rights workers."[52] The administration had little choice but to renew the fight for enactment of the sort of law the conference wanted, for Representative Celler had made it clear that no matter what the White House did he intended to hold hearings on the subject early in the new Congress. Believing that civil rights groups would expect the president to fight again for everything he had requested the year before, including open-housing legislation, Justice Department leaders and Johnson's legislative strategists decided a bit reluctantly to try again for enactment of an omnibus proposal.[53]

The administration bill, as rewritten during January 1967, included a Title V which differed significantly from the one the House had passed in 1966. The Justice Department had deleted the word "lawfully" and, responding to pressure from various quarters for compensation to the victims of racist violence, had included a provision authorizing them to sue their attackers for damages. Perhaps the most important addition was a reluctantly added requirement that the government prove any person prosecuted under Title V had attacked his victim for the purpose of keeping blacks from engaging in a protected activity or preventing other persons from helping them to do so. Louis Claiborne had convinced his Justice Department superiors that without this insertion Title V would be of doubtful constitutionality.[54]

The purpose requirement and the other changes made by the administration disappeared in the House Judiciary Committee, which abandoned the omnibus approach. For Title V, it substituted H.R. 2516, a measure introduced by Celler in January. That bill, which went to the full House on June 29, was the same one the House had passed in 1966, minus its antiriot provisions. Rules Committee Chairman William Colmer (D-Miss.) had insisted that those be considered separately, and Celler agreed in return for a promise from the Mississippi segregationist that he would permit the civil rights violence measure to reach the floor. H.R. 2516, Celler told his House colleagues, was an answer to "the invitation to Congress to act" which the Supreme Court had issued in *Guest*. Although convinced the opinions in that case ensured the validity of legislation to prevent private interference with Fourteenth Amendment rights, Celler did fear the absence of a purpose requirement might make the bill constitutionally defective. At his suggestion the House voted, over the objections of some liberal members, to add one to it.[55]

The Celler bill received strong support from the NAACP, whose members were deeply disturbed by a lengthening list of unpunished racial killings. One of these was the January 10, 1966, arson slaying which claimed the life of Vernon Dahmer, an NAACP leader in Forrest County, Mississippi. Dahmer, also a well-to-do farmer and the owner of a sawmill and grocery store, announced on January 9 that he would collect poll tax payments from would-be black voters at his store near Hattiesburg and deliver the money to the courthouse. That night two carloads of Jones

County White Knights shot up his house and set fire to it, along with his car and the grocery store. The resulting blaze killed the NAACP leader and badly burned his daughter. Attorney General Katzenbach promptly announced that he would make the full resources of the Justice Department available to assist in identifying and apprehending those responsible for this crime, and on June 22 of that year a federal grand jury indicted Sam Bowers and fourteen other klansmen in the case. But the NAACP was also agitated about the February 27, 1967, bomb murder of Wharlest Jackson in Jackson.[56]

Predictably, liberal Democrats, such as William F. Ryan, joined the NAACP in insisting that "racial violence . . . be made an explicit federal crime." More surprising, so did a long list of Republicans, which included McCulloch, Mathias, Ogden Reid of New York, Tom Railsback of Illinois, and Byron Rogers of Colorado. L. H. Fontaine (D-N.C.) complained that the bill would transfer practically all law enforcement jurisdiction from the states to the national government, but many members from both parties apparently concluded that the inability or unwillingness of local authorities in some parts of the country "to enforce the law guaranteeing equal rights to all persons" had rendered federal legislation "appropriate and necessary."[57]

Even some of those who endorsed H.R. 2516, however, seemed more worried about rioting in northern ghettos than about terrorism in the South. When Robert McClory (R-Ill.) announced he was supporting the bill because it was "directed against violence in our cities" (which it clearly was not), he provided dramatic evidence that the House was more enthusiastic about legislation for that purpose than about a law to punish klansmen. Led by Dowdy of Texas, southerners played on fears of ghetto riots (which hit 164 cities during the first nine months of 1967), urging northern colleagues to vote against H.R. 2516 because the measure would encourage urban violence and interfere with efforts to control it. "Now, in this long hot summer of 1967 is not the time to consider any further civil rights legislation that could contribute in any manner or way to any new or further disturbances," William J. Randall (D-Mo.) warned. Supporters of H.R. 2516 countered that, since the House had passed an antiriot bill a month earlier, fairness required that it now legislate against violent attacks on persons seeking to exercise their constitutional rights. A majority of their colleagues apparently agreed with them that the best way to promote law and order was to pass both measures. But the House adopted H.R.

2516 only after adding an amendment by Fletcher Thompson (R-Ga.) which provided that it should never be construed to permit punishment of any police officer for carrying out the lawful duties of his office in a legal manner, and another by Jim Wright (D-Tex.) which made it a crime to interfere with a peace officer or any other public official who was trying to prevent or abate a riot.[58]

Celler and McCulloch both endorsed Wright's amendment. The chairman and ranking Republican member of the Judiciary Committee also accepted one by Whitener which explicitly declared that Congress did not intend to force the states out of any area of law enforcement in which the new statute might operate. As modified, H.R. 2516 passed the House on August 16, 1967, by a vote of 327 to 93, with southerners providing most of the opposition.[59] The *Washington Post* applauded, urging the Senate to "respond with as much determination as the House has manifested."[60]

The upper chamber was slow to act, for the chairman of its Judiciary Committee, James Eastland (D-Miss.), was a segregationist bent on defeating H.R. 2516. He sent the bill to Ervin's Constitutional Rights Subcommittee, which had been holding hearings on the administration's civil rights proposals since August. The North Carolinian already had excoriated Title V as a measure based on "misinterpretations of elementary constitutional law," and he liked H.R. 2516 no better. While again conceding the need for such legislation, Ervin insisted that this bill was unconstitutional. He urged Charles Bloch to come to Washington to explain to his subcommittee that the Equal Protection Clause did not give Congress the power to legislate against private violence. When Attorney General Clark reminded him that six Supreme Court justices had indicated otherwise, Ervin dismissed most of what had been said in *Guest* as dicta. Under Clark's reading of that case, he claimed, the power of the national government would be essentially unlimited. Ervin also objected that H.R. 2516 protected only "one class of persons."[61]

In order to correct that supposed defect, and also to prevent what he and George Autry, chief counsel to the subcommittee, viewed as the excessive expansion of federal police power which would result from adoption of the House bill, Senator Ervin offered a substitute for H.R. 2516. Probably written by Autry, with the assistance of fellow subcommittee staff members Lewis Evans and Wes Hayden, his version was in some respects broader than Celler's. It included six new titles dealing with Indian rights as well as provisions punishing labor violence and protecting union members who refused to participate in strikes. These earned the Ervin substitute endorsements from the Chamber of Commerce and the National Association of Manufacturers. His version of the bill also eliminated the purpose requirement and added four new protected activities: traveling in interstate commerce, instituting civil suits, informing on violations of federal criminal law, and being in the custody of the United States government. The Ervin substitute would make almost any murder a federal offense, the *New York Times* charged. Yet, because it protected only activities dependent on the relationship between the individual and the national government, it was in some ways narrower than the original bill. Ervin's version did not protect service on state juries, participation in state elections or state-sponsored programs, or employment by state or local governments. Noting these deletions and the fact that the substitute exempted from punishment all acts of law enforcement officers and military personnel engaged in suppressing riots, the Justice Department vigorously opposed it.[62]

Ervin nevertheless managed, on October 12, 1967, to get the Constitutional Rights Subcommittee to endorse his measure. Thirteen days later, at the administration's urging, the full Judiciary Committee threw out the substitute and replaced it with another, authored by Philip Hart (D-Mich.). The vote was 8–7, and the White House had to fly supporter Hugh Scott (R-Pa.) home from London in order to prevail. Hart's version of the bill was essentially the same as the one passed earlier by the House.[63]

It went to the floor on November 2, accompanied by two minority reports. In one, diehard segregationists Eastland and Thurmond sought to exploit northern outrage at ghetto disturbances. "The consequences of enacting this bill before the enactment of a meaningful antiriot bill would be disastrous," they warned, "in that the vast majority of the American people would be thus clearly told by Congress that it is not concerned with the problems of violence about which *they* are concerned." In the other minority report, southern Democrat Holland and northern Republicans Dirksen and Hruska (the latter at least attracted by the Ervin substitute's antilabor provisions) joined the North Carolinian in endorsing his version of the bill. The opposition to the administration's version was strong enough that Majority Leader Mike Mansfield (D-Mont.) concluded it might not be possible to bring the bill to a vote before the end of the session, and that prospects for passing it eventually might be dimmed if the measure had to be set aside after lengthy debate. Consequently, he postponed it until January 15, 1968.[64]

The NAACP pressed for action on H.R. 2516, but Ervin remained determined to substitute his measure for the one backed by the administration. Lyndon Johnson was equally committed to his own civil rights proposals. In his January 17, 1968, State of the Union address, the president called for enactment of the bill then before the Senate. Although legislators, still more interested in punishing rioters than in protecting civil rights workers, greeted his words with silence, the president followed this appeal with a special message to Congress a week later in which he endorsed even more explicitly the version reported by the Judiciary Committee.[65]

Efforts soon commenced to resolve the conflict between Johnson and Ervin. Attorneys at the Civil Rights Division entered into quiet negotiations with Autry aimed at working out a compromise. Attorney General Clark, convinced that the North Carolina senator's real objective was to defeat the bill, was "pessimistic about the chances of success." Ervin insisted that, for political reasons, he could not accept any purpose requirement limiting coverage to racially motivated attacks. Since now Assistant Attorney General Pollak (who took over the Civil Rights Division in 1968) believed any bill that did not include such a limitation would affect far too sweeping an extension of federal criminal responsibility, the chances for accommodation did not look good. Senator Dirksen threw himself into the effort to "find a common denominator," holding a series of meetings in his office with a constantly changing lineup of negotiators that included Ervin, Mansfield, the attorney general, Eastland, Jacob Javits, and members of the Judiciary Committee staff. By February 2 the Republican floor leader apparently had the two sides close to agreement. The compromise would have limited federal intervention to cases in which a state, after being afforded an opportunity to prosecute under its own laws, failed to act.[66]

It was destined never to become law. On February 5 a bipartisan liberal coalition led by Javits and Hart (the administration's floor leader on the bill) issued a statement in which thirty-five senators declared their "strong support of the Senate Judiciary Committee version of H.R. 2516." The members of this group expressed the firm belief "that the coverage which is provided by the legislation now pending before the Senate must not be diminished."[67] The next day the liberal coalition forced a test of strength with its foes, moving to table Ervin's substitute. It prevailed 54 to 29, with nine Republicans deserting Dirksen to support H.R. 2516.[68]

This vote came in the midst of a lengthy southern filibuster against civil rights legislation, which had begun on January 15. This flood of obstructionist oratory included a claim by Ernest Hollings (D-S.C.) that the South was already well on the way to eliminating the problem H.R. 2516 was supposed to solve. Senator John Stennis (D-Miss.) attacked what he characterized as a bill that "really scrapes down to the bottom of the civil rights barrel," arguing it would overthrow long established principles of constitutional law and "radically alter the relationship between the States and the Federal Government." Drawing heavily on the arguments of Charles Bloch, Stennis and his allies questioned again and again the power of Congress to enact H.R. 2516. Although supporters of the bill argued that the Brennan and Clark opinions in *Guest* had eliminated all doubt about its constitutionality, six southerners denied that case had altered the traditional interpretation of the Fourteenth Amendment. With particular vehemence, Herman Talmadge (D-Ga.) declared, "To suggest, as sponsors of H.R. 2516 do, that an unbroken line of authority extending over 100 years has been nullified . . . is ridiculous."[69]

Struggling to stay afloat in this sea of hostile rhetoric, the antiviolence bill had to carry the added burden of the housing issue. At the insistence of the Leadership Conference on Civil Rights, liberal senators had agreed to try to attach a proposed national fair-housing law to H.R. 2516. Senator Hart did not believe it was possible to pass housing legislation, which threatened the North's lily-white suburbs, and Assistant Attorney General Pollak considered it unwise to try. As he predicted, this move strengthened the southern filibuster, so that supporters of the bill could not muster the votes needed for cloture.[70]

Then Everett Dirksen, who had been opposing open-housing legislation since 1966, changed his mind. Senator Dirksen had become convinced that the failure of Congress to pass such a law might spark further urban riots. Besides, he was under pressure from Republican liberals Jacob Javits, Charles Percy, and Edward Brooke, and even from his own son-in-law, Howard Baker (R-Tenn.). GOP senators were concerned that if their party did not support the civil rights bill it might be seen as hostile to blacks. Dirksen concluded they were correct. In consultation with Vice-President Hubert Humphrey and the Justice Department, he prepared a

compromise measure covering about 80 percent of the houses and apart-
ments in the country.[71]

To reassure those who feared a federal takeover of law enforcement,
Dirksen included in his version of the bill an explicit disclaimer of intention to withdraw jurisdiction over any offense from the states. The purpose of this provision was to make clear the intent of Congress that federal
prosecution should occur only when state and local law enforcement
proved unable or unwilling to prosecute effectively. To this disclaimer
Dirksen added a requirement that any prosecution brought under the new
law must be authorized in writing by either the attorney general or the
deputy attorney general, who would have to certify that it was "in the
public interest and necessary to secure substantial justice." Jack Miller, an
Iowa Republican, wanted to go even further, explicitly forbidding these
officials to give the necessary permission unless the appropriate state or
local authorities had either refused to prosecute an offense or failed to carry
the prosecution forward promptly and in good faith. Javits argued this
would make it impossible to reach persons prosecuted but protected from
conviction by community prejudice. He and Hart believed the Miller
amendment would gut the bill, but they feared that their Republican
supporters might well desert to the southern Democrats on this issue. In
order to prevent that, they gave assurances that the law would not be used
except in those instances and in those parts of the country where there was
a dereliction of a state's duty to protect civil rights. Their strategy succeeded. Miller's amendment failed, 29 to 51. All of the southerners present but William Spong (D-Va.) and John Sherman Cooper (R-Ky.) voted
for it, but they managed to enlist the support of only a few conservative
Republicans and two nonsouthern Democrats.[72]

Even without the Miller amendment, the Dirksen substitute managed
to achieve what Hart's version of H.R. 2516 could not. One attempt at
cloture failed, but the Johnson administration and Clarence Mitchell of
the NAACP lobbied hard, and even former Vice-President Richard Nixon
reportedly joined in the effort to obtain votes for cloture (urging his fellow
Republican Karl Mundt to support it). On March 4, 1968, the Senate
voted 65 to 32 to limit debate on the bill. Southern Democrats joined half
the Republicans in futile opposition. A week later H.R. 2516 passed, 71
to 20. Southerners cast all but two of the negative votes, receiving support
only from Delaware Republican John J. Williams and Arizona Republican
Paul Fanin.[73]

Because of the changes the Senate had made, the bill had to return to the House. Johnson's staff worried that the housing provisions might drag down to defeat there the civil rights worker protection measure that chamber had passed earlier. Speaker John McCormack did not think he could muster the necessary votes to pass the Senate version of the bill. If the House made changes, this would necessitate the creation of a conference committee, in which H.R. 2516 might well be gutted. For a time it appeared the Senate measure might not even reach the House floor. Despite the efforts of Missouri Democrat Richard Bolling, on March 18 the administration suffered a one-vote defeat on a test vote in the conservative Rules Committee. The Democratic leadership decided to put off action on the bill for some time. Then, on April 4, Martin Luther King, Jr., was felled by an assassin's bullet in Memphis, Tennessee. As word of his death spread across the country, rioting erupted in the black ghettos of more than 125 cities. Soon the army was patrolling the streets of Chicago, Baltimore—and Washington. Rioters did at least $13 million damage to buildings in the District of Columbia, some of them located within a dozen blocks of the White House. Armed troops ringed the executive mansion and the Capitol. While rioting raged, the president sent letters to both McCormack and Minority Leader Gerald Ford (R-Mich.), stressing that the time for action had arrived. The administration lobbied hard over the weekend, and on the day after King's funeral the Rules Committee voted 9 to 6 to send the bill to the floor with a recommendation that the House accept the Senate amendments. Less than twenty-four hours later it did so by a margin of 250 to 172.[74]

Ford insisted that "most members of the House would have voted the same way had there been no murder in Memphis," but he acknowledged that "some votes were changed because of" the ghetto rioting.[75] The escalating racial tensions in the North that had stalled the administration's 1966 civil rights proposals for so long had in the end helped to propel them into law.

Three years after the bloodletting in Alabama that had inspired President Johnson's demands for legislation to suppress racist violence, the obstacles thrown up by Sam Ervin and northern fears of ghetto rioters and open housing had been overcome. With the nation unraveling racially, a civil rights movement that was itself disintegrating had recorded one last triumph. CORE and SNCC, the organizations which had for so long demanded federal protection for civil rights workers, could claim little credit for the legislation passed by Congress, but the NAACP and the Leadership Conference on Civil Rights had lobbied effectively. So had the Johnson administration, which pressed on with its campaign for civil rights legislation in the face of a menacing deterioration in the political situation. Despite ghetto rioting and white backlash, it had achieved success. Now, at last, the Justice Department had a law with which to restore order to the South.[76]

The Restoration of Southern Order

After three years of legislative struggle, the federal government at last had an effective legal weapon with which to combat racist beatings and murders in the South. Yet the Justice Department launched no war against anti–civil rights violence. For the next decade, the new law went largely unused. The reason was that by the time those determined to give the national government the power to protect participants in the civil rights movement accomplished their objective, the problem they were trying to solve had largely disappeared. Fearful of a breakdown of law and order in their communities, southerners had themselves assumed responsibility for controlling and punishing racist violence. By the time extensive federal intervention in the South became possible, it was no longer needed.

That is why 18 U.S.C. §245 went largely unused there. In mid-1969 the Civil Rights Division of the Justice Department, pointing out that the new law had "greatly broadened the protection available against interference by private individuals with anyone's civil rights," boasted of doubling its prosecutions. Routine police brutality cases accounted for most of the increase, however.[1] During the first decade that section 245 was on the statute books, the Justice Department initiated only seventeen prosecutions under it in the eleven former Confederate states. One of these was for acts committed in a national forest. Thus, a maximum of sixteen cases in ten years might have resulted from the sort of abdication of responsibility by southern state criminal justice systems that had concerned proponents of the new law, and one of those was eventually dismissed on motion of the government. During the decade after April 1968, the problem which inspired enactment of section 245 may also have given rise to three section 241 prosecutions, but at most that period produced fewer than twenty examples of the sort of federal legal action that Congress had tried to promote.[2]

Several factors might explain the strange career of section 245. A few months before the new law was enacted the Civil Rights Division had been reorganized to commit a majority of its personnel and the bulk of its resources to problems that were national in scope, such as employment discrimination. The idea for this restructuring came from Ramsey Clark, who had become attorney general in 1967. Clark informed the new head of the division, Stephen Pollak, that with the Voting Rights Act now on the books and the emphasis on desegregating schools in the South declining after October 1967, "the days of walking the red clay roads of the southern rural areas in pursuit of civil rights law enforcement by the federal government were either closed or drawing to a close." But this conversation occurred several months before the passage of section 245, and the new attorney general, who was more of an activist than his predecessors, Nicholas Katzenbach and Robert Kennedy, also stressed to Pollak that "we, the federal government, had to maintain our law enforcement responsibilities in the South," insisting only that "we had to broaden them so as to pursue with more resources equal employment, law enforcement, and school desegregation in the North and West."[3]

Another possible explanation for the limited use of section 245 in the South might be the "southern strategy" of Richard Nixon, who replaced Lyndon Johnson in the White House less than a year after the law's enactment. Nixon entered office intent on building up Republican political strength in the South. In pursuit of that objective his administration made a number of moves intended to curry favor with white southerners. These included modifying (rather than simply extending) the Voting Rights Act and attempting to persuade the Supreme Court to delay school desegregation in Mississippi. When a number of Civil Rights Division lawyers signed a letter protesting the government's role in the Mississippi case, they were forced out of the Justice Department. So alienated did division attorneys become that in May 1972 seven of them resigned to join the campaign staff of Senator George McGovern, Nixon's Democratic opponent in the November presidential election.[4]

Although Nixon's southern strategy might explain the small number of section 245 prosecutions in the South, according to Judge David L. Norman, who served continuously in the Civil Rights Division from the

Eisenhower administration into the Nixon administration at all levels from trial lawyer to assistant attorney general, such is not the case. The new head of the division, Jerris Leonard, was as supportive of criminal civil rights prosecutions as his predecessors had been. The numbers indicate that Norman is correct. Of the sixteen cases brought in the South during the first decade after section 245's enactment, at least as many were commenced while Nixon was in the White House as under the administrations of Lyndon Johnson, Gerald Ford, and Jimmy Carter. Although Leonard's superiors made it clear to him that his division was expected to perform its duties in a manner consistent with the president's political goals, that did not mean it had to overlook violations of the criminal civil rights statutes. The administration's objective was not to thwart enforcement of the law, but merely to shift the onus of integration from the Republican executive branch to a Democratic Congress and an appointed judiciary.[5]

Another possible explanation for the infrequent use of section 245 is that by 1968 the South no longer had much racial violence to prosecute. By the end of the 1960s the civil rights movement had achieved many of its objectives, and besides was falling apart, as SNCC and CORE members, alienated from both white liberals and the government, abandoned its traditional objectives to pursue the chimera of Black Power. A large percentage of the nation's youthful protesters had redirected their energies into opposition to the Vietnam War, and after 1966 the South experienced no further massive civil rights campaigns. Violent bigots had fewer targets and less provocation. Besides, the Ku Klux Klan was once again crumbling into insignificance. Harassed and disrupted by the FBI, groups such as the White Knights and the United Klans of America were torn apart by internal squabbling and crippled by financial problems. By the end of the decade the KKK was approaching impotence and no longer committed large numbers of violent acts.[6]

While southern racial violence did recede considerably following the flood tide of 1964 and early 1965, it remained a serious problem until after the adoption of section 245. The Department of Justice investigated at least eighty alleged incidents of intimidation and harassment connected with desegregation during the 1965–1966 school year, and the following September mobs of white hoodlums assaulted black children in Grenada, Mississippi, while local police stood by, declining to interfere. North Carolina experienced racially motivated shootings and bombings during 1965

and 1966. In January of the latter year SNCC voter registration worker
Sammy Younge was gunned down in Tuskegee, Alabama, and between
August 1965 and June 1966 Mississippi experienced at least seventeen
violent incidents related to black registration and voting. Among these
were the shotgun attack on James Meredith and the shooting of a civil
rights worker at Kosciusko. When some of the civil rights activists who
carried on Meredith's pilgrimage after he was wounded joined Neshoba
County blacks in a memorial march through Philadelphia to commemo-
rate the second anniversary of the murders of Schwerner, Chaney, and
Goodman, white youths attacked the group with fists, stones, bottles,
and clubs. In Canton, Mississippi, state police beat participants in the
Meredith walk. Meanwhile, klansmen conspired to kill an elderly black
man, Ben Chester White, hoping in this way to detract from their march
and to lure Dr. Martin Luther King, Jr., to Natchez, where he could be
assassinated. In Haywood County, Tennessee, several black families huddled together at night for protection, with armed husbands standing
guard outside against menacing whites who prowled the area in trucks
and cars.[7]

On January 10, 1966, an attack of the type these families feared claimed
the life of Vernon Dahmer, an NAACP leader in Forrest County, Mississippi. More than a year later the NAACP was still complaining about the
"abuse and killing of Negro citizens by police officers and white citizens of
Mississippi."[8] During 1966–1967 that state suffered through an epidemic
of racially motivated bombings. Meanwhile, in Alabama, police or white
civilians or both fired into a June 11, 1967, SNCC meeting at Prattville. By
1968 the level of southern violence does seem to have been subsiding, but in
February of that year South Carolina highway patrolmen turned their guns
on a crowd of blacks protesting racial discrimination around South Carolina
State College in Orangeburg, killing three of them and wounding twenty-
seven. A similar incident in May 1970 left two students dead at Mississippi's Jackson State College. The Magnolia State experienced new outbreaks
of bombing in both 1968 and 1970, and as late as September of the latter
year white southerners were still beating civil rights demonstrators.[9]

While anti-civil rights violence was declining, the most important reason why there were few prosecutions under section 245 was that southerners finally began to punish such crimes themselves. By September 1973
the New York Times was able to report the "virtual disappearance" from the
South of unpunished random violence against blacks. There had been, to

be sure, some recent highly publicized instances of whites apparently getting away with killing blacks. A Mississippi grand jury had exonerated all
of the state highway patrolmen who fired on the students at Jackson State.
The South Carolina officers responsible for the "Orangeburg Massacre"
also avoided punishment, but the grand jury and the trial jury which freed
them were federal ones. South Carolina authorities had deferred to the
national government in this case, both the governor and the attorney
general supporting FBI investigation of the incident.[10]

By 1968 they and other southern political leaders and police officials
were far less willing to tolerate racist violence than they had once been. A
notable change of attitude began during the troubled summer of 1964. As
early as June of that year Governor Farris Bryant of Florida invoked emergency powers in order to send 140 highway patrolmen and other law
enforcement personnel into St. Augustine.[11] In 1965, when white hoodlums allegedly attacked civil rights workers in Monticello, Florida, the
sheriff of Jefferson County "gave strong assurances that harassment of civil
rights workers [would] not be tolerated, and that anyone caught
doing same would be prosecuted."[12] In North Carolina, when an NAACP
official informed Governor Dan Moore about racist bombings in Charlotte, Moore ordered state law enforcement agencies to assist in every way
possible "in the apprehension of these vicious criminals."[13] Mecklenburg
County authorities later sent five men to prison just for burning a cross on
a black's lawn. In April 1965 Alabama Attorney General Richmond
Flowers launched an investigation of the Ku Klux Klan in his state, and
the following October the Taliaferro County, Georgia, sheriff, aided by
the state highway patrol and the Georgia Bureau of Investigation, seized
an arsenal of revolvers and shotguns from a group of klansmen that included Howard Sims and Cecil Myers. By the fall of 1965, virtually everywhere in the South, local law enforcement officers, whatever their personal
feelings about school desegregation, were trying to prevent interference
with it.[14]

This crackdown on racist violence extended even into Mississippi. Besides promising to assist in apprehending those responsible for the
Neshoba County murders, Governor Paul Johnson pledged to protect demonstrators who behaved themselves. He set out to purge the Mississippi
Highway Patrol of klansmen and to build it into a force which could be
used to combat vigilantes and control violence in trouble spots such as
McComb. Johnson also called for an all-out effort by law enforcement

agencies to track down the "morally bankrupt criminals" responsible for the Dahmer killing. Although civil rights leaders claimed that the governor failed to provide those who completed Meredith's march through Mississippi with sufficient police protection, highway patrolmen and local peace officers did safeguard the demonstrators most of the time. Special Assistant to the Attorney General Jacob Rosenthal concluded that both the state and the Leflore County sheriff's office were "in fact . . . furnishing adequate protection for the marchers, despite a public statement by Governor Paul Johnson indicating otherwise." Mississippi authorities also arrested a white man, Aubrey James Norvell, for the Meredith shooting, and a DeSoto County grand jury indicted him for assault and battery with intent to kill.[15]

Those responsible for local law enforcement elsewhere in Mississippi also joined the fight against anti–civil rights violence. In Greenville, Police Chief W. C. Burnley and Sheriff John Durham had never tolerated even cross burnings. By 1968 significant advances had been made in the rest of the state in arresting and convicting perpetrators of planned racial violence. In the forefront of this campaign was Meridian Police Chief C. L. Gunn, who ordered his officers to shoot to kill night riders. They did. In June 1968, relying on information supplied by FBI informants, Meridian police ambushed Thomas Albert Tarrants, a klansman suspected of a number of bombings, seriously wounding him and killing his female companion.[16]

Not all southern authorities dealt so firmly with terrorism, and there were exceptions to the general trend that began to develop in late 1964. In Alabama, Prattville law enforcement personnel, according to a federal district court, failed "to provide proper police protection to Negro citizens," and Tuskegee peace officers refused to act when threats were made against a SNCC worker who was subsequently murdered. Similarly, some Mississippi lawmen persisted in refusing to do their duty. City police in Philadelphia made no effort to stop whites from attacking participants in a 1966 Schwerner-Goodman-Chaney memorial march until black youths began fighting back. In Grenada, law enforcement personnel even defied an injunction requiring them to protect Negro protesters.[17]

By 1969, however, in most of the South it was apparent that those responsible for enforcing the law had committed themselves to suppressing racist violence. Over a two-year period ending in March of that year, 132 klansmen were charged with 378 felonies and serious misdemeanors.

While some of these were federal prosecutions, most were not. One local prosecutor in southern Mississippi declared he would seek indictments against "every Klan member I can get my hands on" for every offense from murder to double-parking. More and more, especially by 1968–1969, when confronted with cases of racist violence, all-white grand juries indicted those responsible for it. [18]

Even more surprising, southern trial juries often convicted them. The most dramatic and highly publicized examples of the new willingness of white jurors to send perpetrators of racist violence to jail were the convictions in the Liuzzo, Penn, and Neshoba County cases, but federal courts had no monopoly on precedent-shattering verdicts. Indeed, the first real break in the well-established pattern of white night riders avoiding punishment for their crimes came in a state case. One day before the federal jury in Montgomery convicted Viola Liuzzo's killers, state jurors in Anniston, Alabama, after deliberating for nine hours, found Hubert Damon Strange guilty of second-degree murder in the shooting death of a black man, Willie Lee Brewster. Brewster was not involved in the civil rights movement, but an hour before gunning him down Strange had attended a white supremacy rally at which speakers advocated racial extermination. To Dr. Martin Luther King, Jr., "the verdicts of guilty brought forth by an all-white jury in the state court sitting in Anniston and in a federal court in Montgomery" represented "rays of light and hope" that had penetrated "the darkness which for a long time hung over a long line of unpunished racial killings." [19]

In state as well as federal courts, the hopeful trend which began in those two 1965 trials continued. In late 1968 a Mississippi jury convicted Klan bomber Thomas Tarrants. In other state trials, jurors returned guilty verdicts against four of the men involved in the firebombing which claimed the life of Vernon Dahmer. One of those they convicted had not even participated in the raid on Dahmer's home and store, but only in the Klan meetings at which it was planned. A Mississippi jury also convicted the alleged Dahmer killers' attorney on a related kidnapping charge. [20]

Not all such trials ended in conviction. Jurors continued to acquit some whites accused of killing blacks. Sometimes the victims had been active in the civil rights movement, but in other cases they had not. Generally, the jury was composed entirely of whites, but as federal pressure compelled the increasing integration of southern juries, this was not always so. Even more common than acquittals were hung juries, which produced mistrials in a number of cases. For example, Imperial Wizard Sam Bowers escaped conviction in a state court in Hattiesburg, Mississippi, for his role in the murder of Vernon Dahmer because his racially mixed jury deadlocked, with two whites holding out for acquittal against both black members and eight other whites. A federal civil rights conspiracy prosecution of men implicated in the Dahmer killing also ended in a mistrial because jurors could not agree upon a verdict. While southern trial juries did not always convict those responsible for racial murders, southern grand juries were now regularly indicting them.[21] In 1973 the *New York Times* observed, "Since the middle nineteen-sixties the automatic exoneration of whites accused of assaulting or killing blacks has all but disappeared."[22]

The principal reason for this change was a growing fear among white southerners about a breakdown of law and order. Federal intervention was far less important, although the Justice Department did belatedly begin using the threat of it to goad the South into assuming greater responsibility for combating lawlessness and intimidation. In January 1966 Attorney General Katzenbach declared quite bluntly that if southern authorities failed to move against racist terrorism, night riders would "ride straight into the federal government."[23] John Doar insisted that it was still "the wish of the Department of Justice for agents of the Federal Bureau of Investigation and for Department attorneys to work cooperatively with local authorities."[24]

Still, those authorities had to be concerned about the vast expansion of FBI operations in the civil rights field that began in mid-1964. Most southern law enforcement officials were probably unaware of the Bureau's massive COINTELPRO–White Hate groups, the aims of which included "neutralizing" the Ku Klux Klan and "detering violence." That operation became so large that by late 1965 FBI informants held top leadership positions in at least half of all Klan units. These spies stirred up factional disputes and quarrels over the alleged misuse of KKK funds, lighting fires which the Bureau stoked with mailings from fictitious organizations and even forged letters to klansmen's wives about their supposed infidelity. The COINTELPRO created an "informer panic" within the Klan that led to some expulsions and may well have inspired even more voluntary defections. While wreaking havoc within the KKK, however, this campaign could not have had much of an impact on the thinking of southern law enforcement officials, for on September 2, 1964, J. Edgar Hoover gave strict instructions that the existence of the program was not to be made known to anyone outside the Bureau. On the other hand, the acceleration of FBI civil rights investigations was something southern peace officers could not help but notice. By March 1966 these had increased 143 percent over 1961 levels, and as many as one-third of the Bureau's six thousand agents had devoted at least some of their time to civil rights matters. Southern officials had to be concerned that if they failed to suppress anti–civil rights violence the national government would take over part of their law enforcement function. The *Winston-Salem Journal* recognized that the way to avoid federal intervention was "to assure that property and lives are protected."[25]

It is likely that whites who sat on southern juries also realized that by convicting terrorists they could make federal interference in local affairs less likely, and this may have influenced how they voted. Certainly, the defense attorneys in the Liuzzo case did worry that the jury might convict their clients because of concern about the possible enactment of civil rights worker protection legislation. A desire to save Mississippi from further federal conspiracy prosecutions may explain why, when Mississippians heard the same evidence against men implicated in the Dahmer killing, those serving as state jurors convicted them of murder, while those acting as federal jurors could not agree upon a verdict.[26]

Although prodding by Washington did encourage southerners to assume responsibility for controlling anti–civil rights violence, this was not what precipitated their crackdown on it. Certainly, the Civil Rights Act of 1968 did not goad the South into action, for the crackdown began nearly four years before that law passed Congress. In August 1967 the staff director of the Civil Rights Commission reported to a congressional committee which was considering worker protection legislation that in "many places, political and community leaders have spoken out clearly against violence and have directed law enforcement officials to provide protection for people and ideas they do not like."[27] Of course, the threat that something like section 245 might pass gave the South cause for concern well before April 1968, but the Johnson administration did not even *introduce* its legislation until the spring of 1966. Thus, the 1968 law cannot explain a phenomenon that became noticeable in late 1964. The Civil Rights Act which Congress adopted that year contained no provision that directly addressed the problem of violence. Section 11(b) of the Voting

Rights Act did proscribe coercion, threats, and intimidation directed at
would-be voters and voter registration workers, but even that obscure
provision did not become law until August 6, 1965.[28]

Besides, the Justice Department sought no indictments under section
11(b). Federal prosecutions may eventually have become, as one commentator has suggested, an important stimulus to the development of local
responsibility. But as late as the end of 1965 the Justice Department's
prosecutorial efforts were limited to the cases it had brought against the
killers of Lemuel Penn, Viola Liuzzo, and the three civil rights workers,
and those had up to that point produced only failure. Until Doar obtained
convictions against Wilkins, Eaton, and Thomas at Montgomery in December of 1965, all the Justice Department had to show for its efforts was
the district court dismissals of the *Price* and *Guest* indictments, and federal
criminal prosecutions appeared to be empty and futile gestures. They cannot explain a crackdown on racist violence that was already well underway
before southerners had any reason to fear them.[29]

Nor can the growth of black political power in the South fully account
for this phenomenon. Certainly, it was a factor. A substantial rise in black
registration followed enactment of the Voting Rights Act. By 1970 the
number of blacks in the old Confederacy who could cast ballots had more
than doubled. In some states, such as Louisiana, Alabama, and Mississippi, the increase was particularly dramatic.[30]

As the black electorate expanded, so did the number of blacks holding
elective office. By January 1970 there were 528 elected black officials in
the South, including 89 in law enforcement positions. That autumn Alabamians elected three black sheriffs (one of them in Lowndes County,
where as recently as the summer of 1965 not a single black had been
registered to vote) and reelected a fourth. By 1975 there were nine more
elected black "marshals, sheriffs, and chiefs of police" in the South, as well
as eighty-one black constables, thirty-seven black justices of the peace,
and eleven elected black judges.[31]

The increase in the number of black voters did more than simply put
some law enforcement and judicial jobs in black hands. It also forced
white lawmen to be a good deal more responsive to the wishes of the black
community. As James Silver observed in 1965, "Local officials represent
not the people but the people who vote."[32] After the black electorate in
Green County, Alabama, expanded by four thousand, white Sheriff Bill
Lee, figuring he needed "about 1,000 nigger votes" to win, publicly em-

braced Ralph Abernathy, by then the president of the SCLC, and got that organization's Hosea Williams to teach him the clenched-fist Black Power salute.[33] A black politician, explaining why it was "no longer standard operating procedure for whites to kill blacks at will," declared, "It's all because of politics."[34]

He was not entirely correct. While the growth of black political power did encourage the crackdown on racist violence, the South began getting tough with terrorists nearly a year before passage of the Voting Rights Act. The reason that it did so was white concern about the deterioration of law and order. Prior to 1964 the vast majority of white southerners, although taking no part in anti–civil rights violence, found it difficult to condemn those who did. Gradually, many of them came to realize that toleration of racist terrorism could lead only to anarchy. As the *Atlanta Constitution* observed, "You cannot justify just a little violence or just a little contempt for law and order."[35] The *Constitution* was an unusually progressive publication, but other white southern voices expressed similar sentiments. "Violence is anarchy," Florida's Governor Bryant reminded the public.[36] During the troubled summer of 1964 several southern newspapers expressed concern that unless the bombing, shooting, and killing stopped, anarchy would result. During 1965 papers in Mississippi, Tennessee, and Florida all expressed similar fears.[37]

In Mississippi, where the threat of anarchy was most real, the specter of rampant terrorism impelled a number of prominent citizens to speak out for law and order. In May 1964 Earl Johnson, director of the State Sovereignty Commission, urged Mississippians to cooperate with the police rather than with secret organizations. The following month the president of the Mississippi Economic Council (the equivalent of a Chamber of Commerce), probably concerned about what a reputation for violence and lawlessness would do to the state's chances for economic development, issued a similar statement. In Jackson, Mayor Allen Thompson warned his constituents that they were in danger of taking the road to unbridled lawlessness, and a group of worried citizens issued a statement expressing concern that the concept of law and order was being eroded and urging action to check illegal force and coercion.[38]

When *McComb Enterprise-Journal* editor J. Oliver Emmerich, himself a victim of both beatings and bombings, began trying to raise reward money to bring terrorists to justice, he at first enlisted little support. Eventually, however, Emmerich's efforts and those of the federal Community Relations Service persuaded 650 McComb citizens to publish a signed statement in the November 17 issue of his paper. This group proclaimed: "Order and respect for the law must be re-established and maintained." Soon such statewide groups as the Mississippi Economic Council, the Mississippi Manufacturers Association, and the Mississippi State Bar Association fell in behind McComb. Even Neshoba County clergymen spoke out.[39]

It is possible, of course, that some of the growing number of prominent Mississippians who condemned lawlessness were inspired more by the embarrassment of seeing their state pictured as a land of anarchy on network television newcasts than by fear of a collapse of law and order. But whatever their precise motivation, they created a climate of opinion within which numerous public officials began committing themselves to preserving law and order and to protecting people and ideas they did not like. As early as July 1964, the mayor and city council of Greenville, while condemning civil rights workers as outside agitators, also warned that the police in their city would tolerate no interference from self-appointed vigilante groups such as the Ku Klux Klan. That December, Attorney General Patterson took a similar stand before the state's sheriffs.[40] Two months later Governor Johnson promised the Civil Rights Commission: "Law and order will be maintained in Mississippi by Mississippians. Violence against any person or group will not be tolerated."[41] Later Johnson's successor, John Bell Williams, condemned terrorist bombings. In early 1965 officials in Laurel spoke out for law and order, and in October of that year the city's mayor and law enforcement officers signed a pledge to halt acts of violence. Both Laurel and Jackson offered rewards for the perpetrators of terrorist acts.[42]

In other states as well, public officials adopted tough law and order positions. In July 1964 North Carolina Governor Terry Sanford used the highway patrol to prevent threatened Klan violence. His successor, Dan Moore, condemned antiblack bombings and vowed, "Law and order will be maintained." In 1967 the North Carolina legislature enacted strict antiterrorism legislation. Three years earlier the mayor of Bessemer, Alabama, had committed himself to preserving the law against whites bent on attacking black demonstrators. In Florida, not only the governor but also the state attorney general, the city manager of St. Augustine, and the sheriff of the county in which the troubled community was located pledged that law and order would prevail. In a front-page story in the local newspaper, City Manager Charles Barrier warned that whites who committed acts of interracial violence would be arrested. Indictments and a police crackdown on the Klan backed up this official rhetoric.[43]

Meanwhile, the southern press prodded ordinary citizens to take a stand against terrorism. During the second half of 1964 a number of the region's newspapers condemned violence and endorsed law and order. By 1965 even segregationist publications such as the *Charleston News and Courier* and the *Jackson Daily News* had joined the chorus. "We believe in law and order," the *Daily News* editorialized.[44]

Southern newspapers went beyond such pious generalizations to condemn specifically the very racist murders that had given the rest of the country such a negative impression of southern justice. Although the *Meridian Star* whined about segregationists being unfairly blamed for the Neshoba County killings, the rest of the southern press denounced the murder of the three civil rights workers and demanded that those responsible for the crime be tried and convicted. Even the *Jackson Daily News* denounced the Neshoba County killers, along with the murderers of Lemuel Penn, as "mad beasts." Several southern newspapers, among them Montgomery's *Advertiser,* condemned the Alabama slaying of Viola Liuzzo. That shooting, as well as the killing of Reverend James Reeb and the wounding of James Meredith, drew criticism from major dailies published in the general areas where the crimes had been committed. Lesser-known offenses also generated press condemnation and demands that the perpetrators "be prosecuted fully, convicted, and given stiff sentences."[45]

Southern newspapers urged their readers to take a stand against terrorism. During the second half of 1964 papers in Atlanta, Birmingham, St. Petersburg, and Macon all issued calls to stand up and be counted. Two newspapers in deeply troubled Mississippi spoke out more strongly than any others for public action against terrorism: Emmerich's *McComb Enterprise-Journal* and Hodding Carter's *Delta Democrat-Times.* In September 1964 Carter editorialized that if "Mississippi is to return eventually to security, it is in the long run the obligation of its individual citizens to ensure the realization of that goal by their own adherence to lawful conduct and by their refusal to shrug off the lawlessness of others."[46] The following year several papers urged responsible whites to take a stand against violence, the *Birmingham News* insisting, "Citizens of Birmingham or any community cannot, must not, permit terrorism to continue."[47]

This law-and-order rhetoric reflected a change in attitude among southern whites. Many of them had become convinced that something had to be done to halt anti–civil rights violence. A July 1964 poll disclosed that 54 percent of southerners favored sending federal troops to Mississippi if trouble erupted there.[48] Whites also displayed an increasingly negative attitude toward the Ku Klux Klan. A January 1966 Louis Harris poll discovered in the South "a broad consensus in opposition to the Klan and in favor of those who openly question its purposes."[49] Many public officials and private citizens who in the past had "given either active or passive support to the Klans" now "determined they did not deserve support and joined in denouncing them and the violence they create."[50]

This shift in attitudes probably did not result from reaction against the racism of the hooded order. Nor did it reflect any lessening of animosity toward civil rights activists, whom white southerners continued to regard as outside agitators.[51] The growing hostility toward those who used force to combat integration and black voting indicated instead that the South's level of enthusiasm for violence was becoming considerably less singular than that which had characterized the region in the past. Those scholars, such as Sheldon Hackney, John Shelton Reed, and Raymond D. Gastil, who have branded the South the most violent part of the country, have done so on the basis of data collected primarily in 1965 and earlier.[52] On the other hand, Rodney Stark and James McEvoy III, drawing on an October 1968 survey conducted by Louis Harris Associates for the National Commission on the Causes and Prevention of Violence, conclude, "The South does not appear to be more violent than any other part of the country."[53] Their conclusion receives support from FBI data, which show that in 1967 there were 250 violent crimes per 100,000 population in the former Confederate states, precisely the same number as in the country as a whole. By 1968 the South, at 274, was actually below the national average of 294.[54]

As the FBI pointed out repeatedly during the 1960s, the South remained the most murderous section of the nation.[55] Between 1962 and 1969, however, the number of murders and non-negligent manslaughters per 100,000 population there dropped from 173 percent of the national average to only 147 percent (see Table 1). Homicide was on the rise throughout the United States, but it was actually increasing more slowly in the former Confederate states than in the rest of the country.

By 1969 southern attitudes were even closer to those prevailing else-

TABLE ONE
Murders and Non-Negligent Manslaughters Per 100,000 Inhabitants

	1962	1963	1964	1965	1966	1967	1968	1969
South *	7.8	7.8	8.2	8.5	9.3	9.8	10.8	10.6
			(7.7)†	(8.0)†	(8.9)†	(9.4)†	(10.3)†	(10.4)†
United States	7.5	4.5	4.8	5.1	5.6	6.1	6.8	7.2
Southern figure as percentage of national figure	173%	173%	171%	167%	166%	161%	159%	147%

SOURCE: Federal Bureau of Investigation, *Uniform Crime Reports* (1962–1969).

* Alabama, Arkansas, Florida, Georgia, Louisiana, Mississippi, North Carolina, South Carolina, Tennessee, Texas, and Virginia.

† In 1966 the FBI began reporting figures for murders and non-negligent homicides during the two preceding years in "the South." However, it included within the region the border states of Maryland, Delaware, West Virginia, Kentucky, and Oklahoma.

where than this convergence of conduct might suggest. Male residents of the South, where both tort and criminal law had long permitted a person imperiled by deadly force to respond in kind without first attempting to retreat,[56] did look more favorably on killing in self-defense and to defend one's home than did men elsewhere (see Table 2).[57] However, there was little difference between their opinions and those of other American men about what should be done with murderers. Nearly 76 percent of southern white males agreed with over 71 percent of white respondents elsewhere that those who commit murder should be put to death (see Table 3).

Equally important, by the summer of 1969 no statistically significant difference existed between the value placed on respect for the law by American white men generally and by those living in the supposedly lawless South (see Table 4). Nor, as a 1968 Harris poll disclosed, were southern attitudes concerning vigilantism then out of the national mainstream. A slightly higher percentage of southerners than easterners (51 percent versus 47 percent) found acceptable the proposition that things had worked better in the days of the Old West when justice was rough and ready and there was less legal red tape, but the figure for the South was the same as that for the West and actually lower than the one for the Midwest (53 percent). When asked whether they would participate in a physical assault on antiwar protesters, only 9 percent of southern respondents an-

TABLE TWO
Attitudes Concerning the Defensive Use of Deadly Force

1. Respondents asked to agree or disagree with statement: "A man has a
right to kill another man in a case of self-defense." (Actual number of
respondents in parentheses.)

	Southern Whites	Non-Southern Whites
Disagree a great deal	0.7% (2)	5.5% (57)
Disagree somewhat	4.5% (12)	6.1% (63)
Agree somewhat	20.6% (55)	31.2% (321)
Agree a great deal	74.2% (198)	57.1% (58)

Valid cases: 1,295

Significance: .0000

Gamma: 0.3452

Cramer's V: 0.15244

2. Respondents asked to agree or disagree with the statement: "A man
has the right to kill a person to defend his house." (Actual numbers of
respondents in parentheses).

	Southern Whites	Non-Southern Whites
Disagree a great deal	10.4% (28)	19.7% (203)
Disagree somewhat	20.5% (55)	28.2% (291)
Agree somewhat	31.3% (84)	34.2% (353)
Agree a great deal	37.7% (101)	17.8% (184)

Valid cases: 1,299

Significance: 0.0000

Gamma: 0.33934

Cramer's V: 0.20322

swered yes. The figures for the Midwest, East, and West were 9 percent,
11 percent, and 11 percent respectively. Only on the question of whether
groups had a right to train their members in marksmanship and under-
ground warfare tactics so that they could help put down conspiracies did
the South differ substantially from the rest of the United States. Thirty-
four percent of the southerners polled answered yes, versus 24 percent of
easterners and midwesterners, and 17 percent of westerners.[58] Although

TABLE THREE
Regional Attitudes Concerning Capital Punishment for Murder

Each respondent asked to respond to the statement: "People who commit murder deserve capital punishment." (Actual number of respondents in parentheses.)

	Southern Whites	Non-Southern Whites
Agree	75.9% (202)	71.4% (734)
Disagree	24.1% (64)	28.5% (294)

Valid cases: 1,294

Significance: .0005

Gamma: 0.19024

Cramer's V: 0.11726

comparatively large, the percentage of southerners giving affirmative responses to this question represented barely over one-third of the region's population. Furthermore, the Harris pollsters asked only for respondents' views concerning the rights of Klan-type organizations, not whether they approved of the violence actually perpetrated by such groups.

It was increasingly apparent that most white southerners, including those who served on juries, did not approve of vigilante justice. In April 1965 columnist Kenneth Davis reported that in countless communities across the South "decent men" were becoming so outraged by the conduct of the "few trashy hoodlums in their midst" that they were talking seriously about resorting to vigilante methods if the law failed "to punish the killers and other culprits." Although accurately assessing the strength of the southern reaction against violence, Davis erred in concluding that those middle-class whites he considered respectable wanted to employ the Klan's own tactics to combat it.[59] Actually, what the "decent men" of Dixie feared was that the extralegal violence used by klansmen to defend white supremacy, and the failure of southern legal institutions to control it, would undermine the rule of law.

There had developed in the South a genuine concern about the deterioration of law and order. The Jackson Daily News believed: "Much stronger emphasis on law and order is needed in Mississippi."[60] It expressed this opinion in an editorial endorsing the surprise verdicts in the Meridian trial of the men accused of conspiring to violate the civil rights of Schwerner,

TABLE FOUR
Regional Attitudes Concerning the Importance of Respect for Law

Each respondent asked to rank respect for law against other values in order of importance for type of world he wants to live in. (Actual number of respondents in parentheses)

	Southern Whites	Non-Southern Whites
Rating Respect for Law First	7.5% (20)	7.1% (73)
Rating Respect for Law Second	18.4% (49)	16.6% (160)
Rating Respect for Law Third	22.5% (60)	19.6% (201)
Rating Respect for Law Fourth	26.2% (70)	28.2% (290)
Rating Respect for Law Fifth	16.5% (44)	22.3% (229)
Rating Respect for Law Sixth	9.0% (24)	7.3% (75)

Valid cases 1,295

Significance: 0.2659

Gamma: 0.07065

Cramer's V: 0.7051

Chaney, and Goodman. Even in the town of Philadelphia itself, prominent persons expressed concern about the breakdown of law and order. The *Neshoba Democrat* insisted: "Conscientous citizens of Neshoba County must do everything possible to bring the community around to increasing emphasis on law and order." The same issue in which this editorial appeared carried a warning from the mayor and aldermen of Philadelphia: "Usurpation of legal authority by a lawless individual or group will not be tolerated."[61] Senator John Stennis was correct when he assured President Johnson in June 1966 that "the overwhelming majority of Mississippians stand for law and order."[62]

Their determination to keep it from collapsing, along with the development of similar sentiments in other southern states, inspired the crackdown on anti–civil rights violence that occurred during the late 1960s. Nothing better illustrates the connection between this resolve, felt even by those most anxious to preserve traditional patterns of race relations, and the sudden effectiveness of southern legal institutions against Klan terrorism than one incident involving Judge Cox. After he gave his "dynamite" charge in the Meridian trial, defendents Price and Roberts joked that they had some dynamite for Cox. The judge exploded. If they thought they could intimidate his court, he told the two klansmen, they were badly mistaken.[63] Declaring that he "did not want any more of this strong arm stuff in the Southern District of Mississippi," Cox agreed to release Price and Roberts on bail only for so long as a forty-five county area remained free of terrorist bombings.[64] "We are not going to have anarchy down here, not as long as I sit here," the segregationist judge declared.[65]

Cox also told Roberts he considered any other verdict than the guilty one the jury had returned against him "unthinkable."[66] A growing number of southern jurors arrived at similar conclusions concerning racist killers. Unlike the residents of their region questioned by the Harris poll, jury members had to confront directly the issue of anti–civil rights violence. FBI statistics do not distinguish white attacks on blacks from other violent crimes, and pollsters asked no questions about interracial violence, but jurors required to decide the fate of white extremists charged with killing assertive blacks and northern civil rights workers had to face, in a context in which evasion was next to impossible, precisely the issue confronting the South. While they were relatively few in number and probably not entirely representative even of the white population of the region, their unexpected guilty votes constituted the most dramatic evidence of a regional reaction against anti–civil rights violence and in favor of law and order.

A comparison of the two trials in the Lemuel Penn case highlights the causal relationship between the mounting southern concern about the deterioration of law and order and the verdicts those jurors returned. The federal jury that convicted Howard Sims and Cecil Myers on section 241 charges in July 1966 did not differ significantly from the state one which had acquitted them of murder in September 1964. Both were all-white, predominantly middle-aged, and heavily male, that which heard the state case including only one woman and its federal counterpart just two. Occupationally, the state and federal juries were about the same, consisting mainly of farmers and blue-collar workers, with no professionals on either. Athens, site of the federal trial, is a small city and the home of the University of Georgia. The Justice Department expected to get a more metropolitan jury there than the one which had acquitted the two klansmen in the tiny county seat of Danielsville, but, like all of the jurors in the state trial, most of those who convicted Sims and Myers on civil rights charges were from small towns and rural areas in northeast Georgia. Only one resident of Athens served on the federal jury. Differences in the judicial instructions heard by the two groups of jurors do not appear to explain the differences in the verdicts they returned, and with respect to the actual charges against Sims and Myers the evidence was stronger in the state case than in the federal one. Murder is, of course, a capital crime, but the Danielsville jury could have convicted Sims and Myers of a lesser offense, voluntary manslaughter, which carried a penalty not much greater than that for violation of section 241.[67]

What acounts for the differing outcomes of the two trials is the law-and-order reaction that swept the South between 1964 and 1966. In the wake of the Penn killing, Father John Mulroy warned his flock at Athens's largest Catholic church: "Evil can spread . . . when good men do nothing."[68] The community's leading radio station urged its listeners to join in publicly condemning such lawless acts as the Penn killing. As WGAU saw it, the community had to "take a complete and immediate and unequivocal stand for law and order" or it was "in danger of anarchy and turmoil."[69] United States Attorney Buford was playing on a major concern of northeast Georgians when he asked the federal jury to "return a verdict of guilty as to each defendant in this case and let it be a declaration for law and order."[70]

In Alabama, John Doar and U. S. Attorney Hardeman obtained federal convictions against Viola Liuzzo's killers by successfully exploiting that same sentiment. In their final arguments both stressed the danger of allowing people to take the law into their own hands. Jurors also heard a charge from Judge Frank Johnson which emphasized that "our courts in America and the law that they dispense must remain supreme if our system is to prevail." As journalist Fred Graham noted at the time, this jury was similar to the ones that had twice failed to convict Collie Leroy Wilkins. Like Wilkins's second state jury (the only one on which extensive data is available), it was all-white and all-male. Both juries were drawn mainly from small towns, the single Montgomery resident on the federal jury being the only true urbanite to serve on either. These juries did differ more occupationally than the two that heard the Penn case. At least ten members of the state one were either farmers or blue-collar workers, the other two being county government employees. Occupational information on the federal jurors is less precise, but a majority appear to have been owners or managers of businesses, and the foreman was a school superintendent.[71]

While these occupational differences might account for the contrasting results of the state and federal trials, there is evidence which suggests that in

Alabama, as in Georgia, jurors were greatly influenced by appeals to preserve law and order. Solicitor Arthur Gamble, who prosecuted Wilkins in
the first of his two trials for murder, stressed that theme. Telling members
of the jury that he did not agree with Mrs. Liuzzo, who had driven down
from Detroit to participate in the Selma March, he reminded them that she
nevertheless had a right to be in Alabama. Gamble warned the jury about
the danger of anarchy and urged its members to refuse to put their stamp of
approval on the sort of lawlessness which this case involved. Ten of them
responded to his law-and-order appeal by voting guilty, whereas all of the
jurors in Wilkins's second state trial, confronted instead with an attack on
racism by Richmond Flowers, voted for acquittal.

The case of Hubert Damon Strange demonstrates with particular clarity
that it was heightened concern for law and order which finally made white
southern juries willing to return guilty verdicts against racist killers. In
Anniston, Alabama, where Strange was accused of murdering Willie Lee
Brewster, a black man, and where he later was tried and convicted, the
leading newspaper organized a campaign for law and order that resulted in
the publication by five hundred local citizens of an advertisement proclaiming: "We are determined that those who advocate and commit secret acts of
violence will not control this community." With the aid of the mayor, a city
commissioner, and 263 other civic and business leaders, the *Anniston Star*
collected a $20,000 reward for information leading to the conviction of the
man responsible for the Brewster killing. This money induced a small-time
hoodlum named Jimmy Glenn to step forward with testimony that established Strange's guilt. Despite Glenn's criminal record and defense attacks
upon his credibility, jurors accepted his story and convicted the defendant.
That they should have done so—and thus made the Strange trial the first in
a series of revolutionary proceedings that resulted in the punishment of
white racists for their crimes of violence—is not surprising. The courthouse
bulged with businessmen and lawyers who wanted a guilty verdict. When
the jury returned one, they made their pleasure obvious. "I don't think
we'll have any more trouble with lawlessness," one businessman remarked
happily upon learning what the jury had done.[72]

The determination of whites in Anniston, and throughout the South, to
halt the racist violence that for a time had threatened to plunge their region
into anarchy transformed state criminal justice systems which once had
served as shields for the guilty into weapons for the suppression of night

riding and terrorism. That resolve made largely unnecessary the law which Congress enacted in 1968. The wave of bombings, beatings, and murders which washed over the South during the decade after the *Brown* decision had seriously imperiled not only the lives and safety of civil rights workers and black southerners but also their exercise of rights supposedly guaranteed by the United States Constitution. Under the federal system which the Constitution created, primary responsibility for the prevention and punishment of such crimes rested with state and local authorities. If they chose to abdicate those responsibilities in cases where the victims were blacks or white civil rights workers, terrorists could effectively nullify the constitutional rights of those citizens. Federalism did not require the national government to stand idle while that happened. Yet for too long Congress, judges, presidents, and even the Department of Justice used it as a rationalization for politically convenient inaction. For too long, only when the conduct of state authorities created a major constitutional crisis would they move to protect the victims of anti–civil rights violence. Not until public outrage fueled by an orgy of burning, bombing, beating, and killing in the summer of 1964 generated political pressures too powerful to ignore did they move to create effective legal remedies for racist terrorism. By the time the national government finally acted, white southerners, frightened by the prospect of a breakdown of law and order in their communities, already had moved to deal with the problem themselves.

The federal response to anti–civil rights violence was not too little, but it did come much too late. Although the FBI's COINTELPRO ravaged the Ku Klux Klan and the Civil Rights Division finally sent a few racist killers to prison, it was not the national government but white southerners who were primarily responsible for restoring order in the South. In one sense, history vindicated those, such as Burke Marshall, who had argued for reliance on local institutions and who stressed the need for patience. It took the specter of anarchy to prod white southerners into doing something about racist violence, and they had some federal help in combating terroristic organizations. To a surprising extent, however, the South did solve its own problem. Unfortunately, there were blacks and civil rights workers who did not live to see it do so. "The values of federalism are important," the *Arkansas Gazette* observed in early 1965. "But the values of the human person are important too, and it was decided almost a hundred years ago that states' rights could not be permitted to cloak a state's deprivation of the rights of its residents."[73] For too long, federal officials forgot these truths. If the national government had done all that it had the power to do, numerous tragedies might have been averted. Washington needed to make clear from the beginning that the price of failure to control racist violence which interfered with the exercise of constitutional rights would inevitably be federal intervention and that only local responsibility could preserve local autonomy. Conciliation was a mistake that invited chaos.[74] Washington could not, of course, have policed all of the South permanently, but there was no need for it to do so. All the situation required was for the national government to give white southerners what fear of anarchy eventually provided: a powerful reason for controlling racist violence themselves. Federal law and federal force, used firmly but selectively, might well have prompted them to suppress it considerably sooner than they did. Federal hesitancy and federal inaction served only to delay the restoration of southern order.

NOTES

Abbreviations Used in Notes

C.F.	Confidential File
CORE Papers	Congress of Racial Equality Papers, State Historical Society of Wisconsin, Madison, Wisconsin
CUOHP	Columbia University Oral History Project
DDE	Dwight D. Eisenhower Presidential Library, Abilene, Kansas
D.J.	United States Department of Justice
Ex.	Executive Series
FBI	Federal Bureau of Investigation, Freedom of Information Act Privacy Branch, Reading Room, J. Edgar Hoover Building, Washington, D.C.
Gen.	General Series
GRF	Gerald R. Ford Presidential Library, Ann Arbor, Michigan
JFK	John F. Kennedy Presidential Library, Boston, Massachusetts
JFK Oral	John F. Kennedy Oral History Project, Kennedy Library
King Center	Martin Luther King, Jr., Center for Nonviolent Social Change, Atlanta, Georgia
King Papers–BU	Martin Luther King, Jr., Papers, Mugar Library, Boston University, Boston, Massachusetts
King Papers–King Center	Martin Luther King, Jr., Papers, King Center

LBJ	Lyndon Baines Johnson Presidential Library, Austin, Texas
LC	Manuscript Division, Library of Congress, Washington, D.C.
NAACP Papers	National Association for the Advancement of Colored People Papers, Manuscript Division, Library of Congress
O.F.	Official File
SCLC Papers	Southern Christian Leadership Conference Papers, King Center
SNCC Papers	Student Nonviolent Coordinating Committee Papers, King Center
SRCC	Southern Regional Council Collection, Atlanta University, Atlanta, Georgia
WHCF	White House Central Files

Preface

1 Farmer, telegram to Kennedy, undated, series 1, box 4, folder 4, CORE Papers.

2 Marshall to Professor Russell H. Barrett, January 3, 1964, box 19, Burke Marshall Papers, JFK.

3 For an extended discussion and analysis of Marshall's views, see Michal R. Belknap, "The Vindication of Burke Marshall: The Southern Legal System and the Anti–Civil Rights Violence of the 1960s," *Emory Law Journal* 33 (Winter 1984): 94–97.

4 I am a bit chagrined to admit that I am among those who have been sharply critical of the FBI. See my "Above the Law and Beyond Its Reach: O'Reilly and Theoharis on FBI Intelligence Operations," *American Bar Foundation Research Journal* (Winter 1985): 201–15.

Chapter One

1 On the Waco incident, see "The Waco Horror," *Crisis* 12 (July 1916): Supplement, pp. 1–8.

2 Robert M. Cover, *Justice Accused: Antislavery and the Judicial Process* (New Haven, 1975), pp. 105–107; Kenneth M. Stampp, *The Peculiar Institution: Slavery*

in the Ante-Bellum South (New York, 1956), pp. 171, 174, 210; Winthrop D. Jordan, *White Over Black: American Attitudes Toward the Negro, 1550–1812* (Chapel Hill, 1968), pp. 106, 108; Eugene D. Genovese, *Roll, Jordan, Roll: The World the Slaves Made* (New York, 1974), pp. 31, 37, 41.

3 State v. Mann, 13 N.C. (2 Dev.), 263, 267 (1829).

4 Jordan, *White Over Black*, p. 106; Michael S. Hindus, "Black Justice Under White Law: Criminal Prosecutions of Blacks in Antebellum South Carolina," *Journal of American History* 63 (December 1976): 578; State v. Jowers, 33 N.C. (11 Ired.) 555, 556 (1851). In South Carolina slaves could be subjected to criminal prosecution for insolence toward a white person (Hindus, "Black Justice," p. 579).

5 Stampp, *Peculiar Institution*, pp. 218–19; Genovese, *Roll, Jordan, Roll*, pp. 33–37; Hindus, "Black Justice," pp. 577–78.

6 An Act Concerning Slaves, February 5, 1840, *Laws of the Republic of Texas Passed at the Fourth Congress* 171 (1840); Texas Constitution, art. 8, section 3 (1845).

7 Chandler v. State, 2 Tex. 305, 309–10 (1848).

8 Mark V. Tushnet, "The American Law of Slavery, 1810–1860: A Study in the Persistence of Legal Autonomy," *Law and Society Review* 10 (Fall 1975): 119, 131–32; Tushnet, *The American Law of Slavery, 1810–1860: Considerations of Humanity and Interest* (Princeton, N.J., 1981), pp. 73–75, 84, 102.

9 State v. Jones, 2 Miss. (1 Walker) 83, 84 (1821).

10 Nix v. State, 13 Tex. 575, 578 (1855).

11 Stampp, *Peculiar Institution*, p. 219.

12 Ibid., pp. 219–23; Genovese, *Roll, Jordan, Roll*, p. 39; Stanley Elkins, *Slavery: A Problem in American Institutional and Intellectual Life*, 2d ed. (Chicago, 1963), pp. 56–57; Hindus, "Black Justice," pp. 579–80.

13 Quoted in Hindus, "Black Justice," p. 580.

14 A. E. Keir Nash, "A More Equitable Past? Southern Supreme Courts and the Protection of the Antebellum Negro," *North Carolina Law Review* 48 (February 1970): 197–99, 200, 216–17.

15 Nix v. State at 578.

16 Genovese, *Roll, Jordan, Roll*, pp. 32–33; Walter White, *Rope and Faggot: A Biography of Judge Lynch* (1929; reprint ed., New York, 1969), pp. 87, 92; Gunnar Myrdal, *An American Dilemma: The Negro Problem and Modern Democracy*, 2d ed. (New York, 1962), p. 560; Jacquelyn Dowd Hall, *Revolt Against Chivalry: Jessie Daniel Ames and the Women's Campaign Against Lynching* (New York, 1979), p. 131; James Elbert Cutler, *Lynch Law: An Investigation into the History of Lynching in the United States* (New York, 1905), pp. 91, 124–25, 193; Clement Eaton, *The Freedom-of-Thought Struggle in the Old South*, 2d ed. (New York, 1964), pp. 96, 97,

378; Allen W. Trelease, *White Terror: The Ku Klux Klan Conspiracy and Southern Reconstruction* (New York, 1971), p. xlii.

17   According to the Supreme Court, speaking in the case of *Strauder v. West Virginia*, 100 U.S. 303, 307–308 (1880), the words of the Fourteenth Amendment "contain a necessary implication of a positive immunity of right . . . the right to exemption from unfriendly legislation against them distinctively as colored—exemption from legal discriminations, implying inferiority in civil society, lessening the security of their enjoyment of the rights which others enjoy, and discriminations which are steps towards reducing them to the condition of a subject race."

18   George C. Rable, *But There Was No Peace: The Role of Violence in the Politics of Reconstruction* (Athens, Ga., 1984), pp. 21–58; Trelease, *White Terror,* pp. xliii–xliv, 138; Richard Maxwell Brown, *Strain of Violence: Historical Studies of American Violence and Vigilantism* (New York, 1975), p. 208.

19   Trelease, *White Terror,* pp. 137, 140 (quote at 140). As Rable emphasizes, during Reconstruction "justice appeared to be blind to crimes by whites against blacks" (*No Peace,* p. 21).

20   Quoted in Charles W. Ramsdell, *Reconstruction in Texas* (1910; reprint ed., Gloucester, Mass., 1964), p. 190.

21   Trelease, *White Terror,* pp. xlv–xlvii (quote at xlvi); Rable, *No Peace,* pp. 91–99; David M. Chalmers, *Hooded Americanism: The First Century of the Ku Klux Klan, 1865–1965* (Garden City, N.Y., 1965), p. 20; Pete Daniel, "The Metamorphosis of Slavery, 1865–1900," *Journal of American History* 66 (June 1979): 91.

22   Rable, *No Peace,* pp. 75, 98; White, *Rope and Faggot,* pp. 94–96; Brown, *Strain of Violence,* p. 214; Joel Williamson, *The Crucible of Race: Black-White Relations in the American South Since Reconstruction* (New York, 1983), p. 183; Robert L. Zangrando, *The NAACP Crusade Against Lynching, 1909–1950* (Philadelphia, 1980), pp. 6–7. The peak year was 1892, when 161 blacks were lynched. Figures for the period 1882–1889 range from a low of 49 in 1882 to a high of 94 in 1889, for the 1890s from a low of 78 in 1896 to the high of 161 in 1892, for the early 1900s from a low of 58 in 1907 to a high of 105 in 1901, and for the period 1910–1919 from a low of 36 in 1917 to a high of 76 in 1919.

23   Williamson, *Crucible,* p. 185; Myrdal, *American Dilemma,* p. 561; NAACP, *Thirty Years of Lynching in the United States, 1889–1918* (1919; reprint ed., New York, 1969), p. 7; Southern Commission on the Study of Lynching, *Lynchings and What They Mean* (Atlanta, 1934), pp. 8, 10; Arthur F. Raper, *The Tragedy of Lynching* (New York, 1933), p. 43; Commission on Interracial Cooperation, *Southern Leaders Impeach Judge Lynch: Highlights from Report of Commission on the Study of Lynching* (Atlanta, n.d.), Arthur F. Raper Papers, Southern Historical

Collection, University of North Carolina, Chapel Hill; Lawrence D. Rice, *The Negro in Texas, 1874–1900* (Baton Rouge, 1971), p. 250. Williamson (*Crucible*, pp. 183–84) insists the killing of blacks during Reconstruction was not lynching, which he says began suddenly in 1889.

24 George C. Rable, "The South and the Politics of Antilynching Legislation," *Journal of Southern History* 51 (May 1985): 202; *Dallas Morning News*, June 10, 1897; "What Can Be Done to Stop Lynching," *American Law Review* 39 (January–February 1905): 102; James H. Chadbourn, *Lynching and the Law* (Chapel Hill, 1933), p. 5; Hannis Taylor, "The True Remedy for Lynch Law," *American Law Review* 41 (March–April 1907): 256.

25 Williamson, *Crucible*, p. 186; Donald L. Grant, *The Anti-Lynching Movement, 1883–1932* (San Francisco, 1975), p. 12; "The Waco Horror," p. 2; Chadbourn, *Lynching and the Law*, pp. 6–10.

26 Jordan, *White Over Black*, p. 473.

27 White, *Rope and Faggot*, p. 56.

28 Cutler, *Lynch Law*, p. 176; NAACP, *Thirty Years*, p. 10; White, *Rope and Faggot*, p. 26; Myrdal, *American Dilemma*, p. 562. There is no statistical basis for Joel Williamson's contention (*Crucible*, pp. 183–84) that "whites began the practice of lynching as a reaction against the presumed threat of the black beast to white womanhood."

29 Grant, *Anti-Lynching Movement*, pp. 7, 49; George B. Tindall, *The Emergence of the New South, 1913–1945* (Baton Rouge, 1967), p. 170; White, *Rope and Faggot*, p. 16; Hall, *Revolt Against Chivalry*, pp. 139–40; Richard Maxwell Brown, "The American Vigilante Tradition," in *The History of Violence in America*, ed. Hugh Davis Graham and Ted Robert Gurr (New York, 1969), p. 216; Myrdal, *American Dilemma*, p. 561; H. C. Brearley, "The Pattern of Violence," in *Culture in the South*, ed. W. T. Couch (Chapel Hill, 1934), p. 680; James R. McGovern, *Anatomy of a Lynching: The Killing of Claude Neal* (Baton Rouge, 1982), pp. 5–6. The Tuskegee definition is quoted in a letter from Governor of Florida to Tuskegee Institute Department of Records and Research, March 6, 1946, folder 75-01-33-31, SRCC.

30 Hall, *Revolt Against Chivalry*, p. 141; Brown, "Vigilante Tradition," pp. 216–17; Chadbourn, *Lynching and the Law*, p. 38; Wilbur J. Cash, *The Mind of the South* (New York, 1941), p. 122; Rice, *Negro in Texas*, pp. 250–51; William Ivy Hair, *Bourbonism and Agrarian Protest: Louisiana Politics, 1877–1900* (Baton Rouge, 1969), p. 187; Williamson, *Crucible*, p. 187.

31 Allen D. Grimshaw, "Lawlessness and Violence in America and Their Special Manifestations in Changing Negro-White Relationships," in *Racial Violence in the United States*, ed. Allen D. Grimshaw (Chicago, 1969), pp. 17, 63; Lawrence C. Goodwin, "Populist Dreams and Negro Rights: East Texas as a Case

Study," *American Historical Review* 76 (December 1971): 1439–41; Hall, *Revolt Against Chivalry*, p. 132; Zangrando, *NAACP Crusade*, pp. 6–7; Williamson, *Crucible*, pp. 189–221.

32 Zangrando, *NAACP Crusade*, pp. 6–7; Hall, *Revolt Against Chivalry*, p. 133; Tindall, *Emergence*, p. 171.

33 Zangrando, *NAACP Crusade*, p. 7; Hall, *Revolt Against Chivalry*, p. 129; Jessie Daniel Ames, *The Changing Character of Lynching* (1942; reprint ed., New York, 1973), p. 2.

34 Raper, *Tragedy*, p. 20; Hall, *Revolt Against Chivalry*, pp. 214, 224–25; White, *Rope and Faggot*, p. 172; Notes, Raper Papers; Southern Commission for the Study of Lynching, *Lynchings*, p. 44. The peace officer is quoted in the last of these sources.

35 Myrdal, *American Dilemma*, p. 562; Hall, *Revolt Against Chivalry*, p. 241; Raper, *Tragedy*, pp. 16–18; Chadbourn, *Lynching and the Law*, pp. 23–24.

36 Chadbourn, *Lynching and the Law*, pp. 13–15; Arthur Raper to Thomas Kilby, March 25, 1936, Raper Papers; U.S., Senate, Committee on the Judiciary, *Crime of Lynching: Hearings . . . on H.R. 801 . . .*, 76th Cong., 3d sess., 1940, pp. 60–61.

37 Herman Belz, *Emancipation and Equal Rights: Politics and Constitutionalism in the Civil War Era* (New York, 1978), pp. 123–24; Trelease, *White Terror*, p. 383; Sections 1 and 2, 14 Stat. 27 (1866); Blyew v. United States, 80 U.S. (13 Wall.) 581 (1871); Robert J. Kaczorowski, *The Politics of Judicial Interpretation: The Federal Courts, Department of Justice and Equal Rights, 1866–1876* (New York, 1985), pp. 134–43; Harold Hyman, *A More Perfect Union: The Impact of the Civil War and Reconstruction on the Constitution* (Boston, 1975), p. 444.

38. Belz, *Emancipation and Equal Rights*, pp. 104, 126–27; Ch. 114, 16 Stat. 140 (1870); Harold M. Hyman and William M. Wiecek, *Equal Justice Under Law: Constitutional Development, 1835–1875* (New York, 1982), p. 467.

39 Ch. 22, 17 Stat. 13 (1871); Kaczorowski, *Politics of Judicial Interpretation*, p. 56.

40 Belz, *Emancipation and Equal Rights*, pp. 127–29; Hyman and Wiecek, *Equal Justice*, p. 470; Alfred Avins, "The Ku Klux Klan Act of 1871: Some Reflected Light on State Action and the Fourteenth Amendment," *St. Louis University Law Journal* 11 (1967): 377; Laurent B. Frantz, "Congressional Power to Enforce the Fourteenth Amendment Against Private Acts," *Yale Law Journal* 73 (July 1964): 1353–55; Aviam Soifer, "Protecting Civil Rights: A Critique of Raoul Berger's History," *New York University Law Review* 54 (June 1979): 680.

41 Avins, "Ku Klux Klan Act," p. 379.

42 Belz, *Emancipation and Equal Rights*, p. 136. See also Frantz, "Congressional Power," pp. 1358–62.

43 Trelease, *White Terror*, pp. 399–418; Everett Swinney, "Enforcing the

Fifteenth Amendment, 1870–1877," *Journal of Southern History* 28 (February 1962): 206; Kaczorowski, *Politics of Judicial Interpretation,* p. 94; Kermit L. Hall, "Political Power and Constitutional Legitimacy: The South Carolina Ku Klux Klan Trials," *Emory Law Journal* 33 (Fall 1984): 925–26.

44   Ch. 25, 28 Stat. 36 (1894); Eugene Gressman, "The Unhappy History of Civil Rights Legislation," *Michigan Law Review* 50 (June 1952): 1342.

45   Ch. 321, sections 19 and 20, 35 Stat. 1088 (1909). Section 20's roots ran back to section 2 of the Civil Rights Act of 1866, which was substantially amended by section 17 of 16 Stat. 140 (1870).

46   United States v. Cruikshank, 92 U.S. 542 (1876). For an excellent account of this case and of the massacre, see Kaczorowski, *Politics of Judicial Interpretation,* pp. 175–88.

47   United States v. Cruikshank, 25 F. Cas. 707, 714 (C.C. La. 1874) (No. 14,896).

48   106 U.S. 629 (1883).

49   Ibid. at 640.

50   Ex parte Riggins, 134 F. 404, 409–23 (C.C. N.D. Ala. 1904); United States v. Powell, 151 F. 648, 650–57, 662–64 (C.C. N.D. Ala. 1907).

51   The Supreme Court decision that Jones regarded as controlling was United States v. Waddell, 112 U.S. 76 (1884). In May 1940 a new Civil Liberties Unit in the Department of Justice sent a memorandum to United States attorneys arguing that the failure of a state's officials to protect citizens from lynching could be regarded as a violation by that state of both the Due Process and Equal Protection clauses, and thus as a basis for prosecution under two anti-Klan statutes then known as Penal Code, sections 19 and 20. See John Thomas Elliff, "The United States Department of Justice and Individual Rights, 1936–1962" (Ph.D. diss., Harvard University, 1967), pp. 100–12.

52   United States v. Powell, 212 U.S. 564 (1909).

53   United States v. Shipp, 214 U.S. 386 (1909).

54   144 U.S. 263 (1892); Carrie J. Crouch, *A History of Young County, Texas* (Austin, 1956), pp. 116–20. The victims of this lynching seem to have been white, but the *Shipp* decision (see note 53 above) indicates racism is not an adequate explanation for the differing outcomes of *Logan* and *Harris.*

55   Ex parte Yarbrough, 110 U.S. 65 (1884). The Supreme Court also upheld a conviction for conspiring to drive a farmer (whose race it did not identify) off land he had settled under the Homestead Act. United States v. Waddell, 112 U.S. 76 (1884).

56   325 U.S. 91 (1945).

57   Arthur B. Caldwell, "Civil Rights—A Federal Concern" (speech delivered to the Commission on Human Relations of the City of Chicago, April 28, 1952), box 4, folder 10, and Warren Olney III, Memorandum for William P.

Rogers, January 23, 1956, box 2, folder 6, Arthur Brann Caldwell Papers, University of Arkansas, Fayetteville; Crews v. United States, 160 F.2d 746 (5th Cir. 1947); Elliff, "Department of Justice," pp. 267–68.

58   325 U.S. at 119, 149–57.

59   Ibid. at 119–34 (quote at 119).

60   341 U.S. 70, 87–95 (1951).

61   For Frankfurter's views, see 341 U.S. at 77–78; F.F., "Re: Nos. 26, 365 and 217—The Civil Rights Cases," January 24, 1951, Conference Memoranda 1950 Term, Supreme Court Case File, box 306, Hugo L. Black Papers, LC; F.F., Memorandum for the Conference, March 6, 1951, box 45, Felix Frankfurter Papers, Manuscript Room, Harvard Law School Library, Cambridge, Massachusetts.

62   341 U.S. at 85–86.

63   Caldwell, "Civil Rights—A Federal Concern."

64   Zangrando, NAACP Crusade, pp. 43, 54–71; Rable, "Politics of Antilynching Legislation," p. 204.

65   Zangrando, NAACP Crusade, pp. 111–64.

66   Ibid., pp. 174–96, 191–92, 206; President's Committee on Civil Rights, To Secure These Rights: Report of the President's Committee on Civil Rights (New York, 1947), pp. 156–57; U.S., Congress, Senate, Committee on the Judiciary, Crime of Lynching: Hearings . . . , 80th Cong., 2d sess., 1948, p. 109.

67   "Statement and Analysis by the Attorney General Concerning the Proposed Civil Rights Act of 1949 in Hearings Before Committee on Antilynching and Protection of Civil Rights Bill, 81st Congress, 1st and 2nd sessions (1949–50)," reprinted in U.S., Congress, House, Committee on the Judiciary, Civil Rights:. Hearings on . . . Miscellaneous Bills Regarding the Civil Rights of Persons Within the Jurisdiction of the United States, 84th Cong., 2d sess., 1955, pp. 177–78.

68   Zangrando, NAACP Crusade, p. 165.

69   Ibid., pp. 15–16, 60; Mary Francis Berry, Black Resistance/White Law: A History of Constitutional Racism in America (New York, 1971), pp. 16, 134.

70   McGovern, Anatomy of a Lynching, pp. 119–25; Zangrando, NAACP Crusade, pp. 15, 60, 122, 158; Berry, Black Resistance, pp. 116, 134; Hall, Revolt Against Chivalry, p. 242; Elliff, "Department of Justice," p. 69.

71   Elliff, "Department of Justice," pp. 149–57; Robert K. Carr, Federal Protection of Civil Rights: Quest for a Sword (Ithaca, N.Y., 1947), pp. 164, 169–73; Dominic J. Capeci, Jr., "The Lynching of Cleo Wright: Federal Protection of Constitutional Rights During World War II," Journal of American History 72 (March 1986): 874–83.

72   Screws v. United States, 325 U.S. 91, 159 (1945).

73   Elliff, "Department of Justice," pp. 224–26; Donald R. McCoy and

Richard T. Ruetten, *Quest and Response: Minority Rights and the Truman Administration* (Lawrence, Kans., 1973), pp. 43–49.

74 Memorandum from Director, FBI, to Attorney General, September 12, 1946, box 2, folder 2, Caldwell Papers (also in DJ 144-012).

75 Memorandum from Director, FBI, to the Attorney General, April 29, 1953, box 2, folder 2, Caldwell Papers (also in DJ 144-012); Elliff, "Department of Justice," pp. 302–303; Brooks v. United States, 199 F.2d 336 (4th Cir. 1952); U.S., Department of Justice, *Annual Report of the Attorney General of the United States for the Fiscal Year Ended June 30, 1955* (Washington, D.C., 1955), p. 133.

76 Memorandum from Director, FBI, to the Attorney General, April 29, 1953, Caldwell Papers; Elliff, "Department of Justice," pp. 217–19, 235, 239, 298; United States v. Lynch, 94 F. Supp. 1011 (N.D. Ga. 1950); Tom C. Clark to H. A. Wallace, April 30, 1946, box 28, Tom C. Clark Papers, HST; Ellis Arnall, telegram to Tom C. Clark, July 31, 1946, box 19, Clark Papers.

77 Memorandum from Director, FBI, to the Attorney General, April 29, 1953, Caldwell Papers.

78 Ibid.; Civil Rights Section, Department of Justice, "Protection of the Rights of Individuals," March 1952, box 2, folder 3, Caldwell Papers.

79 White, *Rope and Faggot,* p. 19; Zangrando, *NAACP Crusade,* p. 7: Senate Judiciary Committee, *Crime of Lynching,* p. 100; F. W. Patterson to "Dear Sir," December 31, 1952, folder 75-03-23-33, SRCC.

80 Hall, *Revolt Against Chivalry,* p. 167; Tindall, *Emergence,* p. 174.

81 Undated clipping (apparently from sometime in 1938), box 5, Jessie Daniel Ames Papers, Southern Historical Collection.

82 Chadbourn, *Lynching and the Law,* pp. 29, 48–58, 64–66, 92–93, 105; Cutler, *Lynch Law,* pp. 231–41; White, *Rope and Faggot,* pp. 200–205.

83 White, *Rope and Faggot,* pp. 174–75.

84 Hall, *Revolt Against Chivalry,* pp. 127, 159, 175, 179. The quote is from Arthur Raper, transcript of interview by Jacquelyn D. Hall, January 30, 1974, Southern Historical Collection.

85 Hall, *Revolt Against Chivalry,* pp. 226–28, 236.

86 "Police and the Public," *Light* 5 (February 1952): 4.

87 Arthur Raper, transcript of interview by Morton Sosna, April 4, 1971, Raper Papers.

88 Cash, *Mind of the South,* p. 301; Ames, *Changing Character of Lynching,* p. 7; Chalmers, *Hooded Americanism,* p. 334; Notes on KKK, undated, folder 75-03-22-01, SRCC.

89 Cash, *Mind of the South,* p. 306; White, *Rope and Faggot,* pp. 112, 163.

90 Morton Sosna, *In Search of the Silent South: Southern Liberalism and the Race Issue* (New York, 1971), p. 31; Zangrando, *NAACP Crusade,* p. 11.

91   *Dallas Morning News,* June 11, 1897; Raper, *Tragedy,* p. 4; *Cordele Dispatch,* December 10, 1930.

92   Thurmond to Mrs. M. E. Tully, February 28, 1947, folder 75-01-33-31, SRCC.

93   Cutler, *Lynch Law,* p. 268; Brown, "The American Vigilante Tradition," p. 201.

94   John Hope Franklin, *The Militant South, 1860–1861* (Cambridge, Mass., 1956), p. 35; Bertram Wyatt-Brown, *Southern Honor: Ethics and Behavior in the Old South* (New York: Oxford University Press, 1982), pp. 373, 375–77; Charles Sydnor, "The Southerner and the Laws," *Journal of Southern History* 6 (February 1940): 7–13; Genovese, *Roll, Jordan, Roll,* pp. 43–44; Cash, *Mind of the South,* pp. 33–34; Michael Hindus, *Prison and Plantation: Crime, Justice and Authority in Massachusetts and South Carolina, 1767–1878* (Chapel Hill, 1980), pp. 34–35.

95   Richard Maxwell Brown, "Southern Violence—Regional Problem or National Nemesis? Legal Attitudes Toward Homicide in Historical Perspective," *Vanderbilt Law Review* 32 (January 1979): 229–31; Sheldon Hackney, "The Pattern of Violence," *American Historical Review* 74 (February 1969): 921.

96   Cash, *Mind of the South,* pp. 42–43; Franklin, *Militant South,* p. 35; Wyatt-Brown, *Southern Honor,* pp. 366–68; John Shelton Reed, "To Live—and Die—in Dixie: A Contribution to the Study of Southern Violence," *Political Science Quarterly* 86 (September 1971): 429–43; Raymond D. Gastil, "Homicide and a Regional Culture of Violence," *American Sociological Review* 36 (February 1971): 425. For criticism of the arguments of Hackney and Gastil, see Colin Loftin and Robert H. Hill, "Regional Subculture and Homicide: An Examination of the Gastil-Hackney Thesis," *American Sociological Review* 39 (October 1974): 712.

97   *To Secure These Rights,* p. 23.

98   "The Shape of Things," *Nation,* May 24, 1947, p. 615; "Twelve Good Men and True," *New Republic,* June 2, 1947, p. 9.

99   Commission on Interracial Cooperation, *The Mob Still Rides* (Atlanta, 1936), p. 9.

100   Horace B. Davis, "A Substitute for Lynching," *Nation,* January 1, 1930, p. 12.

101   *Christian Science Monitor,* May 9, 1959.

Chapter Two

1   J. Edgar Hoover, "Racial Tension and Civil Rights" (CONFIDENTIAL), March 1, 1956, Cabinet Meeting of March 9, 1956, Cabinet Series, Papers of Dwight D. Eisenhower as President (Ann Whitman File), DDE.

2 The most important revisionist works on Eisenhower's civil rights record are Robert Frederick Burk, *The Eisenhower Administration and Black Civil Rights* (Knoxville, 1984), and Michael S. Mayer, "Eisenhower's Conditional Crusade: The Eisenhower Administration and Civil Rights, 1953–1957" (Ph.D. diss., Princeton University, 1984). Although both of these works portray Ike's performance in this area more positively than do books written earlier, each author acknowledges that there is a negative side to the story. Burk, for example, writes that Eisenhower "helped institutionalize an official definition of racial inequality, a pattern of federal response, and a public expectation of civil rights advance within a framework of political moderation and consensus that contributed both to the progress of civil rights in the 1960s and to the serious limitations and disillusionment that accompanied it" (p. vi). While challenging the traditional characterization of Ike as a mere obstructionist, Mayer too disclaims any "attempt to resurrect Eisenhower as an unheralded champion of civil rights" (p. 7).

3 *Charleston News and Courier,* October 1, 1957; Numan V. Bartley, *The Rise of Massive Resistance: Race and Politics During the 1950s* (Baton Rouge, 1969), p. 14; Morton Sosna, *In Search of the Silent South: Southern Liberals and the Race Issue* (New York, 1977), p. 171.

4 Hoover, "Racial Tensions"; Sosna, *Silent South,* pp. 171, 207; Southern Regional Council, "Report on Charlotte, Greensboro and Winston-Salem, North Carolina," September 4, 1957, file drawer VII, folder 25, King Papers–BU.

5 Wilkins, *Roy Wilkins Speaks Out* (New York, 1962), p. 7; Leon Friedman, ed., *Southern Justice* (New York, 1965), p. 6; Neil R. McMillen, *The Citizens' Council: Organized Resistance to the Second Reconstruction, 1954–1964* (Urbana, 1971), p. 360. McMillen writes of the White Citizens Council: "Whatever may have been the theoretical relationship between the explosive atmosphere it so often created and the actual outbreak of violence, there is no tangible evidence which suggests it engaged in, or even overtly encouraged, criminal acts" (p. 360). See also Tuskegee Institute, "Tuskegee Race Relations Report, 1955," December 31, 1955, box 2, folder 6, Arthur Brann Caldwell Papers, University of Arkansas, Fayetteville, and American Friends Service Committee et al., *Intimidation, Reprisal and Violence in the South's Racial Crisis* (Atlanta, 1959), p. 1.

6 Bartley, *Massive Resistance,* pp. 202–203, 206–207; Benjamin Muse, *Ten Years of Prelude: The Story of Integration Since the Supreme Court's 1954 Decision* (New York, 1964), pp. 46–47; David M. Chalmers, *Hooded Americanism: The First Century of the Ku Klux Klan, 1865–1965* (Garden City, N.Y., 1965), p. 343; Southern Regional Council, "Pro-Segregation Groups in the South: A Special Report from the Southern Regional Council," May 23, 1957, box 9, Harris L. Wofford, Jr., Files, Papers of President Kennedy, JFK; American Friends Service Committee, *Intimidation, Reprisal and Violence,* p. 2.

7   Supplement to "Pro-Segregation Groups in the South," May 23, 1957, Wofford Files.

8   American Friends Service Committee, *Intimidation, Reprisal and Violence*, pp. 1–9, 15–30; United States Commission on Civil Rights, *Law Enforcement: A Report on Equal Protection in the South* (Washington, 1965), pp. 12–13.

9   American Friends Service Committee, *Intimidation, Reprisal and Violence*, pp. 20–21, 25–26; U.S., Department of Justice, *Annual Report of the Attorney General of the United States for the Fiscal Year Ended June 30, 1956* (Washington, 1956), pp. 119–20; Bartley, *Massive Resistance*, pp. 146–47; Muse, *Ten Years of Prelude*, pp. 53–54, 88–89; *Wilmington Morning News*, February 6, 1956; Mayer, "Eisenhower's Conditional Crusade," p. 261.

10   Muse, *Ten Years of Prelude*, pp. 44, 95–103; Neil R. McMillen, "Organized Resistance to School Desegregation in Tennessee," *Tennessee Historical Quarterly* 30 (Fall 1971): 317–19; *Nashville Tennessean*, September 2, 1956, and February 15, 1957; *Memphis Commercial Appeal*, December 1, 1958; Mayer, "Eisenhower's Conditional Crusade," pp. 265–72.

11   McMillen, "Organized Resistance," p. 322; Muse, *Ten Years of Prelude*, p. 119; *Chattanooga Times*, September 10, 1957; *Christian Science Monitor*, September 5, 1957; E. Frederic Morrow, *Black Man in the White House: A Diary of the Eisenhower Years by the Administrative Officer for Special Projects, the White House, 1955–1961* (New York, 1963), p. 169.

12   *Atlanta Journal*, February 19, 1956; E. C. Smith to Congressman Diggs, May 19, 1957, file drawer VII, folder 19, King Papers–BU; Bartley, *Massive Resistance*, p. 174; *St. Louis Post-Dispatch*, December 21, 1956; *St. Petersburg Times*, January 16, 1957; *Atlanta Journal*, January 17, 1957; *Montgomery Advertiser*, January 29, 1957; *Nashville Banner*, May 31, 1958; Catherine A. Barnes, *Journey from Jim Crow: The Desegregation of Southern Transit* (New York, 1983), p. 122.

13   *Miami Herald*, February 13, 1956; *St. Louis Post-Dispatch*, February 9, 1956; John Thomas Elliff, "The United States Department of Justice and Individual Rights, 1937–1962" (Ph.D. diss., Harvard University, 1967), p. 496; Herbert S. Parmet, *Eisenhower and the American Crusades* (New York, 1972), p. 440.

14   *Washington Post*, September 22, 1955; *Birmingham News*, April 14, 1956; "Background Summary of Violence at Koinoa Farm, Sumter County, Georgia," February 13, 1957, folder 75-01-74-24, SRCC.

15   *Birmingham News*, July 8, 1957, August 14, 1957, September 3, 1957, September 10, 1957, September 20, 1957.

16   Robert L. Zangrando, *The NAACP Crusade Against Lynching, 1909–1950* (Philadelphia, 1980), p. 7.

17   Muse, *Ten Years of Prelude*, pp. 51–52; Memphis Commercial Appeal,

September 24, 1955; St. Louis Post-Dispatch, February 9, 1956; *The State* (Columbia, S.C.), June 27, 1956; *Chattanooga Times,* November 10, 1955.

18 *Nashville Tennessean,* November 21, 1956, and May 30, 1957; "Trial by Jury, Dixie Style," undated, Series III, group B, box 55, NAACP Papers.

19 *Memphis Commercial Appeal,* September 21, 1955; *Montgomery Advertiser,* October 5, 1957.

20 Quoted in *St. Louis Post-Dispatch,* February 9, 1956.

21 *Atlanta Constitution,* November 1, 1957; *Nashville Tennessean,* November 5, 1957; *Birmingham News,* January 7, 1958, February 20, 1958.

22 Quoted in *Nashville Tennessean,* November 5, 1957.

23 *Charleston* (W. Va.) *Gazette,* September 20, 1957; *Richmond Times-Dispatch,* March 7, 1957.

24 U.S., Congress, House, Committee on the Judiciary, *Hearings . . . on . . . Miscellaneous Bills Regarding the Civil Rights of Persons Within the Jurisdiction of the United States,* 86th Cong., 1st sess., 1959, p. 549 (hereinafter cited as House Judiciary Committee, *1959 Hearings*).

25 Benjamin Muse, "Confidential Memorandum on Law Enforcement in Miami—Conversation with Assistant Chief of Police J. J. Youell," folder 75-01-58-38, SRCC.

26 Muse, *Ten Years of Prelude,* p. 90; Mayer, "Eisenhower's Conditional Crusade," p. 247.

27 Miller, "Violence: It Need Not Happen," *New South* 13 (March 1958): 3.

28 Bartley, *Massive Resistance,* p. 284; *St. Petersburg Times,* January 18, 1957; *Charleston News and Courier,* August 23, 1955; Muse, *Ten Years of Prelude,* p. 90.

29 Muse, *Ten Years of Prelude,* p. 90; Bartley, *Massive Resistance,* pp. 63, 163; Emmett John Hughes, *The Ordeal of Power: A Political Memoir of the Eisenhower Years* (New York, 1963), pp. 200, 242; E. Frederic Morrow, transcript of oral history interview, August 13, 1964, p. 13, DDE; Robert Frederick Burk, "Symbolic Equality: The Eisenhower Administration and Black Civil Rights, 1953–1961" (Ph.D. diss., University of Wisconsin, 1982), pp. 44, 239, 243; Dwight D. Eisenhower, *The White House Years: Waging Peace, 1956–1961* (Garden City, N.Y., 1965), p. 149; Mayer, "Eisenhower's Conditional Crusade," pp. 146–47, 189, 203; Memorandum of Conversation, July 24, 1953, box 9, DDE Diaries Series, Ann Whitman File; Robert Griffith, "Dwight D. Eisenhower and the Corporate Commonwealth," *American Historical Review* 87 (February 1982): 114–16. The quote is from Dwight D. Eisenhower to Ralph E. McGill, February 26, 1959, box 39, DDE Diary Series, Ann Whitman File.

30 U.S., Presidents, *Public Papers of the Presidents of the United States: Dwight D. Eisenhower,* 8 vols. (Washington, 1960–1961), 1956: 734–35, 758–59, 913. The position Eisenhower took was one recommended by Deputy Attorney General William Rogers. Mayer, "Eisenhower's Conditional Crusade," p. 262.

31   Judge David L. Norman, personal interview with the author in his chambers, Washington, D.C., October 27, 1980; Mayer, "Eisenhower's Conditional Crusade," pp. 16–17; Robert G. Storey, transcript of oral history interview, August 23, 1971, p. 63, CUOHP; Herbert Brownell, Jr., transcript of oral history interview, January 31, 1968, p. 205, CUOHP; Herbert Brownell, Jr., Order No. 40-54, February 9, 1954, Department of Justice, Office of the Attorney General, box 2, folder 1, Caldwell Papers; Elliff, "Department of Justice," pp. 284–85, 339; Burk, *Eisenhower Administration,* p. 176.

32   U.S. Department of Justice, *Annual Report of the Attorney General of the United States for the Fiscal Year Ended June 30, 1955* (Washington, 1955), pp. 132–33.

33   Arthur B. Caldwell, "The Civil Rights Section: Its Functions and Its Statutes," address delivered July 16, 1953, and revised in October 1955, folder 75-01-71-33, SRCC.

34   Elliff, "Department of Justice," pp. 368–71; A. B. Caldwell, notes from interview with Scott Rafferty, December 16, 1975, box 1, Scott Rafferty Papers, JFK.

35   Memorandum for William P. Rogers, January 23, 1956, box 2, folder 6, Caldwell Papers.

36   Olney to King, January 30, 1957, file drawer IX, folder 16, King Papers–BU.

37   Allan Lichtman, "The Federal Assault Against Voting Discrimination in the Deep South, 1956–1967," *Journal of Negro History* 54 (October 1969): 347–49.

38   Justice, *Annual Report for 1956,* p. 122; Warren Olney III, Memorandum for William P. Rogers, January 23, 1956, box 2, folder 6, Caldwell Papers, and Memorandum for Rogers, January 23, 1956, file 144-76-152, DJ (copy in box 2, folder 16, Caldwell Papers). The quote is from the *Annual Report.*

39   Morrow, Memorandum to Maxwell Rabb, November 29, 1955, box 10, Files of the Administrative Officer for Special Projects, DDE (hereinafter cited as Morrow Papers). On Morrow's background, see Mayer, "Eisenhower's Conditional Crusade," p. 16.

40   *Chicago Defender,* November 3, 1956; *Jackson Daily News,* December 10, 1955; E. Frederic Morrow, Memorandum to Gerald Morgan, March 21, 1956, box 14, DDE Diaries Series, Ann Whitman File. The quote is from the latter source.

41   Elliff, "Department of Justice," pp. 41–42; Burke Marshall, transcript of oral history interview, June 14, 1964, pp. 86–87, and comments by Marshall in Robert F. Kennedy, transcript of oral history interview, December 4, 1964, pp. 534–36, JFK Oral; Mayer, "Eisenhower's Conditional Crusade," pp. 249–52.

42   "President's News Conference of February 8, 1956," in Presidents, *Public Papers: Eisenhower*, 1956: 233–34.

43   Hoxie School District No. 46 of Lawrence County, Arkansas, v. Brewer, 137 F. Supp. 364 (E.D. Ark. 1956); Brewer v. Hoxie School District No. 46 of Lawrence County, Arkansas, 238 F.2d 91 (8th Cir. 1956).

44   137 F. Supp. at 367; Arthur B. Caldwell to J. W. Peltason, January 13, 1962, box 11, folder 15, Caldwell Papers; Elliff, "Department of Justice," pp. 409–17.

45   Elliff, "Department of Justice," pp. 436–37, 448–49; Mayer, "Eisenhower's Conditional Crusade," pp. 270–71; U.S., Department of Justice, *Annual Report of the Attorney General of the United States for the Fiscal Year Ended June 30, 1957* (Washington, 1957), p. 106; *Birmingham News*, December 3, 1956; *Nashville Banner*, December 5, 1956; House Judiciary Committee, *1959 Hearings*, p. 398.

46   Elliff, "Department of Justice," p. 438; *New Orleans Times-Picayune*, December 9, 1956; *Nashville Tennessean*, November 16, 1958.

47   Howard S. Whiteside to John F. Kennedy, December 16, 1955, and "Resolution Presented at Greater Boston Civil Rights Rally December 15, 1955 at Faneuil Hall," "Civil Rights 53-55" folder, Senate Files, Pre-Presidential Papers, Papers of President Kennedy, JFK (hereinafter cited as Kennedy Senate Files); House Judiciary Committee, *Civil Rights: Hearings . . . on . . . Miscellaneous Bills Regarding the Civil Rights of Persons Within the Jurisdiction of the United States*, 84th Cong., 1st sess., 1955, pp. 181, 195–96, 274.

48   Mayer, "Eisenhower's Conditional Crusade," pp. 19–20, 237, 239, 288, 290, 292; Burk, *Eisenhower Administration*, pp. 209, 211.

49   John Weir Anderson, *Eisenhower, Brownell, and the Congress: The Tangled Origins of the Civil Rights Bill of 1956–1957* (Tuscaloosa, Ala., 1964), p. 14; A. B. Caldwell, Memorandum for Harold R. Tyler, Jr., on chronology of the preliminary drafts and memoranda leading to submission to Congress of the civil rights proposals which eventually became the Civil Rights Act of 1957, August 15, 1960, box 2, file 4, Caldwell Papers (hereinafter cited as Caldwell, Chronology).

50   H.B., Memorandum for Mrs. Whitman, September 30, 1957, box 8, Administration Series, Ann Whitman File.

51   Caldwell, Chronology; Elliff, "Department of Justice," pp. 538–39.

52   Caldwell, Chronology; "A. B. Caldwell to St. John Barrett, Re: Attached Draft of Amendment of 18 U.S.C. 242 by Mr. Putzell," August 9, 1960, box 2, folder 5, Caldwell Papers; Elliff, "Department of Justice," p. 538; Mayer, "Eisenhower's Conditional Crusade," pp. 299–300.

53   Caldwell, Chronology; "Draft of Bill to Amend Chapter 13 of Title 18, United States Code, February 24, 1956," box 2, folder 5, Caldwell Papers; "The

Civil Rights Program—Proposed Statement by the Attorney General," CP
56-48, March 7, 1957, box 6, Cabinet Series, Ann Whitman File.

54   Caldwell, Chronology; Anderson, *Eisenhower, Brownell, and the Congress,*
p. 20; "The Civil Rights Program"; "Civil Rights Program—Proposed Statement
of the Attorney General (Revised)," CP 56-48/2, March 20, 1956, "The Civil
Rights Program—Letter and Statement of the Attorney General," CP 56/48/3,
April 10, 1956, and Minutes of Cabinet Meeting, March 23, 1956, box 7, and
Maxwell Rabb, Memorandum for the Attorney General on the President's Views
of the Proposed Civil Rights Program (CP 56-48), undated, box 6, Cabinet Series, Ann Whitman File; Gerald D. Morgan, Memorandum for Ann Whitman,
March 24, 1956, box 14, DDE Diaries Series, Ann Whitman File; Elliff, "De-
partment of Justice," p. 431; Burk, *Eisenhower Administration,* pp. 213–14.

55   Attorney General to the Vice-President, April 9, 1956, in U.S. Congress, Senate, Committee on the Judiciary, *Civil Rights Proposals: Hearings . . . ,*
84th Cong., 2d sess., 1956, pp. 64–68; "The Civil Rights Program—Letter and
Statement by the Attorney General."

56   U.S., Congress, House, Committee on the Judiciary, *Civil Rights: Hear-
ings . . . on . . . Miscellaneous Bills Regarding the Civil Rights of Persons Within the
Jurisdiction of the United States,* 84th Cong., 2d sess., 1956, pp. 17–18, 23 (quote
at 23); Senate Judiciary Committee, *Civil Rights Proposals,* pp. 81–84; Burk,
Eisenhower Administration, pp. 214, 216; Mayer, "Eisenhower's Conditional
Crusade," pp. 323–26.

57   Civil Rights Division, Department of Justice, "The Civil Rights Act of
1957," undated, box 2, file 5, Caldwell Papers; Presidents, *Public Papers:
Eisenhower,* 1957: 23.

58   Civil Rights Division, "The Civil Rights Act of 1957"; Elliff, "Department of Justice," pp. 458–67; Herman Talmadge, transcript of oral history interview, March 10, 1966, pp. 29–30, JFK Oral; "Legislative Leadership Meeting"
(CONFIDENTIAL), July 9, 1957, Memorandum on Telephone Call, July 3,
1957, and supplementary notes on legislative leadership meeting, July 16, 1957,
all in box 25, Gerald D. Morgan, memorandum for the President, August 16,
1957, box 26, and notes on legislative meeting, August 29, 1959, box 48, DDE
Diaries Series, Ann Whitman File; Sherman Adams, *Firsthand Report* (New York,
1961), pp. 336–37; Arthur B. Caldwell to J. W. Peltason, January 13, 1962,
box 11, file 15, Caldwell Papers; Eisenhower, *Waging Peace,* pp. 157–58; Steven
F. Lawson, *Black Ballots: Voting Rights in the South, 1944–1969* (New York,
1976), pp. 167–69, 178–82. According to Lawson, Sam Ervin of North Carolina
was actually the first senator to raise the troops issue.

59   Pub. L. No. 85-315, sections 13(b) and (c), 71 Stat. 634, 637 (1957).

60   NAACP Press Release, July 21, 1957, series III, group B, box 55,
NAACP Papers, LC.

61   NAACP Press Release, September 12, 1957, series III, group B, box 55, NAACP Papers.

62   Tony Freyer, *The Little Rock Crisis: A Constitutional Interpretation* (Westport, Conn., 1984), pp. 16–17, 42–45, 54–59; Attorney General to the President, undated, pp. 1–2, box 8, Administration Series, Ann Whitman File (cited hereinafter as Brownell, Little Rock Legal Opinion); "Chronology of Events in Little Rock, Arkansas," box 5, file 1, Caldwell Papers; Aaron v. Cooper, 1 RRLR 853 (U.S.D.C. E.D. Ark. 1956).

63   Arthur B. Caldwell, Memo for the Files, August 21, 1957, box 5, file 2, Caldwell Papers; Orval Faubus and Brooks Hays, transcript of interview, June 4, 1976, pp. 11–12, box 45, folder 25, Brooks Hays Papers, University of Arkansas, Fayetteville. The quote is from p. 11 of the interview.

64   Caldwell, Memo for the Files; A. B. Caldwell, Memorandum for Warren Olney III, July 24, 1957, DJ 144-100-9 (copy in box 5, file 2, Caldwell Papers).

65   Arthur B. Caldwell, Memorandum for Warren Olney III, August 30, 1957, DJ 144-100-9 (copy in box 5, file 2, Caldwell Papers).

66   Aaron v. Cooper, 156 F. Supp. 220 (E.D. Ark. 1957); Warren Olney III, Memorandum to the Attorney General, September 13, 1957, DJ 144-100-9 (copy in box 5, file 2, Caldwell Papers); FBI, interview with Virgil T. Blossom, September 6, 1957, Summary of Testimony in Arkansas Chancery Court, August 29, 1957, and agent report by Eldon C. Williams on integration in public schools in Little Rock, September 9, 1957, all in FBI file LR 44-341 (copy at University of Arkansas at Little Rock).

67   Caldwell, Memorandum for Warren Olney III, August 30, 1957; FBI, Statement of John R. Thompson, September 10, 1957, box 438, folder 1, Faubus Papers; FBI, statement of J. M. Malone, Sr., September 8, 1957, FBI file LR 44-341; Brooks Hays, *A Southern Moderate Speaks* (Chapel Hill, 1959), p. 154, and transcript of oral history interview, June 27, 1970, p. 50, CUOHP.

68   Bartley, *Massive Resistance,* p. 259; Hays, *A Southern Moderate Speaks,* pp. 171, 193; Sidney McMath, transcript of oral history interview, December 30, 1970, p. 4, CUOHP; Faubus-Hays Interview, pp. 10–13, 17; Orval Faubus, transcript of interview, August 18, 1971, pp. 35–40, CUOHP (quote at 40).

69   Transcript of "Face the Nation" radio and television broadcast, August 31, 1958, box 496, folder 3, Faubus Papers. See also Freyer, *Little Rock Crisis,* p. 109.

70   Caldwell, Memorandum for Warren Olney III, August 30, 1957.

71   Freyer, *Little Rock Crisis,* pp. 101–103; Orval E. Faubus, proclamation, September 2, 1957, box 496, folder 1, and "Speech to the People of Arkansas by Television and Radio, September Crisis of 1957," undated, box 496, folder 1, Faubus Papers; FBI, Statement of Lt. Marion E. Johnson, September 6, 1957, FBI File 44-341; Virgil Blossom, *It Has Happened Here* (New York, 1959), p. 97.

72   Press Release, September 4, 1957, box 496, folder 3, Faubus Papers.

73   Aaron v. Cooper, 156 F. Supp. 220 (E.D. Ark. 1957).

74   Burk, *Eisenhower Administration*, p. 185; Herman E. Lindsay, Memorandum to Department of Arkansas State Police, September 22, 1957, box 498, folder 1, Faubus Papers; Blossom, *It Has Happened Here*, p. 101; Brownell, Little Rock Legal Opinion, p. 19; Freyer, *Little Rock Crisis*, pp. 116–17.

75   Blossom, *It Has Happened Here*, p. 101; Faubus Oral History, p. 35; Freyer, *Little Rock Crisis*, p. 98.

76   Presidents, *Public Papers: Eisenhower*, 1957: 546.

77   Ibid., p. 691.

78   Burk, "Symbolic Equality," pp. 254, 262. James C. Duram, *A Moderate Among Extremists: Dwight D. Eisenhower and the School Desegregation Crisis* (Chicago, 1981), p. 144; Telephone call, September 11, 1957, DDE Diaries Series and Diary: Notes Dictated by the President Concerning Visit of Governor Orval Faubus of Arkansas to Little Rock [*sic*] on September 14, 1957, box 26, Administration Series, Ann Whitman File; Hays CUOHP Oral History, pp. 101–102; Faubus-Hays Oral History, pp. 5–8; White House press release and attached "Statement by the Governor of Arkansas," September 14, 1957, box 6, Papers of Special Counsel and Deputy Assistant to the President (Morgan), DDE (hereinafter cited as Morgan Papers).

79   Memorandum from Arthur B. Caldwell to Warren Olney III, September 23, 1957, DJ 144-100-9 (copy in box 5, folder 2, Caldwell Papers); Hays, *A Southern Moderate Speaks*, pp. 172–73.

80   Bartley, *Massive Resistance*, p. 268; Woodrow Wilson Mann, telegram to President Dwight D. Eisenhower, September 24, 1957, box 26, DDE Diaries Series, Ann Whitman File.

81   Freyer, *Little Rock Crisis*, pp. 123–25; Duram, *A Moderate*, p. 152.

82   Hughes, *Ordeal of Power*, p. 244. See also Duram, *A Moderate*, p. 171.

83   Night letter to Russell, September 27, 1957, box 261, Administration Series, Ann Whitman File. See also Brownell Oral History, p. 33, and Eisenhower, *Waging Peace*, pp. 168–69.

84   Adams, *Firsthand Report*, pp. 351–53; Press conference of Governor Orval E. Faubus, October 2, 1957, box 496, folder 3, Faubus Papers. Adams claims that Faubus added the words "by me" to a promise that court orders would not be obstructed, a promise contained in the statement which he agreed over the telephone to release. When asked by a reporter if he had done what Adams charged, Faubus refused to give a direct answer.

85   Faubus to Major General Edwin A. Walker, October 7, 1957, folder 8, and untitled, September 26, 1957, folder 1, box 496, Faubus Papers; Parmet, *Eisenhower*, p. 512.

86 Aaron v. Cooper, 163 F. Supp. 13 (E.D. Ark. 1958); Aaron v. Cooper, 257 F.2d 33, 39–40 (8th Cir. 1958).
87 Cooper v. Aaron, 358 U.S. 1 (1958).
88 James Hagerty, Press Release, September 12, 1958, and E. Frederick Morrow to Judson N. Walker, November 12, 1958, box 6, Morgan Papers, DDE; Elliff, "Department of Justice," pp. 481–83; Burk, "Symbolic Equality," p. 272; Freyer, *Little Rock Crisis,* p. 127.
89 "Rogers, William P(ierce)," *Current Biography 1958* (New York, 1958), pp. 364–66.
90 *New York Times,* August 28, 1958, pp. 1, 12.
91 *Chattanooga Times,* August 24, 1958; *Arkansas Gazette,* September 11, 1958.
92 *New York Times,* September 10, 1958, pp. 1, 23.
93 *Arkansas Gazette,* September 13, 1958, September 23, 1958.

Chapter Three

1 David L. Lewis, *King: A Critical Biography* (New York, 1970), pp. 66, 70–71, 82–83; Janet Stevenson, "Rosa Parks Wouldn't Budge," *American Heritage* 13 (February 1972): 63, 85; *Montgomery Advertiser,* December 30, 1956, January 10, 1957, January 16, 1957; *Birmingham News,* January 10, 1957, February 11, 1957, February 20, 1975; *Nashville Tennessean,* January 13, 1957; Catherine A. Barnes, *Journey from Jim Crow: The Desegregation of Southern Transit* (New York, 1983), p. 113.
2 U.S., Congress, House, Committee on the Judiciary, *Hearings . . . on . . . Miscellaneous Bills Regarding the Civil Rights of Persons Within the Jurisdiction of the United States,* 86th Cong., 1st sess., 1959, pp. 362–65, 598–99 (cited hereinafter as House Judiciary Committee, *1959 Hearings*); *Chattanooga Times,* October 10, 1958; Neil R. McMillen, "White Citizens' Council and Resistance to School Desegregation in Arkansas," *Arkansas Historical Quarterly* 30 (Spring 1971): 118.
3 House Judiciary Committee, *1959 Hearings,* pp. 362–65; *Birmingham News,* April 27, 1956, December 8, 1957, and July 18, 1958; Montgomery Improvement Association, "Segregation Hasn't Been Licked," undated, drawer II, folder 28A, King Papers—BU.
4 Administrative Committee of the American Jewish Congress, "Anti-Semitic Defamation and Violence: A Statement and Proposed Program by the American Jewish Congress," November 23, 1958, box 459, Emanuel Celler Papers, LC.
5 House Judiciary Committee, *1959 Hearings,* pp. 362–65, 599.

6   David M. Chalmers, *Hooded Americanism: The First Century of the Ku Klux Klan, 1865–1965* (Garden City, N.Y., 1965), p. 351; Clifford J. Durr to Hugo L. Black, January 24, 1957, Family Papers, box 7, Hugo L. Black Papers, LC: United Church Women et al., *The South Speaks Out for Law and Order*, reprinted in U.S., Congress, House, Committee on the Judiciary, *Prohibiting Certain Acts Involving the Use of Explosives: Hearings . . . ,* 85th Cong., 2d sess., 1958, pp. 57–92 (the quote from the *Miami News* appears on p. 71).

7   McMillen, "White Citizens' Council," p. 119; *Charlotte Observer,* March 21, 1958; *Charleston News and Courier,* October 16, 1958; *Nashville Tennessean,* December 14, 1958.

8   Robert J. Murphy, "The South Fights Bombing," *Look,* January 6, 1959, p. 17; *Atlanta Constitution,* January 24, 1959; *Birmingham News,* May 5, 1959.

9   *Charleston News and Courier,* January 24, 1959; *Washington Post,* January 29, 1957, September 11, 1957; *New Orleans Times-Picayune,* January 28, 1957.

10   Murphy, "The South Fights Bombing," pp. 13–14; *Nashville Banner,* May 3, 1958; *Arkansas Gazette,* May 4, 1958.

11   *Nashville Tennessean,* April 29, 1958, November 16, 1958; *Atlanta Journal,* October 13, 1958, October 19, 1958; *Miami Herald,* May 5, 1958.

12   John Thomas Elliff, "The United States Department of Justice and Individual Rights, 1937–1962" (Ph.D. diss., Harvard University, 1967), pp. 621–22; Sidney B. Rose to John F. Kennedy, May 6, 1958, and Alan R. Morse to John F. Kennedy, May 7, 1958, "Civil Rights 10/30/57-5/27/58" folder, Senate Files, Pre-Presidential Papers, Papers of President Kennedy, JFK (hereinafter cited as Kennedy Senate Files); Florence V. Lucas, telegram to the President, May 8, 1958, GF 124-B, WHCF, DDE.

13   E. Frederic Morrow to Edward Avadenka, May 20, 1958, GF 124-B, WHCF, and J. Edgar Hoover to Dwight D. Eisenhower, October 18, 1958, box 21, Administration Series, Papers of Dwight D. Eisenhower as President (Ann Whitman File), DDE; *Atlanta Journal,* October 27, 1958; *Nashville Banner,* October 15, 1958; *New Orleans Times-Picayune,* December 25, 1958; *Montgomery Advertiser,* June 30, 1958; *St. Petersburg Times,* November 20, 1958.

14   "Public Opinion and Civil Rights," box 6, Papers of Special Counsel and Deputy Assistant to the President (Morgan), DDE.

15   Administrative Committee of the American Jewish Congress, "Anti-Semitic Defamation and Violence," pp. 14–16; David Marcus Chapter of the American Jewish Congress, telegram to the President, October 15, 1958, GF 124 B-1 and Edward L. Flaherty, telegram to the President, October 24, 1958, GF 124-B, WHCF, DDE; *Louisville Courier-Journal,* January 12, 1959; *Nashville Tennessean,* November 7, 1958; *Charlotte Observer,* December 16, 1958.

16   *Atlanta Constitution,* October 13, 1958; Herbert S. Parmet, *Eisenhower and the American Crusades* (New York, 1972), p. 504.

17   E. Frederic Morrow, *Black Man in the White House: A Diary of the Eisenhower Years by the Administrative Officer for Special Projects, the White House, 1955–1961* (New York, 1963), pp. 116–17.

18   Ibid., p. 268.

19   House Judiciary Committee, *Prohibiting Certain Acts,* pp. 20–31, 34–35, 44–45, 48–52, 56; R.C.S. to Mrs. Whitman, undated, and Dwight D. Eisenhower to Rabbi Maurice N. Eisendrath, October 16, 1958, OF 142-C, WHCF, DDE.

20   House Judiciary Committee, *Prohibiting Certain Acts,* pp. 1–6, 11–12 (quote at 11); *Atlanta Constitution,* August 18, 1958.

21   *New York Times,* June 6, 1958; U.S., Congress, Senate, Subcommittee on Constitutional Rights of the Committee on the Judiciary, *Civil Rights—1959: Hearings . . . ,* 86th Cong., 1st sess., 1959, 1:256–57, 266–67.

22   Jacob K. Javits to Sam J. Ervin, Jr., December 29, 1958, box 120, and Sam J. Ervin, Jr., to John F. Kennedy, December 3, 1958, box 295, Sam J. Ervin, Jr., Papers, Southern Historical Collection, University of North Carolina, Chapel Hill; Bill S. 3917, May 28, 1958, Bill S. 4327, August 23, 1958, and Press Release, May 28, 1958, "85–2nd Explosives 3917" folder, Kennedy Senate Files; Theodore C. Sorenson, *Kennedy* (New York, 1965), pp. 74–76, 97–99, 102–103.

23   Sam J. Ervin, Jr., to John F. Kennedy, December 3, 1958, box 295, Ervin Papers.

24   John F. Kennedy to Marii Hasegawa, January 13, 1959, "Explosives" folder, Kennedy Senate Files; Senators John F. Kennedy and Sam J. Ervin, Jr., Press Release, December 14, 1958, box 120, Ervin Papers; *Cong. Record,* 86th Cong., 2d sess., March 16, 1960, p. 5726.

25   John F. Kennedy to Herbert E. Tucker, January 16, 1959, "Explosives" folder, Kennedy Senate Files; *Charlotte Observer,* December 14, 1958; House Judiciary Committee, *Prohibiting Certain Acts,* p. 26.

26   Notes on Legislative Leadership Meeting, December 15, 1958, box 2, Legislative Meetings Series, Ann Whitman File.

27   *Birmingham News,* December 23, 1958.

28   U.S., Presidents, *Public Papers of the Presidents of the United States: Dwight D. Eisenhower,* 8 vols. (Washington, D.C., 1960–1961), 1959: 165; House Judiciary Committee, *1959 Hearings,* pp. 209–10; Constitutional Rights Subcommittee, *Civil Rights—1959,* 1:190–91 (quote at 190).

29   Presidents, *Public Papers: Eisenhower,* 1959: 165; Constitutional Rights Subcommittee, *Civil Rights—1959,* pp. 186–87 (quote at 186).

30   House Judiciary Committee, *1959 Hearings,* pp. 190–93, 342; Bill S. 4327, August 23, 1958, "85–2nd Explosives 3917" folder, Kennedy Senate Files; Constitutional Rights Subcommittee, *Civil Rights—1959,* 1:190; Press

Release/Column on Kennedy-Ervin Bill, December 15/18, 1959, box 120, Ervin Papers.

31   House Judiciary Committee, *1959 Hearings,* pp. 146, 274–75, 374–75, 390, 893, 898; Constitutional Rights Subcommittee, *Civil Rights—1959,* 1:276, 307, 392, 909–10; Daniel M. Berman, *A Bill Becomes a Law: Congress Enacts Civil Rights Legislation* (2d ed.; New York, 1966), p. 8; Harold R. Tyler, Memorandum for Lawrence E. Walsh, July 15, 1960, box 2, folder 5, Arthur Brann Caldwell Papers, University of Arkansas at Fayetteville; L. A. Minnich, Jr., Notes on Legislative Meeting, February 3, 1959, box 3, Legislative Meetings Series, Ann Whitman File.

32   Notes on Legislative Meeting, February 3, 1959; J. P. Coleman, telegram to Reverend Martin Luther King, Jr., April 25, 1959, file drawer IV, folder 40, King Papers—BU; *Cong. Record,* 86th Cong., 2d sess., January 26, 1960, p. 1313; Constitutional Rights Subcommittee, *Civil Rights—1959,* 2:1415; Edward Howard Smead, Jr., "The Lynching of Mack Charles Parker in Poplarville, Mississippi, April 25, 1959" (Ph.D. diss., University of Maryland, 1979), p. 332; Elliff, "Department of Justice," pp. 567–68; *Jackson Daily News,* May 21, 1959.

33   *Nashville Tennessean,* May 26, 1959; Smead, "Lynching," pp. 325, 331–32; *Washington Post,* November 8, 1959.

34   *Washington Post,* November 18, 1959; Smead, "Lynching," pp. 333, 362–69; U.S., Department of Justice, *Annual Report of the Attorney General of the United States for the Fiscal Year Ended June 30, 1960* (Washington, 1960), p. 189.

35   Henry Lee Moon book message, April 27, 1959, series III, group B, box 80, NAACP Papers.

36   Herbert E. Tucker, Jr., telegram to John F. Kennedy, Leverett Saltonstall, Lawrence Curtis, and Thomas O'Neill, series III, group B, box 80, NAACP Papers; *Atlanta Journal,* May 3, 1959; House Judiciary Committee, *1959 Hearings,* p. 864.

37   Emanuel Celler to Muriel Symington, June 11, 1959, General Office File, box 257, Celler Papers; John D. Dingell to Dwight D. Eisenhower, December 18, 1959, OF 142-A-2, WHCF, DDE; Bill S. 1842, April 30, 1958, and clipping from *Cong. Record,* "86th–1st Anti-Lynching S. 1848" folder, Kennedy Senate Files; Paul H. Douglas to Dear Friend, May 22, 1959, series III, group B, box 80, NAACP Papers; Smead, "Lynching," pp. 311, 338–39, 377.

38   Dingell to Eisenhower, December 18, 1959, and Eisenhower to Dingell, January 7, 1959, OF 142-A-2, WHCF, DDE.

39   House Judiciary Committee, *1959 Hearings,* pp. 271–73, 338–41, 352–58, 942; Constitutional Rights Subcommittee, *Civil Rights—1959,* 1:410, 412, 598.

40   U.S., Congress, House Committee on the Judiciary, *Civil Rights,* 86th Cong., 1st sess., 1959, H. Rept. 956, p. 28; *Cong. Record,* 86th Cong., 2d sess., March 16, 1960, p. 5769, March 22, 1960, p. 6308, and April 4, 1960, pp. 7218–25.

41   House Judiciary Committee, *1959 Hearings,* pp. 477–78.

42   House Judiciary Committee, *Civil Rights,* p. 34; Subcommittee on Constitutional Rights, *Civil Rights—1959,* 1:488, 797–99, and 2:1094; *Cong. Record,* 86th Cong., 2d sess., March 11, 1960, p. 5336, March 21, 1960, p. 6169, and March 23, 1960, pp. 6373–76, 6389.

43   House Judiciary Committee, *Civil Rights—1959,* pp. 35–37; *Cong. Record,* 86th Cong., 2d sess., March 14, 1960, p. 5461, and March 23, 1960, pp. 6383–87; U.S., Congress, Senate, Committee on the Judiciary, *Civil Rights Act of 1960: Hearings . . . ,* 86th Cong., 2d sess., 1960, p. 11.

44   *Cong. Record,* 86th Cong., 2d sess., March 10, 1960, p. 5184, March 11, 1960, pp. 5264–89, and March 30, 1960, pp. 6945–57. Rep. Samuel Devine (R-Ohio) offered the Lausch amendment in the House on March 23, but on a point of order it was ruled not germane. See ibid., pp. 6369–70.

45   Constitutional Rights Subcommittee, *Civil Rights—1959,* 1:64, 361, 453–54, 471, 489, and 2:1047–56, 1073–74, 1095; House Judiciary Committee, *1959 Hearings,* pp. 540–55, 697–98 (quote at 542); Senate Judiciary Committee, *Civil Rights Act of 1960,* p. 51.

46   *Cong. Record,* 86th Cong., 2d sess., April 17, 1960, pp. 7581–82; Howell Raines, *My Soul Is Rested: Movement Days in the Deep South Remembered* (New York, 1983), pp. 355–58 (interview with Everette Little).

47   *Cong. Record,* 86th Cong., 2d sess., March 10, 1960, p. 5205, March 11, 1960, p. 5447, March 14, 1960, pp. 5461–62, 5467, March 15, 1960, p. 5660, April 8, 1960, p. 7734; Constitutional Rights Subcommittee, *Civil Rights—1959,* pp. 318–19; Jacob K. Javits to Joseph O'Mahoney, February 3, 1960, "Civil Rights 1/4/60-2/29/60" folder, Kennedy Senate Files.

48   House Judiciary Committee, *Civil Rights,* pp. 3, 32.

49   *Cong. Record,* 86th Cong., 2d sess., March 23, 1960, pp. 6378–80 (quote at 6379); Senate Judiciary Committee, *Civil Rights Act of 1960,* pp. 10, 99; Draft of proposed amendment to H.R. 8601, March 29, 1960, series X, box 108, Richard Russell Papers, University of Georgia, Athens, Georgia; *Cong. Record,* 86th Cong., 2d sess., April 8, 1960, pp. 7810–12. Both Berman (*A Bill Becomes a Law,* p. 120) and a U.S. Commission on Civil Rights legislative history entitled "The Civil Rights Act of 1960" (box 2, file 1, Caldwell Papers, p. 31) erroneously state that the bomb threat provision was eliminated from the bill.

50   *Cong. Record,* 86th Cong., 2d sess., March 4, 1960, p. 4520, March 14, 1960, pp. 5419, 5423–24 (quote at 5419).

51   *Cong. Record,* 86th Cong., 2d sess., March 14, 1960, p. 5540; March 16, 1960, pp. 5726–30.

52   Ibid., pp. 5731–37, and March 17, 1960, pp. 5861, 5866–67.

53   Ibid., April 19, 1960, pp. 8205–8206, and April 21, 1960, pp. 8507–8508.

54   Presidents, *Public Papers: Eisenhower,* 1960–1961: 137; Titles I and II, Civil Rights Act of 1960, Pub. L. No. 86-449, 74 Stat. 86.

55   Civil Rights Act of 1960, §203 (e), Pub. L. No. 86-449, 74 Stat. 86.

56   Harold R. Tyler, Jr., "Memorandum for the Attorney General re Accomplishments in the Civil Rights Field During the Past Eight Years," January 18, 1961, box 29, William P. Rogers Papers, DDE.

57   Berman blames Eisenhower for the weakness of the law as a whole. (*A Bill Becomes a Law,* p. 136). The features of the Civil Rights Act of 1960 which excited the most public attention and controversy in Congress were those which dealt with voting.

Chapter Four

1   *Atlanta Journal,* December 12, 1960, June 21, 1961, July 28, 1961, August 12, 1961; *Atlanta Constitution,* May 17, 1961, July 5, 1961; *Washington Post,* February 28, 1961; *Nashville Tennessean,* July 17, 1960, September 4, 1960; *Chattanooga Times,* August 11, 1960, August 13, 1960, August 22, 1960, August 23, 1960; *Arkansas Gazette,* July 12, 1960, July 13, 1960, October 26, 1960; *Memphis Commercial Appeal,* October 14, 1960.

2   *Montgomery Advertiser,* November 20, 1960; David M. Chalmers, *Hooded Americanism: The First Century of the Ku Klux Klan, 1865–1965* (Garden City, N.Y., 1965), p. 354; *Wall Street Journal,* October 4, 1962; *Birmingham News,* April 2, 1961; *Montgomery Advertiser,* April 3, 1961; "Document No. 14 on Human Rights in Alabama," undated, Gen. HU 2/ST 1, WHCF, JFK; *Atlanta Constitution,* January 10, 1961, January 12, 1961; *Chattanooga Times,* August 25, 1960; Thomas G. Dyer, *The University of Georgia: A Bicentennial History, 1785–1985* (Athens, Ga., 1985), pp. 331–33.

3   Clayborne Carson, *In Struggle: SNCC and the Black Awakening of the 1960s* (Cambridge, Mass., 1981), pp. 19, 26; Allen J. Matusow, *The Unraveling of America: A History of Liberalism in the 1960s* (New York, 1984), p. 63; Carl M. Brauer, *John F. Kennedy and the Second Reconstruction* (New York, 1977), p. 35; Harris Wofford, *Of Kennedys and Kings: Making Sense of the Sixties* (New York, 1980), pp. 51–52. The Republicans also had endorsed a variant of Title III. *Knoxville News-Sentinel,* August 3, 1960.

4   Arthur M. Schlesinger, Jr., *A Thousand Days: John F. Kennedy in the White*

House (Boston, 1965), pp. 928–30; Thurgood Marshall, transcript of oral history interview, July 10, 1969, p. 7, JFK Oral; Roy Wilkins, transcript of oral history interview by Berl Bernhard, August 13, 1964, pp. 2–3, JFK Oral; Harris Wofford, transcript of oral history interview by Berl Bernhard, November 29, 1965, pp. 10–11, JFK Oral; Theodore Sorenson, *Kennedy* (New York, 1965), p. 473, and transcript of oral history interview by Berl Bernhard, May 3, 1964, JFK Oral; Matusow, *Unraveling,* pp. 62–63.

    5   Sorenson, *Kennedy,* pp. 473–75; Schlesinger, *A Thousand Days,* pp. 930, 934, 937; *Jackson Daily News,* April 7, 1961; Southern Regional Council, *The Federal Executive and Civil Rights* (Atlanta, 1961), pp. 23–25; Harold C. Fleming to John F. Kennedy, January 12, 1961, folder 75-01-53-28, SRCC; U.S., Presidents, *Public Papers of the Presidents: John F. Kennedy,* 3 vols. (Washington, 1962–1964), 1961: 573.

    6   U.S., Senate, Committee on the Judiciary, *Nomination of Burke Marshall: Hearings . . . ,* 87th Cong., 1st sess., 1961, p. 9; Robert F. Kennedy, transcript of oral history interview by Anthony Lewis, December 4, 1964, pp. 507–11, 526, JFK Oral; Arthur M. Schlesinger, Jr., *Robert Kennedy and His Times* (Boston, 1978), 1:306; Edwin Guthman, *We Band of Brothers* (New York, 1971), pp. 159–65; Draft of RFK's Law Day Address, undated, box 71, President's Office File, JFK.

    7   David Norman, Notes on interview by Scott Rafferty, November 19, 1965, box 1, Scott Rafferty Papers, JFK; Allan Lichtman, "The Federal Assault Against Voting Discrimination in the Deep South, 1957–1967," *Journal of Negro History* 54 (October 1969): 361; Walter Lord, *The Past That Would Not Die* (London, 1965), pp. 118–21.

    8   Matusow, *Unraveling,* pp. 71, 82; Ramsey Clark, personal interview with the author at his office in New York City, October 23, 1980; John Patterson, transcript of oral history interview by John Stewart, May 26, 1967, p. 36, JFK Oral; Robert Kennedy Oral History, pp. 578–80.

    9   Robert Kennedy Oral History, pp. 578–80.

    10   Michal R. Belknap, "The Vindication of Burke Marshall: The Southern Legal System and the Anti–Civil Rights Violence of the 1960s," *Emory Law Journal* 33 (1984): 94; Paul Johnson, transcript of oral history interview, September 8, 1970, pp. 7–8, LBJ; Robert Kennedy Oral History, p. 529; Brauer, *John F. Kennedy,* pp. 93–94.

    11   Senate Judiciary Committee, *Nomination of Burke Marshall,* p. 2.

    12   Burke Marshall, personal interview with the author at the Yale Law School, October 24, 1980; Burke Marshall, *Federalism and Civil Rights* (New York, 1964), pp. 43, 73, 81; Schlesinger, *Robert Kennedy,* 1:304, 317–25; *Norfolk Journal and Guide,* December 22, 1962.

    13   Quoted in *New York Times,* February 20, 1965, p. 13.

14 Burke Marshall to Neil Staebler, July 13, 1964, Gen. HU2/ST 24, WHCF, LBJ.

15 Burke Marshall, "Enforcement of Civil Rights," March 3, 1962, Burke Marshall Papers, JFK; Belknap, "Vindication," pp. 95–97.

16 Marshall Interview. See also Benjamin Muse, *Ten Years of Prelude: The Story of Integration Since the Supreme Court's 1954 Decision* (New York, 1964), p. 152.

17 Victor S. Navasky, *Kennedy Justice* (New York, 1971), pp. 167, 169, 185; Thurgood Marshall Oral History, pp. 23–24; Robert Kennedy Oral History, pp. 577–79; Matusow, *Unraveling,* p. 82; Schlesinger, *A Thousand Days,* p. 956; Burke Marshall, transcript of oral history interview by Anthony Lewis, June 14, 1964, p. 70, JFK Oral (hereinafter cited as Burke Marshall Oral History–JFK).

18 Ben Scheirer to the President, December 30, 1961, and Harris L. Wofford to Ben Scheirer, April 30, 1962, Gen. HU2/ST 18, WHCF, JFK.

19 Stephen J. Pollak, transcript of oral history interview, January 27, 1969, pp. 5–6, LBJ; *New York Times,* September 3, 1963, p. C28; John Lewis, personal interview with the author at the Atlanta City Hall, Atlanta, Georgia, June 5, 1984; John Doar, personal interview with the author at his office in New York City, October 23, 1980; Carson, *In Struggle,* p. 88. Doar is quoted in the *Times* article.

20 "Nine Young Men in Charge of Integrating America," *U.S. News & World Report,* July 29, 1963, pp. 58–60; *Miami Herald,* August 1, 1963; Navasky, *Kennedy Justice,* p. 167; Nicholas Katzenbach, telephonic interview with the author, June 28, 1984; Doar Interview; Robert Kennedy Oral History, p. 577.

21 *New Orleans Times-Picayune,* February 3, 1963; Robert Kennedy Oral History, p. 290; Burke Marshall, transcript of oral history interview, October 28, 1968, p. 19, LBJ (hereinafter cited as Burke Marshall Oral History–LBJ); Schlesinger, *A Thousand Days,* p. 934; *Atlanta Constitution,* June 10, 1968. John Patterson, who served as both attorney general and governor of Alabama, insisted that there was "no room for negotiation with Robert Kennedy" (Patterson Oral History, p. 31), but his is decidedly a minority viewpoint.

22 John Thomas Elliff, "The United States Department of Justice and Individual Rights, 1937–1962" (Ph.D. diss., Harvard University, 1967), pp. 714–16; Matusow, *Unraveling,* p. 79; Wiley Branton, transcript of oral history interview by Steven Lawson, October 21, 1970, pp. 10–11, CUOHP; William Taylor, notes on interview by Scott Rafferty, November 19, 1975, and Burke Marshall, notes on interview by Scott Rafferty, box 1, Rafferty Papers (hereinafter cited as Marshall, Rafferty Notes); United States Commission on Civil Rights, *Law Enforcement: A Report on Equal Protection in the South* (Washington, 1965), p. 117.

23   Brauer, *John F. Kennedy,* pp. 159–60; Robert Kennedy Oral History, p. 588; Thurgood Marshall Oral History, p. 5 (quote is from the latter source).

24   Thurgood Marshall Oral History, p. 23; Howard Sitkoff, *The Struggle for Black Equality, 1954–1980* (New York, 1981), pp. 69–81; William H. Chafe, *Civilities and Civil Rights: Greensboro, North Carolina, and the Black Struggle for Freedom* (New York, 1980), p. 99; Elliff, "Department of Justice," p. 688.

25   Chalmers, *Hooded Americanism,* p. 354; Carson, *In Struggle,* p. 11; *New York Times,* February 15, 1960, p. 18; James Farmer, telegram to Attorney General Robert Kennedy, April 30, 1961, series 3, box 5, folder 8, CORE Papers; Burke Marshall, Memorandum for the Attorney General—Monday Report, December 26, 1961, box 16, Marshall Papers; Sitkoff, *Struggle,* pp. 77–78; Howard Zinn, *SNCC: The New Abolitionists* (Boston, 1964), pp. 25–26.

26   Zinn, *SNCC,* p. 26; James Farmer, telegram to Attorney General Robert Kennedy, April 20, 1961, and untitled memorandum, April 17, 1961, series 3, box 5, folder 8, CORE Papers; Burke Marshall, Memorandum for the Attorney General—Monday Report, December 26, 1961, box 16, Marshall Papers; Jacksonville Youth Counsel of the NAACP, Resolution, August 30, 1960, General Files, 124-A-2, WHCF, DDE; *New York Times,* February 15, 1960, p. 18; Carson, *In Struggle,* p. 11; Benjamin Muse, "Lunch Counter Desegregation: Horace H. Edwards, Richmond City Manager, Albertis Harrison, Virginia State Attorney General, Wed.–Thurs., March 9–10, 1960," March 12, 1960, and "Lunch Counter Desegregation: Preliminary Report, Visit to North Carolina," March 23, 1960, folder 75-01-59-02, SRCC.

27   Catherine A. Barnes, *Journey from Jim Crow: The Desegregation of Southern Transit* (New York, 1983), p. 157; James Peck, *Freedom Ride* (New York, 1962), pp. 116–17; James Farmer, *Lay Bare My Heart: An Autobiography of the Civil Rights Movement* (New York, 1985), pp. 195–96; August Meier and Elliott Rudwick, *CORE: A Study in the Civil Rights Movement, 1942–1968* (New York, 1973), pp. 4–5, 33–35. The Supreme Court decision the Freedom Riders were seeking to implement was Boynton v. Virginia, 364 U.S. 454 (1959).

28   Lewis Interview.

29   Ibid.; Barnes, *Journey from Jim Crow,* p. 159; Peck, *Freedom Ride,* p. 199; Farmer, *Lay Bare,* p. 199.

30   Document No. 9 on Human Rights in Alabama, undated, box 3, Fred L. Shuttlesworth Papers, King Center; Barnes, *Journey from Jim Crow,* pp. 159–60; Burke Marshall, Speech at Notre Dame, April 7, 1962, box 13, Marshall Papers; Testimony of Albert Bigelow before Commission of Inquiry into the Administration of Justice in the Freedom Struggle, May 25, 1962, summarized in Memorandum from Theodore R. Newman, Jr., to Burke Marshall, May 28, 1962 (hereinafter cited as Newman Memorandum).

31   Newman Memorandum; Peck, *Freedom Ride,* pp. 126–27 (quote at 127).

32 Barnes, *Journey from Jim Crow,* p. 160; Robert Corley, "In Search of Racial Harmony: Birmingham Business Leaders and Desegregation, 1950–1963," in *Southern Businessmen and Desegregation,* ed. Elizabeth Jacoway and David Colburn (Baton Rouge, 1982), p. 181.

33 Lewis Interview; Peck, *Freedom Ride,* pp. 119–20. Police in Sumter, South Carolina, provided protection for a later group of Freedom Riders, as did officers in Savannah, Georgia, and Tallahassee, Florida. Testimony of Robert McAffee Brown, May 25, 1962, Commission of Inquiry into the Administration of Justice in the Freedom Struggle, Transcript of Hearings, series 5, box 65, CORE Papers (hereinafter cited as Commission of Inquiry Transcript).

34 Testimony of Albert Bigelow, May 25, 1962, Newman Memorandum.

35 Marshall, Speech at Notre Dame.

36 Testimony of FBI informant Gary Thomas Rowe in U.S., Senate, Select Committee to Study Government Operations with Respect to Intelligence Activities, *Hearings . . . ,* Part VI, *Federal Bureau of Investigation,* 94th Cong., 1st sess., 1975, p. 118. See also Gary Thomas Rowe, *My Undercover Years with the Ku Klux Klan* (New York, 1976), pp. 39–44. Rowe had infiltrated the Klan for the Bureau.

37 Barnes, *Journal from Jim Crow,* p. 159; John Patterson Oral History, p. 32.

38 Senate Select Committee, *Hearings,* pp. 117–18; Frank J. Donner, *The Age of Surveillance: The Aims and Methods of America's Political Intelligence System* (New York, 1980), pp. 204–205, 426; Guthman, *Band of Brothers,* p. 167; Bergman v. United States, 551 F. Supp. 407, 413 (W.D. Mich. 1982). Two federal courts have held that Freedom Riders injured in the attacks on May 14 are entitled to sue FBI personnel allegedly responsible for allowing what happened to them to occur. See Bergman v. United States, also Peck v. United States, 470 F. Supp. 1003 (S.D. N.Y. 1979). Burke Marshall did not know at the time that the FBI had advance knowledge of the plans for an attack on the Freedom Riders. When he found out about this in 1979, he stated that he and the attorney general would have taken prompt action if they had known. Wofford, *Of Kennedys and Kings,* p. 152. Both Robert and John Kennedy, as well as FBI Director J. Edgar Hoover, should have known in advance about the Freedom Ride itself, for CORE leader James Farmer wrote to all three to inform them of his organization's plans. Farmer, *Lay Bare,* p. 197.

39 Barnes, *Journey from Jim Crow,* pp. 161–62; Guthman, *Band of Brothers,* pp. 167–68 (quote at 168); Marshall, Speech at Notre Dame.

40 Guthman, *Band of Brothers,* p. 168; Patterson Oral History, pp. 32–33; Marshall, Speech at Notre Dame.

41 Guthman, *Band of Brothers,* p. 168.

42   Marshall, Speech at Notre Dame; Lewis Interview; Barnes, *Journey from Jim Crow*, p. 161.

43   Farmer, *Lay Bare*, p. 203; Guthman, *Band of Brothers*, p. 169; Marshall, Speech at Notre Dame; Burke Marshall Oral History–JFK, pp. 3–8.

44   Guthman, *Band of Brothers*, p. 170; Burke Marshall Oral History–JFK, pp. 9–10; Marshall, Speech at Notre Dame; *Cong. Record*, 87th Cong., 1st sess., May 24, 1961, p. 8713.

45   Marshall, Speech at Notre Dame. Guthman quotes Patterson as saying he had "the means, ability and the will to keep the peace without outside help." *Band of Brothers*, p. 170.

46   Guthman, *Band of Brothers*, p. 170; Burke Marshall Oral History–JFK, pp. 15–16.

47   Marshall, Speech at Notre Dame; Guthman, *Band of Brothers*, pp. 170–71 (quote at 171); United States v. U.S. Klans, Knights of Ku Klux Klan, Inc., 194 F. Supp. 897, 900-01 (M.D. Ala. 1961); Lewis v. Greyhound Corp., 194 F. Supp. 210, 211 (M.D. Ala. 1961); Lewis Interview; Barnes, *Journey from Jim Crow*, p. 163; Virginia Durr, transcript of oral history interview, October 24, 1974, p. 315, CUOHP.

48   Marshall, Speech at Notre Dame; Guthman, *Band of Brothers*, p. 172; Joseph F. Dolan, transcript of oral history interview by Charles T. Morrissey, December 4, 1964, p. 11, JFK Oral; Matusow, *Unraveling*, pp. 72–73; *Cong. Record*, 87th Cong., 1st sess., May 24, 1961, p. 8713; Reporter's Transcript of Conference Sunday, May 21, 1961, box 509, file 4, Orval E. Faubus Papers, University of Arkansas Library, Fayetteville; Hugh Scott, telegram to the President, May 20, 1960, Ex. HU2/ST 1, WHCF, JFK; Record of telephone call at 7:30 P.M., Saturday, May 20, 1961, box 10, Attorney General's General Correspondence, Robert F. Kennedy Papers, JFK.

49   Matusow, *Unraveling*, p. 73; Tinsley E. Yarbrough, *Judge Frank Johnson and Human Rights in Alabama* (University, Ala., 1981), pp. 25–36, 81; United States v. U.S. Klans, Knights of Ku Klux Klan, Inc., 194 F. Supp. 897, 903 (M.D. Ala. 1961).

50   Reporter's Transcript of Conference. For a good sketch of Byron White, see Bob Woodward and Scott Armstrong, *The Brethren: Inside the Supreme Court* (New York, 1979), pp. 65–66.

51   Patterson, telegram to Robert Kennedy, box 10, Attorney General's General Correspondence, Robert F. Kennedy Papers.

52   Lewis Interview; Guthman, *Band of Brothers*, p. 173; Burke Marshall Oral History–JFK, pp. 25–26; Farmer, *Lay Bare*, pp. 204–206.

53   Guthman, *Band of Brothers*, pp. 173, 176; Barnes, *Journey from Jim Crow*, p. 164.

54 Guthman, *Band of Brothers,* pp. 176–77.

55 *Cong. Record,* 87th Cong., 1st sess., May 24, 1961, pp. 8712–13, and
May 25, 1961, p. 8922; Untitled memo, May 22, [1961], and Wilbur D. Mills,
telegram to Robert F. Kennedy, box 10, Attorney General's General Correspon-
dence, Robert F. Kennedy Papers; Orval E. Faubus, telegram to Senators John
McClellan and J. W. Fulbright and Congressmen Dale Alford, J. W. Trimble,
Oren Harris, Wilbur Mills, E. C. Gathings, and Catherine Norrell, May 22,
1961, Wilbur D. Mills, telegram to John F. Kennedy and Robert F. Kennedy,
May 22, 1961, and E. C. Gathings, telegram to John F. Kennedy, all in box 539,
folder 4, Faubus Papers; Edgar W. Stuart and Ben Wilbanks, telegram to the
President, May 22, 1961, and untitled statement of Alabama State Chamber of
Commerce, May 25, 1961, Gen. HU2/ST 1, WHCF, JFK.

56 Lester Holtzman to John F. Kennedy, May 22, 1961, Ex. HU2/ST 1,
WHCF, JFK.

57 Guthman, *Band of Brothers,* p. 176.

58 "Statement by the Honorable Robert F. Kennedy," May 24, 1961, box
10, Attorney General's General Correspondence, Robert F. Kennedy Papers.

59 Barnes, *Journey from Jim Crow,* p. 165; Ross R. Barnett, telegram to
Robert F. Kennedy, May 23, 1961, and transcript of telephone conversation be-
tween Burke Marshall and Attorney General Patterson of Jackson, Mississippi,
May 22, 1961, box 10, Attorney General's General Correspondence, Robert F.
Kennedy Papers.

60 Ross R. Barnett, telegram to Robert F. Kennedy, May 23, 1961, box 10,
Attorney General's General Correspondence, Robert F. Kennedy Papers.

61 Guthman, *Band of Brothers,* p. 176; Robert Kennedy Oral History, p.
575.

62 Burke Marshall Oral History–JFK, p. 37.

63 Robert Kennedy Oral History, pp. 572–76; "Remarks of Roy Wilkins . . . at a Mass Meeting of the Jackson, Miss. Branch of the NAACP," sched-
uled for delivery Wednesday, June 7, 1961, box 11, Harris L. Wofford, Jr., Files,
Papers of President Kennedy, JFK; Transcript of telephone conversation between
Robert F. Kennedy and Governor Ross Barnett of Mississippi, May 23, 1961, box
10, Attorney General's General Correspondence, Robert F. Kennedy Papers;
Barnes, *Journey from Jim Crow,* p. 165; Guthman, *Band of Brothers,* p. 176.

64 Barnes, *Journey from Jim Crow,* pp. 165–67; Bailey v. Patterson, 199 F.
Supp. 595 (S.D. Miss. 1961); Bailey v. Patterson, 368 U.S. 346, 346 (1961);
James Farmer to "Dear Friend," April 27, 1962, series 1, box 4, folder 8, CORE
Papers; Allen Knight Charles to "Dear Friend," November 20, 1961, file drawer
VII, folder 2, King Papers–BU.

65 Wofford, *Of Kennedys and Kings,* pp. 155–56; Brauer, *John F. Kennedy,* pp.
106–107; *Washington Post,* June 15, 1961.

66   Wyatt T. Walker and Henry Schwarzcheld, Memorandum to Robert F. Kennedy, Interstate Commerce Commission & Civil Rights Division of the Department of Justice, July 3, 1961, file drawer VII, folder 44, King Papers–BU.

67   Testimony of Dave Dennis, May 26, 1962, Commission of Inquiry Transcript, pp. 332–33; Meier and Rudwick, *CORE,* pp. 143–44.

68   Robert Kennedy Oral History, pp. 582–83. Marshall was present during this interview with Kennedy and sometimes spoke.

69   Ibid.; Burke Marshall, Memorandum for the Attorney General—Monday Report, December 4, 1961, box 16, Marshall Papers.

70   *McComb Enterprise-Journal,* August 2, 1962; Congress of Racial Equality v. Douglas, 311 F.2d 95 (5th Cir. 1963).

71   John Patterson, telegram to the Attorney General, August 28, 1961, box 9, Attorney General's General Correspondence, Robert F. Kennedy Papers.

72   Meier and Rudwick, *CORE,* p. 202; James Forman, *The Making of Black Revolutionaries* (New York, 1972), pp. 187–99; "Facts in the Monroe, N.C. Kidnap Case," undated, series 5, box 57, folder 5, CORE Papers; Hugh Cannon to John Seigenthaler, August 2, 1961, and John Patterson, telegram to Robert F. Kennedy, August 28, 1961, box 9, Attorney General's General Correspondence, Robert F. Kennedy Papers.

73   Marshall, *Federalism and Civil Rights,* pp. 69–70; Marshall, "The Enforcement of Civil Rights"; "Report of the Attorney General to the President on the Department of Justice's Activities in the Field of Civil Rights," December 29, 1961, box 97, President's Office Files, Papers of President Kennedy, JFK; Elliff, "United States Department of Justice," p. 675; U.S. Department of Justice, *Annual Report of the Attorney General of the United States for the Fiscal Year Ended June 30, 1962* (Washington, 1962), pp. 174, 182. One of the nine indicted bus burners was not tried because of ill health. Trial of the others resulted in one not-guilty verdict and a hung jury for the remaining seven defendants. Six of these seven eventually pleaded *nolo contendere,* with five receiving suspended sentences and the other being sentenced to one year and a day in prison. Indictments against the other two defendants were dismissed on motion of the United States attorney.

74   Ross Barnett, transcript of oral history interview by Dennis O'Brien, May 6, 1969, p. 29, JFK Oral.

75   Guthman, *Band of Brothers,* p. 184; Brauer, *John F. Kennedy,* pp. 180–81; Lord, *Past,* p. 144.

76   Robert Kennedy Oral History, p. 731.

77   Lord, *Past,* pp. 144–45; Guthman, *Band of Brothers,* p. 189; Brauer, *John F. Kennedy,* p. 182; Elliff, "United States Department of Justice," p. 693.

78   Ramsey Clark, transcript of oral history interview, February 11, 1969, pp. 2–3, LBJ; Burke Marshall Oral History–JFK, pp. 73–75.

79   James E. Folsom, telegram to the President, September 19, 1962, box 11, Attorney General's Personal Correspondence, Robert F. Kennedy Papers; Guthman, *Band of Brothers,* p. 185; Elliff, "Department of Justice," p. 707.

80   Elliff, "Department of Justice," pp. 707–708; Ross Barnett, telegram to Robert Kennedy, September 25, 1962, box 10, Attorney General's Personal Correspondence, Robert F. Kennedy Papers; Directive to All Sheriffs and Law Enforcement Officers of the State of Mississippi, Including Law Enforcement Officers of all Counties and Municipalities, September 25, 1962, and Public Proclamation of the Governor of Mississippi, September 24, 1962, box 11, Attorney General's Personal Correspondence; Transcripts of Conversations Between RFK and Governor Ross Barnett, Tuesday, September 25, 1962 at 12:20 P.M. and 3:25 P.M., box 20, Marshall Papers; Brauer, *John F. Kennedy,* pp. 183–84.

81   Transcript of RFK–Barnett Conversation at 12:20 P.M., September 25.

82   Transcript of Conversation Between RFK and Governor Barnett, Tuesday, September 25, 1962, at 7:25 P.M., box 20, Marshall Papers.

83   Transcript of RFK–Barnett Conversation at 12:20 P.M., September 25; Transcript of Conversation Between RFK and Governor Ross Barnett, Monday, September 24, 1962, at 9:50 P.M., box 20, Marshall Papers; Guthman, *Band of Brothers,* p. 189; Robert Kennedy Oral History, pp. 744–45.

84   "Barnett, Ross Robert," in *Biographical Directory of the Governors of the United States, 1789–1978,* ed. Robert Sobel and John Raimo, 4 vols. (Westport, Conn., 1978), 2:831; Robert Kennedy Oral History, pp. 728, 731; Burke Marshall Oral History–JFK, pp. 72–75; Guthman, *Band of Brothers,* pp. 192–96; Lord, *Past,* p. 169; Brauer, *John F. Kennedy,* p. 186; Transcript of Conversation Between RFK and Governor Barnett, Thursday, September 27, 1962, at 2:50 P.M., box 20, Marshall Papers.

85   Guthman, *Band of Brothers,* p. 196; Burke Marshall Oral History–JFK, p. 75; Transcripts of Conversations Between RFK and Governor Barnett, Thursday, September 27, 1962 at 3:50 P.M. and 6:35 P.M., box 20, Marshall Papers; Benjamin Muse, "University of Mississippi," August 23, 1961, folder 75-01-59-01, SRCC; *Birmingham News,* September 27, 1962; *Jackson Daily News,* September 27, 1962.

86   Lord, *Past,* pp. 176–77, 184–85. Guthman, *Band of Brothers,* p. 203.

87   Lord, *Past,* p. 169; Burke Marshall Oral History–JFK, pp. 76–77; Guthman, *Band of Brothers,* p. 198; Brauer, *John F. Kennedy,* p. 191; Transcript of Telephone Conversation Between Attorney General and Governor Barnett, 12:45 P.M., September 30, 1962, box 20, Marshall Papers.

88   Burke Marshall Oral History–JFK, p. 77; White House Press Release, September 29, 1962, box 97, President's Office Files, Papers of President Kennedy, JFK; Transcript of Conversation at 12:45 P.M. on September 30.

89   John F. Kennedy, telegram to Ross Barnett, September 29, 1962, Attorney General's Personal Correspondence, Robert F. Kennedy Papers.

90   September 29, 1962, White House Press Release.

91   Statement of Norbert S. Schlei, Assistant Attorney General, Office of Legal Counsel, undated, box 32, Ramsey Clark Papers, LBJ; Guthman, *Band of Brothers,* p. 199; Proclamation No. 3497, September 30, 1962, 76 Stat. 1506 (1962); Ex. Order 11,053, September 30, 1960.

92   Transcript of Conversation at 2:45 P.M. on September 30; Ross Barnett, Press Release, September 30, 1962, telegram sent at 5:45 P.M., September 29, 1962, and White House Press Release, October 1, 1962, box 11, Attorney General's Personal Correspondence, Robert F. Kennedy Papers.

93   Joseph F. Dolan, transcript of oral history interview by Charles T. Morrissy, December 4, 1964, p. 114, JFK Oral; Guthman, *Band of Brothers,* p. 206; Lord, *Past,* p. 204; Statement of Norbert Schlei; *Who's Who in American Law,* 4th ed. (Chicago, 1985), p. 288.

94   Statement of Norbert Schlei; Statements of Carl E. Enders, Assistant Chief Patrol Inspector, James Whiteford, reporter for the *Baltimore Sun,* Donald R. Copoch, Assistant Commissioner of Enforcement, Immigration Border Patrol, and Bobby Christensen, Patrol Inspector, all in box 32, Clark Papers; Johnson Oral History, pp. 15–17; Brauer, *John F. Kennedy,* p. 194.

95   Guthman, *Band of Brothers,* pp. 202–203; Sorenson, *Kennedy,* p. 487; Pollak Oral History, pp. 8–9; Katzenbach Interview. Sorensen gives the number of marshals shot as thirty-five, while Guthman says it was twenty-eight. I have used the latter figure because Guthman was actually in Oxford while Sorenson was not.

96   Presidents, *Public Papers: Kennedy,* 1962: 726; Guthman, *Band of Brothers,* p. 203; Burke Marshall Oral History–JFK, p. 80; Katzenbach Interview; Statement of Norbert Schlei; Sorenson, *Kennedy,* p. 487.

97   Burke Marshall, Memorandum to the Attorney General—Monday Report, April 23, 1963, box 16, Marshall Papers; Attorney General to Ross Barnett, March 8, 1963, box 8, Marshall Papers; Ramsey Clark, Memorandum to the Attorney General, May 7, 1963, box 32, Clark Papers; Florence Mars, *Witness in Philadelphia* (Baton Rouge, 1977), p. 75.

98   Brauer, *John F. Kennedy,* pp. 198–99; Strom Thurmond, telegram to the President, September 30, 1962, Ex. HU2/ST 24, WHCF, JFK; Joe D. Waggoner, Jr., to the President, October 1, 1962, Gen. HU2/ST 24, WHCF; Samuel D. Thurman to the President, October 3, 1962, Ex. HU2/ST 1, WHCF; *New York Times,* October 5, 1962, p. 19; *Washington Post,* October 3, 1962.

99   Paul S. Lofton, Jr., "Calm and Exemplary: Desegregation in Columbia, South Carolina," in *Southern Businessmen and Desegregation,* ed. Elizabeth A. Jacoway and David R. Colburn (Baton Rouge, 1982), p. 80; "Desegregation at the

University of Alabama: Racial Matters" [May 28, 1963], box 18, Marshall Papers; Robert Kennedy Oral History, p. 524; *Delta Democrat-Times* (Greenville, Miss.), May 2, 1963.

100   Draft telegram to Governor Wallace from the President, undated, box 80, President's Office Files, JFK; *Public Papers: Kennedy*, 1963: 374; Robert Kennedy Oral History, p. 815; Guthman, *Band of Brothers*, p. 209; Brauer, *John F. Kennedy*, p. 258; "Wallace, George C.," in Sobel and Raimo, eds., *Governors of the United States*, 1:37; Buford Boone, "Southern Newsmen and Local Pressure," in *Race and the News Media*, ed. Paul L. Fisher and Ralph L. Lowenstein (New York, 1967), p. 49.

101   "Desegregation at the University of Alabama"; Robert Kennedy Oral History, pp. 812–13, 824; Marshall, Rafferty Notes; Guthman, *Band of Brothers*, pp. 212–17; Presidents, *Public Papers: Kennedy*, 1963: 467–68; Howell Raines, *My Soul Is Rested: Movement Days in the Deep South* (New York, 1977), p. 174.

102   *Washington Post*, June 18, 1963; John F. Kennedy, telegram to George C. Wallace, June 14, 1963, Ex. HU2/ST 1, WHCF, JFK (quote is from this source); *Birmingham News*, November 19, 1963; *Montgomery Advertiser*, June 18, 1963, December 20, 1963, January 9, 1964, February 1, 1964, May 19, 1964.

103   *St. Louis Post-Dispatch*, June 13, 1963; *Birmingham News*, June 13, 1963.

104   Yarbrough, *Judge Frank Johnson*, p. 93 (Wallace quoted at 93); White House Press Release, September 10, 1963, box 97, President's Office Files, Subject Files: Civil Rights, JFK; Dolan Oral History, p. 116; Burke Marshall to John Lewis, September 16, 1963, box 16, folder 125, SNCC Papers.

105   Elliff, "United States Department of Justice," pp. 706, 710; William L. Taylor, Memorandum for Lee C. White, October 10, 1962, box 24, Lee C. White Files, Papers of President Kennedy, JFK.

106   Cleve McDowell to the Justice Department, September 23, 1923 [*sic*], box 19, Marshall Papers.

107   Stephen G. Spottsword to John F. Kennedy, October 17, 1962, Gen. HU2/ST 24, WHCF, JFK.

108   Brauer, *John F. Kennedy*, p. 231; Stephen B. Oates, *Let the Trumpet Sound: The Life of Martin Luther King, Jr.* (New York, 1982), pp. 209–11.

109   Quoted in David J. Garrow, *The FBI and Martin Luther King, Jr.* (New York, 1983), p. 58.

110   Oates, *Trumpet*, p. 211.

111   Robert Corley, "In Search of Harmony: Birmingham Business Leaders and Desegregation, 1950–1963," in *Southern Businessmen and Desegregation*, p. 180; *Pittsburgh Courier*, October 5, 1963.

112   Alabama Advisory Committee of the United States Civil Rights Commission, Special Memorandum to U.S. Civil Rights Commission and Civil

Rights Division, U.S. Department of Justice, September 1962, box 17, Marshall Papers; Rowe, *My Undercover Years*, p. 92; *Atlanta Constitution*, March 29, 1963; *Jackson Daily News*, December 15, 1962; *Birmingham News*, December 15, 1962, February 15, 1964; *New York Times*, August 30, 1962, p. 17C; Brauer, *John F. Kennedy*, p. 259; Schlesinger, *Thousand Days*, p. 959.

113 Forman, *Making of Black Revolutionaries*, p. 312.

114 News Memorandum of Statement by Mayor Sam Yorty, undated, box 19, Papers of President Kennedy, Lee C. White Files, JFK.

115 Theodore Sorenson, transcript of oral history interview by Karl Kaysen, May 3, 1964, p. 130, JFK Oral; Burke Marshall Oral History–JFK, p. 98; *Birmingham News*, October 13, 1963; John H. Gilbert to the President, May 8, 1963, and Jacob Javits, telegram to the President, Ex. HU2/ST 1, WHCF, JFK; Joseph Beaver to John Kennedy, May 7, 1963, and Jackie Robinson, telegram to the President, May 7, 1963, Gen. HU2/ST 1, WHCF, JFK.

116 Matusow, *Unraveling*, pp. 87–88; Schlesinger, *Thousand Days*, p. 959; Brauer, *John F. Kennedy*, p. 236; Sorenson Oral History, p. 130; *Washington Post*, September 17, 1963; *St. Louis Post-Dispatch*, September 19, 1963; Burke Marshall, Memorandum for the Attorney General—Monday Report, May 29, 1962, box 16, Marshall Papers; Leonard W. Holt, "Birmingham's Harlem," *Folkways* 3 (Summer 1963): 438; J. Edgar Hoover to the President (CONF.), April 10, 1964, C.F. HU2/ST 1, WHCF, LBJ. Although both the *Post* and the *Post-Dispatch* asserted that the FBI made no effort to investigate Birmingham bombings until May 1963, and Hoover included none before that date in his list of the ones it had investigated, the Justice Department consistently stated that agents had been on the scene immediately after the Bethel Baptist Church bombing and that the Bureau's identification and laboratory facilities had been made available to state authorities working on that case. See Statement in Connection with the Bombing of the Bethel Baptist Church, Birmingham, Alabama, December 14, 1962, box 17, Marshall Papers; Burke Marshall to Walter Jenkins, February 28, 1963, Gen. HU2/ST 1, WHCF, JFK; "Justice Department Statement in Connection with the Bombing of the Bethel Baptist Church, Birmingham, Alabama, on December 14, 1962," undated, box 19, White Files.

117 Presidents, *Public Papers: Kennedy*, 1963: 397.

118 Ibid., pp. 397–98; Sorenson, *Kennedy*, p. 491; George Wallace, telegrams to the President, May 12, 1963 [2], and May 13, 1963, Ex. HU2/ST 1, WHCF, JFK.

119 Sorenson, *Kennedy*, p. 491; Draft of telegram from John F. Kennedy to George C. Wallace, May 13, 1963, Ex. HU2/ST 1, WHCF, JFK.

120 House Joint Resolution No. 16, May 21, 1963, Ex. HU2/ST 1, WHCF, JFK; Birmingham City Council Resolution, May 14, 1963, Gen. HU2/ST 1, WHCF, JFK.

121 Draft of telegram from John F. Kennedy to George C. Wallace, May 13, 1962, Ex. HU2/ST 1, WHCF, JFK; Telegrams from Representatives George Grant, Albert Rains, George Huddleston, Jr., Armistad Sheldon, Robert E. Jones, George Andrews, and Carl Elliot to the President, May 13, 1963, and Representative Kenneth A. Roberts to the President, May 13, 1963, Gen. HU2/ST 1, WHCF, JFK.

122 Pierre Salinger, Memorandum of Conversation Between President Kennedy and Governor George C. Wallace of Alabama on May 18, 1963, undated, box 96, President's Office Files.

123 Ibid.; "Civil Rights: The Sunday School Bombing," *Time*, September 27, 1963, p. 17 (quote); "Birmingham After the Bombing," *U.S. News & World Report*, September 30, 1963, p. 39; Jack Mendelsohn, *The Martyrs: Sixteen Who Gave Their Lives for Racial Justice* (New York, 1966), p. 95.

124 "Birmingham After the Bombing," p. 39.

125 *New York Times*, September 18, 1963, p. 36; Roy Wilkins, telegram to John F. Kennedy, September 15, 1963, group III, series B, box 248, NAACP Papers; "Birmingham: 'My God, You're Not Even Safe in Church,' " *Newsweek*, September 30, 1963, p. 22; *Montgomery Advertiser*, September 19, 1963; Brauer, *John F. Kennedy*, p. 295; Martin Luther King, Jr., Statement re Violence in Birmingham, September 16, 1963, series IV, King Papers—King Center.

126 Presidents, *Public Papers: Kennedy*, 1963: 681; John Sparkman, draft telegram to Melvin Bailey, et al., May 15, 1963, Ex. HU2/ST 1, WHCF, JFK; *Washington Post*, September 13, 1963; *Dallas Morning News*, September 13, 1963; *Chattanooga Times*, September 20, 1963; *Birmingham News*, September 16, 1963; Sorenson Oral History, p. 131.

127 *New York Times*, September 22, 1963, p. E3.

128 Both he and Baldwin are quoted in " 'My God,' " p. 23.

129 Kenneth Royall [?], Preliminary Report to the President on Birmingham by Royall-Blaik Committee, November 5, 1963, box 18, Marshall Papers.

130 Kenneth C. Royall and Earl H. Blaik, "Report to the President of the United States," October 10, 1963, box 96, President's Office Files.

131 Colonel Earl H. "Red" Blaik, transcript of oral history interview by Charles T. Morrissy, December 2, 1964, p. 11, JFK Oral.

132 Robert Kennedy Oral History, p. 766. See also p. 851 and Attorney General Kennedy's October 15, 1964, testimony before the House Judiciary Committee in U.S., Congress, House, Committee on the Judiciary, *Civil Rights: Hearings . . . ,* 89th Cong., 1st sess., 1963, 4:2652.

133 *Houston Post*, August 18, 1963; Matusow, *Unraveling*, p. 88; Sorenson, *Kennedy*, pp. 494, 496.

134 House Judiciary Committee, *Civil Rights*, 4:2656; Matusow, *Unraveling*, pp. 90–92; *Cong. Record*, 88th Cong., 1st sess., June 11, 1963, p. 9966;

Leadership Conference on Civil Rights, Attachment #1, October 17, 1963, box 15, folder 214, SNCC Papers; Forman, *Making of Black Revolutionaries,* p. 336; James Farmer to Roland Gibson, October 28, 1963, series 1, box 5, folder 1, CORE Papers.

135 Arnold Aronson, Memo #5 to Cooperating Organizations, August 30, 1963, series 3, box 25, folder 1, CORE Papers; Marshall, *Federalism and Civil Rights,* pp. 61–63; Marshall Interview; "Address by Burke Marshall . . . Before the Executive Board of the American Jewish Committee, Chicago, Illinois," November 2, 1963, box 13, Marshall Papers.

136 House Judiciary Committee, *Civil Rights,* 4:2657–58 (quote at 2658); Press Conference of Attorney General Robert F. Kennedy, October 15, 1963, box 30, Theodore Sorenson Papers, JFK.

137 Matusow, *Unraveling,* p. 93; Leadership Conference on Civil Rights, Attachment 1, October 17, 1963, folder 214, SNCC Papers; Senator Jacob K. Javits, Press Release, October 17, 1963, folder 192, box 15, SNCC Papers.

Chapter Five

1 August Meier and Elliott Rudwick, *CORE: A Study in the Civil Rights Movement* (New York, 1973), pp. 172–75; Allen J. Matusow, *The Unraveling of America: A History of Liberalism in the 1960s* (New York, 1984), pp. 74–75; James Forman, *The Making of Black Revolutionaries* (New York, 1972), p. 266; Steven F. Lawson, *Black Ballots: Voting Rights in the South 1944–1969* (New York, 1976), pp. 262–64.

2 Meier and Rudwick, *CORE,* p. 174; Lawson, *Black Ballots,* p. 265; Matusow, *Unraveling,* p. 75; Forman, *Making of Black Revolutionaries,* p. 266; Allen J. Matusow, "From Civil Rights to Black Power: The Case of SNCC, 1960–1966," in *Twentieth Century America: Recent Interpretations,* ed. Allen J. Matusow and Barton Bernstein, 2d ed. (New York, 1972), p. 499.

3 Wiley Austin Branton, transcript of oral history interview by Steven Lawson, October 21, 1970, p. 8, CUOHP.

4 Howard Zinn, *SNCC: The New Abolitionists* (Boston, 1964), pp. 124–34; Clayborne Carson, *In Struggle: SNCC and the Black Awakening of the 1960s* (Cambridge, Mass., 1981), pp. 56–61; Forman, *Making of Black Revolutionaries,* p. 248.

5 SNCC Press Release, September 10, 1962, box 8, folder 16, CORE Papers; SNCC, "Southwest Georgia Project Report and Proposals," December 27, 1963, box 21, folder 341, SNCC Papers.

6 Howard Zinn, *Albany* (Atlanta, 1962), pp. 12–14 (quote at 14); Zinn, *SNCC,* pp. 135–36; SNCC Press Release, March 26, [1962], series 1, box 8, folder 16, CORE Papers; Peter Tileman, Report on Albany, Georgia, box 95,

folder 32, SNCC Papers; Carl M. Brauer, *John F. Kennedy and the Second Reconstruction* (New York, 1977), pp. 170–71.

7   SNCC, "Southwest Georgia Project Report"; John L. Murphy, "For Mr. Marshall's Informal Report to the Attorney General," September 18, 1962, box 16, Burke Marshall Papers, JFK; SNCC Press Release, September 14, 1962, series 1, box 8, folder 16, CORE Papers; CORE, telegram to Attorney General Robert Kennedy, August 15, 1962, series 1, box 4, folder 8, CORE Papers; SNCC Press Release, September 10, 1962, box 49, folder 116, SNCC Papers. McDew is quoted in the press release.

8   Murphy, "For Mr. Marshall's Informal Report"; Burke Marshall, Memoranda for the Attorney General—Monday Reports, September 4, 1962, and September 10, 1962, box 16, Marshall Papers; Carson, *In Struggle*, p. 92; Howard Zinn to Leslie Dunbar, July 28, 1962, folder 75-01-77-45, SRCC; Forman, *Making of Black Revolutionaries*, p. 277; Fact Sheet, Americus, Georgia, box 95, folder 37, SNCC Papers. A three-judge federal district court held the Georgia insurrection statute unconstitutional and enjoined the Americus prosecution. John L. Murphy to Ethel Cohen, December 10, 1963, series 1, box 4, folder 4, CORE Papers.

9   John Dittmer, "The Movement in McComb, 1961–1964" (paper delivered at the annual meeting of the Organization of American Historians, Los Angeles, California, April 1984), pp. 1, 3; John Doar and Dorothy Landsberg, "The Performance of the FBI in Investigating Violations of Federal Laws Protecting the Right to Vote—1960–1967," in U.S. Senate, Select Committee to Study Governmental Operations with Respect to Intelligence Activities, *Hearings . . . ,* pt. VI: *Federal Bureau of Investigation,* 94th Cong., 1st sess., 1975, pp. 911–12; *A Chronology of Violence and Intimidation in Mississippi Since 1961* (Atlanta, 1964 [?]), pp. 5–18.

10   Doar and Landsberg, "Performance of the FBI," pp. 912, 921–22; Testimony of Robert Moses, May 25, 1962, Commission of Inquiry into the Administration of Justice in the Freedom Struggle, Transcript of Hearings, pp. 105–107, series 5, box 5, CORE Papers (hereinafter cited as Commission of Inquiry Transcript); Bob Moses, "Report on Registration Attempt at Liberty," undated, folder 75-06-11-15, SRCC; *Jackson Daily News,* February 3, 1964; Dittmer, "Movement in McComb," p. 5.

11   John Thomas Elliff, "The United States Department of Justice and Individual Rights, 1937–1962" (Ph.D. diss., Harvard University, 1967), pp. 657–59; United States v. Wood, 295 F.2d 772, 776 (5th Cir. 1961). Wood is quoted by the Court of Appeals in *Wood.*

12   Carson, *In Struggle,* pp. 73–74, 79; *A Chronology,* p. 11; SNCC Press Release, September 11, 1962, series 1, box 8, folder 6, CORE Papers; Zinn, *SNCC,* p. 94.

13   Zinn, *SNCC,* pp. 89–90; *A Chronology,* pp. 12–13; Burke Marshall,

Memoranda for the Attorney General—Monday Reports, March 4, 1963, and March 26, 1963, box 16, Marshall Papers; SNCC Press Release, March 25, 1963, box 21, folder 360, SNCC Papers; Brauer, *John F. Kennedy*, p. 224; SNCC Press Release, March 1, 1963, series 1, box 8, folder 16, CORE Papers; Jack Minnis, Memo for the Files, March 1, 1963, folder 75-06-11-16, SRCC; Lee C. White to Michael Rosenbaum, March 22, 1963, Gen. HU2/ST 24, WHCF, JFK.

14 "Coahoma County Branch, NAACP," March 13, 1963, folder 75-16-11-16, SRCC; Testimony of Robert Moses, May 25, 1962, Commission of Inquiry Transcript, pp. 100–101; Aaron E. Henry, telegram to the President, March 27, 1963, Gen. HU2/ST 24, WHCF, JFK; Ivanhoe Donaldson, "Field Report Covering 30 October thru 5 November '63," box 17, folder 242, SNCC Papers; Carson, *In Struggle*, pp. 47–49; Forman, *Making of Black Revolutionaries*, p. 224; Burke Marshall, Memorandum to the President, re: Civil Rights Commission Resolution, April 8, 1963, box 8, Marshall Papers.

15 Aaron Henry, telegram to the President, April 5, 1963, Gen. HU2/ST 24, WHCF, JFK; Charles McDew, telegrams to Robert F. Kennedy, January 18, 1961, November 19, 1961, and December 6, 1961, box 1, folder 27, SNCC Papers; SNCC Press Releases, August 29, 1962, January 21, 1963, and February 21, 1963, box 21, folder 360, SNCC Papers; SNCC Press Releases, April 6, 1962, and March 1, 1963, series 1, box 8, folder 16, CORE Papers; James Forman, telegram to John F. Kennedy, March 25, 1963, Gen. HU2/ST 24, WHCF, JFK; *Baltimore Afro-American*, February 2, 1963.

16 Forman, *Making of Black Revolutionaries*, p. 243; Jack Minnis, Memo for the Files, March 1, 1963, folder 75-06-11-16, SRCC; Carson, *In Struggle*, pp. 81, 85–86; James Forman, telegram to the President, September 10, 1962, Gen. HU2/ST 24, WHCF, JFK.

17 *Atlanta Journal*, November 12, 1962; Roy Wilkins, telegram to the President, March 7, 1963, and A. Phillip Randolph, telegram to the President, March 27, 1963, Gen. HU2/ST 24, WHCF, JFK; James Farmer, telegram to Robert Kennedy, August 15, 1962, series 1, box 4, folder 8, CORE Papers; Charles McDew, telegram to James Farmer, September 13, 1962, series 1, box 4, folder 16, CORE Papers; Wiley Branton, telegram to Attorney General Robert F. Kennedy, March 29, 1963, folder 75-06-37-05, SRCC; Brauer, *John F. Kennedy*, pp. 173–74; Southern Conference Education Fund, telegram to Robert Kennedy, March 1, 1963, box 22, folder 365, SNCC Papers; SNCC Press Release, September 13, 1962, box 49, folder 16, SNCC Papers.

18 King to Kennedy, March 28, 1963, box 14, folder 5, King Papers—King Center.

19 Benjamin J. Davis, Jr., et al., telegram to the President, December 6, 1961, box 3, Harris Wofford, Jr., Files, Papers of President Kennedy, JFK; Arthur Gorson, telegram to the President, March 4, 1963, Richard P. Sullmeier

to John F. Kennedy, March 13, 1963, and Michael Rosenbaum and Leonard
Cohen, telegram to the President, March 8, 1963, all in Gen. HU2/ST 24,
WHCF, JFK; William F. Schnitzler, telegram to the President, July 12, 1962,
Gen. HU2/ST 10, WHCF, JFK.

20   Reuther to the President, April 1, 1963, Ex. HU2/ST 24, WHCF, JFK.

21   See 4-1-63—4-15-63 folder, Gen. HU2/ST 24, WHCF, JFK.

22   Robert F. Kennedy, transcript of oral history interview by Anthony
Lewis, December 4, 1964, p. 193, JFK Oral; Andrew Tully, *The FBI's Most
Famous Cases* (New York, 1965), p. 227; Doar and Landsberg, "Performance of the
FBI," p. 928; Lee C. White to Michael Rosenbaum, March 22, 1963, Gen.
HU2/ST 24, WHCF, JFK; Burke Marshall, Memorandum to the President, re:
Civil Rights Commission Resolution; *Pittsburgh Courier,* November 24, 1964;
Washington Post, September 2, 1963, September 11, 1963; *Nashville Banner,* Sep-
tember 10, 1963; *Atlanta Journal,* December 7, 1962; Victor Navasky, *Kennedy
Justice,* (New York, 1971), p. 19.

23   Doar and Landsberg, "Performance of the FBI," p. 928.

24   Burke Marshall, notes of interview by Scott Rafferty, box 1, Scott Rafferty
Papers, JFK (hereinafter cited as Marshall, Rafferty Notes); Testimony of Nicholas deB. Katzenbach, November 12, 1975, Senate Select Committee, *Hearings,*
p. 213; Brauer, *John F. Kennedy,* pp. 163–64.

25   Senate Select Committee, *Hearings,* p. 213.

26   Ibid., pp. 124–30, 134; Burke Marshall, transcript of oral history inter-
view, October 28, 1968, pp. 24–25, LBJ (hereinafter cited as Marshall Oral
History—LBJ); Nicholas deB. Katzenbach, telephonic interview with the au-
thor, June 20, 1984; Navasky, *Kennedy Justice,* pp. 107–108; testimony by Robert
Moses, May 25, 1962, Commission of Inquiry Transcript, p. 109; Richard
Haley, Memorandum to James Farmer, June 5, 1963, series 2, box 2, folder 4,
CORE Papers; Zinn, *Albany,* p. 28; *St. Petersburg Times,* October 5, 1963;
Matusow, *Unraveling,* p. 80; Pat Watters and Reese Cleghorn, *Climbing Jacob's
Ladder: The Arrival of Negroes in Southern Politics* (New York, 1967), p. 225.

27   Quoted in "Enforcing the Law: Interview with J. Edgar Hoover," *U.S.
News & World Report,* December 21, 1964, p. 36.

28   Ibid.; Katzenbach Interview; Robert Kennedy Oral History, p. 664;
Arthur M. Schlesinger, Jr., *Robert Kennedy and His Times* (Boston, 1978), 1:304;
William C. Sullivan with the assistance of Bill Brown, *The Bureau: My Thirty
Years in Hoover's FBI* (New York, 1979), p. 125.

29   Quoted in "Department of Justice: Off Hoover's Chest," *Newsweek,*
November 30, 1964, p. 29, and James Wechsler, "The Decline of J. Edgar
Hoover," *Progressive* 29 (January 1965): 12.

30   Ramsey Clark, transcript of oral history interview, February 11, 1969, p.
30, LBJ.

31   Ibid., pp. 29–30; Navasky, *Kennedy Justice*, p. 103; *Pittsburgh Courier*, November 3, 1962; Norman Thomas to Burke Marshall, December 3, 1968, box 8, Marshall Papers; Norman C. Jimerson to Lee C. White, February 6, 1963, Gen. HU2/ST 1, WHCF, JFK; *Jackson Daily News*, November 22, 1964; "First Status Report: Voter Education Project," September 20, 1961, series 5, box 23, folder 9, CORE Papers.

32   Quoted in Wechsler, "Decline," p. 12.

33   *New York Times*, November 19, 1962, p. 26C; David J. Garrow, *The FBI and Martin Luther King, Jr.* (New York, 1983), pp. 55–56, 122–24 (quote at 55).

34   Howard Zinn to Shad Polier, December 20, 1962, folder 75-01-77-45, SRCC; Garrow, *FBI and King*, p. 96; Matusow, *Unraveling*, p. 76; U.S., Presidents, *Public Papers of the Presidents of the United States: John F. Kennedy*, 3 vols. (Washington, 1962–1964), 1962: 378–79; Branton Oral History, p. 9; Lawson, *Black Ballots*, p. 279; Neil R. McMillen, "Black Enfranchisement in Mississippi: Federal Enforcement and Black Protest in the 1960s," *Journal of Southern History* 43 (August 1977): 360.

35   Forman, *Making of Black Revolutionaries*, pp. 285–86; Zinn, *Albany*, pp. vi–vii, 32; Watters and Cleghorn, *Climbing Jacob's Ladder*, p. 215; Lawson, *Black Ballots*, p. 267.

36   Burke Marshall, Memoranda for the Attorney General—Monday Reports, January 3, 1962, January 16, 1962, February 13, 1962, February 19, 1962, March 27, 1962, July 3, 1962, July 17, 1962, July 24, 1962, November 19, 1962, December 11, 1962, February 25, 1963, and March 11, 1963, box 16, Marshall Papers.

37   Elliff, "United States Department of Justice," p. 661; Marshall, Rafferty Notes; Burke Marshall to Wiley A. Branton, March 29, 1963, folder 75-06-37-05, SRCC; Burke Marshall, Memoranda for the Attorney General—Monday Reports, January 8, 1963, and January 29, 1963, box 16, Marshall Papers; Zinn, *Albany*, p. vi; "A Report on the Progress in the Field of Civil Rights by Attorney General Robert F. Kennedy to the President," January 24, 1963, box 9, Attorney General's General Correspondence, Robert F. Kennedy Papers, JFK.

38   "Report on the Progress"; Doar and Landsberg, "Performance of the FBI," p. 889; Burke Marshall, "Federal Protection of Negro Voting Rights," *Law and Contemporary Problems* 27 (1962): 458–59; Elliff, "United States Department of Justice," p. 659; United States v. Wood, 295 F.2d 772, 774 (5th Cir. 1961); Burke Marshall to Walter P. Reuther, April 26, 1963, Ex. HU2/ST 24, WHCF, JFK; Forman, *Making of Black Revolutionaries*, pp. 299–303; Zinn, *Albany*, p. 28.

39   Benjamin Muse, *Ten Years of Prelude: The Story of Integration Since the Supreme Court's 1954 Decision* (New York, 1964), p. 156; Commission of Inquiry Transcript, title page; "Suggested Recommendations of the Committee of Inquiry,"

September 10, 1962, series 1, box 2, folder 11, CORE Papers; Brauer, *John F. Kennedy,* p. 156. The "commission" was originally referred to by those planning it as a "Committee of Inquiry," and it is erroneously so identified in a May 28, 1962, memorandum on the hearings which Theodore R. Newman, Jr., of the Civil Rights Division's Constitutional Rights Unit prepared for Burke Marshall (box 31, Marshall Papers), hereinafter cited as Newman Memorandum. Newman also erred in his identification of some of the commission members.

40 James Farmer to Burke Marshall, series 1, box 2, folder 11, CORE Papers. For a complete record of the hearings, see Commission of Inquiry Transcript. Attorney Theodore R. Newman, Jr., provided a summary of the proceedings in a memorandum he prepared for Burke Marshall and attached to that memorandum written statements of the witnesses, as well as of other persons who did not actually attend the hearings (Newman Memorandum).

41 Newman Memorandum.

42 Ibid.; Commission of Inquiry Transcript, pp. 45–47, 304–306, 322.

43 James Farmer to Charlotte Devrie, June 15, 1962, series 1, box 2, folder 11, CORE Papers; Marvin Rich to Eleanor Roosevelt, June 20, 1962, series 5, box 5, folder 5, ibid.; Burke Marshall to James Farmer, May 10, 1962, series 1, box 4, folder 4, ibid.; Brauer, *John F. Kennedy,* p. 156.

44 Marvin Rich to Eleanor Roosevelt, June 20, 1962, series 5, box 5, folder 5, CORE Papers; Meier and Rudwick, *CORE,* p. 180; *Baton Rouge State-Times,* September 12, 1962.

45 Mississippi Advisory Committee to the U.S. Commission on Civil Rights, *Administration of Justice in Mississippi* (N.p., 1963), pp. 23–25; Arthur M. Schlesinger, Jr., *A Thousand Days: John F. Kennedy in the White House* (Boston, 1965), p. 952; Brauer, *John F. Kennedy,* p. 225.

46 Interim Report of the United States Commission on Civil Rights, April 16, 1963, box 50, folder 19, SNCC Papers.

47 Burke Marshall, Memorandum to the President, April 8, 1963, box 8, Marshall Papers; White House Press Release, April 19, 1962, box 97, President's Office Files, Subjects, Civil Rights—General, Papers of President Kennedy, JFK; Burke Marshall to John Lewis, September 16, 1963, box 16, folder 225, SNCC Papers.

48 Carson, *In Struggle,* p. 90; Jerome K. Heilbrom, Memorandum for the Files, July 22, 1963, box 31, Marshall Papers; SNCC Press Release, undated, box 96, folder 64, SNCC Papers; *Student Voice,* December 9, 1963; Edward S. Hollander, "Report on Canton, Madison County, Mississippi," February 26, 1964, series 5, box 15, folder 2, CORE Papers.

49 Samuel Block, Report, September 26, 1963, box 42, folder 23, SNCC Papers.

50 Forman, *Making of Black Revolutionaries,* pp. 317–22, 328, 349–51;

Meier and Rudwick, *CORE,* pp. 221–23, 260–67; "Home Burns as La. Negro Tries to Vote," *Jet,* November 21, 1963, p. 7; *Baltimore Afro-American,* June 16, 1963; *Baton Rouge State-Times,* August 27, 1963; James W. Ely, Jr., "Negro Demonstrations and the Law," *Vanderbilt Law Review* 27 (October 1974): 932, 935; Carson, *In Struggle,* p. 90.

51 *Washington Post,* April 14, 1963; Memorandum from Mr. Gabel to Mr. Marshall, July 22, 1963, box 32, Marshall Papers; Walter L. Kirschenbaum to Robert Kennedy, June 1, 1963, box 9, Attorney General's General Correspondence, Robert F. Kennedy Papers; John Fisher, "A Small Band of Practical Heroes," *Harper's* 227 (October 1963): 24; Mike Miller, "Report on Holmes County," July 22, 1963, folder 75-06-08-03, SRCC; SNCC Press Release, May 10, 1963, box 21, folder 360, SNCC Papers; SNCC Press Release, September 23, 1963, box 95, folder 37, SNCC Papers; Commission of Inquiry Transcript, pp. 204–205; SNCC Newsletter, March 1, 1963, series 1, box 8, folder 16, CORE Papers; Watters and Cleghorn, *Climbing Jacob's Ladder,* pp. 235–36.

52 *Chicago Defender,* July 20–26, 1963; W. Gabel, Memorandum to Burke Marshall, July 20, 1963 [?], box 32, Marshall Papers; "Police Brutality, Jails," n.d., folder 75-03-11-36, SRCC; St. John Barrett, untitled report, June 18, 1963, box 16, Marshall Papers; *Richmond News Leader,* June 12, 1963.

53 Southern Regional Council, *Southern Justice: An Indictment* (N.p., 1965), pp. 12, 20 (quote at 12); Peggy B. Thomson, "A Visit to Danville," *Progressive* 27 (November 1963): 25, 28; *Norfolk Virginian-Pilot,* June 25, 1963. In fairness to Judge Aiken, it should be pointed out that in both Danville and Baton Rouge federal judges also dealt with violence against protesters by enjoining their demonstrations. See Ely, "Negro Demonstrations," p. 94; Congress of Racial Equality v. Clemmons, 323 F.2d 54 (5th Cir. 1963).

54 Southern Regional Council, *Southern Justice,* p. 12; *Atlanta Constitution,* September 5, 1963; "S. C. White Gets Hard Labor, Slapped Girl 15," *Jet,* July 25, 1963, p. 53; *Norfolk Journal and Guide,* August 17, 1963; *Baltimore Afro-American,* August 3, 1963. See also *Atlanta Constitution,* May 3, 1964; *Montgomery Advertiser,* June 8, 1963.

55 Southern Regional Council, *Southern Justice,* p. 2; *New York Times,* December 3, 1965, pp. 1, 35; *Dual Justice in the Courts—Unconcerned Community* (Atlanta, n.d.), p. 1; *Miami Herald,* March 30, 1965.

56 Jack Mendelsohn, *The Martyrs: Sixteen Who Gave Their Lives for Racial Justice* (New York, 1966), pp. 104–105; "Alabama: Rewards for Bombers Mount; Eight Indicted by Federal Jury," *South,* September 30, 1963, p. 5; W. W. McTyeire, Jr., to [?] Levett, October 8, 1963, box 1, folder 10, King Papers–King Center; George McMillan, "The Birmingham Church Bomber," *Saturday Evening Post,* June 6, 1964, pp. 17–18; *New York Times,* October 2, 1963, p. 22; B. M. [Burke Marshall], Memorandum to the Attorney General, October 4,

1963, box 3, Marshall Papers; Robert Kennedy Oral History, pp. 923–24; J. Edgar Hoover to the President (CONF.) April 10, 1964, C.F. HU2/ST 1, WHCF, LBJ.

57   B.M., Memorandum to the Attorney General; Robert Kennedy Oral History, pp. 923–24; McMillan, "Birmingham Church Bomber," p. 17.

58   Statement by Rev. Fred L. Shuttlesworth, October 1, 1963, Fred L. Shuttlesworth Papers, King Center.

59   James Farmer, Memorandum to CORE Group Leaders, April 24, 1963, series 2, box 2, folder 4, CORE Papers; Mendelsohn, *Martyrs*, pp. 43, 47, 53, 57, 63; "William Moore," undated, series 5, box 40, folder 3, CORE Papers; *New York Times*, September 14, 1963, p. 11; Clarence Mitchell III, telegram to the President, April 27, 1963 [?], Gen. HU2/ST 1, WHCF, JFK; Forman, *Making of Black Revolutionaries*, p. 308; Complaint, Zellner v. Lingo, undated, box 94, folder 5, SNCC Papers; Meier and Rudwick, *CORE*, p. 215.

60   *Jackson Daily News*, June 12, 1963; Mendelsohn, *Martyrs*, pp. 76–80; *New Orleans Times-Picayune*, June 16, 1963; Schlesinger, *Thousand Days*, p. 966.

61   Mendelsohn, *Martyrs*, p. 74; Charles Sallis and John Quincy Adams, "Desegregation in Jackson," in *Southern Businessmen and Desegregation*, ed. Elizabeth Jacoway and David R. Colburn (Baton Rouge, 1982), p. 241; *New York Times*, June 24, 1963, p. 1; *Memphis Commercial Appeal*, June 25, 1963; "Star Prisoner," *Newsweek*, December 13, 1963.

62   January 25, 1964.

63   Mendelsohn, *Martyrs*, pp. 83–84; *New Orleans Times-Picayune*, July 3, 1963; "Civil Rights: A Little Abnormal," *Time*, July 5, 1963, p. 15; "Crime: The Colonel's Grandson," *Newsweek*, July 8, 1963, p. 22; *Jackson Daily News*, February 6, 1964, February 12, 1964; Larry Still, "Ambush Evers-Type Killing, Race," *Jet*, February 20, 1964, p. 14; *New York Times*, February 8, 1964, p. 1, April 8, 1964, p. 1, April 12, 1964, p. 42, April 18, 1964, p. 1; *Birmingham News*, February 7, 1964; *Washington Post*, February 8, 1964; *Delta Democrat-Times* (Greenville, Miss.), April 23, 1964.

64   *Washington Post*, June 14, 1963.

65   Theodore H. Brown to Attorney General Robert Kennedy, June 14, 1963, box 31, Marshall Papers.

66   Charles Diggs, telegrams to the President, May 29, 1963, and May 30, 1963, Ex. HU2/ST 24, WHCF, JFK; A. Phillip Randolph, telegram to the President, March 27, 1963, Gen. HU2/ST 24, WHCF, JFK.

67   Wiley A. Branton to Aaron Henry and Robert Moses, November 12, 1963, folder 75-06-07-21, SRCC.

68   *Baltimore Afro-American*, September 28, 1963; Shad Polier to "Dear Colleague," November 15, 1963, box 95, folder 32, SNCC Papers; Resolution of

New Jersey Branch of Women's International League for Peace and Freedom, May 18, 1963, Gen. HU2/ST 1, WHCF, JFK.

69 *New Orleans Times-Picayune,* September 2, 1963; St. John Barrett, Memorandum to Mr. Marshall, September 2, 1963, box 32, Marshall Papers; James Farmer, telegram to President John Kennedy, series 5, box 26, folder 8, CORE Papers.

70 James Farmer, telegram to Attorney General Robert Kennedy, series 1, box 4, folder 4, CORE Papers.

71 SNCC, Action Memo: Selma, October 9, 1963, folder 75-06-05-24, SRCC; Chicago Area Friends of the Student Nonviolent Coordinating Committee to the President, December 21, 1963, Gen. HU2/ST 1, WHCF, LBJ; Timothy Jenkins to "Dear Friends of Freedom," June 14, 1963, box 29, SNCC Papers; SNCC Press Release, May 20, 1963, box 21, folder 360, SNCC Papers.

72 Complaint, Moses v. Kennedy, 219 F. Supp. 762 (D.D.C. 1963), box 35, folder 17, SCLC Papers; Moses v. Kennedy, 219 F. Supp. 762 (D.D.C. 1963); *Atlanta Constitution,* January 3, 1963; Burke Marshall, Memorandum for the Attorney General—Monday Report, January 8, 1963, box 16, Marshall Papers. Although the *Constitution* referred to Higgs as a Jackson lawyer, he identified himself as practicing out of Washington, D.C. See 219 F. Supp. at 763.

73 Moses v. Kennedy, 219 F. Supp. 762 (D.D.C. 1963).

74 Brauer, *John F. Kennedy,* p. 288; *Baltimore Afro-American,* September 21, 1963; B.M., Memorandum to the Attorney General, September 18, 1963, box 8, Marshall Papers; Burke Marshall, personal interview with author at the Yale Law School, October 24, 1980; Burke Marshall to Charles McDew, May 23, 1963, and Burke Marshall to Sandra Hayden, July 23, 1963, box 16, folder 225, SNCC Papers; David H. Martin, Memorandum to Burke Marshall [September 1963?], box 22, Marshall Papers.

75 Marshall to Professor Russell H. Barrett, January 3, 1964, box 19, Marshall Papers.

76 Lewis, telegram to Robert F. Kennedy, September 16, 1963, box 22, folder 365C, SNCC Papers.

Chapter Six

1 Merle Miller, *Lyndon: An Oral Biography* (New York, 1980), pp. 118, 210–11, 226–29; Doris Kearns, *Lyndon Johnson and the American Dream* (New York, 1976), pp. 230–32; Eric F. Goldman, *The Tragedy of Lyndon Johnson* (New York, 1969), pp. 316–17; Lyndon Baines Johnson, *The Vantage Point: Perspectives on the Presidency* (New York, 1971), pp. 155–56; Paul B. Johnson, transcript of oral

history interview, September 8, 1970, p. 3, LBJ; Edwin Guthman, *We Band of Brothers* (New York, 1971), p. 188, n. 2.

2   Johnson, *Vantage Point,* p. 157.

3   Ibid.; Lee C. White, transcript of oral history interview, March 2, 1971, p. 23, LBJ; Roy Wilkins, transcript of oral history interview, April 1, 1969, pp. 23–24, LBJ; Reverend Theodore Hesburgh, transcript of oral history interview, February 1, 1970, pp. 3–4, LBJ; Vaughn Davis Bornet, *The Presidency of Lyndon B. Johnson* (Lawrence, Kans., 1983), p. 98.

4   He said so during his acceptance speech at the 1964 Democratic National Convention, but of course that address was not given until August. See *Dallas Times-Herald,* August 31, 1964.

5   *Chicago Sun-Times,* June 29, 1964, p. 26.

6   David J. Garrow, *The FBI and Martin Luther King, Jr.* (New York, 1983), p. 127; Richard A. Wasserstram, review of Burke Marshall, *Federalism and Civil Rights,* in *University of Chicago Law Review* 33 (Winter 1966): 407–409; "Comment: Theories of Federalism and Civil Rights," *Yale Law Journal* 75 (May 1966): 1041.

7   Pub. L. No. 88-352, 78 Stat. 241, (1964); U.S., Presidents, *Public Papers of the Presidents of the United States: Lyndon B. Johnson,* 5 vols. (Washington, D.C., 1965–1970), 1964: 844.

8   Sherman Harris, "Present Status of Klans in the South," May 20, 1964, folder 75-01-41-19, SRCC; *Washington Post,* October 8, 1964; *Atlanta Constitution,* April 5, 1965.

9   *Washington Post,* October 8, 1964; Harris, "Present Status."

10   *Washington Post,* July 5, 1964, October 8, 1964; *Louisville Courier-Journal,* July 18, 1964; *Atlanta Constitution,* April 5, 1965; Harold H. Martin and Kenneth Fairly, " 'We Got Nothing to Hide,' " *Saturday Evening Post,* January 3, 1965, pp. 32–33; Don Whitehead, *Attack on Terror: The FBI Against the Ku Klux Klan in Mississippi* (New York, 1970), pp. 9, 22–25; Florence Mars, *Witness in Philadelphia* (Baton Rouge, 1977), pp. 120–21. Contemporary estimates of Klan strength, which appear to have been little more than educated guesses, vary widely. For example, writing in May 1964, Sherman Harris ("Present Status") reported it as 45,000–65,000, while the *Washington Post* on July 5, 1964, supplied a figure of 75,000 as the total *national* strength of the Ku Klux Klan. On the other hand, Martin and Fairly ("Nothing to Hide," p. 33) claimed that in January 1965 there were only 10,000 dues-paying klansmen in the South, and Bill Shipp of the *Atlanta Constitution,* writing on April 5, 1965, gave that figure for the entire country. Of course, a decline in Klan strength between 1964 and 1965 could explain some of these differences. But on April 23 of the latter year the *Birmingham News* estimated there were 50,000–60,000 klansmen in the South, and three days later the *Memphis Commercial Appeal* put the figure at 9,000.

11   *Miami Herald,* March 25, 1964, July 26, 1964; Notes, undated, folder

75-03-17-14, SRCC; *Nashville Banner,* March 4, 1964; *Florida Times-Union* (Jacksonville), March 24, 1964, April 20, 1964; *New York Times,* March 24, 1964, p. 24; *Chattanooga Times,* March 24, 1964; U.S., Department of Justice, *Annual Report of the Attorney General of the United States for the Fiscal Year Ended June 30, 1965* (Washington, 1965), p. 185.

12   Berl I. Bernhard to Lee White, October 25, 1963, box 24, Lee White Files, Papers of President Kennedy, JFK; Joseph F. Dolan, Memorandum for Burke Marshall, June 5, 1964, box 6, Files of Lee C. White, LBJ; Emile Schmeidler, "Shaping Ideas and Actions: CORE, SCLC, and SNCC in the Struggle for Equality, 1960–1966" (Ph.D. diss., University of Michigan, 1980), p. 150; David R. Colburn, "The St. Augustine Business Community: Desegregation, 1963–1964," in *Southern Businessmen and Desegregation,* ed. Elizabeth Jacoway and David R. Colburn (Baton Rouge, 1982), p. 216; Stephen B. Oates, *Let the Trumpet Sound: The Life of Martin Luther King, Jr.* (New York, 1982), pp. 293–94; *St. Augustine Record,* June 19, 1963; *Florida Times-Union,* October 17, 1963, November 6, 1963; *Pittsburgh Courier,* September 28, 1963; *Atlanta Daily World,* October 27, 1963, *St. Petersburg Times,* November 22, 1963; *Daytona Beach Morning Journal,* September 20, 1963; BM, Memorandum for the Attorney General, November 5, 1963, box 3, Burke Marshall Papers, JFK.

13   Colburn, "St. Augustine," pp. 221–22; Oates, *Trumpet,* p. 294; Walter I. Pozen to Lee C. White, box 6, White Files, LBJ; David R. Colburn, *Racial Change and Community Crisis: St. Augustine, Florida, 1877–1980* (New York, 1985), p. 61.

14   Colburn, "St. Augustine," p. 222; Oates, *Trumpet,* pp. 295, 298; *St. Petersburg Times,* June 10, 1964, June 11, 1964; Schmeidler, "Shaping Ideas and Actions," pp. 150, 160.

15   "Ku Klux Klan" *Life,* June 24, 1961, p. 21; Reverend Elizabeth J. Miller, "Report on St. Augustine, Florida," box 20, folder 43, King Papers–King Center; Colburn, *Racial Change,* pp. 89, 93.

16   Martin Luther King, Jr., telegram to the President, May 29, 1964, White Files, LBJ.

17   Martin Luther King, Jr., telegram to Attorney General Robert F. Kennedy, March 30, 1964, folder 37, box 27, SCLC Papers; Lee C. White, Memorandum for the Files, June 10, 1964; Wyatt Tee Walker, telegram to the President, June 9, 1964, and Martin Luther King, Jr., and Robert B. Hayling, telegram to the President, June 10, 1964, box 5, White Files, LBJ.

18   Lee C. White, Memorandum for the Files, June 1, 1964, box 6, White Files, LBJ.

19   Lee C. White, Memorandum for the Files, June 10, 1964, box 5, White Files, LBJ. For biographical information on White, see *Who's Who in America,* 43d ed., 2 vols. (Chicago, 1984), 2:3470.

20   Lee C. White to Wyatt Tee Walker, June 10, 1964, Lee C. White, Memorandum for the Files, June 13, 1964, and Carl Holman, Memorandum to William L. Taylor, June 11, 1964, all in box 5, White Files, LBJ; *Miami Herald,* June 16, 1964; Miller, "Report on St. Augustine"; Colburn, *Racial Change,* p. 105.

21   Leon Friedman, "The Federal Courts in the South: Judge Bryan Simpson and His Reluctant Brethren," in *Southern Justice,* ed. Leon Friedman (New York, 1965), pp. 203–207; Lee C. White, Memoranda for the Files, June 22, 1964, and June 26, 1964, box 6, White Files, LBJ; *Florida Times-Union* (Jacksonville), July 26, 1964; *St. Petersburg Times,* January 26, 1964.

22   *Florida Times-Union,* June 26, 1964.

23   Ibid., June 27, 1964; *New York Times,* June 27, 1964, p. 1; *Chicago Sun-Times,* June 27, 1964, Lee C. White, Memorandum for the Files, June 26, 1964, and Memorandum for the President, July 15, 1964, both in box 6, White Files, LBJ; Colburn, "St. Augustine," p. 229 and *Racial Change,* p. 107.

24   August Meier and Elliott Rudwick, *CORE: A Study in the Civil Rights Movement, 1942–1968* (New York, 1973), pp. 261–68; Judy Bollins, "CORE's Chronological Listing of Intimidations and Harassments in Louisiana," undated, series 5, box 12, folder 4, CORE Papers; "Chronology on Jonesboro," undated, and CORE, "Bogalusa, Louisiana, Incident Summary January 25–February 21," undated, series 5, box 12, folder 7, CORE Papers; Paul Good, "Klantown USA," *Nation,* February 1, 1965, pp. 110–12; *Washington Post,* January 11, 1965; *Atlanta Daily World,* August 2, 1964; James Farmer, "It's Going To Be an Expensive Summer," undated, group III, series B, box 327, NAACP Papers.

25   Reverend Francis Gedden, telegram to Lee White, April 7, 1965, Gen. HU2/ST 18, WHCF, LBJ.

26   Peter R. Teachout, "Louisiana Underlaw," in Friedman, ed., *Southern Justice,* p. 58.

27   Bollins, "CORE's Chronological Listing."

28   CORE, "Bogalusa, Louisiana."

29   "Chronology on Jonesboro."

30   Bollins, "CORE's Chronological Listing"; Maceo W. Hubbard, Memorandum to Burke Marshall, September 23, 1963, box 32, Marshall Papers; Meier and Rudwick, *CORE,* p. 268; James Farmer to "Dear Friend," February 16, 1965, series 5, box 12, folder 7, CORE Papers; Ronnie Moore, telegram to Attorney General Robert Kennedy, July 25, 1964, series 1, box 12, folder 5, CORE Papers.

31   Plaintiffs Trial Brief, United States v. Clark, No. 3438-64 Civ. (S.D. Ala. 1964); SNCC Press Release, July 9, 1964, box 35, folder 141, SNCC Papers; "What Will the Future Be," undated, box 96, folder 59, SNCC Papers; *Jackson Daily News,* July 6, 1964; Zev to Nooker, Marcia, Marv, et al., July 26,

1964, series 5, box 11, folder 1, CORE Papers; "Newsmen Attacked as Police Look On," *Editor & Publisher,* February 27, 1965, p. 15.

32 SNCC Press Release, July 9, 1964; Untitled and undated notes, folder 75-03-17-14, SRCC; *Raleigh News and Observer,* August 25, 1964.

33 Meier and Rudwick, *CORE,* p. 269; Clayborne Carson, *In Struggle: SNCC and the Black Awakening of the 1960s* (Cambridge, Mass., 1981), p. 78; "What is COFO," COFO publication #6, undated, series 5, box 22, folder 4, CORE Papers; James Forman, *The Making of Black Revolutionaries* (New York, 1972), pp. 288, 372; Allen J. Matusow, "From Civil Rights to Black Power: The Case of SNCC, 1960–1966," in *Twentieth Century America: Recent Interpretations,* ed. Barton J. Bernstein and Allen J. Matusow, 2d ed. (New York, 1972), p. 499; Untitled and undated document in "Miss. Summer Project" folder, box 170, SNCC Papers; Louis E. Lomax, "The Road to Mississippi," in *Mississippi Eyewitness: The Three Civil Rights Workers—How They Were Murdered,* ed. John Howard Griffin (Menlo Park, Calif., 1964), p. 10; "Summer Project: Mississippi," *Lawyers Guild Practitioner* 24 (Winter 1965): 35, 40.

34 Carson, *In Struggle,* p. 98; Schmeidler, "Shaping Ideas and Actions," p. 290; Howell Raines, *My Soul Is Rested: Movement Days in the Deep South* (New York, 1977), p. 287 (interview with Lawrence Guyot); Robert D. Owen, Memorandum to Burke Marshall, May 6, 1964, box 8, Marshall Papers; *New York Times,* November 30, 1963, p. 8; Neil R. McMillen, "Black Enfranchisement in Mississippi: Federal Enforcement and Black Protest in the 1960s," *Journal of Southern History* 43 (August 1977): 364–67. SNCC's James Forman claimed later that, although forcing a confrontation between the federal government and Mississippi was part of the original thinking behind the Summer Project, through discussion and analysis this idea changed, as it was concluded that Washington was unlikely to crack down on Mississippi by using troops there. *Making of Black Revolutionaries,* p. 373. Little in the planning or conduct of the project supports this ambiguous account, but as a reflection of the feelings of participants in the project, it may be accurate.

35 Quoted in Carson, *In Struggle,* p. 99.

36 Ibid., pp. 112–14; Undated and untitled document cited in n. 33; "Washington Hearings on Mississippi," undated, box 182, folder 494, SNCC Papers; Raines, *My Soul Is Rested,* pp. 287–88 (interview with Lawrence Guyot); Pat Watters and Reese Cleghorn, *Climbing Jacob's Ladder: The Arrival of Negroes in Southern Politics* (New York, 1967), pp. 66–67; McMillen, "Black Enfranchisement," p. 367. When interviewed by the author, John Lewis denied that SNCC deliberately set out to get white students killed, but he acknowledged that the Summer Project created a high likelihood that this would happen. Councilman John Lewis, personal interview with the author at the Atlanta City Hall, Atlanta, Georgia, June 5, 1984.

37   *Louisville Courier-Journal,* June 16, 1964; John Doar, personal interview with the author at his office in New York City, October 23, 1980; John Dittmer, "The Movement in McComb" (unpublished paper presented at the annual meeting of the Organization of American Historians, April 1984); Arthur M. Schlesinger, Jr., *Robert Kennedy and His Times,* 2 vols. (Boston, 1978), 2:669; Howard Zinn, *SNCC: The New Abolitionists* (Boston, 1964), p. 198.

38   William Bradford Huie, *Three Lives for Mississippi* (New York, 1965), p. 143; Lomax, "The Road to Mississippi," pp. 8–9; Whitehead, *Attack on Terror,* pp. 43–44.

39   Cleveland Sellers (with Robert Terrell), *The River of No Return: The Autobiography of a Black Militant and the Life and Death of SNCC* (New York, 1973), p. 94.

40   Benjamin Muse, Confidential Memorandum Re: The Problem of Law Enforcement in Mississippi, n.d. [June 1964], folder 75-10-59-10, SRCC; *Memphis Commercial Appeal,* May 21, 1964; David Welsh, "Valley of Fear," in Griffin, ed., *Mississippi Eyewitness,* p. 54; Whitehead, *Attack on Terror,* p. 6; Benjamin Muse, "Report on Mississippi," January 1964, box 8, Marshall Papers.

41   John Doar, Memorandum to Burke Marshall, May 19, 1964, box 8, Marshall Papers; Welsh, "Valley of Fear," p. 54; COFO, "Case Studies of Intimidation," May 6, 1964 [?], series 5, box 22, folder 3, CORE Papers; Untitled and undated COFO publication, box 14, folder 9, CORE Papers; *New York Times,* May 30, 1964, p. 1; Benjamin Muse, *The American Negro Revolution: From Non-Violence to Black Power* (Bloomington, Ind., 1968), p. 140; *Delta Democrat-Times* (Greenville, Miss.), May 11, 1964; COFO, Report Submitted to Mississippi Advisory Committee, U.S. Commission on Civil Rights, March 18, 1964, box 141, folder 12, SCLC Papers; Robert Moses and Aaron Henry to Dr. A. B. Britton, March 5, 1964, box 100, folder A:XV 160, SNCC Papers.

42   Mississippi Summer Project, "Running Summary of Incidents," undated, series 3, box 22, CORE Papers.

43   "Bombings in McComb, Mississippi," September 23, 1964, and Nicholas deB. Katzenbach, Memorandum for the President, undated, both in box 8, Marshall Papers. "McComb Incident Summary," located in series 5, box 14, folder 11, CORE Papers, lists only twelve bombings for this same period, but it often lumps multiple incidents together in a single entry.

44   "McComb Incident Summary"; "The Ku Klux Klan on the Way Back," *Newsweek,* October 19, 1964, p. 51; Report on Beatings in McComb, June 8, 1964, box 35, folder 141, SNCC Papers; Watters and Cleghorn, *Climbing Jacob's Ladder,* p. 103.

45   Mr. and Mrs. G. L. Sweeny, telegram to the President, July 8, 1964, Gen. HU2/ST 24, WHCF, LBJ.

46   Mississippi Summer Project, "Running Summary of Incidents"; Calvin Trillin, "Letters from Jackson," *New Yorker,* August 29, 1964, p. 80.

47   *Atlanta Journal-Constitution,* May 17, 1964; "Johnson, Paul Burney, Jr.," *Biographical Directory of the Governors of the United States, 1789–1978,* ed. Robert Sobel and John Raimo, 4 vols. (Westport, Conn., 1978), 2:831–32; Paul Johnson Oral History, pp. 27–29, 34; Walter Lord, *The Past That Would Not Die* (London, 1965), p. 235; Muse, Confidential Memorandum Re: Law Enforcement.

48   Burke Marshall, transcript of oral history interview, October 28, 1968, p. 31, LBJ; Huie, *Three Lives,* pp. 37–38; Muse, Confidential Memorandum Re: Law Enforcement; "Mississippi: Terror on Schedule," *Newsweek,* October 15, 1964, p. 72.

49   Mississippi Summer Project, "Running Summary."

50   Southern Regional Council, *Law Enforcement,* p. 70.

51   Al Carmines et al., "To Whom It May Concern," series 5, box 22, folder 4, CORE Papers; Affidavits 1–5, Columbus, Mississippi, Beatings Press Release, June–July folder, box 35, SNCC Papers; Welsh, "Valley of Fear," pp. 53–54; Southern Regional Council, *Law Enforcement,* p. 18.

52   Muse, Confidential Memorandum Re: Law Enforcement.

53   Charles Evers, telegram to the President, October 23, 1964, Gen. HU2/ST 24, WHCF, LBJ; SNCC, Press Release, November 27, 1964, box 171, SNCC Papers; Martin and Fairly, "Nothing to Hide," p. 31; James H. Rener, "The Case of the Disappearing Docket," in Friedman, ed., *Southern Justice,* pp. 104–105.

54   Nhagwin M. Jackson, telegram to Robert Kennedy, May 14, 1964, box 10, Attorney General's General Correspondence, Robert F. Kennedy Papers, JFK.

55   Charles Evers, telegram to the President, February 2, 1964, and Dave Dennis, telegram to the President, May 20, 1964, Gen. HU2/ST 24, WHCF, LBJ; James Farmer, telegram to J. Edgar Hoover, May 20, 1964, series 5, box 15, folder 2, CORE Papers; SNCC Press Release, January 10, 1964, box 99, SNCC Papers; *Atlanta Daily World,* May 21, 1964.

56   Unofficial Transcript of the Open Session of the Hearings Held by the Mississippi Advisory Committee to the United States Civil Rights Commission, Natchez, Mississippi, May 6, 1964, series 5, box 14, folder 9, CORE Papers.

57   Bob Moses, Memo to "Friends of Freedom in Mississippi," April 6, 1964, series 5, box 22, folder 2, CORE Papers. For Zinn's views, see his *SNCC,* pp. 192, 197.

58   Mimeograph copy of letter from Bob Moses to President Lyndon B. Johnson, June 14, 1964, and COFO Press Release, June 17, 1964, June–July folder, box 35, SNCC Papers.

59   Memorandum for the President, June 17, 1964, Ex. HU2/ST 24, WHCF, LBJ.

60   Meier and Rudwick, *CORE*, p. 277.

61   Lee C. White, Memorandum for the President, June 17, 1964; Clarence J. Harris et al. to President Lyndon B. Johnson, April 27, 1964, box 5, White Files, LBJ; Los Angeles Field Office Report, March 16, 1964, document LA 10-63822, SNCC File, FBI; Julie Davis Jewitt to Burke Marshall, April 30, 1964, A:I:76, CORE Papers, Addendum 1944–1968.

62   Noel Day to Clifford Alexander, June 9, 1964, and attachment, box 5, White Files, LBJ.

63   Mike Thelwell to William [*sic*] Penn Warren, May 14, 1964, box 182, folder 38, SNCC Papers; *Atlanta Daily World,* June 5, 1964; Summary of Major Points in Testimony by Citizens of Mississippi, [June 8, 1964], box 100, folder 162, SNCC Papers; Press release copy of letter from Harold Taylor to President Lyndon B. Johnson, June 11, 1964, and attached summary of testimony, box 35, folder 141, SNCC Papers.

64   Taylor to Johnson, June 11, 1964, SNCC Papers.

65   Mike Thelwell to Representative John Lindsay, June 16, 1964, Mike Thelwell to Representative Silvio O. Conte, June 6, 1964, and Silvio O. Conte to Mike Thelwell, all in box 164, folder 100, SNCC Papers; Memorandum from Council of Federated Organizations to Members of the United States Congress, June 3, 1964, box 164, folder 100, SNCC Papers.

66   Lee C. White, Memorandum for the President, June 17, 1964, Ex. HU2/ST 24, WHCF, LBJ; Lee C. White, Memorandum for Burke Marshall, June 17, 1964, Gen. HU2/ST 24, WHCF, LBJ; COFO Press Release, June 17, 1964, box 35, folder 141, SNCC Papers.

67   *Baton Rouge State-Times,* March 26, 1964; Stephen Sokoloff and Mr. and Mrs. M. Sokoloff to the President, July 9, 1964, Gen. HU2/ST 24, WHCF, LBJ; Burke Marshall, Memorandum for the Attorney General, June 5, 1964, box 3, Marshall Papers; Attorney General, Memorandum for the President, June 5, 1964, Ex. HU2/ST 24, LBJ.

68   Attorney General, Memorandum for the President, June 5, 1964, LBJ.

69   Burke Marshall to Neil Staebler, July 13, 1964, Gen. HU2/ST 24, WHCF, LBJ.

70   Nicholas Katzenbach, Memorandum for the President, July 1, 1964, box 6, White Files, LBJ. For the views of the law professors, see SNCC Press Release, July 9, 1964, box 35, folder 103, SNCC Papers, and "See Here, General Kennedy," *Time,* July 10, 1964, p. 45.

71   Quoted in James Farmer, form letter, June 29, 1964, series 5, box 14, folder 9, CORE Papers.

72   Meier and Rudwick, *CORE*, p. 276; Lomax, "Road to Mississippi," pp. 9–12; Huie, *Three Lives*, pp. 70–71, 88–89, 99–102; Whitehead, *Attack on Terror*, pp. 30–31, 44; Muse, *American Negro Revolution*, pp. 141–44; Mars, *Witness in Philadelphia*, p. 86.

73   Lomax, "Road to Mississippi," pp. 12–13; Whitehead, *Attack on Terror*, pp. 47–52; Anna Johnston Diggs, telegram to the President, June 25, 1964, Gen. HU2/ST 24, WHCF, LBJ. While Lomax says the three young men did not learn about what had happened in Longdale until they reached Meridian, Whitehead, who had access to the FBI's investigative files on the case, says Schwerner heard about the events there before leaving Ohio and learned further details after reaching Meridian.

74   Whitehead, *Attack on Terror*, pp. 53–61.

75   Ibid., pp. 57–58; Huie, *Three Lives*, pp. 155, 173; "The Philadelphia, Mississippi Case: Chronology of Contacts with Agents of the Federal Government," box 5, White Files, LBJ.

76   "Philadelphia, Mississippi Case"; Whitehead, *Attack on Terror*, pp. 63–65; Lee C. White, Memorandum to the Files, June 23, 1964, box 6, White Files, LBJ; *St. Louis Post-Dispatch*, June 24, 1964; Mars, *Witness in Philadelphia*, p. 93.

77   Mars, *Witness in Philadelphia*, pp. 87–88, 92; Welsh, "Valley of Fear," p. 58; "Civil Rights: The Grim Roster," *Time*, July 3, 1964, p. 20; Anna Johnston Diggs, telegram to the President, June 24, 1964, Gen. HU2/ST 24, WHCF, LBJ; "Summer Project: Mississippi 1964," pp. 38–39.

78   Whitehead, *Attack on Terror*, pp. 65–70, 75–81; *Delta Democrat-Times*, June 23, 1964; Lee C. White, Memorandum for the Files, June 23, 1964, box 6, White Files, LBJ.

79   Whitehead, *Attack on Terror*, pp. 125–35; A. Rosen, Memoranda to Mr. Belmont, September 16, 1964, and September 21, 1964, MIBURN File, FBI; Transcript of Record, at 400-33, United States v. Price, Crim. No. 5291 (S.D. Miss. 1967); David M. Spain, "Post Mortem Examination Report on the Body of James Chaney," box 100, folder 158, SNCC Papers and "Mississippi Autopsy," in Griffin, ed., *Mississippi Eyewitness;* Paul Johnson Oral History, p. 33. Although Spain's autopsy supports Johnson's account of what was done to Chaney, the governor's assertion that the klansmen intended only to hang the three civil rights workers up in a big cotton bag to frighten them, and murdered Schwerner and Goodman only to eliminate witnesses to the extemporaneous killing of their black companion, is contradicted by the confessions of two participants in the crime, which were made public during a federal trial in 1967.

80   Record at 401-13, Meyers v. United States, 377 F.2d 412 (5th Cir. 1967); Statement of James Lackey, undated, document 44-25873-151, PENVIC

File, FBI; Michal R. Belknap, "The Legal Legacy of Lemuel Penn," *Howard Law Journal* 25 (1982): 467, 470; Bill Shipp, *Murder at Broad River Bridge* (Atlanta, 1981), pp. 5–10.

81 Loretta Markman et al., night letter to President Lyndon B. Johnson, undated, Gen. HU2/CO 1 (South), WHCF, LBJ. The telegrams are in Gen. HU2/ST 10, WHCF, LBJ.

82 LBJ to Mrs. Lemuel H. Penn, July 13, 1964, and Horace Busby, Memorandum for Jack Valenti, July 13, 1964, Lemuel Penn Name File, WHCF, LBJ.

83 A. Rosen, Memorandum to Mr. Belmont, August 6, 1964, document 44-25873-151, PENVIC File; Note to Mr. White and Lee C. White, Memorandum for Jack Valenti, July 17, 1964, box 6, White Files, LBJ; Whitehead, *Attack on Terror*, p. 69; *Washington Post*, June 24, 1964; Meier and Rudwick, *CORE*, p. 277.

84 *Washington Post*, June 30, 1964; Mrs. Louis Levant to President Lyndon B. Johnson, November 11, 1964, Gen. HU2/ST 24, WHCF, LBJ; [Mr. and Mrs. Robert Goodman] to President Lyndon B. Johnson, August 17, 1964, and Nathan H. Schwerner to Lyndon Johnson, August 17, 1964, Ex. HU2/ST 24, WHCF, LBJ.

85 *Baltimore Sun*, June 26, 1964; Mrs. E. M. Stetzer to Mr. Farmer, July 9, 1964, series 5, box 14, folder 9, CORE Papers; COFO, Memorandum to Parents of All Mississippi Volunteers, undated, box 100, folder 160, SNCC Papers; *Parents Mississippi Freedom Committee of Southern California Newsletter*, vol. 1, no. 1, September 1964, box 102, SNCC Papers; Mrs. Mildred H. Smith et al. to President Lyndon B. Johnson, July 9, 1964, Mr. and Mrs. Marcus Morse to President Lyndon Johnson, December 6, 1964, and Joseph F. Dolan to Elmer J. Maloney, July 27, 1964, all in Gen. HU2/ST 24, WHCF, LBJ; Wiley Austin Branton, transcript of oral history interview by Steven Lawson, October 21, 1970, p. 29, CUOHP.

86 Joseph F. Dolan to Elmer J. Maloney, July 27, 1964, Gen. HU2/ST 24, WHCF, LBJ.

87 SNCC Press Release, June 30, 1964, box 35, June–July folder, SNCC Papers.

88 SNCC Press Release, undated, box 100, folder 158, SNCC Papers.

89 John Lewis to Lyndon B. Johnson, August 19, 1964, Ex. HU2/ST 24, WHCF, LBJ; *Providence Journal*, June 28, 1964; *St. Louis Post-Dispatch*, June 28, 1964; *Jackson Daily News*, June 29, 1964; *Washington Post*, October 15, 1964; Forman, *Making of Black Revolutionaries*, p. 381.

90 Council of Federated Organizations v. Mize, 339 F.2d 898 (5th Cir. 1964); COFO Policy Statement, July 10, 1964, box 141, folder 13, SCLC Papers; William Kunstler to Robert F. Kennedy, series 5, box 5, folder 8, CORE Papers.

91   339 F.2d at 900; Southern Regional Council, *Law Enforcement in Missis-sippi* (Atlanta, 1964), p. 33; NAACP, *Triple Murder: States Rights, Mississippi Style* (New York, 1964), p. 2; *Atlanta Daily World,* April 25, 1964; "Report of the Special Mississippi Investigation Committee of the National Board of Directors of the National Association for the Advancement of Colored People," July 23, 1964, box 11, Attorney General's General Correspondence, Robert F. Kennedy Papers; Lee C. White, Memorandum to Mrs. Junita Roberts, June 18, 1964, Lee C. White to Bishop Stephen Gill Spotswood, July 17, 1964, and Stephen Gill Spotswood, telegram to the President, June 26, 1964, all in Ex. HU2/ST 24, WHCF, LBJ; *Washington Post,* June 24, 1964; *Baltimore Sun,* June 27, 1964; *Jackson Daily News,* June 29, 1964.

92   Petition to the President of the United States, undated, and William B. Stanley et al. to President Lyndon B. Johnson, Gen. HU2/ST 24, WHCF, LBJ; Petitions headed "To President Lyndon B. Johnson," undated, WHCF, LBJ; *New York Times,* July 8, 1964, p. 20.

93   Edward L. Schieffen to the President, June 27, 1964, Gen. HU2/ST 24, WHCF, LBJ.

94   *New York Times,* June 25, 1964, p. 32; *Baltimore Afro-American,* July 4, 1964; *Atlanta Constitution,* July 15, 1964; *Arkansas Gazette,* September 28, 1964, and October 7, 1964.

95   *Washington Post,* June 25, 1964; Robert F. Ellsworth to the President, July 1, 1964, and Leona Goodell to Lee White, July 13, 1964, both in Gen. HU2/ST 24, WHCF, LBJ; Press Release, entitled "18 Congressmen Send Open Letter to President Johnson to Ask Aid to Stop Anti-Rights Violence in Mis-sissippi," October 2, 1964, box 171, folder 433, SNCC Papers. The petitions submitted by Ryan on July 30 and July 31 are in Gen. HU2/ST 24, WHCF, LBJ.

96   Lee C. White to William F. Ryan, October 26, 1964, Ex. HU2/ST 24, WHCF, LBJ.

97   A. Rosen, Memorandum for Mr. Belmont, July 14, 1964, document 44-25873-3, PENVIC File.

98   John Edgar Hoover, Memorandum for Mr. Tolson et al., July 16, 1964, C. A. Evans to Mr. Belmont, July 12, 1964, document 44-25873-10, C. A. Evans, Memorandum for Mr. Belmont, July 11, 1964, document 44-25873-15, and A. Rosen, Memorandum for Mr. Belmont, July 13, 1964, document 44-25873-31, all in PENVIC File (the quote is from the last of these sources).

99   SAC, Atlanta, AIRTEL to Director, FBI, August 5, 1964, document 44-25873-143, M. A. Jones, Memorandum to Mr. DeLoach, August 7, 1964, document 44-25873-164, A. Rosen, Memorandum for Mr. Belmont, August 6, 1964, document 44-25873-151, and Statement of James S. Lackey, undated, document 44-25873-151, all in PENVIC File; FBI Press Release, August 6,

1964, Department of Justice, Administrative History, vol. 8, pt. 19a, Documentary Supplement, LBJ; William Bradford Huie, "Murder: The Klan on Trial," *Saturday Evening Post,* June 19, 1965, p. 86; *New York Times,* August 7, 1964, p. 13.

100   White Oral History, p. 12.

101   Ibid.; Whitehead, *Attack on Terror,* p. 71; John Edgar Hoover, Memorandum to Mr. Tolson, July 16, 1964, and C. D. DeLoach, Memorandum to Mr. Mohr, August 5, 1964, PENVIC File; Lee White, proposed press release, August 5, 1964, Ex. HU2/ST 24, WHCF, LBJ.

102   *St. Louis Post-Dispatch,* June 24, 1964; *Nashville Banner,* June 24, 1964; *Los Angeles Times,* June 25, 1964; White House Statement, June 23, 1964, Ex. HU2/ST 24, WHCF, LBJ; Whitehead, *Attack on Terror,* pp. 71–73.

103   Doar Interview; *Delta Democrat-Times,* June 25, 1964; *Jackson Daily News,* June 25, 1964; *St. Louis Post-Dispatch,* June 25, 1964; *New York Times,* June 26, 1964, p. 1; Raines, *My Soul Is Rested,* p. 289; Muse, Confidential Memorandum Re: Law Enforcement; "Briefing by Mr. Allen Dulles re: His Trip to Mississippi for the President," June 26, 1964, Ex. HU2/ST 24, WHCF, LBJ.

104   *St. Louis Post-Dispatch,* June 26, 1964; "Briefing by Mr. Dulles"; Muse, Confidential Memorandum Re: Law Enforcement; Robert F. Kennedy, Transcript of oral history interview by Anthony Lewis, December 4, 1964, p. 663, JFK Oral; Nicholas deB. Katzenbach, Memorandum for the President, July 1, 1964, box 6, White Files.

105   Whitehead, *Attack on Terror,* pp. 80, 89; *Louisville Courier-Journal,* June 27, 1964; Lee C. White to William F. Ryan, October 26, 1964, and J. Edgar Hoover to Walter W. Jenkins, July 13, 1964, Ex. HU2/ST 24, WHCF, LBJ; *Christian Science Monitor,* June 29, 1964; Doar Interview; *New York Herald Tribune,* July 11, 1964; John Doar and Dorothy Landsberg, "The Performance of the FBI in Investigating Violations of Federal Laws Protecting the Right to Vote— 1960–1967," in U.S., Senate, Select Committee to Study Governmental Operations with Respect to Intelligence Activities, *Hearings . . . ,* pt. VI, *Federal Bureau of Investigation,* 94th Cong., 1st sess. 1975, p. 950; Dorothy Landsberg, personal interview with the author at her office in Washington, D.C., October 22, 1980.

106   Frank J. Donner, *The Age of Surveillance: The Aims and Methods of America's Political Intelligence System* (New York, 1980), p. 206; F. J. Baumgardner, Memorandum to W. C. Sullivan, August 27, 1964, document 157-9-2, and J. H. Gale, Memorandum for Mr. Tolson, July 30, 1964, document 157-9-3, White Hate File, FBI; U.S. Senate, Select Committee, *Hearings,* pp. 602–603, and *Final Report,* book III, *Intelligence Activities and the Rights of Americans,* 94th

Cong., 2d sess., S. Rept. 755, 1976, pp. 18–20; William C. Sullivan (with Bill Brown), *The Bureau: My Thirty Years in Hoover's FBI* (New York, 1979), p. 129.

107 Director, FBI, Memorandum, September 2, 1964, in Senate Select Committee, *Hearings,* p. 378.

108 Senate Intelligence Committee, *Rights of Americans,* p. 19.

109 Director, FBI, Memorandum to the Attorney General, September 2, 1965, in Senate Intelligence Committee, *Hearings,* p. 514.

110 Ibid.; A. H. Belmont, Memorandum to Mr. Tolson, August 31, 1965, document 157-9-?, White Hate File; Donner, *Age of Surveillance,* p. 207; Schlesinger, *Robert Kennedy,* 2:671.

111 *Jackson Clarion-Ledger,* July 11, 1964; *Memphis Commercial Appeal,* July 10, 1964; "Next: A National Police Force?" *U.S. News & World Report,* December 7, 1964, p. 44; *New York Herald Tribune,* July 11, 1964; *St. Louis Post-Dispatch,* August 6, 1964; Mars, *Witness in Philadelphia,* pp. 113–14, 117; Calvin Trillin, "Letter from Jackson," *New Yorker,* August 29, 1964, p. 80.

112 Quoted in "J. Edgar Hoover and the FBI," *Newsweek,* December 7, 1964, p. 24.

113 Nicholas deB. Katzenbach, Memorandum for the President, July 1, 1964, box 6, White Files, LBJ.

114 Burke Marshall to Samuel S. Stratton, July 10, 1964, box 164, SNCC Papers.

115 Joseph F. Dolan to Elmer J. Maloney, July 27, 1964, Gen. HU2/ST 24, WHCF, LBJ; Nicholas deB. Katzenbach, Memorandum for the President, undated, box 8, Marshall Papers.

116 Nicholas deB. Katzenbach, Memorandum for the President, July 1, 1964, box 6, White Files, LBJ.

117 Joseph F. Dolan to Elmer J. Maloney, July 27, 1964, Gen. HU2/ST 24, WHCF, LBJ; *Louisville Courier-Journal,* December 27, 1964.

118 Whitehead, *Attack on Terror,* pp. 175–95; Mars, *Witness in Philadelphia,* p. 140; Lee C. White to Mrs. Louis Levant, December 16, 1964, Gen. HU2/ST 24, WHCF, LBJ.

119 Mars, *Witness in Philadelphia,* p. 142. Arrested along with Rainey, Price, and Burkes on section 241 charges were the following: Olen Burrage, owner of the farm where the bodies were found; Jimmy Lee Townsend, a service station attendant; Herman Tucker, the bulldozer operator who built Burrage's dam; Billy Wayne Posey, a service station operator; Jerry McGrew Sharpe, a used car salesman; Edgar Ray Killen, a sawmill owner and Baptist preacher; Bernard Akin, owner of a mobile home park; Frank Herndon, a restaurant manager; Oliver Warner, Jr., operator of a drive-in grocery; James "Pete" Harris, a truck driver; James Edward Jordan, a truck driver; Horace Doyle Barnette, a truck driver;

Travis Barnette, half-owner of a garage and Horace's brother; Alton Wayne Roberts, a nightclub bouncer; and Jimmy Snowden, a laundry truck driver. Ibid., p. 144. In addition, two other men, Earl B. Akin (Bernard's son) and Tommy Horne, were charged with misprision of a felony. See ibid., p. 143; Whitehead, *Attack on Terror*, p. 201.

120 For an example of their use in this way, see Augusta Levant to President Lyndon B. Johnson, November 11, 1964, and Lee C. White to Mrs. Louis Levant, December 16, 1964, both in Gen. HU2/ST 24, WHCF, LBJ.

121 December 6, 1964.

Chapter Seven

1 Quoted in Don Whitehead, *Attack on Terror: The FBI Against the Ku Klux Klan in Mississippi* (New York, 1970), p. 203.

2 383 U.S. 745 (1966).

3 *Atlanta Constitution,* August 15, 1964.

4 SAC, Atlanta, AIRTEL to Director, FBI, August 10, 1964, document 44-25873-164, PENVIC File, FBI.

5 FBI, Atlanta, teletype to the Director, August 11, 1964, document 44-25873-208, and A. Rosen, Memorandum to Mr. Belmont, August 10, 1964, document 25873-162, PENVIC File.

6 *Atlanta Constitution,* August 15, 1964.

7 A. Rosen, Memorandum to Mr. Belmont, August 14, 1964, document 44-25873-191, Memorandum to Solicitor General Clete D. Johnson, August 15, 1964, document 44-25873-180, FBI, Atlanta, teletype to Director, FBI, August 11, 1964, document 44-25873-208, A. Rosen, Memorandum to Mr. Belmont, August 21, 1964, document 44-25873-234, FBI, Atlanta, teletype to Director, FBI, August 21, 1964, document 44-25873-194, and A. Rosen, Memorandum to Mr. Belmont, August 22, 1964, document 44-25873-236, all in PENVIC File; Bill Shipp, *Murder at Broad River Bridge* (Atlanta, 1981), pp. 51–52.

8 Shipp, *Murder,* p. 50; *New York Times,* August 26, 1964, p. 20. The fourth man the FBI had arrested, Herbert Guest, was not indicted. He had not been in the car from which the fatal shots were fired. Guest had been present at his garage when the other three klansmen returned there after the shooting to clean the guns (one of which belonged to him) that they had used. Consequently, consideration was given to prosecuting him as an accessory after the fact. The state prosecutors concluded, however, that under Georgia law they did not have a strong case against him on that charge. See A. Rosen, Memorandum to Mr. Belmont, August 21, 1964, document 44-25873-236, PENVIC File.

9 Statement of James S. Lackey, given August 6, 1964, serial 44-25873-184, pp. 696–99, PENVIC File.

10   *Athens Banner-Herald,* August 31, 1964, September 1, 1964, September 2, 1964, September 3, 1964; *Macon Telegraph,* September 4, 1964; Shipp, *Murder,* pp. 50–63. If two persons are engaged in a conspiracy, the declarations of one made while the conspiracy is actually in progress and in furtherance of it are admissible against the other because, under the substantive law of conspiracy, coconspirators are criminally liable for each other's actions and statements. The requirement that the statement be made in furtherance of the conspiracy should result in the exclusion of those statements, such as Lackey's, possessing evidential value solely as admissions; nevertheless, if one of this type was made during the continuance of the conspiracy, courts will generally admit it. See Edward W. Cleary et al., *McCormick's Handbook of the Law of Evidence,* 2d ed. (St. Paul, 1972), p. 645.

11   FBI Atlanta, teletype to Director, FBI, September 8, 1964, document 44-25873-273, PENVIC File; *Macon Telegraph,* September 4, 1964; Shipp, *Murder,* pp. 52–64. Both Shipp and the *Telegraph* are sketchy concerning the substance of the testimony given by the two alibi witnesses, Ruth Bertling and Clyde Harper. On the assumption that it was essentially the same as that which they gave at the federal civil rights trial of Myers and Sims, I have supplemented these accounts with details drawn from Record, at 575–615, Myers v. United States, 377 F.2d 412 (1967), hereinafter cited as Myers Transcript. The law permitting criminal defendants in Georgia to make unsworn statements, Georgia Code Annotated section 38-415 (1963), was repealed in 1973. For a more detailed discussion of this trial, see Michal R. Belknap, "The Legal Legacy of Lemuel Penn," *Howard Law Journal* 25 (1982): 471–74.

12   SAC, Atlanta, AIRTEL to Director, FBI, September 14, 1964, document 44-25873-300, PENVIC File.

13   *Athens Banner-Herald,* September 6, 1964; *New York Times,* September 5, 1965, pp. 1, 9; *Atlanta Journal and Constitution,* September 6, 1964; William Bradford Huie, "Murder: The Klan on Trial," *Saturday Evening Post,* June 19, 1965, pp. 86–88; FBI, Atlanta, teletype to Director, FBI, September 8, 1964, document 44-25873-273, PENVIC File.

14   *Athens Banner-Herald,* September 6, 1964.

15   *New York Times,* September 5, 1964, p. 9.

16   *Athens Banner-Herald,* September 6, 1964. In an account written many years later, a journalist who covered the Penn murder trial quotes Darsey as saying: "Never let it be said that a Madison County jury converted an electric chair into a sacrificial altar on which the pure flesh of a member of the human race was sacrificed to the savage, revengeful appetite of a raging mob." Shipp, *Murder,* p. 68.

17   Shipp, *Murder,* pp. 68, 72; *Athens Banner-Herald,* September 6, 1964; FBI, Atlanta, teletype to Director, FBI, September 8, 1964, document 44-25873-273,

PENVIC File; *New York Times*, September 5, 1964, p. 9. The FBI told Wayne there were only three persons in the jury panel who had "Klan affiliation or association," and none of these was selected as a juror. However, the Bureau did not actually investigate the people on the petit jury list, but only ran a file check of their names. A. Rosen, Memorandum to Mr. Belmont, September 1, 1964, document 44-25873-260, PENVIC File.

18 SAC, Atlanta, AIRTEL to Director, FBI, September 11, 1964, document 44-25873-300, and A. Rosen, Memorandum to Mr. Belmont, September 15, 1964, document 44-25873-295, PENVIC File; Former Second Assistant Attorney General St. John Barrett, personal interview with the author at his office in Washington, D.C., October 23, 1981.

19 Former Assistant Attorney General Burke Marshall, personal interview with the author at the Yale Law School, New Haven, Connecticut, October 24, 1980. There was case law to support Marshall's position. See Bartkus v. Illinois, 359 U.S. 121, 132–39 (1959).

20 Former Assistant Attorney General John Doar, personal interview with the author at his office in New York City, October 23, 1980; Former Attorney General Ramsey Clark, personal interview with the author at his office in New York City, October 23, 1980; Former Assistant Attorney General Stephen Pollak, personal interview with the author at his office in Washington, D.C., October 22, 1980; Dorothy Landsberg, former assistant to John Doar, personal interview with the author at her office in Washington, October 22, 1980.

21 *Augusta Chronicle,* October 17, 1964; Barrett Interview; United States v. Guest, 246 F. Supp. 475, 477 n. 1 (M.D. Ga. 1964).

22 Marshall Interview.

23 Judge David L. Norman, personal interview with the author at his chambers in Washington, D.C., October 23, 1980.

24 When the Supreme Court later held that there was a federal right of interstate travel that was constitutionally protected against interference by private individuals, the *Harvard Law Review* characterized this ruling as an unexpected shift in constitutional doctrine. "The Supreme Court, 1965 Term," *Harvard Law Review* 80 (November 1966): 157.

25 *Law Enforcement: A Report on Equal Protection in the South* (Washington, 1965), p. 111.

26 Clark Interview.

27 A. Rosen, Memorandum to Mr. Belmont, September 17, 1964, document 44-25706-1192, MIBURN File, FBI; Marshall Interview; Lee White, transcript of oral history interview, February 18, 1971, pp. 11–12, LBJ; Lee C. White to Anthony Town, February 5, 1965, Gen. HU2/ST 24, WHCF, LBJ. According to Marshall, the Civil Rights Division received no direct pressure from

the White House with respect to the case. The reason was that there was "no occasion" for such pressure. Marshall Interview.

28   Paul B. Johnson, transcript of oral history interview, September 8, 1970, p. 31, LBJ.

29   Florence Mars, *Witness in Philadelphia* (Baton Rouge, 1977), p. 127; Whitehead, *Attack on Terror,* p. 179; Nicholas Katzenbach, Memorandum for the President, September 4, 1964, Ex. HU 2/ST 24, WHCF, LBJ.

30   Johnson Oral History, pp. 31—32.

31   Ibid., pp. 32, 34; Whitehead, *Attack on Terror,* p. 196; Doar Interview; Nicholas Katzenbach, telephonic interview with the author, June 20, 1984; Norman Interview.

32   Mars, *Witness in Philadelphia,* pp. 129—30; Whitehead, *Attack on Terror,* pp. 171—72, 174; J. Edgar Hoover to Walter Jenkins, September 18, 1964, document 44-25076-1193, A. Rosen, Memorandum to Mr. Belmont, September 21, 1964, document 44-25076-1195, and A. Rosen, Memorandum for Mr. Belmont, September 25, 1964, document 44-25706-1215, all in MIBURN File.

33   Whitehead, *Attack on Terror,* pp. 172—73 (quote at 173); Mars, *Witness in Philadelphia,* pp. 130—31; J. Edgar Hoover, telegram to O. H. Barnett, September 25, 1964, document 44-25706-1211; A. Rosen, Memorandum to Mr. Belmont, September 25, 1964, document 44-25706-1226, A. Rosen to Mr. Belmont, September 25, 1964, document 44-25706-1277, A. Rosen, Memorandum to Mr. Belmont, September 27, 1964, document 44-25706-1224, and A. Rosen, Memorandum for Mr. Belmont, September 24, 1964, document 44-25706-1217, all in MIBURN File.

34   A. Rosen, Memorandum to Mr. Belmont, December 1, 1964, document 44-25706-1413, A. Rosen, Memorandum to Mr. Belmont, December 2, 1964, document 44-25706-1414, A. Rosen, Memorandum to Mr. Belmont, December 3, 1964, document 44-25706-1417, [deleted] to Mr. Rosen, December 3, 1964, document 44-25706-1418, Jackson Field Office, telegram to the Director, December 3, 1964, document 44-25706-1420, A. H. Belmont, Memorandum to Mr. Tolson, December 3, 1964, document 44-25706-1424, A. Rosen, Memorandum to Mr. Belmont, December 4, 1964, document 44-25706-1427, [?] to Bill Moyers, December 4, 1964, document 44-25706-1435, and John W. Douglas, Memorandum for Nicholas Katzenbach, September 29, 1964, document 44-25706-123 and attached "Statement on Behalf of Department of Justice," all in MIBURN File; Whitehead, *Attack on Terror,* pp. 196—97; Mars, *Witness in Philadelphia,* pp. 142, 150.

35   *New Orleans Times-Picayune,* October 18, 1967; Mars, *Witness to Philadelphia,* pp. 262—63.

36   Whitehead, *Attack on Terror,* pp. 203—204.

37   Ibid., pp. 204–205; Investigative Summary, document 44-25706-1613, p. 996, MIBURN File (hereinafter cited as Investigative Summary); "Mississippi: 'Jesus No!'" *Newsweek,* December 21, 1964, pp. 21–22. The Supreme Court had ruled in Costello v. United States, 350 U.S. 359 (1956), that for a grand jury to consider hearsay would not make any indictment which it subsequently returned defective.

38   Whitehead, *Attack on Terror,* p. 205 (quote at 205); *Dallas Morning News,* December 12, 1964; *Nashville Tennessean,* December 12, 1964; *Chattanooga Times,* December 12, 1964; *Nashville Banner,* December 11, 1964.

39   *Delta Democrat-Times* (Greenville, Miss.), January 13, 1965; Transcript of Record, at 1–2, 11–16, United States v. Price, 383 U.S. 787 (1966); Whitehead, *Attack on Terror,* pp. 215–16. Two of the men arrested by the FBI on civil rights conspiracy charges, police officer Otha Neal Burkes and grocer Oliver Warner, Jr., were not indicted by the grand jury. Nor did it indict Earl Akin and Tommy Horne, the two men charged earlier with misprision of a felony. On the other hand, the grand jury added a new name to the list of alleged conspirators: Philadelphia police officer Richard Andrew Willis (who had been in the car with Neshoba County Deputy Sheriff Cecil Price when the three murdered civil rights workers left Philadelphia). Whitehead, *Attack on Terror,* p. 216. Jordan had erroneously identified Burkes as the policeman who was with Price. See Investigative Summary, p. 794.

40   Whitehead, *Attack on Terror,* p. 216.

41   Mars, *Witness in Philadelphia,* pp. 228–29; Carl M. Brauer, *John F. Kennedy and the Second Reconstruction* (New York, 1977), pp. 120, 123; Leon Friedman, "The Federal Courts in the South: Judge Bryan Simpson and His Reluctant Brethren," in *Southern Justice,* ed. Leon Friedman (New York, 1965), pp. 188–89.

42   United States v. Price, No. 5215 Crim. (S.D. Miss. Feb. 24, 1965).

43   Ibid., at 4.

44   United States v. Price, No. 5216 Crim. (S.D. Miss. Feb. 25, 1965); Norma K. VanAuken to the President, December 11, 1964, Gen. HU2/ST 24, WHCF, LBJ; *Baltimore Afro-American,* March 13, 1965.

45   J. W. Peltason, *Fifty-eight Lonely Men: Southern Federal Judges and School Desegregation* (New York, 1961), pp. 113–14, 178, 195.

46   United States v. Guest, 246 F. Supp. 475 (M.D. Ga. 1964).

47   Barrett Interview; *Washington Post,* January 3, 1965.

48   Barrett Interview.

49   See his remarks in United States v. Guest, 246 F. Supp. at 477–78.

50   Ibid. at 478.

51   Ibid. at 484.

52   Ibid. at 487.

53   Memorandum from Burke Marshall to the Solicitor General, January 11, 1965, in Administrative History of the Department of Justice, Documentary Supplement, vol. 7, pt. 10B, LBJ (hereinafter cited as Documentary Supplement).

54   Ibid.; Memorandum from Louis F. Claiborne to the Solicitor General, January 15, 1965, and Memorandum from Ralph F. Spritzer to the Solicitor General, January 19, 1965, both in Documentary Supplement; A. Rosen, Memorandum to Mr. Belmont, January 21, 1965, document 44-25873-368, PENVIC File.

55   Spritzer Memorandum.

56   Marshall Memorandum.

57   Ibid.

58   Jurisdictional Statement, United States v. Guest, 383 U.S. 745 (1966); Brief for the United States, at 7 n.2, United States v. Guest, 383 U.S. 745 (1966).

59   Doar Interview.

60   Lee C. White to Anthony Towne, February 5, 1965, Gen. HU2/ST 24, LBJ.

61   Jurisdictional Statement, Motion to Consolidate Appeals, Motion for Expedited Hearing, at 9, United States v. Price, 383 U.S. 787 (1966).

62   United States v. Price, 380 U.S. 940 (1965).

63   Katzenbach Interview. Solicitor General Cox apparently made the decision personally. See A. Rosen, Memorandum to Mr. Belmont, January 21, 1965, document 44-25873-368, PENVIC File. Cox can no longer remember precisely when or why the decision to appeal Guest was made. He does recall, however, "We knew that Guest would be a very difficult case. On the other hand, the issue was one that had to be faced and the Guest case was as good a vehicle as any." Archibald Cox to Michal R. Belknap, May 30, 1984 (hereinafter cited as Cox Letter). On the violence around Selma and the public and presidential reaction to it, see chapters 8 and 9.

64   Jurisdictional Statement, at 5, United States v. Guest, 383 U.S. 745 (1966).

65   Ibid. at 6.

66   United States v. Guest, 381 U.S. 932 (1965); United States v. Price, 380 U.S. 970 (1965). In both cases the Supreme Court postponed consideration of the jurisdictional question to the hearing on the merits.

67   Stephen J. Pollak, transcript of oral history interview, January 27, 1969, p. 22, LBJ; Cox Letter; New York Times, September 12, 1965, p. 73, November 10, 1965, p. 7. Pollak is the source of the information that Johnson pressured Cox, who was closely tied to the Kennedys, into leaving the Justice Department.

68   Ibid., November 10, 1965, p. 7; Brief for Appellees, at 8, 10–13, United States v. Price, 383 U.S. 787 (hereinafter cited as Brief for Price Appellees).

69   Brief for Appellees Herbert Guest, Cecil William Myers, Denver Willis Phillips, Joseph Howard Sims, and George Hampton Turner, at 3, United States v. Guest, 383 U.S. 745 (1966), hereinafter cited as Brief for Guest Appellees.

70   Ibid. at 609; Brief for Appellee James Lackey, at 14-52, United States v. Guest, 383 U.S. 745 (1966), hereinafter cited as Lackey Brief.

71   Brief for the United States, at 10–17, United States v. Price, 383 U.S. 787 (1966), hereinafter cited as Government's *Price* Brief.

72   Brief for the United States, at 8–10, 18–28, 31 (quote at 31), United States v. Guest, 383 U.S. 745 (1966), hereinafter cited as Government's *Guest* Brief.

73   Ibid. at 9–10; Brief for *Guest* Appellees, at 8–9; Lackey Brief, at 40–45; Brief for *Price* Appellees, at 21–22, 32.

74   Government's *Price* Brief, at 11.

75   United States v. Price, 383 U.S. 787, 794 (1966).

76   Ibid. at 795.

77   United States v. Guest, 383 U.S. 745, 751 (1966). It was far from obvious that Bootle's ruling was based on what he regarded as a deficiency in the pleading, rather than on his construction of the statute. Furthermore, as the government pointed out, this pleading objection had been neither raised nor noticed below. Neither of the briefs filed by appellees had even mentioned the issue, and the government had addressed it rather tangentially only after the Court indicated it entertained doubts about its jurisdiction. Government's *Guest* Brief, at 62–65, 81 n.35.

78   United States v. Guest, 383 U.S. at 757–61, 762–74. Part III of Justice Stewart's opinion for the Court upheld the portion of the indictment alleging conspiracy to deprive blacks of a right to travel freely to and from the state of Georgia. Concurring in part and dissenting in part, Harlan argued that section 241 reached state interference with interstate travel, but not private interference with it. Also concurring in part and dissenting in part, Justice Brennan (writing also for Justice Douglas and Chief Justice Warren) expressly agreed with Part III of Stewart's opinion. Justice Clark, concurring for himself and Justices Fortas and Black, expressed general agreement with "the opinion of the Court."

79   United States v. Price, 383 U.S. at 797–98.

80   United States v. Guest, 383 U.S. at 753.

81   See United States v. Price, 383 U.S. at 798–806.

82   Ibid. at 806.

83   Ibid. at 798.

84   Ibid. at 806.

85   United States v. Guest, 383 U.S. at 756–57.

86   Justice Brennan to Justice Stewart, February 22, 1966, box 139, William J. Brennan, Jr., Papers, LC.

87   George Richard Poehner, "Comment: Fourteenth Amendment Enforcement and Congressional Power to Abolish the States," *California Law Review* 55 (April 1967): 316; Howard M. Feurstein, "Civil Rights Crimes and the Federal Power to Punish Private Individuals for Interference with Federally Secured Rights," *Vanderbilt Law Review* 19 (June 1966): 674.

88   383 U.S. at 782.

89   Ibid. at 784. That is how a student writer for the *Harvard Law Review* read the Brennan opinion. "Supreme Court, 1965 Term," p. 156. For a contrasting analysis, see John G. Niles, "Note: Constitutional Law—Civil Rights—Congressional Power Under Section 5 of the Fourteenth Amendment May Extend to Punishment of Private Conspiracies to Interfere with the Equal Enjoyment of State-Owned Public Facilities," *Texas Law Review* 45 (November 1966): 173.

90   383 U.S. at 762; "No. 65 United States v. Guest," box 139, Brennan Papers.

91   A note in Justice Clark's file on the Price case, which indicates only that it was appended to the initial circulation of Fortas's opinion (dated February 15, 1966), says, "Vote in #59 [the case based on the section 241 indictment] show unanimous except for Stewart, J. and by his name ??"

"Nothing recorded for #60 [the section 242 case]." Case File 59 and 60, October Term, 1965, Tom C. Clark Papers, Tarleton Law Library, University of Texas Law School, Austin, Texas. Justice Brennan's conference notes show that Stewart passed in *Price,* indicating he wished to postpone casting a vote until he saw the opinion that was written. Box 412, Brennan Papers.

92   Brennan's conference notes on United States v. Guest, box 412, Brennan Papers; Preliminary Circulation, Opinion of the Court, United States v. Guest (January 26, 1966), p. 8, Case File 65, October Term, 1965, Clark Papers.

93   Preliminary Circulation, Opinion of the Court, pp. 9–10.

94   383 U.S. 301 (1966). In this case the Court ruled that section 2 of the Fifteenth Amendment empowered Congress to enact a number of key provisions of the Voting Rights Act of 1965.

95   Memorandum from WJB, Jr., to the Conference, Re: No 65 United States v. Guest, February 4, 1966, Clark Case File 65 (hereinafter cited as Brennan Memorandum); Memorandum for the Conference from Stewart, January 26, 1966, Clark Case File 65.

96   Brennan Memorandum; Memorandum from PS to the Conference, February 21, 1966, Preliminary Circulation, Opinion of the Court, United States v.

Guest, February 21, 1966, Preliminary Circulation, Concurring Opinion of Mr. Justice Brennan, United States v. Guest, March 10, 1966, Preliminary Circulation, Concurring Opinion of Mr. Justice Brennan, United States v. Guest, March 22, 1966, and Preliminary Circulation, Concurring Opinion of Mr. Justice Brennan, United States v. Guest, March 25, 1966, all in Clark Case File 65; William J. Brennan, Jr., to Potter Stewart, March 9, 1966, box 139, Brennan Papers.

97   Note from Clark to Stewart, January 27, 1966, Clark Case File 65.

98   Note from Clark to Stewart, February 23, 1966, undated typed draft of concurring opinion by Mr. Justice Clark, and Preliminary Circulation, Concurring Opinion of Mr. Justice Clark, United States v. Guest, Clark Case File 65. On the typed draft is a note written in pen which says: "Dear Abe: What about something like this? I welcome suggestions, TCC."

99   Steve Salch, "Note: Protection of Fourteenth Amendment Rights Under Section 241 of the United States Code," *Southwestern Law Journal* 20 (1966): 919.

100   Poehner, "Fourteenth Amendment Enforcement," pp. 298, 302; Feurstein, "Civil Rights Crimes," p. 675; "Comment: Congressional Power Under the Civil War Amendments," *Duke Law Journal* 1969 (December 1969): 1273–78; John E. Moye, "Note: Fourteenth Amendment Congressional Power to Legislate Against Private Discrimination: The *Guest* Case," *Cornell Law Quarterly* 52 (Spring 1967): 587–89; Barbara C. Schwartzbaum, "Note: Federal Prosecution of Private Violence—Arrests Resulting from Private Conspirators' False Reports to Police Constitutes State Denial of Equal Protection Indictable Under Civil Rights Conspiracy Statute," *Howard Law Journal* 13 (1967): 192.

101   Poehner, "Fourteenth Amendment Enforcement," p. 316; Alfred Avins, "Federal Power to Punish Individual Crimes Under the Fourteenth Amendment: The Original Understanding," *Notre Dame Lawyer* 43 (February 1968): 343, 347.

102   Bruce H. Spector, "Comment: The Fourteenth Amendment, Congressional Power, and Private Discrimination: *United States v. Guest*," *U.C.L.A. Law Review* 14 (January 1967): 553–54; Thomas P. Ruane, "Note, Constitutional Law—Congress By Appropriate Legislation May Have the Power to Punish Private Conspiracies That Interfere with Fourteenth Amendment Rights," *Duquesne University Law Review* 5 (Winter 1966): 201; "Note: Civil Rights—Federal Criminal Code Protects Rights Secured by Fourteenth Amendment," *Vanderbilt Law Review* 20 (December 1966): 175; Laurent B. Frantz, "Federal Power to Protect Civil Rights: The Price and Guest Cases," *Law in Transition Quarterly* 4 (March 1967): 69–73; "Note: Double Prosecution by State and Federal Governments: Another Exercise in Federalism," *Harvard Law Review* 80 (May 1967): 1539.

103   *New York Times,* March 29, 1966, p. 1; "Civil Rights: Toward Outlawing Murder," *Time,* April 8, 1966, p. 28.

Chapter Eight

1 "Dallas County," box 146, folder 8, SCLC Papers; Tinsley E. Yarbrough, *Judge Frank Johnson and Human Rights in Alabama* (University, Ala., 1981), pp. 113–14; Allen J. Matusow, *The Unraveling of America: A History of Liberalism in the 1960s* (New York, 1984), pp. 184–85.

2 Complaint, Miles v. Dixon, United States District Court for the Middle District of Alabama, box 60, folder 327, SNCC Papers.

3 Statement at SCLC Executive Board Meeting, Baltimore, Maryland, April 2, 1965, folder 10, box 12, SCLC Papers.

4 SNCC, "What Are You Waiting For, Mr. President," box 47, folder 70, SNCC Papers; Mr. and Mrs. F. G. Hayden to the President, March 8, 1965, Joachim Prinz, telegram to the President, March 10, 1965, Reverend David H. Harris, telegram to the President, March 12, 1965, Charles H. Percy, telegram to the President, March 9, 1965, and Gail B. Schmidt to the President, March 9, 1965, all in Gen., HU2/ST 1, WHCF, LBJ.

5 Governor John Dempsey, telegram to President Lyndon B. Johnson, March 9, 1965, Gen. HU2/ST 1, WHCF, LBJ.

6 Robert Evans and Robert Novak, *Lyndon B. Johnson: The Exercise of Power* (New York, 1966), p. 494; *Atlanta Constitution,* April 10, 1965; Burke Marshall, transcript of oral history interview, October 28, 1968, p. 39, LBJ; Lyndon B. Johnson, *The Vantage Point: Perspectives of the Presidency* (New York, 1971), pp. 162–63; George Wallace, telegram to the President, March 12, 1965, Ex. HU2/ST 1, WHCF, LBJ.

7 Williams v. Wallace, 240 F. Supp. 100, 109 (M.D. Ala. 1965).

8 George C. Wallace, telegram to the President, March 18, 1965, Lieutenant Governor James B. Allen, telegram to the President, March 19, 1965, and Lyndon B. Johnson to George Wallace, March 20, 1965, all in Ex. HU2/ST 1, WHCF, LBJ; David J. Garrow, *Protest at Selma: Martin Luther King, Jr., and the Voting Rights Act of 1965* (New Haven, 1978), p. 114.

9 Johnson, *Vantage Point,* p. 163.

10 Burke Marshall, "The Protest Movement in the South," May 6, 1965, box 13, Burke Marshall Papers, JFK; Lyndon B. Johnson to George Wallace, March 20, 1965, Ex. HU2/ST 1, WHCF, LBJ; International Situation Room for Mr. Valenti, OPORD 1, March 21, 1965 (CONFIDENTIAL), C.F. HU2/ST 1, WHCF, LBJ; Yarbrough, *Judge Johnson,* p. 120; Stephen J. Pollak, transcript of oral history interview, January 29, 1969, pp. 34–40, LBJ.

11 Earl D. James, Franklin W. Parks, and L. B. Sullivan to Fred Gray, March 23, 1965, box 43, folder 12, SCLC Papers; Lyndon B. Johnson to George Wallace, March 20, 1965, Ex. HU2/ST 1, WHCF, LBJ.

12 *New York Times,* March 21, 1965, pt. III, p. 10; *Washington Post,* March 20, 1965; *Montgomery Advertiser,* March 21, 1965; *The State* (Columbia, S.C.), March 22, 1965.

13 Special Agent's Report, March 30, 1965, Mobile Field Office file MO 44-1245, copy in Viola Liuzzo File, FBI; Don Whitehead, *Attack on Terror: The FBI Against the Ku Klux Klan in Mississippi* (New York, 1970), p. 305; Garrow, *Protest at Selma,* p. 117; Transcript of Record, at 257–65, 413–18, United States v. Wilkins, 376 F.2d 552 (5th Cir. 1967). The quote is from p. 264 of the latter source, which is hereinafter cited as Wilkins Transcript.

14 "Dallas County," undated, box 146, folder 8, SCLC Papers; Benjamin Muse, *The American Negro Revolution: From Nonviolence to Black Power, 1963–1967* (Bloomington, 1968), pp. 167–68; "Jinksi" [Virginia Foster Durr] to Elizabeth and Hugo [Black], March 18, 1965, box 7, Family Papers, Hugo L. Black Papers, LC.

15 SNCC Press Release, August 21, 1965, box 171, SNCC Papers; Muse, *Negro Revolution,* pp. 220–21; John Doar, Memorandum for the Attorney General, August 28, 1965, box 14, Ramsey Clark Papers, LBJ.

16 "Jinksi" [Virginia Foster Durr] to Elizabeth and Hugo [Black], September 23, 1965, box 7, Family Papers, Black Papers; Muse, *Negro Revolution,* pp. 221–22; *New York Times,* September 16, 1965, p. 33.

17 Whitehead, *Attack on Terror,* pp. 305–306; A. H. Belmont, Memorandum to Mr. Tolson, March 26, 1965, document 44-28601-129, and C. D. DeLoach, Memorandum to Mr. Mohr, March 28, 1965, document 44-28601-?, Viola Liuzzo File.

18 Special Agent's Report, March 30, 1965, Mobile Field Office file MO 44-1245, pp. 108–10, 148, C. D. DeLoach, Memorandum to Mr. Mohr, March 28, 1965, document 44-28601-?, C. L. McGowan, Memorandum to Mr. Rosen, March 27, 1965, document 44-28601-[illegible], JDH, note concerning information furnished to St. John Barrett, March 27, 1965, SAC, Mobile, teletype to Director, FBI, March 27, 1965, document 44-28601-108, Director, FBI, teletype to SAC Mobile, April 9, 1965, document 44-28601-174, C. L. McGowan, Memorandum to Mr. Rosen, April 14, 1965, document 44-28601-208, and Director, FBI, teletype to SAC, Mobile November 29, 1965, document 44-28601-573, all in Viola Liuzzo File.

19 SAC, Mobile, teletype to Director, FBI, March 27, 1965, document 44-28601-108, and FBI, Mobile, teletype to Director, FBI, May 7, 1965, document 44-28601-328, Viola Liuzzo File; Muse, *Negro Revolution,* pp. 219–20; *New York Times,* April 27, 1965, p. 21, and May 8, 1965, pp. 1, 15; Yarbrough, *Judge Johnson,* p. 128; Virginia Durr, transcript of oral history interview, October 24, 1974, p. 327, CUOHP; Gary Thomas Rowe, *My Undercover Years with the Ku Klux Klan* (New York, 1971), p. 195.

20   FBI, Mobile, teletype to Director, FBI, May 3, 1965, document 44-28601-328, Viola Liuzzo File.

21   Yarbrough, *Judge Johnson*, p. 129; R. H. Jevons, Memorandum to Mr. Conrad, October 25, 1965, document 44-28601-525, Viola Liuzzo File; *New York Times*, October 17, 1965, p. 1, October 20, 1965, p. 1, October 21, 1965, p. 1, October 23, 1965, p. 1; Flowers v. Thagard, 278 Ala. 537, 179 So. 2d 286 (1965).

22   Rowe, *My Undercover Years*, pp. 205–206.

23   "Jinksi" [Virginia Foster Durr] to Elizabeth and Hugo [Black], September 23, 1965, box 7, Family Papers, Black Papers.

24   "Life with Lyndon in the Great Society," vol. 1, no. 16, May 20, 1965, Box 177, SNCC Papers.

25   *New York Times*, December 11, 1965, pp. 1, 22.

26   U.S., Congress, Senate, Subcommittee on Constitutional Rights of the Committee on the Judiciary, *Civil Rights Hearings on S 3296 . . . and S 3170*, 89th Cong., 2d sess., 1966, 1:497.

27   A story by Nelson appeared in the *Charleston* (W. Va.) *Gazette* on July 1, 1965.

28   *Washington Post*, February 27, 1965.

29   *Atlanta Constitution*, April 10, 1965; John Doar, personal interview with the author at his office in New York City, October 23, 1980; John Doar to Senator Philip Hart, April 22, 1965, Gen. HU2/ST 1, WHCF, LBJ; *New York Times*, May 8, 1965, p. 1, October 23, 1965, p. 1, December 4, 1965, p. 35; Nicholas Katzenbach, telephonic interview with the author, June 20, 1984; *New York Times* (international edition), October 2, 1965, p. 1; Transcript of Hearing on Pretrial Motions, at 5–16, Wilkins v. United States, 376 F.2d 552 (5th Cir. 1967); Wilkins Transcript, pp. 12–13.

30   Rowe, *My Undercover Years*, p. 192; *New York Times*, February 8, 1964, p. 1, April 18, 1964, p. 1, May 3, 1965, p. 28, May 9, 1965, p. 41; *Charlotte Observer*, August 11, 1964; *Montgomery Advertiser*, May 11, 1964; Murray Kempton, "Trial of the Klansmen: A Ranting Attorney, A Hung Jury," *New Republic*, May 22, 1965, p. 10.

31   Wilkins Transcript, pp. 292–603, 711; Rowe, *My Undercover Years*, pp. 207–208.

32   Wilkins Transcript, pp. 123–86, 225–368, 520–24, 579–81 (quotes at 258 and 264).

33   Ibid., pp. 619–25, 632–33, 636–41, 647–68, 672–82.

34   Ibid., pp. 71–72, 705, 707–10.

35   Ibid., pp. 691–95, 711–18 (quote at 695).

36   Excerpt Transcript, at 11–12, 23–24, United States v. Wilkins, 376 F.2d 55 (5th Cir. 1967), hereinafter cited as Excerpt Transcript.

37   Ibid., pp. 29–40; *New York Times,* December 4, 1965, p. 35.

38   Excerpt Transcript, pp. 42–43.

39   *New York Times,* December 4, 1965, pp. 1, 35 (quote at 1).

40   Wilkins v. United States, 376 F.2d 552 (5th Cir. 1967).

41   Ibid. at 559.

42   Myers v. United States, 377 F.2d 412, 414 (5th Cir. 1967); C. D. De-Loach, Memorandum to Mr. Tolson, March 30, 1966, document 44-25873-?, PENVIC File, FBI; *New York Times,* June 29, 1966, p. 28.

43   Record, at 703, Myers v. United States, 377 F.2d 412 (5th Cir. 1967), hereinafter cited as Myers Record. See also his remarks at pp. 707 and 708.

44   Ibid., pp. 712, 725, 726, 739 (quote at 739).

45   Ibid., pp. 814–15; *New York Times,* July 3, 1966, p. 28, July 9, 1966, p. 1; *Athens Banner-Herald,* July 10, 1966; St. John Barrett, personal interview with the author at his office in Washington, D.C., October 23, 1981.

46   Barrett Interview; SAC, Atlanta, AIRTEL, to Director, FBI, July 11, 1966, document 44-25873-496, PENVIC File.

47   *Athens Banner-Herald,* July 10, 1966.

48   United States v. Guest, 246 F. Supp. 475, 477 n.1 (M.D. Ga. 1964); FBI Press Release, August 6, 1964, Department of Justice Administrative History, vol. 8, pt. 19A, Documentary Supplement, LBJ.

49   Myers Record, pp. 482–514, 571 (quote at 571).

50   Ibid., pp. 9–10.

51   Ibid., pp. 33–562; *New York Times,* July 1, 1966, p. 19.

52   Myers Record, pp. 764, 768.

53   Ibid., p. 571; *Athens Banner-Herald,* July 7, 1966; Chambers v. State, 194 Ga. 773, 22 S.E. 2d 487 (1942).

54   Myers Record, p. 729.

55   United States v. Myers, 377 F.2d 412 (5th Cir. 1967).

56   *Washington Post,* December 5, 1964; *New York Times,* December 6, 1964, p. 8E; *Nashville Tennessean,* January 18, 1965.

57   Barrett Interview; Doar Interview; C. D. DeLoach, Memorandum to Mr. Tolson, March 30, 1966, document 44-25873-?, PENVIC File.

58   Transcript of Record, at 2323, United States v. Price, Crim. No. 5291 (S.D. Miss. 1967), hereinafter cited as Price Transcript.

59   Doar Interview; Florence Mars, *Witness in Philadelphia* (Baton Rouge, 1977), pp. 225–26; Justice Department, Administrative History, vol. VII, pt. 10, p. 92; Rabinowitz v. United States, 366 F.2d 34 (5th Cir. 1966); *New York Times,* January 13, 1967, p. 12. Although reindicted with the other defendants, James Jordan was to be tried separately in Atlanta.

60   "Mississippi: Time of Trial," *Time,* October 20, 1967, p. 22; "Mississippi:

Reckoning in Meridian," *Time,* October 27, 1967, p. 33; "Mississippi: Changing Times," *Newsweek,* October 30, 1967, p. 28.

61 Price Transcript, pp. 2479, 2505. Cox's surprising fairness may well have been due to his developing concern that law and order was breaking down in Mississippi. For more about his thinking on this subject and its effect on his actions, see chapter 10.

62 Ibid., pp. 56–543, 725–40.

63 Ibid., pp. 581–613, 1134–44.

64 Ibid., pp. 755–99, 818, 908–25.

65 Ibid., pp. 1116–25, 951–88, 992–95, 1028, 1032.

66 Ibid., p. 475–76, 1173–74, 1252–60, 1266, 1271–79 (quote at 1277).

67 Ibid., pp. 1–2, 1634–2292; Mars, *Witness in Philadelphia,* pp. 229, 253–54; *Birmingham News,* October 17, 1967; *Jackson Daily News,* October 17, 1967. What seemed to be the best alibi was that which Finis McAdory provided for Deputy Price. He said he had filed a complaint with Price at 10:30 P.M. at the Philadelphia police station and that Price had gone with him, his brother-in-law, and his wife to look for his daughter and two of her male friends. They had found the three youths around 11:30 P.M., and Price had then taken the two boys to jail, where he, McAdory, saw the deputy again around 1:00–1:30. Mrs. McAdory corroborated her husband's story and also claimed to have seen Price at 12:30 A.M. Price Transcript, pp. 2053–71.

68 Price Transcript, pp. 110, 113–17, 155–56, 1144, 2371, 2374, 2376, 2382–83, 2400, 2402, 2424, 2431, 2446–47, 2452, 2460 (quote at 113).

69 Ibid., p. 2472.

70 Ibid., p. 2235.

71 Ibid., pp. 2477–2555; Mars, *Witness in Philadelphia,* p. 234; *New York Times,* October 10, 1967, p. 21. The jury was comprised of a grocery store owner, a pipe fitter, a textile worker, an electrician, an oil exploration operator, a production worker, a secretary, a clerk, a school cafeteria worker, and three housewives.

72 *Birmingham News,* October 21, 1967; Mars, *Witness in Philadelphia,* pp. 260, 264; Price Transcript, pp. 1978–2012, 2358, 2548–56; "Potential Subjects," document 44-25707-1222, MIBURN File, FBI. Evidence gathered by the FBI showed that Herndon had "participated in making plans as well as selecting and obtaining individuals from Meridian, Mississippi to proceed to Philadelphia to participate in the assault and later murder of" Schwerner, Goodman, and Chaney, which clearly would have made him guilty of conspiracy. Investigative Summary, p. 798, document 44-25706-1613, MIBURN File.

73 *Birmingham News,* October 30, 1967.

74 Quoted in *Jackson Daily News,* October 21, 1967.

75 Price Transcript, pp. 2411–20. For some unexplained reason, the tran-

script fails to record the number of years to which Jimmy Arledge was sentenced. James Jordan, who entered a plea of no contest in federal district court in Atlanta a few days after the Meridian trial ended, received a four-year sentence. Mars, *Witness in Philadelphia,* p. 261; *New York Times,* January 15, 1968, p. 25.

76 *New York Times,* October 1, 1967, p. 18.

77 *Atlanta Constitution,* October 26, 1967; *Jackson Daily News,* October 21, 1967; *New York Times,* October 22, 1967, sec. IV, p. 10.

Chapter Nine

1 Memorandum for the Solicitor General, March 29, 1966, United States v. Herbert Guest folder, reel 52, Records of the Civil Rights Division, United States Department of Justice, LBJ (hereinafter cited as CRD Records).

2 David J. Garrow, *Protest at Selma: Martin Luther King, Jr., and the Voting Rights Act of 1965* (New Haven, 1978), pp. 133–35; Voting Rights Act of 1965, Pub. L. No. 89-110, 79 Stat. 437 (1965).

3 Sections 11(b) and 12(a), Voting Rights Act of 1965, Pub. L. No. 89-110, 79 Stat. 437 (1965); U.S., House, Committee on the Judiciary, *Voting Rights: Hearings Before Subcommittee No. 5 . . . on H.R. 6400,* 89th Cong., 1st sess., 1965, pp. 11, 62–65, 667, 691, and *Voting Rights Legislation,* 89th Cong., 1st sess, 1965, H. Rept. 439, pp. 20–21; U.S., Senate, Committee on the Judiciary, *Voting Rights: Hearings . . . on S. 1564,* 89th Cong., 1st sess., 1: 2–3, 16–17, and *Voting Rights Legislation,* 89th Cong., 1st sess., S. Rept. 162, 3:28–29; U.S., House, Committee on Conference, 89th Cong., 1st sess., 1965, H. Rept. 711, p. 13. The only case which the Justice Department brought under section 11(b) between its August enactment and July 1, 1966, was a civil action against Louisiana landowners whose tenants alleged they had been evicted for registering to vote. See U.S., Department of Justice, *Annual Report of the Attorney General of the United States for the Fiscal Year Ended June 30, 1966* (Washington, 1966), p. 191.

4 Malcolm E. Peabody et al., telegram to the President, August 23, 1965, Ex. HU2/ST 1, WHCF, LBJ.

5 Clayborne Carson, *In Struggle: SNCC and the Black Awakening of the 1960s* (Cambridge, Mass., 1981), p. 160; *New York Times,* May 9, 1965, pt. IV, p. 12, October 2, 1965, p. 4, October 24, 1965, p. 1, December 14, 1965, p. 42; Robert Edward Jones to the President, October 27, 1965, Edwin Peets, telegram to the President, October 28, 1965, and Lee C. White to Mathew Ahmann, October 8, 1965, all in Ex. HU2/ST 1, WHCF, LBJ; Herman B. Glaser to President Lyndon B. Johnson, May 11, 1965, LIUB Name File, WHCF, LBJ; *Baltimore Afro-American,* April 10, 1965; *Greensboro Daily News,* April 2, 1965.

6   December 14, 1965, p. 42.

7   Stephen J. Pollak, transcript of oral history interview, January 29, 1969, p. 43, LBJ; Pat Watters and Reese Cleghorn, *Climbing Jacob's Ladder: The Arrival of Negroes in Southern Politics* (New York, 1967), p. 268; Lee C. White to Mathew Ahmann, October 8, 1965, Ex. HU2/ST 1, WHCF, LBJ; John Edgar Hoover, Memorandum for Mr. Tolson et al., March 26, 1965, document 44-28601-16, Viola Liuzzo File, FBI; "Suggested Response to Inquiries on Bogalusa," July 15, 1965, box 6, Files of Lee White, LBJ; John Doar to Sam Ridge, August 24, 1965, Gen. HU2/ST 18, WHCF, LBJ; *New York Times,* December 2, 1965, pp. 1, 36; Jack Rosenthal, Memorandum for Clifford Alexander, Jr., March 25, 1966, Ex. SP 2-3/1966/HU2, Message on Civil Rights 4/28/66, Back-up Material, WHCF, LBJ (hereinafter cited as Back-up Material); John Doar and Dorothy Landsberg, "The Performance of the FBI in Investigating Violations of Federal Laws Protecting the Right to Vote—1960–1967," in U.S., Senate, Select Committee to Study Governmental Operations with Respect to Intelligence Activities, *Hearings . . . ,* Part VI, *Federal Bureau of Investigation,* 94th Cong., 1st sess., 1975, pp. 937–47 (quote at 940).

8   Don Whitehead, *Attack on Terror: The FBI Against the Ku Klux Klan in Mississippi* (New York, 1970), pp. 305–306; John Edgar Hoover, Memorandum for Mr. Tolson et al., March 26, 1965, document 44-78601-15, Viola Liuzzo File; U.S., Presidents, *Public Papers of the Presidents of the United States: Lyndon B. Johnson,* 5 vols. (Washington, D.C., 1965–1970), 1965: 333. Hoover did not want the president to talk to Mrs. Liuzzo's husband because "he is well known as a teamster strongarm man and on the woman's body we found numerous needle marks indicating she had been taking dope." John Edgar Hoover, Memorandum for Mr. Tolson et al., March 26, 1965, document 44-78601-16, Viola Liuzzo File.

9   Lee C. White to Upton Sinclair, April 7, 1965, Ex. HU2/ST 24 WHCF, LBJ; Jim Devine, buck slip to the Deputy Attorney General, April 8, 1965, and J. Walter Yeagley, Memorandum for Ramsey Clark, box 17, Ramsey Clark Papers, LBJ.

10   Francis X. Worthington, Memorandum to J. Walter Yeagley, April 21, 1965, box 17, Clark Papers.

11   James T. Devine, Memorandum to Messrs. Barnett, Yeagley, Willens, Pollak, and Creame, April 21, 1965, box 17, Clark Papers; Johnson to Volpe, May 14, 1965, Ex. HU2/ST 1, WHCF, LBJ.

12   George Reedy, Memorandum to the President, October 2, 1965, Joe Califano, Memorandum to the President, October 25, 1965, and Lee C. White, Memorandum to the President, October 13, 1965, all in C.F. HU 2, WHCF, LBJ.

13 *New York Times,* March 30, 1965, p. 1, June 10, 1965, p. 38, February 25, 1966, p. 18, July 21, 1966, p. 18; *Birmingham News,* March 30, 1965; *Columbia* (S.C.) *Record,* October 20, 1965; Garrow, *Protest at Selma,* p. 119.

14 Ramsey Clark, transcript of oral history interview, April 16, 1969, 4:1–3, LBJ; United States Commission on Civil Rights, *Law Enforcement: A Report on Equal Protection in the South* (Washington, D.C., 1965), pp. 177–78; William L. Taylor to Lee C. White, December 8, 1965, and attachments, box 25, Office Files of Harry McPherson, LBJ; Marvin Watson, telegram from Lee C. White, November 13, 1965, box 3, White Files; Nicholas deB. Katzenbach, Memorandum for Joseph Califano, December 13, 1965, Ex. LE HU2, WHCF, LBJ; "President's Annual Message to Congress on the State of the Union," in Presidents, *Public Papers: Johnson,* 1966: 5; Leadership Conference on Civil Rights, Memo No. 80, January 25, 1966, folder 4, box 44, SCLC Papers, Memorandum from Stephen J. Pollak to David L. Norman, January 26, 1966, Memorandum from Pollak to Norman and Alan Marer, February 1, 1966, Memorandum from Marer to Norman, February 11, 1966, and alternative draft bills, all in "Legislation Against Intimidation and Violence" folder, reel 51, CRD Records; Steven F. Lawson, *In Pursuit of Power: Southern Blacks and Electoral Politics, 1965–1982* (New York, 1985), pp. 64–65; Former Assistant Attorney General, Stephen J. Pollak, personal interview with the author at his office in Washington, D.C., October 22, 1980.

15 "The President's T.V. Remarks on Civil Rights," box 5, Will Sparks Aide Files, LBJ; Routing slip from Harold D. Koffsky to Barefoot Sanders, February 1, 1966, in Department of Justice, "Administrative History," vol. VII, part 10b, LBJ; Nicholas deB. Katzenbach, Memorandum for Joseph Califano, December 13, 1965, Ex. LE HU2, WHCF, LBJ; Memorandum from Ramsey Clark to Joseph A. Califano, Jr., February 26, 1966, Memorandum from Califano to the President, March 15, 1966, Memorandum from Califano for the President, March 25, 1966, yellow slip, dated March 28, 1966, attached to draft address, and Califano to Bill Moyers, April 4, 1966, all in Back-up Material; Ramsey Clark, Memo to Lawrence F. O'Brien, April 17, 1966, box 19, Reports on Legislation, Clark Papers; Former Attorney General Ramsey Clark, personal interview with the author at his office in New York City, October 23, 1980.

16 Joe Califano, Memorandum for the President, April 13, 1966, Back-up Material.

17 Attorney General, Memorandum for Joseph Califano, March 8, 1966, and drafts of the message in Back-up Material.

18 Presidents, *Public Papers: Johnson,* 1966: 463.

19 Attorney General to the Vice-President, April 28, 1966, "Civil Rights Bill Proposed in 1966" folder, reel 51, CRD Records. Other titles of the bill dealt

with the selection of state and federal juries, with the desegregation of public schools and facilities, and with housing discrimination.

20   Henry Wilson, Memorandum for the President, March 11, 1966, box 11, Office Files of Henry Wilson, LBJ; Roy Wilkins, telegram to the President, January 13, 1966, "Civil Rights (1)" folder, Clifford Alexander, Jr., Memorandum to Harry McPherson, June 8, 1966, Civil Rights (4) folder, box 22, Files of Harry McPherson, LBJ; Dore Schary, telegram to the President, February 16, 1967, box 552, Files of Fred Panzer, LBJ; SNCC Press Release, February 4, 1966, box 171, SNCC Papers; Resolution adopted by Iowa Conference of the United Church of Christ, June 9, 1966, Gen. HU2/ST 24, WHCF, LBJ; William M. Klin to Lyndon B. Johnson, June 8, 1966, Gen. LE/HU2, WHCF, LBJ; Lawson, *In Pursuit of Power,* pp. 52, 72.

21   Press release, June 7, 1966, Gen. LE/HU 2, WHCF, LBJ.

22   Lawson, *Pursuit of Power,* pp. 5, 31–32, 44–46, 51–53, 57, 61–62; Harvard Sitkoff, *The Struggle for Black Equality, 1954–1980* (New York, 1981), pp. 212–15; Allen J. Matusow, *The Unraveling of America: A History of Liberalism in the 1960s* (New York, 1984), pp. 349, 353–55; Cleveland Sellers (with Robert Terrell), *The River of No Return: The Autobiography of a Black Militant and the Life and Death of SNCC* (New York, 1973), pp. 149–50.

23   Sitkoff, *Struggle,* p. 202; Matusow, *Unraveling,* p. 362; Lawson, *Pursuit of Power,* pp. 5, 74.

24   *Unraveling,* p. 196.

25   Sitkoff, *Struggle,* p. 222; Lawson, *Pursuit of Power,* p. 6.

26   Sitkoff, *Struggle,* p. 222, Lawson, *Pursuit of Power,* pp. 45–57.

27   *Washington Post,* March 28, 1965.

28   NAACP, "Congress Gets the Civil Rights Protection Act of 1966," undated, box 114, SNCC Papers.

29   "Republican Policy Committee Statement on the Civil Rights Act of 1966," August 1, 1966, box 11, files of Henry Wilson, LBJ.

30   Charles D. Roche, Memorandum for General O'Brien, March 11, 1966, box 11, Wilson Files; Attorney General, Memorandum for the President, March 17, 1966, box 21, "Civil Rights (1)" folder; McPherson Files; Attorney General, Memorandum for Henry H. Wilson, March 13, 1966, Larry O'Brien, Memorandum to Joe Califano, March 14, 1966, and Nicholas deB. Katzenbach, Memorandum for Joseph A. Califano, Jr., March 11, 1966, all in Ex. SP 2/3/1966/HU2, Message on Civil Rights 4/28/66, Back-up Material; White House Conference on Civil Rights, *To Fulfill These Rights* (Washington, 1966), pp. 111, 133–35 (hereinafter cited as *To Fulfill These Rights*).

31   U.S., Congress, House, Committee on the Judiciary, *Civil Rights Act of 1966,* 89th Cong., 2d sess., 1966, H. Rept. 1678, 1:1, 15–16, 28; *Cong. Re-*

cord, 89th Cong., 2d sess., July 25, 1966, p. 16849. The second new title gave the attorney general the authority to authorize destruction of certain records required by existing law to be retained.

32   U.S., Congress, House, Committee on the Judiciary, *Civil Rights 1966: Hearings . . . ,* 89th Cong., 2d sess., 1966, p. 1061, and *Civil Rights Act of 1966: Additional and Minority Views,* 89th Cong., 2d sess., 1966, H. Rept. 1678, 2:21–23 (quote at 23); *Cong. Record,* 89th Cong., 2d sess., August 8, 1966, p. 18475.

33   Lawson, *Pursuit of Power,* p. 71; House Judiciary Committee, *Civil Rights Act of 1966,* 1:12, 60, and 2:48, *Cong. Record,* 89th Cong., 2d sess., July 28, 1966, pp. 17487–88, 17496, and August 8, 1966, pp. 18474–78.

34   William Higgs, "Analysis of Civil Rights Act of 1966 as Reported by the House Judiciary Committee on June 30, 1966," and "Summary of a Statement by Stokely Carmichael . . . on the Civil Rights Bill of 1966 . . . ," July 1, 1966, box 175, SNCC Papers; James C. Harvey, *Black Civil Rights During the Johnson Administration* (Jackson, Miss., 1973), p. 39; *Cong. Record,* 89th Cong., 2d sess., July 25, 1966, p. 16832; Lawson, *In Pursuit of Power,* p. 71.

35   *Cong. Record,* 89th Cong., 2d sess., August 2, 1966, pp. 17846–48, and August 3, 1966, pp. 18107–108.

36   Ibid., July 25, 1966, p. 17181, and July 27, 1966, p. 17226.

37   Ibid., July 28, 1966, p. 17497, and August 8, 1966, pp. 18474, 18481, 18489.

38   Ibid., July 28, 1966, pp. 17522, 17525, and August 8, 1966, pp. 18485–89. The amendment authorized the attorney general to bring suit to recover the amount of the award from the person who had injured the victim.

39   Ibid., August 8, 1966, pp. 18474–80.

40   Ibid., pp. 18455–74, and August 9, 1966, pp. 18739–40.

41   Sam J. Ervin, Jr., *Preserving the Constitution: The Autobiography of Senator Sam J. Ervin, Jr.* (Charlottesville, 1984), pp. 163–64; Paul R. Clancy, *Just a Country Lawyer: A Biography of Senator Sam Ervin* (Bloomington, 1974), p. 175.

42   Sam J. Ervin to Charles W. Brown, May 6, 1966, and Ervin to L. M. Bankright, May 6, 1966, box 36, Sam J. Ervin, Jr., Papers, Southern Historical Collection, University of North Carolina, Chapel Hill.

43   Sam J. Ervin to Thomas J. Schwab, August 15, 1966, Ervin to Mrs. Murray Newman, May 27, 1966, and Ervin to Barbara Moffitt, June 13, 1966, all in box 36, Ervin Papers; Ervin to Ray E. Jones, June 21, 1966, and Ervin to John Menapace, September 28, 1966, both in box 52, Ervin Papers; U.S., Congress, Senate, Subcommittee on Constitutional Rights of the Committee on the Judiciary, *Civil Rights: Hearings on S. 3296 . . . and S 3170,* 89th Cong., 2d sess., 1966, 1:97. (Hereafter cited as CRS, *1966 Hearings.*)

44   CRS, *1966 Hearings,* 1:66, 96, 103–106.

45 Ibid., p. 66.

46 Ibid., pp. 93–97, 124.

47 Ibid., pp. 94, 103–105, 123–24, 175, 412, 468, 846 (quote at 175); Erving to Bloch, February 5, 1960, box 193, Ervin Papers; Ervin to Bloch, box 36, Ervin Papers.

48 Richard Russell to Milton Tipton, August 15, 1966, box 108, series X, Richard Russell Papers, University of Georgia, Athens, Georgia; Justice, "Administrative History," vol. 7, part X, p. 107; Harvey, *Black Civil Rights*, pp. 39–40; Russell D. Renka, "Bargaining with Legislative Whales in the Kennedy and Johnson Administrations" (paper delivered at the annual meeting of the American Political Science Association, August 28–31, 1980), pp. 17–18; Lawson, *Pursuit of Power*, p. 76.

49 Ervin to Bernard J. Schmidt, September 26, 1966, box 36, Ervin Papers.

50 Quoted in Lawson, *Pursuit of Power*, p. 6.

51 Sitkoff, *Struggle*, p. 218; Lawson, *Pursuit of Power*, 64, 78; Ramsey Clark, Memorandum for Joseph H. Califano, undated, box 1, Legislative Background of Civil Rights Act of 1968, LBJ; Ramsey Clark to the Vice-President, February 17, 1967, "Civil Rights Bill Proposed in 1966" folder, Reel 51, CRD Records; Barefoot Sanders, Memorandum to the Acting Attorney General, January 26, 1967, box 7, Clark Papers; Pollak Oral History.

52 White House Conference, *To Fulfill These Rights*, pp. 133–35.

53 Press release, October 18, 1966, Special Legislative File, box 471, Emanuel Celler Papers, LC; Jim Gaither, Memorandum for Joe Califano, January 23, 1965, "Civil Rights" folder, box 3, Files of James Gaither, LBJ.

54 John Doar, Memorandum for the Acting Attorney General, January 26, 1967, in Justice, "Administrative History," vol. VII, part 10b, Documentary Supplement; Justice, "Administrative History," vol. VII, part 10b, pp. 107–108; White House Conference, *To Fulfill These Rights*, pp. 135–36; Louis F. Claiborne, Memorandum to Ramsey Clark, July 18, 1966, "Legislation Against Intimidation and Violence" folder, Reel 51, CRD Records; Stephen Pollak, Memorandum for John Doar, January 20, 1967, box 7, Clark Papers.

55 "Fact Sheet 10—Civil Liberties: Penalties for Interference with Civil Rights (H.R. 2516)," undated, Special Legislative File, box 475, Celler Papers; Harvey, *Black Civil Rights*, p. 44; "Title V of the Proposed Civil Rights Act of 1967," undated, in Justice, "Administrative History," vol. VII, part 10b, Documentary Supplement; U.S. Congress, House, Committee on the Judiciary, *Penalties for Interference with Civil Rights*, 90th Cong., 1st sess., 1967, H. Rept. 705; *Cong. Record*, 90th Cong., 1st sess., August 15, 1967, pp. 22076–77, 22680, and August 16, 1967, pp. 22743–45.

56 Whitehead, *Attack on Terror*, pp. 236–38; Florence Mars, *Witness in Philadelphia* (Baton Rouge, 1977), p. 224; Watters and Cleghorn, *Climbing Jacob's*

Ladder, p. 140; "Write Your Congressman About Death in the Night with Killers Going Free," Group III, series B, box 304, NAACP Papers; Roy Wilkins to "Dear Friend," February 1966, box 114, SNCC Papers; "Other Litigation," p. 3–314, undated, box 151, Clark Papers; Petition, undated, Group III, series B, box 304, NAACP Papers; Roy Wilkins, telegram to Emanuel Celler, August 14, 1967, Special Legislative File, box 475, Celler Papers.

57 *Cong. Record,* 90th Cong., 1st sess., August 15, 1967, pp. 22681–88, 22689 (Ryan), and August 16, 1967, pp. 22771 (Helstoski) and 22773 (Fontain). For expressions of views similar to those of Helstoski by Representatives James Corman (D-Calif.) and Andrew Jacobs (D-Ind.), see ibid., August 15, 1967, p. 22688, and August 16, 1967, p. 22748.

58 Ibid., August 15, 1967, pp. 22676, 22684–88 (McClory quote at 22685), and August 16, 1967, pp. 22756–59, 22772–73, 22775–79 (Randall quote at 22775–76); Matusow, *Unraveling,* p. 362; Lawson, *Pursuit of Power,* p. 79.

59 *Cong. Record,* 90th Cong., 1st sess., August 16, 1967, pp. 22745, 22757–59, 22777–78.

60 August 18, 1967.

61 Harvey, *Black Civil Rights,* p. 46; U.S., Congress, Senate Committee on the Judiciary, *Interference with Civil Rights,* 90th Cong., 1st sess., 1967 S. Rept. 721, p. 3; U.S. Senate, Subcommittee on Constitutional Rights of the Committee on the Judiciary, *Civil Rights Act of 1967: Hearings . . . ,* 90th Cong., 1st sess., 1967, pp. 61, 350–73; Ervin to Reverend Robert E. Seymore, November 8, 1967, box 53, and Ervin to Charles J. Bloch, September 12, 1967, box 224, Ervin Papers.

62 Senate Judiciary Committee, *Interference with Civil Rights,* pp. 21–33; George B. Autry to Ralph Hemphill, October 6, 1967, box 20, and Wes Hayden, Memorandum for Lewis Evans, December 29, 1967, box 19, Records of the Senate Committee on the Judiciary's Subcommittee on Constitutional Rights, 85–92nd Congs., Record Group 46, National Archives (hereinafter cited as CRS Records); *New York Times,* October 16, 1967, p. 44; Sam Ervin, Jr., to *New York Times,* October 17, 1967, and Sam Ervin to Roman L. Hruska, October 20, 1967, box 224, Ervin Papers; "Inadequacies of Coverage in the Substitute Version of H.R. 2516," undated, "Legislation Against Intimidation and Violence" folder, Reel 51, CRD Records.

63 Senate Judiciary Committee, *Interference with Civil Rights,* pp. 1–3; Sam J. Ervin, Jr., to Steve Tilley, February 19, 1968, box 53, and Ervin to Reverend Tom A. Cutting, April 9, 1968, box 27, Ervin Papers; Steve Pollak, Memorandum for the Attorney General, box 49, Clark Papers.

64 Sam Ervin to Roman Hruska, October 20, 1967, box 224, Ervin Papers; Senate Judiciary Committee, *Interference with Civil Rights,* pp. 13–20 (quote at

20); Senator Philip Hart to Clarence Mitchell, December 19, 1967, box 306, Philip A. Hart Papers, Bentley Historical Library, University of Michigan.

65 Clarence Mitchell to Philip Hart, December 12, 1967, box 306, Hart Papers; Sam Ervin, Jr., to N. B. Smith, November 8, 1967, box 53, Ervin Papers; Lyndon B. Johnson to Roy Wilkins, November 20, 1967, Ex. HU2, WHCF, LBJ; Presidents, *Public Papers: Lyndon Johnson,* 1968–1969:31, 58–59; Lawson, *Pursuit of Power,* p. 81.

66 Justice, "Administrative History," vol. VII, part 10b, p. 114; Stephen J. Pollak, Memorandum to the Deputy Attorney General, January 25, 1968, in ibid., Documentary Supplement; Larry Temple, Memorandum to the President, January 22, 1968, box 4, Legislative Background, Fair Housing Act of 1968, LBJ; Grady Norris, Memorandum for Stephen J. Pollak, January 26, 1968, "Legislation Against Intimidation and Violence" folder, Reel 51, CRD Records; Robert S. Rankin to Sam Ervin, February 3, 1968, and Ervin to Rankin, February 7, 1968, box 21, CRS Records; Everett Dirksen, "The Continuing Battle of Civil Rights," radio-TV message, February 12–18, 1968, Remarks and Releases 1968 file and "Civil Rights Legislation—H.R. 2516 and Senator Dirksen's Amendment #544," Working Papers File, Everett M. Dirksen Papers, Dirksen Center, Pekin, Illinois. Senator James Eastland (D-Miss.) candidly acknowledged to Clark that he planned to vote for the Ervin amendment and then against the bill as amended. The attorney general seems to have believed Ervin's intentions were similar. Larry Temple, Memorandum for the President, January 22, 1968.

67 Dirksen, "Continuing Battle of Civil Rights"; Birch Bayh et al., "Joint Statement of Senators on Legislation to Protect Against Violent Interference with Civil Rights," February 5, 1968, Special Legislative File, box 475, Celler Papers.

68 "Civil Rights Legislation"; Harvey, *Black Civil Rights,* pp. 49–50.

69 *Cong. Record,* 90th Cong., 2d sess., January 18, 1968, p. 319, January 22, 1968, pp. 536–37, 542, January 24, 1968, pp. 914–15 (Talmadge quote at 914), January 25, 1968, pp. 1023, 1026, 1033, January 26, 1968, p. 1162, January 29, 1968, pp. 1277 (Stennis quote), 1282–83, January 31, 1968, p. 1796; Sam J. Ervin, Jr., to Charles J. Bloch, January 30, 1968, box 53, Ervin Papers.

70 Harvey, *Black Civil Rights,* pp. 49–50; Leadership Conference on Civil Rights, Press Release, January 12, 1968, Gen. LE/HU2, WHCF, LBJ; "Statement Adopted by the Annual Board Meeting of the Leadership Conference on Civil Rights," January 30, 1968, folder 5, box 44, SCLC Papers; Merle Miller, *Lyndon: An Oral Biography* (New York, 1980), p. 515; Memo to Terry Segal, January 15, 1968, box 456, Hart Papers; [Stephen Pollak], Memorandum for the Attorney General, January 9, 1968, box 18, Clark Papers.

71 Miller, *Lyndon,* p. 515; Harvey, *Black Civil Rights,* p. 51; Neil MacNeil, "How Old Ev Foiled the Filibuster," *Life,* March 15, 1968, p. 328; Ramsey to the

Vice-President, February 28, 1968, box 45, Clark Papers; Pollak Oral History, p. 50; Lawson, *Pursuit of Power*, pp. 84–85.

72   Joseph Thomas Sees, "Federal Power to Combat Private Racial Violence in the Aftermath of *Price, Guest,* and the Civil Rights Act of 1968" (Ph.D. diss., Georgetown University, 1971), pp. 290–97; *Cong. Record*, 90th Cong., 2d sess., February 28, 1968, pp. 4570–71, and March 8, 1968, pp. 5831–33.

73   *Cong. Record*, 90th Cong., 2d sess., March 4, 1968, p. 4960, and March 11, 1968, p. 5992; Harvey, *Black Civil Rights*, p. 51; Mike Manatos, Memorandum for the President, March 5, 1968, box 4, Legislative Background.

74   Matusow, *Unraveling*, pp. 208, 396; Barefoot Sanders, Memorandum for the President, February 29, 1962, Ex. LE HU2, WHCF, LBJ; John W. McCormack to John J. Wright, April 4, 1968, box 131, folder 6, John W. McCormack Papers, Mugar Library, Boston University; Barefoot Sanders to Richard Bolling, April 11, 1968, Gen. LE/HU2, WHCF, LBJ; Lyndon B. Johnson, *The Vantage Point: Perspectives on the Presidency* (New York, 1971), pp. 177–78; Harvey, *Black Civil Rights,* p. 54; Notes on the President's Meeting with the Congressional Democratic Leadership, March 19, 1968, box 2, Meeting Notes Files, Papers of Lyndon B. Johnson, President, LBJ; Untitled and undated memo attached to letter from Gerald R. Ford to Dwight W. Johnson, box 85, folder 42, Ford Congressional Papers, GRF; Harry McPherson, transcript of oral history interview, undated, tape 8, p. 4, LBJ; U.S., Congress, House, Committee on Rules, *Providing for Agreeing to the Senate Amendments to the Bill (H.R. 2516) to Prescribe Penalties for Certain Acts of Violence and Intimidation and for Other Purposes,* 90th Cong., 2d sess., 1968, H. Rept. 1289; *Cong. Record,* 90th Cong., 2d sess., March 14, 1968, pp. 6489–90, and April 10, 1968, pp. 9620–21.

75   Gerald R. Ford to Dwight W. Johnson, box B85, folder 42, Ford Congressional Papers.

76   For the provisions of the new law, see Title I, Pub. L, No. 90-284, 82 Stat. 23 (1968).

Chapter Ten

1   U.S., Department of Justice, *The Annual Report of the Attorney General of the United States: Fiscal 1969* (Washington, 1969), pp. 46–47.

2   Assistant Attorney General Drew S. Days III to the author, October 23, 1980 (hereinafter cited as Days Letter). Six of the nineteen possible abdication cases resulted in the conviction of all defendants, and four in the acquittal of all defendants. In five all defendants entered pleas of guilty. One case was dismissed on motion of the government, and in two cases grand juries refused to indict the accused. One case produced mixed results: ten convictions, three pleas of guilty, three acquittals, and four dismissals. Days's compilation does not include one

police brutality case in which a white peace officer who had beaten a black suspect was tried under both section 245 and section 242 but convicted only on the latter charge. United States v. Hearod, 499 F.2d 1003 (5th Cir. 1974). For a more detailed discussion of how section 245 was used during the first decade after its enactment, see Michal R. Belknap, "The Legal Legacy of Lemuel Penn," *Howard Law Journal* 25 (1982): 516–21.

3   Stephen J. Pollak, transcript of oral history interview, January 30, 1969, pp. 26–38, LBJ (quotes at 34). For the assessment of Clark as more "activist" than his predecessors, see Allen Wolk, *The Presidency and Black Civil Rights* (Rutherford, N.J., 1971), p. 77.

4   Steven F. Lawson, *In Pursuit of Power: Southern Blacks and Electoral Politics, 1965–1982* (New York, 1985), pp. 131–32; Jonathan Schell, *The Time of Illusion* (New York, 1976), pp. 35–43; Alexander v. Holmes, 396 U.S. 19, 19–20 (1969); *New York Times,* October 17, 1969, p. 24, May 11, 1972, p. 13; Councilman John Lewis, personal interview with the author at the Atlanta City Hall, Atlanta, Georgia, June 5, 1984.

5   Judge David L. Norman, personal interview with the author in his chambers in Washington, D.C., October 27, 1980; Days Letter; Schell, *Time of Illusion,* p. 43; "Apologist," *Time,* October 31, 1969, p. 77.

6   Milton Viorst, *Fire in the Streets: America in the 1960s* (New York, 1979), pp. 165–92, 364–65; *Baltimore Sun,* March 9, 1969; Dwayne Walls, *The Klan: Collapsed and Dormant* (Nashville, 1970); U.S., Senate, Committee to Study Governmental Operations with Respect to Intelligence Activities, *Hearings . . . , pt. VI, Federal Bureau of Investigation,* 94th Cong., 1st sess., 1975, p. 145; Memo from the Director of the FBI to the Attorney General, December 19, 1967, in the same source, pp. 516–27 (hereinafter cited as FBI Memo).

7   United States Commission on Civil Rights, *Survey of School Desegregation in Southern and Border States, 1965–1966* (Washington, 1966), p. 38; Southern Regional Council, "Justice in Grenada, Mississippi," mimeographed, November 1966, folder 75-03-60, and Voter Education Press Release, June 13, 1966, folder 75-01-76-17, SRCC; Florence Mars, *Witness in Philadelphia* (Baton Rouge, 1977); pp. 207–10; Gene Livingston, Memorandum to James L. Kelly, June 16, 1967, and "Recent Acts of Racial Violence in North Carolina," undated, box 145, Ramsey Clark Papers, LBJ; Braxton Bryant to the President, May 23, 1966, Gen. HU2/ST 42, WHCF, LBJ; Lawson, *Pursuit of Power,* pp. 20, 31, 50–51, 59–60.

8   Aaron E. Henry and Charles Evers, telegram to the President, October 4, 1967, Gen. HU2/ST 24, WHCF, LBJ.

9   Jeanette Strong, telegram to the President, March 1, 1967, Gen. HU2/ST 24, WHCF, LBJ; Memorandum from Kathy Coyne to Wilkins et al., November 17, 1966, group III, series B, box 294, NAACP Papers; *New York World-Journal-Tribune,* March 5, 1967; *Jackson Daily News,* April 11, 1968; *New Orleans Times-*

Picayune, May 16, 1968; *Memphis Commercial Appeal,* April 5, 1970; Wilkins "Dear Friend" letter; Houser v. Hill, 278 F. Supp. 920, 924–25 (M.D. Ala. 1968); John Doar, Memorandum for the Attorney General, June 30, 1967, box 145, Clark Papers; Viorst, *Fire in the Streets,* pp. 525, 541; *Arkansas Gazette,* September 17, 1970; SNCC Press Release, January 4, 1966, box 141, SNCC Papers.

10 *New York Times,* September 19, 1973; "The Law: Hotheads and Professionals," *Time,* August 10, 1970, pp. 42–43; *Charleston News and Courier,* November 8, 1968; *Charlotte Observer,* September 14, 1968; Memorandum from the Attorney General to the President, February 12, 1968, EX HU2/ST 40, WHCF, LBJ. Ramsey Clark, the attorney general at the time of the Orangeburg Massacre, was extremely disappointed by the Justice Department's inability to obtain indictments and convictions in the case (Ramsey Clark, personal interview with the author in his office in New York City, October 23, 1980).

11 *Miami Herald,* July 2, 1964; Memorandum for the Files by Lee C. White, June 10, 1964, box 5, Files of Lee C. White, LBJ.

12 John Doar to Lee C. White, December 31, 1965, Gen. HU2/ST 9, WHCF, LBJ.

13 Dan Moore to Mrs. Margaret Bush Wilson, November 30, 1965, group III, series B, box 294, NAACP Papers. William H. Chafe (*Civilities and Civil Rights: Greensboro, North Carolina, and the Black Struggle for Freedom* [New York, 1980], p. 28) claims that despite his law and order posture Governor Moore failed really to crack down on the Ku Klux Klan. However, his principal evidence for this contention is the fact that Moore allowed klansmen to exercise their constitutionally protected right of free speech by operating a booth at the North Carolina State Fair from which antiblack taunts were broadcast.

14 Senator Sam Ervin to Ramsey Clark, September 22, 1967, box 224, Sam J. Ervin, Jr., Papers, Southern Historical Collection, University of North Carolina, Chapel Hill; *Chicago Sun-Times,* May 3, 1965; Transcript of Record, at 360–85, United States v. Myers, 277 F.2d 412 (5th Cir. 1967); *Alabama Journal,* September 5, 1965.

15 Harold Marty and Kenneth Fairley, "'We Got Nothing to Hide,'" *Saturday Evening Post,* January 30, 1965, p. 31; "The Ku Klux Klan on the Way Back," *Newsweek,* October 19, 1964, p. 51; *Miami Herald,* August 6, 1964; *Baltimore Afro-American,* October 10, 1964; Whitehead, *Attack on Terror: The FBI Against the Ku Klux Klan in Mississippi* (New York, 1970), p. 237; Steven Rosenthal, Memorandum for Bill Moyers, June 17, 1966, Ex FG 135, WHCF, LBJ; John Doar to Congressman Byron Rogers, August 11, 1966, Gen. HU2/ST 24, WHCF, LBJ; *New York Times,* November 19, 1966, p. 22; Lawson, *Pursuit of Power,* p. 58. For the complaints of civil rights activists about the amount of protection provided, see the comments in Harry McPherson, undated handwrit-

ten notes, box 22, "Civil Rights (5)" folder, Office Files of Harry McPherson, LBJ, and Floyd McKissick to the President, June 19, 1966, Gen. HU2/ST 24, WHCF, LBJ.

16 *Delta Democrat-Times* (Greenville, Miss.), September 27, 1964; *Christian Science Monitor,* July 10, 1968; *New York Times,* March 2, 1968; Whitehead, *Attack on Terror,* pp. 289–95.

17 Houser v. Hill, 278 F. Supp. 920, 927 (M.D. Ala. 1968); SNCC Press Release, January 4, 1966, box 171, SNCC Papers; Mars, *Witness in Philadelphia,* pp. 207, 210; Lawson, *Pursuit of Power,* p. 59; Mal Gissen to the President, undated, Gen. HU2/ST 24, WHCF, LBJ. It should be noted that when the local police in Grenada defaulted on their responsibilities, Mississippi state troopers were sent into that community to restore order. *Memphis Commercial Appeal,* September 15, 1966; Clayborne Carson, *In Struggle: SNCC and the Black Awakening of the 1960s* (Cambridge., Mass, 1981), p. 210.

18 *Baltimore Sun,* March 9, 1969.

19 "The South: Turn in a Dark Road," *Time,* December 10, 1965, pp. 27–28; Benjamin Muse, *The American Negro Revolution: From Nonviolence to Black Power, 1963–1967* (Bloomington, Ind., 1968), p. 222; *New York Times,* December 3, 1965, pp. 1, 35; "Statement by Dr. Martin Luther King, Jr.," December 3, 1965, series III, box 9, King Papers–King Center.

20 *New Orleans Times-Picayune,* December 1, 1968; Memorandum from Stephen J. Pollak to the Attorney General, February 12, 1968, and Memorandum from Stephen J. Pollak to the Attorney General, March 18, 1968, Weekly Reports of the Attorney General, Reel 52, Records of the Civil Rights Division, Department of Justice, LBJ (hereinafter cited as CRD Records); *New York Times,* March 16, 1968, p. 17, November 11, 1968, p. 23, February 1, 1969, p. 32; *Los Angeles Times,* January 19, 1969; *Birmingham News,* November 25, 1969.

21 Memorandum from John Doar to the Attorney General, December 4, 1967, Memorandum from Stephen J. Pollak to the Attorney General, February 12, 1968, Memorandum from Pollak to the Attorney General, March 18, 1968, Memorandum from Pollak to the Attorney General, March 23, 1968, all on Reel 52, CRD; *New York Times,* March 16, 1968, p. 17, November 11, 1968, p. 23, January 26, 1969, p. 49, February 1, 1969, p. 32, September 19, 1973, p. 33; *Los Angeles Times,* July 29, 1968, and January 19, 1969; *Memphis Commercial Appeal,* January 19, 1969, October 12, 1971; *Birmingham News,* February 5, 1971; *Charlotte Observer,* January 20, 1968; *Baltimore Sun,* March 9, 1969; *National Observer,* May 26, 1969.

22 September 19, 1973, p. 33.

23 *Milwaukee Journal,* October 22, 1967; U.S. Department of Justice, Press Release, January 2, 1966, folder 75-01-71-33, SRCC; Former Attorney General Nicholas Katzenbach, telephonic interview with the author, June 20, 1984.

24 John Doar to W. W. Godbold, Jr., October 31, 1966, Gen. HU2/ST 24, LBJ.

25 FBI Memo, p. 519; Frank J. Donner, *The Age of Surveillance: The Aims and Methods of America's Political Intelligence System* (New York, 1980), pp. 204, 207–11; Athan Theoharis, *Spying on Americans: Political Surveillance from Hoover to the Huston Plan* (Philadelphia, 1978), pp. 141–42; *Winston-Salem Journal*, July 16, 1964; Jack Rosenthal, Memorandum for Clifford L. Alexander, Jr., March 25, 1966, box 4, Legislative Background, Fair Housing Act of 1968, LBJ.

26 Transcript of Record, at 3, United States v. Wilkins, 376 F.2d 55 (5th Cir. 1967); *National Observer*, May 26, 1969.

27 U.S., Senate, Subcommittee on Constitutional Rights of the Committee on the Judiciary, *Civil Rights Act of 1967: Hearings . . .*, 90th Cong., 1st sess., 1967, p. 211.

28 Section 11(b), Voting Rights Act of 1965, Pub. L, No. 89–110, 79 Stat. 437 (1965).

29 Joseph Thomas Sees, "Federal Power to Combat Racial Violence in the Aftermath of *Price, Guest,* and the Civil Rights Act of 1968" (Ph.D. diss., Georgetown University, 1971), p. 24. The only case the Justice Department brought under section 11(b) between its enactment and June 30, 1966, was a civil action directed at Louisiana landlords who had evicted their black tenants for registering to vote. U.S., Department of Justice, *Annual Report of the Attorney General of the United States for the Fiscal Year Ended June 30, 1965* (Washington, 1966), p. 191. Attorney General Katzenbach declined to use that provision against the man who allegedly shot James Meredith. Lawson, *Pursuit of Power*, p. 54.

30 Norman Interview; Lewis Interview; Katzenbach Interview; Voter Education Project Press Release, August 5, 1966, folder 75-01-76-10, SRCC; Charles V. Hamilton, *The Bench and the Ballot: Southern Federal Judges and Black Voters* (New York, 1973), pp. 331, 341; "Black Power at Southern Polls," *U.S. News & World Report*, January 5, 1970, p. 6; Allen Matusow, *The Unraveling of America: A History of Liberalism in the 1960s* (New York, 1984), pp. 187–88.

31 *New York Times*, August 30, 1970, p. 66; Voter Education Project Press Release, December 15, 1970, and "Black Elected Officials in the South" (January 1965), Files of the Voter Education Project, Atlanta, Georgia.

32 Review of *Federalism and Civil Rights* by Burke Marshall, *Georgetown Law Journal* 53 (Spring 1965): 860.

33 "Black Power at the Dixie Polls," *Time*, June 15, 1970, p. 17.

34 *New York Times*, September 19, 1973, p. 33.

35 October 4, 1964.

36 Quoted in *Christian Science Monitor*, July 3, 1964. In July 1964 Florida Attorney General James Kynes made much the same point when he observed that St. Augustine restaurant and motel owners had allowed young toughs to take

over their city, only to find it impossible to resume control of the community when it no longer suited their purposes to have groups of violent whites roaming the streets. David R. Colburn, "The St. Augustine Business Community," in *Southern Businessmen and Desegregation,* ed. Elizabeth Jacoway and David R. Colburn (Baton Rouge, 1982), pp. 229–30.

37 *Charlotte Observer,* August 6, 1964; *The State* (Columbia, S.C.), August 7, 1964; *Delta Democrat-Times,* June 11, 1965; *Nashville Tennessean,* February 27, 1965; *Miami Herald,* March 13, 1965. As late as the fall of 1967 one Mississippi newspaper continued to worry that if bombings were not stopped, "this criminal element will soon take over our society." *Lexington Advertiser,* October 12, 1967.

38 Confidential Memorandum by Benjamin Muse on the Problem of Law Enforcement in Mississippi, June 1964, folder 75-01-59-01, SRCC; United States Commission on Civil Rights, *Law Enforcement: A Report on Equal Protection in the South* (Washington, 1965), p. 97; Charles Sallis and John Quincy Adams, "Desegregation in Jackson, Mississippi," in *Southern Businessmen and Desegregation,* p. 247; *Dallas Morning News,* October 3, 1964; *Delta Democrat-Times,* July 23, 1964.

39 Civil Rights Commission, *Law Enforcement,* pp. 39–41; Robert W. Brumfield to President Johnson, November 20, 1964, and Memorandum from John A. Griffin to Governor Collins, October 2, 1964, Ex. HU2/ST 24, WHCF, LBJ; *Charlotte Observer,* April 27, 1965; Benjamin Muse, *The American Negro Revolution: From Nonviolence to Black Power, 1963–1967* (Bloomington, 1968), p. 135; *Memphis Commercial Appeal,* June 27, 1965; *Delta Democrat-Times,* February 5, 1965; *Norfolk Virginian-Pilot,* January 19, 1965; Mars, *Witness in Philadelphia,* pp. 142–43.

40 U.S., Congress, House, Committee on the Judiciary, *Hearings Before Subcommittee Number 5 on Miscellaneous Proposals Regarding the Civil Rights of Persons Within the Jurisdiction of the United States,* 89th Cong., 2d sess., 1966, p. 1407; *Jackson Daily News,* July 1, 1964; *Birmingham News,* December 10, 1964. Although there is no good study of the impact of television news coverage of the civil rights struggle in the South, William B. Monroe, Jr., has commented on the effect it had on the understanding and attitudes of white southerners. See his "Television: The Chosen Instrument of the Revolution," in *Race and the News Media,* ed. Paul L. Fisher and Ralph C. Lowenstein (New York, 1967), pp. 87–88.

41 Quoted in *Arkansas Gazette,* February 18, 1965.

42 *Christian Science Monitor,* July 10, 1968; *Delta Democrat-Times,* February 21, 1965; *Nashville Tennessean,* November 10, 1965; "Newspaper Bombed: UPI Man Injured," *Editor & Publisher,* September 5, 1964, p. 11.

43 *Greensboro Daily News,* July 13, 1964, January 27, 1965; Governor Dan Moore to Mrs. Margaret Bush Wilson, November 30, 1965, group III, series B,

box 294, NAACP Papers; *Greensboro Daily News,* January 27, 1965; *Atlanta Constitution,* January 4, 1970; *Birmingham News,* July 9, 1964; Notes (abstracting newspaper article), July 25, 1964, folder 75-03-17-14, SRCC; Colburn, "The St. Augustine Business Community," p. 232.

44 *St. Petersburg Times,* July 2, 1964; *Miami Herald,* July 28, 1964; *Dallas Times-Herald,* August 31, 1964; *Raleigh News and Observer,* September 13, 1964; *Arkansas Gazette,* October 7, 1964; *Birmingham News,* December 3, 1964; *Jackson Daily News,* June 23, 1964; *Charleston News and Courier,* September 1, 1965.

45 *Baton Rouge State-Times,* August 7, 1964; *Chattanooga Times,* December 12, 1964; *Delta Democrat-Times,* August 5, 1964, August 9, 1964, December 10, 1964, January 13, 1965, March 12, 1965, May 9, 1965; *Greensboro Daily News,* August 8, 1964; *Knoxville News-Sentinel,* August 6, 1964; *Nashville Tennessean,* December 12, 1964; *Nashville Banner,* August 10, 1964, December 11, 1964; *Norfolk Virginian-Pilot,* August 7, 1964; *Richmond News Leader,* January 4, 1965; *St. Petersburg Times,* August 7, 1964, December 5, 1964; *Jackson Daily News,* September 10, 1964, June 7, 1966; *Montgomery Advertiser,* March 11, 1965, March 27, 1965; *Arkansas Gazette,* October 26, 1964, May 9, 1965; *Birmingham News,* March 12, 1965; *Memphis Commercial Appeal,* June 8, 1966; *The State* (Columbia, S.C.), December 8, 1964; *Winston-Salem Journal,* August 6, 1964.

46 *Atlanta Constitution,* July 13, 1964; *Birmingham News,* December 10, 1964; *St. Petersburg Times,* October 6, 1964; *Macon Telegraph,* March 29, 1965; Muse, *American Negro Revolution,* p. 135; *Delta Democrat-Times,* September 29, 1964. See also the *Delta Democrat-Times,* issues of October 30, 1964, and November 30, 1964.

47 *Birmingham News,* April 1, 1965; *Dallas Morning News,* April 6, 1965; *Delta Democrat-Times,* March 7, 1965.

48 Press Release, July 6, 1964, Ex. HU2/ST 24, WHCF, LBJ.

49 Press Release, January 17, 1966, Ex. SP 2-3/1966 HU2, Message on Civil Rights 4/28/66, Back-up Material III, WHCF, LBJ.

50 Lee C. White to Bobby C. Pappas, May 7, 1965, Ku Klux Klan Name File, WHCF, LBJ.

51 Leroy Collins, Report to the President, March 24, 1965, box 21, "Civil Rights (1)" folder, Files of Harry McPherson, LBJ. Although impressionistic evidence suggests that other white southerners continued to share the Klan's racist attitudes, Paul B. Sheatsly found that between May 1963 and June 1965 there was a remarkable change in their feelings about having a few blacks in their childrens' schools. The percentage which would object to this dropped from 61 percent to 37 percent. Sheatsly, "White Attitudes Toward the Negro," *Daedalus* 75 (1966): 235–36.

52 Sheldon Hackney, "Southern Violence," *American Historical Review* 74

(February 1969): 906–25; John Shelton Read, "To Live—and Die—in Dixie: A Contribution to the Study of Southern Violence," *Political Science Quarterly* 86 (September 1971): 429–43; Raymond D. Gastil, "Homicide and a Regional Culture of Violence," *American Sociological Review* 36 (February 1971): 412–27. Reed does use responses to one question from a 1969 survey asking whether respondents had guns in their homes.

53   "Middle Class Violence," *Psychology Today* 4 (November 1970): 53. The data on which Stark and McEvoy rely support their characterization of the South, just as that used by the authors cited in note 52 above support theirs. Due to differences in the factors on which these scholars have based their respective conclusions concerning regional propensities for violence, however, direct comparisons between 1968 and the period down to 1965 are difficult. The only comparisons which can be drawn between Reed's data and that of Stark and McEvoy involve attitudes about corporal punishment of children in the schools.

54   Federal Bureau of Investigation, *Crime in the United States: Uniform Crime Reports—1968* (Washington, 1969), pp. 60, 62, 64. The southern figures presented here are for the eleven states which once comprised the Confederate States of America. The South for which the FBI presents totals of its own includes the border states of Delaware, Maryland, West Virginia, Kentucky, and Oklahoma.

55   Ibid., p. 7; FBI, *Crime in the United States: Uniform Crime Reports—1963* (Washington, 1964), p. 6, *Crime in the United States: Uniform Crime Reports—1964* (Washington, 1965), p. 6, *Crime in the United States: Uniform Crime Reports—1965* (Washington, 1966), p. 6, *Crime in the United States: Uniform Crime Reports—1966* (Washington, 1967), p. 6, *Crime in the United States: Uniform Crime Reports—1967* (Washington, 1968), p. 5, and *Uniform Crime Reports for the United States—1969* (Washington, 1970), p. 7.

56   For discussion of regional differences with respect to this "stand-your-ground" doctrine and the consequences thereof, see William L. Prosser, *Handbook of the Law of Torts*, 4th ed. (St. Paul, 1971), p. 111, and Richard Maxwell Brown, "Southern Violence—Regional Problem or National Nemesis? Legal Attitudes Toward Southern Homicide in Historical Perspective," *Vanderbilt Law Review* 32 (January 1979): 234. Brown's article should be compared with the cases cited in "Annotation: Homicide: The Duty to Retreat When Not on One's Own Premises," *American Law Reports* 18 (1922): 1279–95.

57   The data utilized in Tables 2–4 was made available by the Inter-University Consortium for Political and Social Research. The data was originally collected for the *Justifying Violence* (1969) study done by Monica D. Blumenthal, Robert L. Kahn, and Frank M. Andrews. Neither the original source, nor the collectors of the data, nor the consortium bear any responsibility for the analyses or interpretations presented here.

58   Stark and McEvoy, "Middle Class Violence," p. 111.

59   *Charlotte Observer,* April 1, 1965; *Memphis Commercial Appeal,* April 8, 1965.

60   October 21, 1967.

61   Both the editorial and the statement are quoted in Mars, *Witness in Philadelphia,* pp. 147–48.

62   Senator John Stennis, telegram to the President, June 23, 1966, Ex. HU2/ST 24, WHCF, LBJ.

63   Transcript of Record, at 2558–59, United States v. Price, Crim. No. 5291 (S.D. Miss. 1967), hereinafter cited as Price Transcript.

64   Ibid., pp. 2567–70; *New Orleans Times-Picayune,* October 21, 1967.

65   Price Transcript, p. 2563.

66   Ibid., pp. 2562–63.

67   *New York Times,* September 1, 1964, p. 20, June 28, 1966, p. 25, June 29, 1966 p. 28; *Athens Banner-Herald,* September 1, 1964, September 6, 1964; Typed list of Athens Division petit jury panel, June 27, 1966, United States v. Myers, 377 F.2d 412 (5th Cir. 1967), FRC Container 53897, box 85, Crim. No. 2732, Federal Records Center, East Point, Georgia; St. John Barrett, personal interview with the author at his office in Washington, D.C., October 23, 1981; Belknap, "Legal Legacy," pp. 511–13. Even as to the murder of Lemuel Penn itself, the evidence against Sims and Myers was weaker in the federal trial than in the state one because Lackey's confession was not admitted into evidence against them.

In 1964 voluntary manslaughter was punishable in Georgia by one to twenty years in prison. Ga. Code section 16-1008 (1933).

68   Quoted in William Bradford Huie, "Murder: The Klan on Trial," *Saturday Evening Post,* June 19, 1965, p. 87.

69   WGAU Editorial on Lawlessness and Violence, Gen. HU2/ST 10, WHCF, LBJ.

70   Record, at 777, Myers v. United States, 377 F.2d 412 (1967).

71   Wilkins Transcript, pp. 693–95, 718; Excerpt Transcript, p. 26 (Johnson quote); *New York Times,* December 5, 1965, sec. IV, p. 7, April 27, 1965, p. 21, November 30, 1965, p. 33; Wilkins Transcript, pp. 32–43; Tinsley E. Yarbrough, *Judge Frank Johnson and Human Rights in Alabama* (University, Ala., 1981), p. 131.

72   "Alabama: The Trial," *Time,* May 14, 1965, p. 29; *New York Times,* October 23, 1965, p. 1, October 28, 1965, p. 28, December 3, 1965, p. 15 (quotes at 15); Muse, *American Negro Revolution,* p. 222; "Turn in a Dark Road," p. 27.

73   March 10, 1965.

74   As far back as 1871, Attorney General Amos T. Akerman had declared that in his opinion nothing was "more idle than to attempt to conciliate by kindness that portion of the southern people who are still malcontent. They take

all kindness on the part of the Government as evidence of timidity, and hence are emboldened to lawlessness by it. It appears impossible for the Government to win their affection. But it can command their respect by the exercise of its powers." Quoted in Robert J. Kaczorowski, *The Politics of Judicial Interpretation: The Federal Courts, Department of Justice and Civil Rights, 1866–1876* (New York, 1985), p. 83.

The long struggle of the civil rights movement to obtain federal protection from violence and intimidation generated a wealth of manuscript source material. Particularly valuable are the holdings of the Martin Luther King, Jr., Center for Nonviolent Social Change in Atlanta, Georgia. The King Center's Student Nonviolent Coordinating Committee Collection is especially rich. Also useful are its Southern Christian Leadership Conference, Martin Luther King, Jr., and Fred L. Shuttlesworth Papers, as well as its addendum to the Congress of Racial Equality Papers (1944–1968). The more valuable part of the CORE collection is housed at the Wisconsin State Historical Society in Madison, along with the files of CORE's Southern Regional Office. The King Papers are divided too, with those from the Nobel Peace Prizewinner's early career (including the period of the Montgomery bus boycott) located at Boston University's Mugar Library. Particularly valuable to anyone interested in the civil rights movement, its relations with the federal government, or racial violence in the South is the Southern Regional Council Collection at the Atlanta University Library. The National Association for the Advancement of Colored People Papers at the Library of Congress also contain a good deal of important information. The Leadership Conference on Civil Rights Collection at the Library of Congress and the files of the Voter Education Project in Atlanta are not as rich, but they too include some useful material.

For the government side of the story, the most valuable manuscript collections are those housed in the Dwight D. Eisenhower Presidential Library in Abilene, Kansas, the John F. Kennedy Presidential Library in Boston, Massachusetts, and the Lyndon B. Johnson Presidential Library in Austin, Texas, although there is some useful background material in the Tom C. Clark Papers at the Harry S. Truman Presidential Library in Independence, Missouri. By far the most valuable collection at the Eisenhower

Library is Papers of Dwight D. Eisenhower as President (Ann Whitman File). Also informative concerning the Eisenhower administration's response to racist violence in the South are the White House Central Files and the papers of Ike's black aide, E. Frederic Morrow. The Gerald Morgan Collection is useful too. Although a valuable source of information on other subjects, the Bryce Harlow Papers are not of much help on this one. The papers of Attorney General William Rogers lack substance on most matters of importance.

Those of Attorney General Robert Kennedy at the John F. Kennedy Library, on the other hand, yield a good deal of information about developments in the field of civil rights. Even richer are the papers of Assistant Attorney General Burke Marshall, also housed in the Kennedy Library. Other collections at that facility which provide useful information on Kennedy administration civil rights policies are the White House Central Files (especially the HU2 category) and the files of presidential assistant Lee C. White. Senate Files, Legislation, Pre-Presidential Papers, Papers of President Kennedy contains a good deal of material on then-Senator John Kennedy's efforts to promote passage of legislation to combat racist bombings. Far less useful are the Theodore Sorenson and Brooks Hays collections.

At the Johnson Library, those interested in anti–civil rights violence during the period 1964–1968 and in the changing role of the federal government in combating it should consult first the White House Central Files, especially category HU2 (confidential, executive, and general). Also of great value are the LBJ Library's Lee White Files and its Ramsey Clark Papers (which contain material on the Ole Miss rioting as well as on Justice Department activity during the Johnson administration). In addition, the library has a typescript Administrative History of the Department of Justice for the Johnson years that includes documentary supplements and emphasizes the *Guest* case and civil rights worker protection legislation. The LBJ Library also holds microfilm copies of selected files originated by the department's Civil Rights Division. Useful on passage of the Civil Rights Act of 1968 are the Barefoot Sanders Papers and the office files of LBJ White House aides Harry McPherson, Fred Panzer, Henry Wilson, and James Gaither.

One can also find information on that legislation in the Congressional Papers at the Gerald R. Ford Presidential Library in Ann Arbor, Michigan, in the Philip Hart Papers at the Bentley Historical Library of the

University of Michigan, also in Ann Arbor, and in the Everett M. Dirksen Papers at the Dirksen Center in Pekin, Illinois. Even more informative concerning the negotiations that made passage of the 1968 law possible are the records of the Senate Committee on the Judiciary's Subcommittee on Constitutional Rights, 85–92nd Congs., Record Group 46, at the National Archives in Washington. Extremely valuable on civil rights legislation in general are the papers of one of its leading supporters, Congressman Emanuel Celler, which are located in the Library of Congress, and those of one of its most vigorous opponents, Senator Sam J. Ervin, Jr., which are part of the Southern Historical Collection of the University of North Carolina in Chapel Hill. Much less helpful, at least with respect to those provisions of civil rights bills dealing with violence, are the papers of Senator Richard B. Russell in the Richard B. Russell Library at the University of Georgia in Athens and the papers of Congressman John W. McCormack at Boston University's Mugar Library.

For manuscript material on the Supreme Court's handling of the *Price* and *Guest* cases, the most important sources are the William J. Brennan, Jr., Papers at the Library of Congress and the Tom Clark Papers at the University of Texas Law School (Texas has Clark's Supreme Court case files, while material from his earlier career with the Justice Department is housed at the Truman Library). The William O. Douglas and Harold Burton collections at the Library of Congress and the Felix Frankfurter Papers at the Harvard Law School contain files on *United States v. Williams*. So do the Hugo L. Black Papers at the Library of Congress, although what makes that collection particularly valuable are letters to Black from his sister-in-law, Virginia Durr, describing conditions and attitudes in Alabama during the 1950s and 1960s.

The best source of information on the violence which the Ku Klux Klan perpetrated in that state, and especially on the Viola Liuzzo murder, is the FBI's Viola Liuzzo File, available in the Freedom of Information/Privacy Act Branch reading room of the J. Edgar Hoover Building in Washington, D.C. That file contains not only investigative reports but also a good deal of information about the work of Justice Department lawyers on the Liuzzo case. The same is true of the MIBURN File on the 1964 murder of the three civil rights workers near Philadelphia, Mississippi, and the PENVIC File on the Lemuel Penn case. Another important source of information on the latter is the "Lemuel Penn" folder in the vertical files of the University of Georgia library in Athens. The FBI's COIN-

TELPRO–White Hate Groups File was of some help in writing this book, but, surprisingly, its SNCC File was not. The reason is that most of the material it contains relates to SNCC activities in the North after 1964. Much more valuable for this study was FBI report Little Rock 44-12284-933, which contains much information on the situation in that Arkansas city in 1957. A copy of the report is deposited in the library of the University of Arkansas–Little Rock.

The University of Arkansas at Fayetteville has the papers of Governor Orval Faubus. Those of Congressman Brooks Hays are also housed there. For students of Justice Department civil rights policy, that library's most valuable collection is the Arthur Brann Caldwell Papers. Containing copies of many government documents, this collection is particularly rich for the Eisenhower years.

Far less important than the Caldwell Papers, but still useful for background on the situation in the South after 1954, are the Arthur Raper Papers, the Jessie Daniel Ames Papers, and the Mark Ethridge Papers. All are part of the Southern Historical Collection at the University of North Carolina. That collection also contains an oral history interview with Raper, which likewise provides some useful background information. The library at the University of Arkansas at Fayetteville contains an especially illuminating joint interview with Governor Faubus and Congressman Hays. Very informative on the civil rights policies of the Eisenhower administration is an interview with Attorney General Herbert Brownell, Jr., done by the Columbia University Oral History Project. Other useful interviews in the Columbia collection include those with Wiley Austin Branton, Virginia Durr, Congressman Brooks Hays, Governor Faubus, and Governor Sidney McMath. The Columbia project's interviews with Attorney General William P. Rogers, Senator Kenneth Keating, and Robert G. Storey, on the other hand, provide little information about the federal response to southern violence. Columbia oral histories on Eisenhower administration figures are available at the Eisenhower Library as well as at Columbia. The Eisenhower Library also did an important interview of its own with black White House aide E. Frederic Morrow, as well as others with Brownell and Rocco Siciliano, which proved far less useful for this project.

The Kennedy and LBJ libraries both have vigorous oral history programs that have interviewed many of the major actors in the civil rights dramas of the 1960s. Particularly rich are the Kennedy Library's long and fact-filled Robert F. Kennedy and Burke Marshall oral histories. Also valuable are its interviews with Governor John Patterson, Justice Thurgood Marshall, Governor Carl Sanders, Joseph F. Dolan, and Norbert Schlei. On the other hand, although the subjects of the Harris Wofford, Louis P. Oberdorfer, Theodore Sorenson, Governor Ross R. Barnett, Senator Herman Talmadge, Senator Joseph S. Clark, Roy Wilkins, and Colonel Earl H. "Red" Blaik oral histories all played important roles in civil rights during the Kennedy years, none of those interviews contains much information about southern violence or the federal government's reaction to it. One good place to look for information on those subjects is the notes which Scott Rafferty took on the interviews he did for his Princeton senior thesis and subsequently deposited with the Kennedy Library. The most valuable oral histories at the LBJ Library are those with Governor Paul Johnson and Assistant Attorney General Stephen J. Pollak. Also of some help were its interviews with Burke Marshall, Ramsey Clark, Clarence Mitchell, Roy Wilkins, and Reverend Theodore Hesburgh.

I supplemented these oral histories with a number of personal interviews. These included talks with former Attorneys General Nicholas Katzenbach (June 28, 1984) and Ramsey Clark (October 23, 1980) and with former Assistant Attorneys General Burke Marshall (October 24, 1980), John Doar (October 23, 1980), Stephen Pollak (October 22, 1980), and Judge David L. Norman (October 23, 1980). I also interviewed St. John "Slim" Barrett, who was a Civil Rights Division lawyer in the 1960s (October 23, 1981), Atlanta City Councilman John Lewis, the former head of SNCC (June 5, 1984), and Dorothy Landsberg, one-time assistant to Doar (October 22, 1980).

Interviews are, however, not the only way to recover the recollections and determine the beliefs and attitudes of the public officials who dealt with racial violence during the 1950s and 1960s, or of the civil rights activists who suffered from it. Together these groups have produced a voluminous memoir literature. A particularly moving victim's account is James Peck, *Freedom Ride* (New York: Simon and Schuster, 1962). Also touching are some of the recollections recorded in Howell Raines, *My Soul Is Rested: Movement Days in the Deep South* (New York: G. P. Putnam's Sons, 1977). Cleveland Sellers (with Robert Terrell), *The River of No Return: The Autobiography of a Black Militant and the Life and Death of SNCC* (New York: William Morrow, 1973), contains useful comments and information on the Mississippi Freedom Summer, but James Forman, *The Making of*

Black Revolutionaries (New York: Macmillan, 1972), is far more informative concerning SNCC and its activities during the early 1960s. On the NAACP, see Roy Wilkins, *Standing Fast: The Autobiography of Roy Wilkins* (New York: Viking Press, 1982).

Edwin Guthman, *We Band of Brothers* (New York: Harper & Row, 1971), is a rich source of information on the Kennedy Justice Department and its handling of anti–civil rights violence. William C. Sullivan (with Bill Brown), *The Bureau: My Thirty Years in Hoover's FBI* (New York: W. W. Norton, 1979), contains some intriguing tidbits, but it is questionable whether Sullivan could have had firsthand knowledge of some of the matters he discusses. Gary Thomas Rowe, a longtime Bureau informant within the Ku Klux Klan, clearly was in a position to observe the incidents on which he reports in *My Undercover Years with the Ku Klux Klan* (New York: Bantam, 1976), but his veracity has been questioned. For presidential views on the racial crises of the 1950s and 1960s, see Lyndon Johnson, *The Vantage Point: Perspectives on the Presidency* (New York: Holt, Rinehart and Winston, 1971), and Dwight D. Eisenhower, *The White House Years: Waging Peace, 1956–1961* (Garden City, N.Y.: Doubleday, 1965). Other memoirs providing information on and insights into Eisenhower's attitudes and actions are Sherman Adams, *Firsthand Report* (New York: Harper & Brothers, 1961), Emmett John Hughes, *The Ordeal of Power: A Political Memoir of the Eisenhower Years* (New York: Atheneum, 1963), and E. Frederic Morrow, *Black Man in the White House: A Diary of the Eisenhower Years by the Administrative Officer for Special Projects, the White House, 1955–1961* (New York: Coward-McCann, 1963). The Morrow book is especially moving. For Arkansas perspectives on the biggest racial crisis of the Eisenhower presidency, Little Rock, see Brooks Hays, *A Southern Moderate Speaks* (Chapel Hill: University of North Carolina Press, 1959), Virgil T. Blossom, *It Has Happened Here* (New York: Harper & Brothers, 1959), and Orval Faubus, *Down from the Hills* (Little Rock: Pioneer, 1980). Sam J. Ervin, Jr., *Preserving the Constitution: The Autobiography of Senator Sam J. Ervin, Jr.* (Charlottesville, Va.: Michie Company, 1984), is also a useful memoir, although it provides more insights into the author's thinking about civil rights legislation in general than information about his efforts to defeat specific bills.

In addition to these memoirs, there are several books containing a good deal of information about anti–civil rights violence and efforts to control it which combine personal recollections with more traditional history.

Three of these are by Kennedy aides: Arthur Schlesinger, Jr.'s *A Thousand Days: John F. Kennedy in the White House* (Boston: Houghton Mifflin, 1965), Theodore Sorenson's *Kennedy* (Harper & Row, 1965), and Harris Wofford, *Of Kennedys and Kings: Making Sense of the Sixties* (New York: Farrar, Straus & Giroux, 1980). Another is Florence Mars, *Witness in Philadelphia* (Baton Rouge: Louisiana State University Press, 1977). This book, by a longtime resident of Philadelphia, Mississippi, is by far the best account of the Neshoba County murder case.

The only better source of information on that crime and the legal proceedings that flowed from it is Transcript of Record, United States v. Price, Crim. No. 5291 (S.D. Miss. 1967). Equally valuable on the Lemuel Penn slaying and the trial of the alleged killers is Record, Myers v. United States, 377 F.2d 412 (5th Cir. 1967). On the Liuzzo case, see Transcript of Record, Transcript of Hearings on Motions, and Excerpt Transcript, United States v. Wilkins, 376 F.2d 552 (5th Cir. 1967). Although held in the Federal Records Center at East Point, Georgia, each of these trial records must be obtained through the clerk of the court in which the case was tried. Another important source of information on *Price* and *Guest* is the United States Supreme Court Records and Briefs, which contain, among other treasures, some unpublished opinions filed by Judge Harold Cox in the Mississippi case. The Supreme Court's decisions in that case and in *Guest* are reported in the *United States Reports.* Additional rulings in those cases and opinions in other legal proceedings involving southern racist violence are found in *Federal Reporter* (2d series) and the *Federal Supplement.* The *Southern Reporter* (2d series) and the *South Eastern Reporter* (2d series) also contain relevant rulings.

In addition, there is some information about court decisions in the *Annual Reports of the Attorney General of the United States* for the fiscal years 1955–1977. These reports devote more attention, however, to the activities of the Civil Rights Division and the FBI. The sections dealing with those agencies, which they prepared themselves, tend to be unduly self-congratulatory. For a more candid and less flattering picture of the Bureau, see U.S., Senate, Select Committee to Study Governmental Operations with Respect to Intelligence Activities, *Final Report,* Book III, 94th Cong., 2d sess., 1976, S. Rept. 755, and the same committee's *Hearings,* vol. VI, *Federal Bureau of Investigation,* 94th Cong., 1st sess., 1975. The latter document contains, at pp. 888–991, a very fine analysis of the FBI's work in the civil rights field by John Doar and Dorothy Landsberg, entitled "The Performance of the FBI in Investigating Violations of Federal Laws Protecting the Right to Vote—1960–1967." Book II of the Select Committee's *Final Report,* entitled *Intelligence Activities and the Rights of Americans,* contains a limited amount of information on the FBI's operations against the Ku Klux Klan. The Bureau's *Crime in the United States: Uniform Crime Reports* for the years 1963–1969 provides data which can be used to compare the rate of violent crimes in the South with the rate in the rest of the country. Unfortunately, the reports do not break offenses down in such a way that one can isolate those committed by persons of one race against those of another.

Although ignored by FBI statisticians, interracial violence was of interest to occupants of the White House. For presidential pronouncements on it, readers should consult the *Public Papers of the Presidents of the United States,* published by the Government Printing Office. Early recommendations for strengthening the federal laws against racially motivated violence appear in President's Committee on Civil Rights, *To Secure These Rights: Report of the President's Committee on Civil Rights* (New York: Simon and Schuster, 1947). The White House Conference on Civil Rights made rather similar suggestions two decades later in *To Fulfill These Rights* (Washington: Government Printing Office, 1966). The reasons why legislation such as these groups recommended seemed necessary become quite apparent if one reads the United States Commission on Civil Rights' *Law Enforcement: A Report on Equal Protection in the South* (Washington: U.S. Commission on Civil Rights, 1965), a devastating expose of the inadequate protection given blacks in the South. The commission's *Summary of School Desegregation in the Southern and Border States, 1965–1966* (Washington: U.S. Commission on Civil Rights, 1966) contains some information on the use of violence and intimidation to keep Negro students out of white schools. The commission's Mississippi Advisory Committee criticizes both state and federal authorities in *Administration of Justice in Mississippi* (N.p.: Mississippi Advisory Committee, 1963).

One can also find criticism of both the southern states and the federal government in the small mountain of documents which Congress generated during the long years before it finally passed meaningful legislation to combat racist violence. Useful for background are U.S., Senate, Committee on the Judiciary, *Crime of Lynching: Hearings . . . on H.R. 801 . . . ,* 76th Cong., 3d sess., 1940, and U.S., Congress, Senate, Committee on the Judiciary, *Crime of Lynching: Hearings . . . on S.42, S. 1352 and S.*

1465 . . . , 80th Cong., 2d sess., 1948. Among the documents that provide insights into the failure of efforts to obtain legislation against violence in 1956–1957 are U.S. Congress, House, Committee on the Judiciary, *Civil Rights: Hearings . . . on . . . Miscellaneous Bills Regarding the Civil Rights of Persons Within the Jurisdiction of the United States,* 84th Cong., 1st sess., 1955; *Hearings . . . on Legislation Regarding the Civil Rights of Persons Within the Jurisdiction of the United States: Executive Session,* 84th Cong., 2d sess., 1956, and *Hearings . . . on . . . Miscellaneous Bills Regarding the Civil Rights of Persons Within the Jurisdiction of the United States,* 84th Cong., 2d sess., 1956. The last two documents are particularly important because they reveal a good deal about the true position of Attorney General Brownell. So does U.S., Senate, Committee on the Judiciary, *Civil Rights Proposals: Hearings . . . ,* 84th Cong., 2d sess., 1956. The important congressional documents on the 1960 bombing legislation are U.S., Congress, House, Committee on the Judiciary, *Prohibiting Certain Acts Involving the Use of Explosives: Hearings . . . on . . . H.R. 11806 . . . and H.J. Res. 526,* 85th Cong., 2d sess., 1958; *Hearings . . . on . . . Miscellaneous Bills Regarding the Civil Rights of Persons Within the Jurisdiction of the United States,* 86th Cong., 1st sess., 1959, and *Civil Rights,* 85th Cong., 1st sess., 1959, H. Rept. 956; U.S., Congress, Senate, Subcommittee on Constitutional Rights of the Committee on the Judiciary, *Civil Rights— 1959: Hearings . . . on . . . Proposals to Secure, Protect and Strengthen Civil Rights of Persons Under the Constitution and Laws of the United States,* 86th Cong., 2d sess., 1960, and *Civil Rights Act of 1960,* 86th Cong., 1st sess., 1959; and U.S., Congress, Senate, Committee on the Judiciary, *Civil Rights Act of 1960: Hearings . . . on H.R. 8601 . . . ,* 86th Cong., 2d sess., 1960, and *Civil Rights Act of 1960,* 86th Cong., 2d sess., 1960, S. Rept. 1205. Robert Kennedy expressed his opposition to the inclusion of a "Part III" provision in the Civil Rights Act of 1964 during testimony reported in U.S., Congress, House, Committee on the Judiciary, *Civil Rights: Hearings . . . ,* 89th Cong., 1st sess., 1963. Those with any interest in the legislative history of the hugely unimportant section 11(b) of the Voting Rights Act of 1965 can trace it through U.S., Congress, House, Committee on the Judiciary, *Voting Rights: Hearings Before Subcommittee No. 5 . . . on H.R. 6400 . . . ,* 89th Cong., 1st sess, 1965, *Voting Rights,* 89th Cong., 1st sess., 1965, H. Rept. 711, and *Voting Rights Legislation,* 89th Cong., 1st sess., 1965, H. Rept. 433; and U.S., Congress, Senate, Committee on the Judiciary, *Voting Rights Legislation,* 89th Cong., 1st sess.,

S. Rept. 162. Government documents recording the long struggle for enactment of the antiviolence provisions of the Civil Rights Act of 1968 include U.S., Congress, House, Committee on the Judiciary, *Civil Rights Act of 1966: Hearings* . . . , 89th Cong., 2d sess., 1966, *Civil Rights Act of 1966,* 89th Cong., 2d sess., 1966, H. Rept. 1678, and *Penalties for Interference with Civil Rights,* 90th Cong., 1st sess., 1967, H. Rept. 473; U.S., Senate, Subcommittee on Constitutional Rights of the Committee on the Judiciary, *Civil Rights: Hearings on S. 3296* . . . *and S. 3170,* 89th Cong., 2d sess., 1966, and *Civil Rights Act of 1967: Hearings* . . . , 90th Cong., 1st sess., 1967; U.S. Congress, Senate, Committee on the Judiciary, *Interference with Civil Rights,* 90th Cong., 1st sess., 1967, S. Rept. 721; and U.S., Congress, House, Committee on Rules, *Providing for Agreeing to the Senate Amendments to the Bill (H.R. 2516) to Prescribe Penalties for Certain Acts of Violence and Intimidation and for Other Purposes,* 90th Cong., 2d sess., 1968, H. Rept. 1289. The *Congressional Record* is an important source for all civil rights legislation, but the fact that southerners regularly filibustered bills of this type in the Senate makes locating remarks on one subject, such as violence, a protracted and frustrating undertaking. Also worth consulting, although more for biographical data than for insights into the subject's views on federalism, is U.S., Senate, Committee on the Judiciary, *Nomination of Burke Marshall: Hearings* . . . , 87th Cong., 1st sess., 1961.

While the vast majority of the published primary sources on racist violence in the South and efforts to suppress it are government documents, a number of private organizations also issued books, pamphlets, and reports on the subject. Important as background for developments in the post-1954 period are National Association for the Advancement of Colored People, *Thirty Years of Lynching in the United States* (1919; reprint ed., New York: Arno Press and the New York Times, 1969) and Jessie Daniel Ames, *The Changing Character of Lynching* (1942; reprint ed., New York: AMS Press, 1973). Roy Wilkins, *Roy Wilkins Speaks Out* (New York: NAACP, 1962), comments perceptively on the causes of the violence that followed the *Brown* decision. Southern Regional Council and American Civil Liberties Union, *Southern Justice: An Indictment* (N.p.: Southern Regional Council and ACLU, 1965), is a stinging critique of racially biased court systems which also exposes the failure of law enforcement in the South to protect blacks and civil rights workers, while Southern Regional Council, "The Federal Executive and Civil Rights" (Atlanta: Southern Regional Council, 1961, mimeographed), calls for federal action to control racist violence, as does the same organization's "Law Enforcement in Mississippi" (Atlanta: Southern Regional Council, 1964, mimeographed). Department of Records and Research, Tuskegee Institute, *Race Relations in the South, 1961: Forty-eighth Annual Report to the American People on Developments in Race Relations* (Tuskegee, Ala.: Tuskegee Institute, 1962), contains perceptive comments on the impact and significance of the Freedom Rides. Howard Zinn, *Albany* (Atlanta: Southern Regional Council, 1962), discusses the violence in that Georgia city and criticizes the federal government for failing to do anything about it. Jack Minnis, *A Chronology of Violence and Intimidation in Mississippi Since 1961* (Atlanta: Student Nonviolent Coordinating Committee, 1964), is a useful list of incidents, but National Association for the Advancement of Colored People, *Triple Murder: States Rights, Mississippi Style* (New York: NAACP, 1964), is little more than a few pages of anti-Goldwater political propaganda. Dwayne Walls, *The Klan: Collapsed and Dormant* (Nashville: Race Relations Information Center, 1970), is another short pamphlet of rather limited value.

Also not very helpful on the subject of southern violence after 1954 is George M. Gallup, *The Gallup Poll: Public Opinion, 1935–1971,* 3 vols. (New York: Random House, 1972). It is an outstanding collection of public opinion poll data, but unfortunately Gallup's interviewers almost never asked questions relevant to this study.

For southern public opinion, as well as for information on violent incidents in the South, one must look primarily to the southern press. When researching a topic related to civil rights, the best way to do this is to use the microfilmed "Facts on Film" clipping file assembled by the Southern Education Reporting Service. It is reasonably well indexed and contains news stories and editorials from both southern and nonsouthern newspapers on events in the South. In addition to "Facts on Film," I made extensive use of the *New York Times,* which provided excellent coverage of major racial crises and legal proceedings arising out of racially motivated killings. I also consulted the *Athens* (Ga.) *Banner-Herald* for information on the murder of Lemuel Penn and the trials of his killers.

Like newspapers inside and outside the South, popular periodicals devoted a great deal of attention to the southern racial violence of the late 1950s and early 1960s, to the trials of those allegedly responsible for it, to federal initiatives in the civil rights field, and to the Ku Klux Klan. The coverage provided by *Newsweek* and *Time* was especially extensive. *U.S. News & World Report* devoted considerable attention to the FBI. Significant articles also appeared in *Jet, New Republic, Nation, Life, Look, Saturday Evening Post, New Yorker, Harper's, Christian Century, Progressive, Commentary, South, Folkways,* and *Editor & Publisher.*

Legal periodicals also devoted substantial attention to the racial violence in the South, focusing most of their attention on the appellate litigation that it spawned and on the issue of the extent to which the Constitution empowered the federal government to combat it. Especially important are "Summer Project: Mississippi 1964," *National Lawyers Guild Practitioner* 24 (Winter 1965): 32–43; Laurent B. Frantz, "Congressional Power to Enforce the Fourteenth Amendment Against Private Acts," *Yale Law Journal* 73 (July 1964): 1353–84; the same author's "Federal Power to Protect Civil Rights: The *Price* and *Guest* Cases," *Law in Transition Quarterly* 4 (March 1967): 63–73; Howard Feurstein, "Civil Rights Crimes and the Federal Power to Punish Private Individuals for Interference with Federally Secured Rights," *Vanderbilt Law Review* 19 (June 1966): 641–81; John E. Moye, "Note: Fourteenth Amendment: Congressional Power to Legislate Against Discrimination: The *Guest* Case," *Cornell Law Quarterly* 52 (Spring 1967): 586–99; George Richard Poehner, "Comment: Fourteenth Amendment Enforcement and Congressional Power to Abolish the States," *California Law Review* 55 (April 1967): 293–317; and "Comment: Theories of Federalism and Civil Rights," *Yale Law Journal* 75 (May 1976): 1007–52. Alfred Avins's "The Ku Klux Klan Act of 1871: Some Reflected Light on State Action and the Fourteenth Amendment," *St. Louis University Law Journal* 11 (1967): 331–81, and "Federal Power to Punish Individual Crimes Under the Fourteenth Amendment: The Original Understanding, "*Notre Dame Lawyer* 43 (February 1968): 317–43, are also important articles, although they advance some rather dubious conclusions. Of lesser value are "Comment: Congressional Power Under the Civil War Amendments," *Duke Law Journal* 1969 (December 1969): 1247–84; Steve Salch, "Note: Protection of Fourteenth Amendment Rights Under Section 241 of the United States Criminal Code," *Southwestern Law Journal* 20 (1966): 913–22; Thomas P. Ruane, "Note: Constitutional Law—Congress by Appropriate Legislation May Have the Power to Punish Conspiracies That Interfere with Fourteenth Amendment Rights," *Duquesne University Law Review* 5 (Winter 1966): 197–201; "Review of Recent Supreme Court Decisions," *American Bar Association Journal* 52 (June 1966): 574–81; "Note: Double Prosecution by State and Federal Governments: Another Exercise in Federalism," *Har-*

vard Law Review 80 (May 1967): 1538–65; "The Supreme Court, 1965 Term," *Harvard Law Review* 80 (November 1966): 124–272; John G. Niles, "Note: Constitutional Law—Civil Rights—Congressional Power Under Section 5 of the Fourteenth Amendment May Extend to Punishment of Private Conspiracies to Interfere with Equal Enjoyment of State-Owned Public Facilities," *Texas Law Review* 45 (November 1966): 168–76; Barbara C. Schwartzbaum, "Note: Federal Prosecution of Private Violence—Arrests Resulting from Private Conspirators' False Reports to Police Constitutes State Denial of Equal Protection Indictable Under Civil Rights Conspiracy Statute," *Howard Law Journal* 13 (1967): 189–93; and Bruce H. Spector, "Comment: The Fourteenth Amendment, Congressional Power and Private Discrimination: *United States v. Guest,*" *U.C.L.A. Law Review* 14 (January 1967): 553–80. Useful for the background they provide on the problems of the 1950s and 1960s are "What Can Be Done to Stop Lynching," *American Law Review* 39 (January/February 1905): 101–103, and Hannis Taylor, "The True Remedy for Lynch Law," *American Law Review* 41 (March/April 1907): 255–66.

Burke Marshall wrote two law review articles while he was head of the Civil Rights Division: "Federal Protection of Negro Voting Rights," *Law and Contemporary Problems* 27 (Summer 1962): 455–67, and "The Protest Movement and the Law," *Virginia Law Review* 51 (June 1965); 785–803. These articles do not reveal nearly as much about Marshall's philosophy, however, as does his book *Federalism and Civil Rights* (New York: Columbia University Press, 1964). Readers interested in Marshall's thinking should also consult two reviews of that book, one by James Silver in the *Georgetown Law Journal* 53 (Spring 1965): 559–61, and the other by Richard A. Waserstram in the *University of Chicago Law Review* 65 (Winter 1966): 406–13.

Contemporary works on the relationship between anti–civil rights violence and federalism are considerably more numerous than secondary sources on that subject. The best available book is Mary Francis Berry, *Black Resistance/White Law: A History of Constitutional Racism in the United States* (New York: Appleton-Century-Crofts, 1971). It touches upon a number of the matters dealt with in this study, but is rather polemical in tone and covers all of American history. Scott Rafferty, "Federal Protection of Civil Rights Against Acts of Violence" (Undergraduate thesis, Princeton University, 1976), is good on the period 1939–1960, but weaker on the Kennedy-Johnson era. Michal R. Belknap, "The Vindication of Burke

Marshall: The Southern Legal System and the Anti-Civil-Rights Violence of the 1960s, "*Emory Law Journal* 33 (Winter 1984): 93–133, focuses on the latter period. Joseph Thomas Sees, "Federal Power to Combat Racial Violence in the Aftermath of *Price, Guest* and the Civil Rights Act of 1968" (Ph.D. diss., Georgetown University, 1971), is a good analysis of the law concerning federal punishment of racial violence as of the time it was written and also contains a rather narrow legislative history of 18 U.S.C. section 245, based entirely on published sources. Gregory Padgett, "Racially-Motivated Violence and Intimidation: Inadequate State Enforcement and Federal Civil Rights Remedies," *Journal of Criminal Law and Criminology* 75 (Spring 1984): 103–38, is considerably less relevant than its title suggests, for it is really just an analysis of the situation that existed when it was written in the 1980s.

While historical treatments of the federal responses to unpunished racial violence are rare, there are numerous books and articles which examine the southern attitudes that gave rise to this problem. Wilbur J. Cash, *The Mind of the South* (New York: Alfred A. Knopf, 1941), is a classic work that is undocumented but extremely perceptive. Bertram Wyatt-Brown, *Southern Honor: Ethics and Behavior in the Old South* (New York: Oxford University Press, 1982), is more scholarly and equally insightful. John Hope Franklin, *The Militant South, 1800–1861* (Cambridge, Mass.: Belknap Press, 1956), is excellent too, but less valuable to students of recent southern history. The same is true of Clement Eaton, *The Freedom-of-Thought Struggle in the Old South,* 2d ed. (New York: Harper & Row, 1964), which does, however provide some insights into southern vigilantism. Charles Sydnor's "The Southerner and the Law," *Journal of Southern History* 6 (February 1940): 3–23, also deals with the antebellum period, but despite rather thin documentation and heavy reliance on secondary sources, it is most illuminating concerning southern legal attitudes. More useful to those primarily interested in the recent history of the South is James W. Silver, *Mississippi: The Closed Society,* 3d ed. (New York: Harcourt, Brace and World, 1966), which does an excellent job of putting the Ole Miss riot into perspective. Also extremely valuable is Gunnar Myrdal's classic work, *An American Dilemma: The Negro Problem and Modern Democracy,* 2d ed. (New York: Harper & Row 1962).

The vast literature on the southern proclivity for violence includes John Shelton Reed's "To Live—and Die—in Dixie: A Contribution to the Study of Southern Violence," *Political Science Quarterly* 86 (September

1971): 429–43; Raymond D. Gastil's "Homicide and a Regional Culture of Violence," *American Sociological Review* 36 (February 1971): 412–27; Sheldon Hackney's "Southern Violence," *American Historical Review* 74 (February 1969): 906–25; H. C. Brearley's "The Pattern of Violence," in *Culture in the South,* ed. W. T. Couch (Chapel Hill: University of North Carolina Press, 1934), pp. 678–92; Colin Loftin and Robert H. Hill's "Regional Subculture and Homicide: An Examination of the Gastil-Hackney Thesis," *American Sociological Review* 39 (October 1974): 712–24; Richard Maxwell Brown's *Strain of Violence: Studies in American Violence and Vigilantism* (New York: Oxford University Press, 1975) and "Southern Violence—Regional Problem or National Nemesis? Legal Attitudes Toward Homicide in Historical Perspective," *Vanderbilt Law Review* 32 (January 1979): 225–50; Dennis R. Nolan's "Comment: Southern Violence—Regional Problem or National Nemesis? Legal Attitudes Toward Southern Violence in Historical Perspective," *Vanderbilt Law Review* 32 (January 1979): 251–69; and Allen D. Grimshaw's "Lawlessness and Violence in America and Their Manifestations in Changing Negro-White Relationships," *Journal of Negro History* 44 (January 1959): 52–72. Helpful on the general phenomenon of vigilantism is Richard Maxwell Brown, "The American Vigilante Tradition," in *The History of Violence in America,* ed. Hugh Davis Graham and Ted Robert Gurr (New York: Bantam, 1969), pp. 45–84. Readers interested in comparing the South with the rest of the country should also consult Rodney Stark and James McEvoy III, "Middle Class Violence," *Psychology Today* 4 (November 1970): 52–54, 110–12.

Those looking for information on the way the white South used legally sanctioned private violence to control its black slaves before the Civil War should start with Kenneth Stampp, *The Peculiar Institution: Slavery in the Ante-Bellum South* (New York: Alfred A. Knopf, 1956). Also worth consulting on this subject are Eugene D. Genovese, *Roll, Jordan, Roll: The World the Slaves Made* (New York: Pantheon Books, 1974), and Winthrop D. Jordan, *White Over Black: American Attitudes Toward the Negro, 1550–1812* (Chapel Hill: University of North Carolina Press, 1968). The extent to which antebellum southern law protected slaves from violence by whites has been a matter of some controversy among scholars. The most important books and articles on this subject are A. E. Keir Nash, "A More Equitable Past? Southern Supreme Courts and the Protection of the Antebellum Negro," *North Carolina Law Review* 48 (February 1970): 197–242; the same author's "Fairness and Formalism in the Trials of Blacks in the

State Supreme Courts of the Old South," *Virginia Law Review* 56 (1970): 64–100; Mark V. Tushnet, "The American Law of Slavery, 1810–1860: A Study in the Persistence of Legal Autonomy," *Law and Society Review* 10 (Fall 1975): 119–84; the same author's *The American Law of Slavery, 1810–1860: Considerations of Humanity and Interest* (Princeton, N.J.: Princeton University Press, 1981); Michael S. Hindus, "Black Justice Under White Law: Criminal Prosecutions of Blacks in Antebellum South Carolina," *Journal of American History* 63 (December 1976): 575–99; the same author's *Prison and Plantation: Crime, Justice and Authority in Massachusetts and South Carolina, 1767–1878* (Chapel Hill: University of North Carolina Press, 1980); and Stanley Elkins, *Slavery: A Problem in American Institutional and Intellectual Life,* 2d ed. (Chicago: Grosset & Dunlap, 1963).

The federal government's legal efforts to protect blacks from white violence during the years just after the Civil War have also received substantial scholarly attention. The best books dealing with this subject are Robert J. Kaczorowski, *The Politics of Judicial Interpretation: The Federal Courts, Department of Justice and Civil Rights, 1866–1876* (New York: Oceana, 1985); Harold M. Hyman, *A More Perfect Union: The Impact of the Civil War and Reconstruction on the Constitution* (Boston: Houghton Mifflin, 1975); Harold M. Hyman and William Wiecek, *Equal Justice Under Law: Constitutional Development, 1835–1875* (New York: Harper & Row, 1982); Herman Belz, *Emancipation and Equal Rights: Politics and Constitutionalism in the Civil War Era* (New York: W. W. Norton & Co., 1978); and Allen W. Trelease, *White Terror: The Ku Klux Klan Conspiracy and Southern Reconstruction* (New York: Harper & Row, 1977). Important articles include Kermit L. Hall, "Political Power and Constitutional Legitimacy: The South Carolina Ku Klux Klan Trials," *Emory Law Journal* 33 (Fall 1984): 921–51; Everette Swinney, "Enforcing the Fifteenth Amendment, 1870–1877," *Journal of Southern History* 28 (February 1962): 202–18; and William Gillette, "Anatomy of a Failure: Federal Enforcement of the Right to Vote in the Border States During Reconstruction," in *Radicalism, Racism and Party Realignment,* ed. Richard O. Curry (Baltimore: Johns Hopkins University Press, 1969), pp. 265–304. Aviam Soifer, "Protecting Civil Rights: A Critique of Raoul Berger's History," *New York University Law Review* 54 (June 1979): 651–706, is also helpful on Reconstruction efforts to protect blacks. George C. Rable, *But There Was No Peace: The Role of Violence in the Politics of Reconstruction* (Athens, Ga.: University of

Georgia Press, 1984), is an excellent study of the use of force and violence against the freedmen, while Trelease's *White Terror* and David A. Chalmers, *Hooded Americanism: The First Century of the Ku Klux Klan, 1865–1965,* 2d ed. (New York: F. Watts, 1981), are both good on organized racist terrorism during Reconstruction.

The recent book which is most informative concerning racial violence in the post-Reconstruction South is Joel Williamson, *The Crucible of Race: Black-White Relations in the American South Since Reconstruction* (New York: Oxford University Press, 1984), although, strangely, Williamson emphasizes race riots rather than lynching. So does Charles Crowe, whose article "Racial Violence and Social Reform—Origins of the Atlanta Race Riot of 1906," *Journal of Negro History* 53 (April 1968): 234–56, stresses the racial control function of rioting. One can also find brief but perceptive discussions of racist violence in Pete Daniel, "The Metamorphosis of Slavery, 1865–1900," *Journal of American History* 66 (June 1979): 88–99; C. Vann Woodward, *Origins of the New South,* 2d ed. (Baton Rouge: Louisiana State University Press, 1971); and George B. Tindall, *The Emergence of the New South* (Baton Rouge: Louisiana State University Press, 1976). Lawrence C. Goodwyn, "Populist Dreams and Negro Rights: East Texas as a Case Study," *American Historical Review* 76 (December 1971): 1435–56; Albert C. Smith, "Down Freedom's Road: The Contours of Race, Class and Property Crimes in Black-Belt Georgia, 1866–1910" (Ph.D. diss., University of Georgia, 1982); and Dan T. Carter, *Scottsboro: A Tragedy of the American South,* 2d ed. (Baton Rouge: Louisiana State University Press, 1979), provide useful perspective.

The best books on lynching are older studies published during the first one-third of the twentieth century. They include Walter White, *Rope and Faggot: A Biography of Judge Lynch* (1929; reprinted, New York, Arno Press and the New York Times, 1969); Arthur F. Raper, *The Tragedy of Lynching* (New York: Negro Universities Press, 1933); James Elbert Cutler, *Lynch Law: An Investigation into Lynching in the United States* (New York: Longmans, Green and Co., 1905); and James H. Chadbourn, *Lynching and the Law* (Chapel Hill: University of North Carolina Press, 1933). The best recent works on this subject are two case studies of Roosevelt-era crimes: James R. McGovern, *Anatomy of a Lynching: The Killing of Claude Neal* (Baton Rouge: Louisiana State University Press, 1982), and "The Lynching of Cleo Wright: Federal Protection of Constitutional Rights During World War II," *Journal of American History* 72 (March 1986): 859–87.

While not much has been written lately on lynching itself, the 1970s
and 1980s produced some excellent studies of campaigns to eradicate that
form of racial violence. The best of these books are Jacquelyn Dowd Hall's
superb *Revolt Against Chivalry: Jessie Daniel Ames and the Women's Campaign
Against Lynching* (New York: Columbia University Press, 1979) and
Robert L. Zangrando's excellent *The NAACP Crusade Against Lynching,
1909–1950* (Philadelphia: Temple University Press, 1980). Donald L.
Grant, *The Anti-Lynching Movement, 1883–1932* (San Francisco: R&E Associates, 1975), is solid too. Useful on southern opposition to efforts to
secure enactment of a federal law against lynching is George C. Rable,
"The South and the Politics of Anti-lynching Legislation," *Journal of
Southern History* 51 (May 1985): 201–20.

John Thomas Elliff's brilliant dissertation "The United States Department of Justice and Individual Rights, 1936–1962" (Ph.D. diss., Harvard
University, 1967) begins while Congress was haggling over antilynching
legislation and carries the story of federal action against racial violence and
other civil rights violations through the Roosevelt, Truman, and
Eisenhower presidencies and well into the Kennedy administration. Although written by a political scientist, it is solidly grounded in Justice
Department manuscript sources. His "Aspects of Federal Civil Rights En-
forcement: The Justice Department and the FBI, 1939–1964," *Perspectives
in American History* 5 (1971): 605–73, is also of interest. Robert K. Carr's
Federal Protection of Civil Rights: Quest for a Sword (Ithaca, N.Y.: Cornell
University Press, 1947) is not nearly as good as Elliff's dissertation, but it
too contains useful information on the Civil Rights Section of the Justice
Department as well as on enforcement of 18 U.S.C. sections 241 and 242.
Donald R. McCoy and Richard T. Ruetten, *Quest and Response: Minority
Rights and the Truman Administration* (Lawrence, Kans.: University of Kan-
sas Press, 1973), is a detailed and well researched study, but it devotes
only limited attention to federal action against southern racial violence.

Such violence was, of course, less common during the Truman presidency than it became after *Brown v. Board of Education.* The best works on
southern resistance to the Supreme Court's 1954 school desegregation decision are Numan V. Bartley, *The Rise of Massive Resistance: Race and Politics
in the South During the 1950s* (Baton Rouge: Louisiana State University
Press, 1969), and Neil R. McMillen, *The Citizens' Council: Organized Resistance to the Second Reconstruction, 1954–1964* (Urbana: University of Illinois Press, 1971). Also important are McMillen's articles "White Citizens

Council and Resistance to School Desegregation in Arkansas," *Arkansas Historical Quarterly* 30 (Spring 1971): 95–122, and "Organized Resistance to School Desegregation in Tennessee," *Tennessee Historical Quarterly* 30 (Fall 1971): 315–28. The latter, which deals extensively with the activities of agitator John Kasper, is particularly valuable. Tony Fryer, *The Little Rock Crisis: A Constitutional Interpretation* (Westport, Conn.: Greenwood Press, 1984), is the best book on that subject.

Robert Burk deals extensively with both Little Rock and the Civil Rights Act of 1957 in his *The Eisenhower Administration and Black Civil Rights* (Knoxville: University of Tennessee Press, 1984), a book which is somewhat ambivalent about Eisenhower's civil rights record. So is the same author's "Symbolic Equality: The Eisenhower Administration and Black Civil Rights, 1953–1961" (Ph.D. diss., University of Wisconsin—Madison, 1982). Michael S. Mayer's "Eisenhower's Conditional Crusade: The Eisenhower Administration and Civil Rights, 1953–1957" (Ph.D. diss., Princeton University, 1984) is more frankly revisionist. Mayer's failure to consider either Little Rock or the Civil Rights Act of 1960 seriously flaws his interpretation, however. Unlike "Eisenhower's Conditional Crusade," Donald M. Berman, *A Bill Becomes a Law: Congress Enacts Civil Rights Legislation,* 2d ed. (New York: Macmillan, 1966), does explore the legislative history of the 1960 act, but its author devotes little attention to either Title I or Title II and errs in what he does say about the second of these two antiviolence provisions. John Weir Anderson, *Eisenhower, Brownell, and the Congress: The Tangled Origins of the Civil Rights Bill of 1956–1957* (University, Ala.: University of Alabama Press, 1964), is also disappointing. Like Berman's book, it is inadequately documented, and in addition it relates only half of the legislative history of the Civil Rights Act of 1957. James C. Duram, *A Moderate Among Extremists: Dwight D. Eisenhower and the School Desegregation Crisis* (Chicago: Nelson-Hall, 1981), is adequately researched, but it is poorly organized and some of the author's interpretations of his documentary evidence are highly questionable. David Daniel Potenziani, "Look to the Past: Richard B. Russell and the Defense of Southern White Supremacy" (Ph.D. diss., University of Georgia, 1981), is a well-written and interesting dissertation on a leading congressional opponent of civil rights legislation, while Edwin Howard Smead, Jr., "The Lynching of Mack Charles Parker in Poplarville, Mississippi, April 25, 1959" (PhD. diss., University of Maryland, 1979), deals with an important incident from the Eisenhower years in a much more interesting fashion than its pedestrian title would suggest. Robert Griffith, "Dwight D. Eisenhower and the Corporate Commonwealth," *American Historical Review* 87 (February 1982): 87–122, comments briefly but perceptively on Ike's racial views and policies. Herbert S. Parmet, *Eisenhower and the American Crusades* (New York: Macmillan, 1972), and Charles C. Alexander, *Holding the Line: The Eisenhower Era, 1952–1961* (Bloomington: Indiana University Press, 1975), are both good surveys of the Eisenhower presidency, but Parmet deals more extensively and effectively with Ike's reluctance to take action to halt attacks on southern blacks. Allen Wolk, *The Presidency and Black Civil Rights: Eisenhower to Nixon* (Rutherford, N.J.: Fairleigh Dickinson University Press, 1971), is a work of rather limited value that ignores the problem of southern violence, is based entirely on published sources, and is not of high quality.

Those interested in the civil rights policies of the Kennedy administration should consult instead Carl M. Brauer's *John F. Kennedy and the Second Reconstruction* (New York: Columbia University Press, 1977). The book is a bit too defensive of JFK's record, and Brauer fails to uncover his subject's role in the passage of federal legislation against bombing. Nevertheless, this is a detailed survey of Kennedy administration civil rights policies which is informative concerning both the White House and the Justice Department. Also excellent on this administration's handling of southern racial problems, as well as on the conduct of the FBI while Robert Kennedy was attorney general, is Arthur M. Schlesinger, Jr., *Robert Kennedy and His Times* (Boston: Houghton Mifflin, 1978). Schlesinger's biography tends to be excessively laudatory, while Victor Navasky's less impressively researched *Kennedy Justice* (New York: Atheneum, 1971) is harshly critical. Walter Lord, *The Past That Would Not Die* (London: Hamish Hamilton, 1966), is a fact-filled but undocumented journalistic account of the Ole Miss crisis. Thomas G. Dyer, on the other hand, provides a scholarly treatment of violence at the University of Georgia in *The University of Georgia: A Bicentennial History, 1785–1985* (Athens, Ga.: University of Georgia Press, 1985). The best secondary source on Ku Klux Klan attacks upon the Freedom Riders and the way state and federal authorities dealt with them is Catherine Barnes's impressively researched and engagingly written *Journey from Jim Crow: The Desegregation of Southern Transit* (New York: Columbia University Press, 1983). Allen J. Matusow, *The Unraveling of America: A History of Liberalism in the 1960s* (New York: Harper &

Row, 1984), also deals impressively with that issue, as well as with other aspects of the Kennedy administration's civil rights record. Matusow has surprisingly little to say about the evolution of federal policy during the summer of 1964 or about the passage of the Civil Rights Act of 1968.

By far the best history of the 1968 legislation is that presented by Steven Lawson in his fine monograph *In Pursuit of Power: Southern Blacks and Electoral Politics, 1965–1982* (New York: Columbia University Press, 1985). The same author's "Civil Rights," in *Exploring the Johnson Years,* ed. Robert A. Divine (Austin: University of Texas Press, 1981), pp. 93–125, deals with this subject too, but its treatment is neither as detailed nor as accurate. James C. Harvey, *Black Civil Rights During the Johnson Administration* (Jackson: University and College Press of Mississippi, 1973), also contains a rather good legislative history of the 1968 act, but unlike *In Pursuit of Power,* it is not based on manuscript research. James L. Sundquist's *Politics and Policy: The Eisenhower, Kennedy and Johnson Years* (Washington, D.C.: Brookings Institution, 1968) is of some use on the failure of the Johnson administration's 1966 civil rights bill. So is Russell D. Renka, "Bargaining with Legislative Whales in the Kennedy and Johnson Administrations" (paper delivered at the annual meeting of the American Political Science Association, August 1980), which provides insights into the role Senator Dirksen played in the defeat of that legislation. Paul R. Clancy, *Just a Country Lawyer: A Biography of Senator Sam Ervin* (Bloomington: Indiana University Press, 1974), is an undocumented book that devotes a chapter to its subject's opposition to civil rights legislation but largely ignores his fight against the 1968 act. Steven F. Lawson, *Black Ballots: Voting Rights in the South, 1944–1966* (New York: Columbia University Press, 1976), is excellent on the struggle that led to enactment of the Voting Rights Act in 1965, as is David J. Garrow, *Protest at Selma: Martin Luther King, Jr., and the Voting Rights Act of 1965* (New Haven: Yale University Press, 1978). Both of these books deal extensively with the violence that was directed at those trying to increase black registration in the South. One would expect Vaughn Davis Bornet's *The Presidency of Lyndon Johnson* (Lawrence, Kans.: University of Kansas Press, 1983) to also treat southern racial violence and the way the Johnson administration responded to it, but this disappointing monograph ignores that topic entirely and badly slights the whole subject of civil rights. Merle Miller's *Lyndon: An Oral Biography* (New York: G. P. Putnam's Sons, 1980) and Eric F. Goldman's *The Tragedy of Lyndon Johnson* (New York: Alfred A.

Knopf, 1969) make much more interesting reading than does Bornet's turgid monograph, but they are really useful only for the light they shed on LBJ's attitudes about civil rights. The best source for insights into those, and into the president's racial views as well, is Monroe Billington, "Lyndon B. Johnson and Blacks: The Early Years," *Journal of Negro History* 62 (January 1977): 26–42.

The literature on race relations during the presidency of Johnson's successor is not nearly as extensive as that focusing on LBJ's administration. Lawson's *In Pursuit of Power* is the best treatment of civil rights during the Nixon years. Jonathan Schell's *The Time of Illusion* (New York: Alfred A. Knopf, 1976) is also useful.

The civil rights movement has received much more attention from historians than has the race relations record of the Nixon administration. The best book on the Student Nonviolent Coordinating Committee is Claybourne Carson's brilliant *In Struggle: SNCC and the Black Awakening of the 1960s* (Cambridge, Mass.: Harvard University Press, 1981). Howard Zinn, *SNCC: The New Abolitionists* (Boston: Beacon Press, 1965) is a contemporary history by a scholar who was close to the organization. Also quite perceptive, especially on the way the failure of the federal government to protect voter registration workers affected the thinking of young SNCC activists, is Allen J. Matusow, "From Civil Rights to Black Power: The Case of SNCC, 1960–1966," in *Twentieth Century America: Recent Interpretations,* ed. Barton J. Bernstein and Allen J. Matusow, 2d ed. (New York: Harcourt Brace Jovanovich, 1972), pp. 494–520. Unfortunately, this essay was written before the SNCC Papers became available. August Meier and Elliott Rudwick, *CORE: A Study in the Civil Rights Movement* (New York: Oxford University Press, 1973), is an impressively researched study which adopts the perspective of CORE's national office, and consequently provides a view of that organization's activities from the top down. Emile Schmeidler, "Shaping Ideas and Action: CORE, SLC and SNCC in the Struggle for Equality, 1960–1966" (PhD. diss., University of Michigan, 1980), is a sociology dissertation based mainly on secondary sources, but it does provide valuable insights into SNCC's strategy, as well as a good summary of what occurred in St. Augustine, Florida, during the SCLC's 1964 campaign there. David R. Colburn puts that year's tensions and conflicts into historical perspective in his solid study *Racial Change and Community Crisis: St. Augustine, Florida, 1877–1980* (New York: Columbia University Press, 1985). Also good on the SCLC's St. Augustine campaign is Stephen B. Oates, *Let the Trumpet Sound: The Life of Martin Luther King, Jr.* (New York: Harper & Row, 1982), a scholarly but also very readable biography. David Lewis, *King: A Critical Biography* (New York: Praeger, 1970), is, as its title implies, less laudatory than Oates's study.

For an interesting account of the incident that launched King's career as a civil rights leader, see Janet Stevenson, "Rosa Parks Wouldn't Budge," *American Heritage* 13 (February 1972): 56–64, 85, which discusses not only the Montgomery bus boycott but also the bombings that it inspired. William H. Chafe, *Civilities and Civil Rights: Greensboro, North Carolina, and the Black Struggle for Freedom* (New York: Oxford University Press, 1980), is a superb account of developments in the city where the sit-ins began, while John Dittmer, "The Movement in McComb" (paper delivered at the annual meeting of the Organization of American Historians, April 1984), is an excellent study of the civil rights movement in a violence-plagued Mississippi community.

Harvard K. Sitkoff's *The Struggle for Black Equality* (New York: Hill & Wang, 1981), although lacking footnotes, is a solid survey of the whole civil rights crusade. It is of much higher quality than most of the books dealing with the violence to which some white racists resorted in a futile attempt to halt that movement. Jack Mendelsohn's *The Martyrs: Sixteen Who Gave Their Lives for Racial Justice* (New York: Harper & Row, 1966), which has chapters on most of the major racial killings of the early 1960s, is a popular and undocumented work. William Bradford Huie's *Three Lives for Mississippi* (New York: W. C. Books, 1965) is an interesting account of the Goodman-Chaney-Schwerner slaying, written by a skilled journalist, but unfortunately it was done before the federal trial of the alleged killers and the transcript of that proceeding disproves some of Huie's conclusions and contentions. *Mississippi Eyewitness: The Three Civil Rights Workers—How They Were Murdered* (Menlo Park, Calif.: Ramparts Magazine, 1964) is even more inaccurate. Readers interested in this crime should rely instead on Mars's *Witness in Philadelphia*. Len Holt, *The Summer That Didn't End* (London: Heineman, 1966), is an account by a lawyer of events in Mississippi during the summer of 1964.

The best book on the Lemuel Penn killing is *Murder at Broad River Bridge: The Slaying of Lemuel Penn by Members of the Ku Klux Klan* (Atlanta: Peachtree Publishers, 1981), by Bill Shipp of the *Atlanta Constitution*. Michal R. Belknap, "The Legal Legacy of Lemuel Penn," *Howard Law*

Journal 25 (1982): 457–524, is less entertaining, but it is more scholarly and much stronger on the legal aspects of the case. Benjamin Muse's impressively detailed but undocumented *The American Negro Revolution: From Non-Violence to Black Power, 1963–1967* (Bloomington: Indiana University Press, 1968) relates numerous incidents of violence against blacks and civil rights workers.

Articles in Elizabeth Jacoway and David R. Colburn, eds., *Southern Businessmen and Desegregation* (Baton Rouge: Louisiana State University Press, 1982), report on how local authorities in Jackson, Mississippi, Birmingham, Alabama, and St. Augustine, Florida, dealt with anti–civil rights violence. Leon Friedman, ed., *Southern Justice* (New York: Random House, 1965), a collection of articles by lawyers and law students who worked with the civil rights movement, illuminates the quality of justice available to those laboring to bring about racial change in various parts of the South. So does Steven E. Barkan's *Protesters on Trial: Criminal Justice in the Southern Civil Rights and Vietnam Antiwar Movements* (New Brunswick: Rutgers University Press, 1985), a perceptive but poorly researched and error-plagued work by a sociologist.

For criticism of the federal government for not protecting voter registration workers in the South, see Pat Watters and Reese Cleghorn, *Climbing Jacob's Ladder: The Arrival of Negroes in Southern Politics* (New York: Harcourt, Brace & World, 1971). Neil R. McMillen, "Black Enfranchisement in Mississippi: Federal Enforcement and Black Protest in the 1960s," *Journal of Southern History* 43 (August 1977): 351–72, and Allan Lichtman, "The Federal Assault Against Voting Discrimination in the Deep South, 1957–1967," *Journal of Negro History* 54 (October 1969): 346–67, also call attention to the Justice Department's inaction where violence was concerned.

One federal agency that did act against it, finally, was the FBI. Frank J. Donner discusses what the Bureau eventually did to the Ku Klux Klan in his *The Age of Surveillance: The Aims and Methods of America's Political Intelligence System* (New York: Alfred A. Knopf, 1980). So does Athan Theoharis in his *Spying on Americans: Political Surveillance from Hoover to the Huston Plan* (Philadelphia: Temple University Press, 1978). Much the most detailed discussion of this subject, however, is in Don Whitehead's *Attack on Terror: The FBI Against the Ku Klux Klan in Mississippi* (New York: Funk and Wagnalls, 1970). This book was written with the full cooperation of the Bureau, but its author is a known apologist for former

Director J. Edgar Hoover, and its reliability is somewhat difficult to assess. *The FBI and Martin Luther King, Jr.* (New York: W. W. Norton, 1981) by David J. Garrow is a heavily documented and extremely interesting account of one of the most controversial facets of the Bureau's relationship with the civil rights movement.

Good on the interaction between that movement and the federal judiciary is J. W. Peltason, *Fifty-eight Lonely Men: Southern Federal Judges and School Desegregation* (New York: Harcourt, Brace & World, 1961). James W. Ely, Jr., "Negro Demonstrations and the Law," *Vanderbilt Law Review* 27 (October 1974): 927–68, is an important article on one aspect of that subject. Charles V. Hamilton, *The Bench and the Ballot: Southern Federal Judges and Black Voting Rights* (New York: Oxford University Press, 1973), is another useful study, which contains some valuable data on increases in black voter registration. Of particular importance to anyone interested in the interrelated problems of anti–civil rights violence and state-federal relations is Tinsley E. Yarbrough's *Judge Frank Johnson and Human Rights in Alabama* (University, Ala.: University of Alabama Press, 1981). It is a solid biography of a jurist who wrestled repeatedly with these issues, in litigation involving the Freedom Rides and the Selma March and as the trial judge in the Viola Liuzzo case. If anyone came to really understand the relationship between federal law and southern order, it was Judge Frank Johnson.

INDEX

Abernathy, Ralph David, 85, 107, 238–39
Abolitionists, 4
Adams, Sherman, 270 (n. 84)
Afro-Americans. *See* Blacks
Aiken, Archibald, 121, 295 (n. 53)
Akerman, Amos T., 340 (n. 74)
Akin, Bernard, 200, 309 (n. 119)
Akin, Earl B., 310 (n. 119), 314 (n. 39)
Alabama, 21, 23, 98, 120, 183–90 passim, 232, 234, 238–39, 240; University of, 29, 37, 96; officials, 78, 184–86, 188; Highway Patrol, 82, 86, 97, 98, 120, 122, 123, 135, 183, 186; congressional delegation, 96; National Guard, 97–98, 101, 186; Legislature, 101; House delegation, 102; Department of Public Safety, 188; Supreme Court, 189. *See also* Anniston; Birmingham; Lowndes County; Montgomery; Selma
Albany, Georgia, 107–8, 114, 116, 118, 119; "Albany Movement," 107, 109
Allen, Louis, 109
Allen, Ralph, 108
American Civil Liberties Union (ACLU), 154
American Jewish Congress, 54, 56
American Negro Leadership Conference on Africa, 124
Americus, Georgia, 109, 135
Ames, Jessie Daniel, 22, 23
Amite County, Mississippi, 109
Anarchy, 247, 248, 249, 250

Ancient City Hunting Club, 132
Anniston, Alabama, 79, 80, 89, 235, 249
Anti–civil rights violence, ix, xi, xii, 28–31, 46, 74, 106, 109, 110, 112, 135, 136, 147–48, 158, 174, 182, 183, 184, 196, 205, 206, 229, 231–32, 250–51; legislation to control, 208–11, 212, 214–19, 219–28, 237; decline of, 231–32; change in white attitudes about, 239–42, 247–50; southern juries begin to convict perpetrators, 247–50
Anti-Defamation League of B'Nai B'Rith, 55, 58, 130, 211
Arkansas, 135; National Guard, 46–49. *See also* Hoxie; Little Rock
Arkansas Gazette, 151, 158, 250
Arledge, Jimmy, 200
Arnall, Ellis, 20
Arson, 108, 110, 112, 114, 116, 120, 134, 138, 145, 156, 158, 250
Ashbrook, John, 209
Ashmore, Robert T., 217
Association of Southern Women for the Prevention of Lynching, 22
Athens, Georgia, 196, 247
Atlanta Constitution, 151, 239
Atlanta Daily World, 151
Atlanta temple bombing, 56
Attorney General (U.S.), 104, 105, 129, 226. *See also* Brownell, Herbert, Jr.; Clark, Ramsey; Katzenbach, Nicholas; Kennedy, Robert F; Rogers, William
Autrey, George, 222, 224